Python Geospatial Development

Second Edition

Learn to build sophisticated mapping applications from scratch using Python tools for geospatial development

Erik Westra

PUBLISHING

BIRMINGHAM - MUMBAI

Python Geospatial Development
Second Edition

First published: December 2012

Second Edition: May 2013

Production Reference: 1170513

Published by Packt Publishing Ltd.
Livery Place
35 Livery Street
Birmingham B3 2PB, UK.

ISBN 978-1-78216-152-3

www.packtpub.com

Cover Image by Karl Moore (karl@karlmoore.co.uk)

Credits

Author
Erik Westra

Reviewers
Will Cadell

Richard Marsden

Silas Toms

Acquisition Editor
Kartikey Pandey

Lead Technical Editor
Susmita Panda

Technical Editors
Sharvari Baet

Meenakshi Gupta

Chirag Jani

Project Coordinator
Arshad Sopariwala

Proofreaders
Stephen Silk

Katherine Tarr

Indexers
Hemangini Bari

Rekha Nair

Tejal Daruwale

Graphics
Ronak Dhruv

Abhinash Sahu

Production Coordinator
Manu Joseph

Cover Work
Manu Joseph

About the Author

Erik Westra has been a professional software developer for over 25 years, and has worked almost exclusively in Python for the past decade. Erik's early interest in graphical user-interface design led to the development of one of the most advanced urgent courier dispatch systems used by messenger and courier companies worldwide. In recent years, Erik has been involved in the design and implementation of systems matching seekers and providers of goods and services across a range of geographical areas. This work has included the creation of real-time geocoders and map-based views of constantly changing data. Erik is based in New Zealand, and works for companies worldwide.

I would like to thank Ruth, the love of my life, for all of her support and encouragement.

About the Reviewers

Richard Marsden has over 15 years of professional software development experience. After starting in the field of geophysics and oil exploration, he has spent the last ten years running the Winwaed Software Technology LLC, an independent software vendor. Winwaed specialize in geospatial tools and applications including web applications, and operate the `http://www.mapping-tools.com` website for tools and add-ins for Microsoft's MapPoint product.

Richard also manages the technical aspects of the EcoMapCostaRica.com project for the Biology Department at the University of Dallas. This includes the website, online field maps, field surveys, and the creation and comparison of panoramic photographs.

Richard is also active in the field of natural language processing, especially with Python's NLTK package.

Will Cadell is a principal consultant with Sparkgeo.com. He builds next generation web mapping applications, primarily using Google Maps, geoDjango, and PostGIS. He has worked in academia, government, and natural resources but now mainly consults for the start-up community in Silicon Valley. His passion has always been the implementation of geographic technology and with over a billion smart, mobile devices in the world it's a great time to be working on the geoweb.

Will lives in Prince George, Northern British Columbia, and when he's not writing code or talking about geographic web technology you can find him on a ski hill with his family.

Silas Toms is a GIS programmer with ICF International. His main professional interests are programming in Python and automation of large-scale environmental impact analyses. He has lived in San Francisco for 6 years while finishing a masters in GIS at San Francisco State University on temperature interpolation. He wishes to thank his girlfriend and his family for being supportive of his many interests.

www.PacktPub.com

Support files, eBooks, discount offers and more

You might want to visit www.PacktPub.com for support files and downloads related to your book.

Did you know that Packt offers eBook versions of every book published, with PDF and ePub files available? You can upgrade to the eBook version at www.PacktPub.com and as a print book customer, you are entitled to a discount on the eBook copy. Get in touch with us at service@packtpub.com for more details.

At www.PacktPub.com, you can also read a collection of free technical articles, sign up for a range of free newsletters and receive exclusive discounts and offers on Packt books and eBooks.

http://PacktLib.PacktPub.com

Do you need instant solutions to your IT questions? PacktLib is Packt's online digital book library. Here, you can access, read and search across Packt's entire library of books.

Why Subscribe?
- Fully searchable across every book published by Packt
- Copy and paste, print and bookmark content
- On demand and accessible via web browser

Free Access for Packt account holders

If you have an account with Packt at www.PacktPub.com, you can use this to access PacktLib today and view nine entirely free books. Simply use your login credentials for immediate access.

Table of Contents

Preface

With the explosion of map-based websites and spatially-aware devices and applications, geospatial development is becoming increasingly important. The geospatial market is growing rapidly, and as a Python developer you can't afford to be left behind. In today's location-aware world, all commercial Python developers can benefit from an understanding of geospatial concepts and development techniques.

Working with geospatial data can get complicated because you are dealing with mathematical models of the Earth's surface. Since Python is a powerful programming language with high-level toolkits, it is well-suited to geospatial development. This book will familiarize you with the Python tools required for geospatial development. It introduces basic geospatial concepts with a clear, detailed walkthrough of the key concepts such as location, distance, units, projections, datums, and geospatial data formats. We then examine a number of Python libraries and use these with freely-available geospatial data to accomplish a variety of tasks. The book provides an in-depth look at the concept of storing spatial data in a database and how you can use spatial databases as tools to solve a variety of geospatial problems.

It goes into the details of generating maps using the Mapnik map-rendering toolkit, and helps you to build a sophisticated web-based geospatial map editing application using GeoDjango, Mapnik, and PostGIS. By the end of the book, you will be able to integrate spatial features into your applications and build a complete mapping application from scratch.

This book is a hands-on tutorial. It teaches you how to access, manipulate, and display geospatial data efficiently using a range of Python tools for GIS development.

What this book covers

Chapter 1, Geospatial Development Using Python, gives an overview of the Python programming language and the concepts behind geospatial development. Major use-cases of geospatial development and recent and upcoming developments in the field are also covered.

Chapter 2, GIS, introduces the core concepts of location, distance, units, projections, shapes, datums, and geospatial data formats, before discussing the process of working with geospatial data manually.

Chapter 3, Python Libraries for Geospatial Development, explores the major Python libraries available for geospatial development, including the available features, how the library is organized, and how to install and use it.

Chapter 4, Sources of Geospatial Data, investigates the major sources of freely-available geospatial data, what information is available, the data format used, and how to import the downloaded data.

Chapter 5, Working with Geospatial Data in Python, uses the libraries introduced earlier to perform various tasks using geospatial data, including changing projections, importing and exporting data, converting and standardizing units of geometry and distance, and performing geospatial calculations.

Chapter 6, GIS in the Database, introduces the spatial capabilities of PostGIS, MySQL, and SQLite. It discusses best practices for storing different types of spatial data, and looks at how to access these databases from Python.

Chapter 7, Working with Spatial Data, works through the design and implementation of a complete geospatial application called DISTAL, using freely-available geospatial data stored in a spatial database. It investigates the performance of this application and then works to optimize it using best-practice techniques.

Chapter 8, Using Python and Mapnik to Produce Maps, gives an in-depth look at the Mapnik map-generation toolkit, and how to use it to produce a variety of maps.

Chapter 9, Putting it all Together: a Complete Mapping Application, introduces the "ShapeEditor", a complete and sophisticated web application built using PostGIS, Mapnik and GeoDjango. We start by designing the overall application, and then build the ShapeEditor's database models.

Chapter 10, ShapeEditor: Implementing List View, Import, and Export, continues the implementation of the ShapeEditor system, concentrating on displaying a list of imported shapefiles, along with the logic for importing and exporting shapefiles via a web browser.

Chapter 11, ShapeEditor: Selecting and Editing Features, concludes the implementation of the ShapeEditor, adding logic to let the user select and edit features within an imported shapefile. This involves the creation of a custom Tile Map Server, and the use of the OpenLayers JavaScript library to display and interact with geospatial data.

Bonus chapter, Web Frameworks for Geospatial Development, examines the concepts of web application frameworks, web services, JavaScript UI libraries, and slippy maps. It introduces a number of standard web protocols used by geospatial applications, and finishes with a survey of the tools and frameworks available for building geospatial applications that run via a web interface.

You can download this chapter from: `http://www.packtpub.com/sites/default/files/downloads/1523OS_Bonuschapter.pdf`

What you need for this book

To follow through this book, you will need to have Python Version 2.5 to 2.7. You will also need to download and install the following tools and libraries; full instructions are given in the relevant sections of this book:

- GDAL/OGR
- GEOS
- Shapely
- Proj
- `pyproj`
- `MySQL`
- MySQLdb
- SpatiaLite
- `pysqlite`
- PostgreSQL
- PostGIS
- `pyscopg2`
- Mapnik
- Django

Who this book is for

This book is aimed at experienced Python developers who want to get up to speed with open source geospatial tools and techniques in order to build their own geospatial applications, or to integrate geospatial technology into their existing Python programs.

Conventions

In this book, you will find a number of styles of text that distinguish between different kinds of information. Here are some examples of these styles, and an explanation of their meaning.

Code words in text are shown as follows: " The `pyproj` Geod class allows you to perform various geodetic calculations based on points on the Earth's surface."

A block of code is set as follows:

```
import mapnik

symbolizer = mapnik.PolygonSymbolizer(
                    mapnik.Color("darkgreen"))

rule = mapnik.Rule()
rule.symbols.append(symbolizer)
```

When we wish to draw your attention to a particular part of a code block, the relevant lines or items are set in bold:

```
 import mapnik

symbolizer = mapnik.PolygonSymbolizer(
                    mapnik.Color("darkgreen"))
rule = mapnik.Rule()
rule.symbols.append(symbolizer)
```

Any command-line input or output is written as follows:

```
python setup.py build
sudo python.setup.py install
```

New terms and **important words** are shown in bold. Words that you see on the screen, in menus or dialog boxes for example, appear in the text like this: "clicking the **Next** button moves you to the next screen".

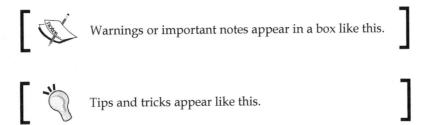

Warnings or important notes appear in a box like this.

Tips and tricks appear like this.

Reader feedback

Feedback from our readers is always welcome. Let us know what you think about this book—what you liked or may have disliked. Reader feedback is important for us to develop titles that you really get the most out of.

To send us general feedback, simply send an e-mail to feedback@packtpub.com, and mention the book title via the subject of your message.

If there is a topic that you have expertise in and you are interested in either writing or contributing to a book, see our author guide on www.packtpub.com/authors.

Customer support

Now that you are the proud owner of a Packt book, we have a number of things to help you to get the most from your purchase.

Downloading the example code

You can download the example code files for all Packt books you have purchased from your account at http://www.packtpub.com. If you purchased this book elsewhere, you can visit http://www.packtpub.com/support and register to have the files e-mailed directly to you.

Errata

Although we have taken every care to ensure the accuracy of our content, mistakes do happen. If you find a mistake in one of our books—maybe a mistake in the text or the code—we would be grateful if you would report this to us. By doing so, you can save other readers from frustration and help us improve subsequent versions of this book. If you find any errata, please report them by visiting http://www.packtpub.com/submit-errata, selecting your book, clicking on the **errata submission form** link, and entering the details of your errata. Once your errata are verified, your submission will be accepted and the errata will be uploaded on our website, or added to any list of existing errata, under the Errata section of that title. Any existing errata can be viewed by selecting your title from http://www.packtpub.com/support.

Piracy

Piracy of copyright material on the Internet is an ongoing problem across all media. At Packt, we take the protection of our copyright and licenses very seriously. If you come across any illegal copies of our works, in any form, on the Internet, please provide us with the location address or website name immediately so that we can pursue a remedy.

Please contact us at copyright@packtpub.com with a link to the suspected pirated material.

We appreciate your help in protecting our authors, and our ability to bring you valuable content.

Questions

You can contact us at questions@packtpub.com if you are having a problem with any aspect of the book, and we will do our best to address it.

1
Geospatial Development Using Python

This chapter provides an overview of the Python programming language and geospatial development. Please note that this is not a tutorial on how to use the Python language; Python is easy to learn, but the details are beyond the scope of this book.

In this chapter, we will cover:

- What the Python programming language is, and how it differs from other languages
- An introduction to the Python Standard Library and the Python Package Index
- What the terms "geospatial data" and "geospatial development" refer to
- An overview of the process of accessing, manipulating, and displaying geospatial data
- Some of the major applications for geospatial development
- Some of the recent trends in the field of geospatial development

Python

Python (http://python.org) is a modern, high level language suitable for a wide variety of programming tasks. It is often used as a scripting language, automating and simplifying tasks at the operating system level, but it is equally suitable for building large and complex programs. Python has been used to write web-based systems, desktop applications, games, scientific programming, and even utilities and other higher-level parts of various operating systems.

Python supports a wide range of programming idioms, from straightforward procedural programming to object-oriented programming and functional programming.

While Python is generally considered to be an "interpreted" language, and is occasionally criticized for being slow compared to "compiled" languages such as C, the use of byte-compilation and the fact that much of the heavy lifting is done by library code means that Python's performance is often surprisingly good.

Open-source versions of the Python interpreter are freely available for all major operating systems. Python is eminently suitable for all sorts of programming, from quick one-off scripts to building huge and complex systems. It can even be run in interactive (command-line) mode, allowing you to type in commands and immediately see the results. This is ideal for doing quick calculations or figuring out how a particular library works.

One of the first things a developer notices about Python compared with other languages such as Java or C++ is how *expressive* the language is: what may take 20 or 30 lines of code in Java can often be written in half a dozen lines of code in Python. For example, imagine that you wanted to print a sorted list of the words that occur in a given piece of text. In Python, this is trivial:

```
words = set(text.split())
for word in sorted(words):
    print word
```

Implementing this kind of task in other languages is often surprisingly difficult.

While the Python language itself makes programming quick and easy, allowing you to focus on the task at hand, the **Python Standard Libraries** make programming even more efficient. These libraries make it easy to do things such as converting date and time values, manipulating strings, downloading data from websites, performing complex maths, working with e-mail messages, encoding and decoding data, XML parsing, data encryption, file manipulation, compressing and decompressing files, working with databases — the list goes on. What you can do with the Python Standard Libraries is truly amazing.

As well as the built-in modules in the Python Standard Libraries, it is easy to download and install custom modules, which can be written in either Python or C.

The **Python Package Index** (http://pypi.python.org) provides thousands of additional modules which you can download and install. And if that isn't enough, many other systems provide python "bindings" to allow you to access them directly from within your programs. We will be making heavy use of Python bindings in this book.

 It should be pointed out that there are different versions of Python available. Python 2.x is the most common version in use today, while the Python developers have been working for the past several years on a completely new, non-backwards-compatible version called Python 3. Eventually, Python 3 will replace Python 2.x, but at this stage most of the third-party libraries (including all the GIS tools we will be using) only work with Python 2.x. For this reason, we won't be using Python 3 in this book.

Python is in many ways an ideal programming language. Once you are familiar with the language itself and have used it a few times, you'll find it incredibly easy to write programs to solve various tasks. Rather than getting buried in a morass of type-definitions and low-level string manipulation, you can simply concentrate on what you want to achieve. You end up almost thinking directly in Python code. Programming in Python is straightforward, efficient, and, dare I say it, *fun*.

Geospatial development

The term "geospatial" refers to information that is located on the earth's surface using coordinates. This can include, for example, the position of a cell phone tower, the shape of a road, or the outline of a country:

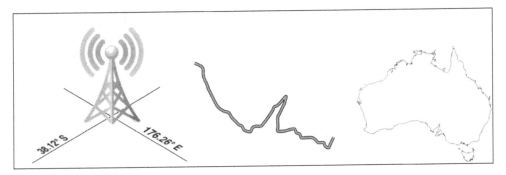

Geospatial data often associates some piece of information with a particular location. For example, the following is an interactive map from the http://www.bbc.co.uk/ website, showing the percentage of people in each country with access to the Internet in 2008:

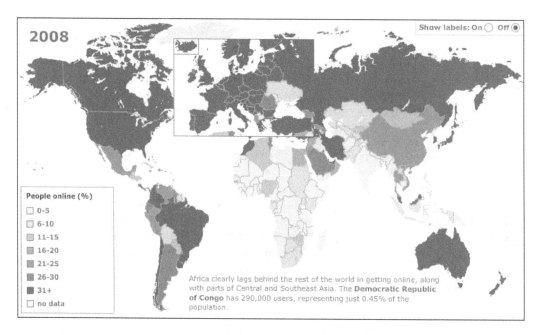

Geospatial development is the process of writing computer programs that can access, manipulate, and display this type of information.

Internally, geospatial data is represented as a series of **coordinates**, often in the form of latitude and longitude values. Additional **attributes** such as temperature, soil type, height, or the name of a landmark are also often present. There can be many thousands (or even millions) of data points for a single set of geospatial data. For example, the following outline of New Zealand consists of almost 12,000 individual data points:

Because so much data is involved, it is common to store geospatial information within a database. A large part of this book will be concerned with how to store your geospatial information in a database, and how to access it efficiently.

Geospatial data comes in many different forms. Different **Geographical Information System (GIS)** vendors have produced their own file formats over the years, and various organizations have also defined their own standards. It is often necessary to use a Python library to read files in the correct format when importing geospatial data into your database.

Unfortunately, not all geospatial data points are compatible. Just like a distance value of 2.8 can have a very different meaning depending on whether you are using kilometers or miles, a given latitude and longitude value can represent any number of different points on the earth's surface, depending on which **projection** has been used.

A projection is a way of representing the curved surface of the earth in two dimensions. We will look at projections in more detail in *Chapter 2, GIS*, but for now just keep in mind that every piece of geospatial data has a projection associated with it. To compare or combine two sets of geospatial data, it is often necessary to convert the data from one projection to another.

 Latitude and longitude values are sometimes referred to as **unprojected coordinates**. We'll learn more about this in the next chapter.

In addition to the prosaic tasks of importing geospatial data from various external file formats and translating data from one projection to another, geospatial data can also be manipulated to solve various interesting problems. Obvious examples include the task of calculating the distance between two points, or calculating the length of a road, or finding all data points within a given radius of a selected point. We will be using Python libraries to solve all of these problems, and more.

Finally, geospatial data by itself is not very interesting. A long list of coordinates tells you almost nothing; it isn't until those numbers are used to draw a picture that you can make sense of it. Drawing maps, placing data points onto a map, and allowing users to interact with maps are all important aspects of geospatial development. We will be looking at all of these in later chapters.

Applications of geospatial development

Let's take a brief look at some of the more common geospatial development tasks you might encounter.

Analyzing geospatial data

Imagine that you have a database containing a range of geospatial data for San Francisco. This database might include geographical features, roads, the location of prominent buildings, and other man-made features such as bridges, airports, and so on.

Such a database can be a valuable resource for answering various questions. For example:

- What's the longest road in Sausalito?
- How many bridges are there in Oakland?
- What is the total area of the Golden Gate Park?
- How far is it from the Pier 39 to the Moscone Center?

Many of these types of problems can be solved using tools such as the **PostGIS** spatially-enabled database. For example, to calculate the total area of the Golden Gate Park, you might use the following SQL query:

```
select ST_Area(geometry) from features
  where name = "Golden Gate Park";
```

To calculate the distance between two places, you first have to **geocode** the locations to obtain their latitude and longitude. There are various ways to do this; one simple approach is to use a free geocoding web service, such as this:

`http://nominatim.openstreetmap.org/search?q=Pier 39, San Francisco,CA`

This returns a latitude value of 37.82 and a longitude value of -122.42.

 These latitude and longitude values are in **decimal degrees**. If you don't know what these are, don't worry; we'll talk about decimal degrees in *Chapter 2, GIS*.

Similarly, we can find the location of the Moscone Center using this query:

`http://nominatim.openstreetmap.org/search?q=Moscone Center, San Francisco,CA`

This returns a latitude value of 37.80 and a longitude value of -122.44.

Now that we have the coordinates for the two desired locations, we can calculate the distance between them using the **Proj** Python library:

```
import pyproj

lat1,long1 = (37.82,-122.42)
lat2,long2 = (37.80,-122.44)

geod = pyproj.Geod(ellps="WGS84")
angle1,angle2,distance = geod.inv(long1, lat1, long2, lat2)

print "Distance is %0.2f meters" % distance
```

This prints the distance between the two points:

Distance is 2833.64 meters

 Don't worry about the "WGS84" reference at this stage; we'll look at what this means in *Chapter 2, GIS*.

Of course, you wouldn't normally do this sort of analysis on a one-off basis like this — it's much more common to create a Python program that will answer these sorts of questions for any desired set of data. You might, for example, create a web application that displays a menu of available calculations. One of the options in this menu might be to calculate the distance between two points; when this option is selected, the web application would prompt the user to enter the two locations, attempt to geocode them by calling an appropriate web service (and display an error message if a location couldn't be geocoded), then calculate the distance between the two points using Proj, and finally display the results to the user.

Alternatively, if you have a database containing useful geospatial data, you could let the user select the two locations from the database rather than typing in arbitrary location names or street addresses.

However you choose to structure it, performing calculations like this will usually be a major part of your geospatial application.

Visualizing geospatial data

Imagine that you wanted to see which areas of a city are typically covered by a taxi during an average working day. You might place a GPS recorder into a taxi and leave it to record the taxi's position over several days. The results would be a series of timestamps, latitude and longitude values as follows:

```
2010-03-21 9:15:23   -38.16614499   176.2336626
2010-03-21 9:15:27   -38.16608632   176.2335635
2010-03-21 9:15:34   -38.16604198   176.2334771
2010-03-21 9:15:39   -38.16601507   176.2333958
. . .
```

By themselves, these raw numbers tell you almost nothing. But when you display this data visually, the numbers start to make sense:

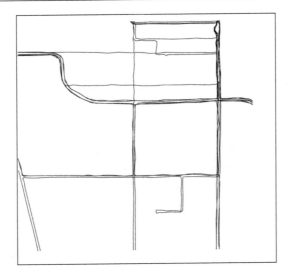

You can immediately see that the taxi tends to go along the same streets again and again. And if you draw this data as an **overlay** on top of a street map, you can see exactly where the taxi has been:

(Street map courtesy of `http://openstreetmap.org`).

While this is a very simple example, visualization is a crucial aspect of working with geospatial data. How data is displayed visually, how different data sets are overlaid, and how the user can manipulate data directly in a visual format are all going to be major topics of this book.

Creating a geospatial mash-up

The concept of a "mash-up" has become popular in recent years. Mash-ups are applications that combine data and functionality from more than one source. For example, a typical mash-up may combine details of houses for rent in a given city, and plot the location of each rental on a map, as follows:

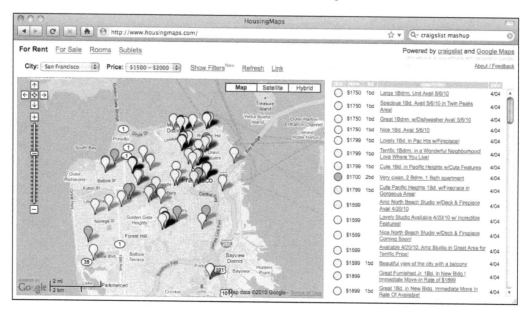

This example comes from `http://housingmaps.com`.

The **Google Maps API** has been immensely popular in creating these types of mash-ups. However, Google Maps has some serious licensing and other limitations—as does Google's main competitor, Bing. Fortunately, these are not the only options; tools such as **Mapnik**, **Openlayers**, and **MapServer**, to name a few, also allow you to create mash-ups that overlay your own data onto a map.

Most of these mash-ups run as web applications across the Internet, running on a server that can be accessed by anyone who has a web browser. Sometimes the mash-ups are private, requiring password access, but usually they are publicly available and can be used by anyone. Indeed, many businesses (such as the housing maps site shown in the previous image) are based on freely-available geospatial mash-ups.

Recent developments

A decade ago, geospatial development was vastly more limited than it is today. Professional (and hugely expensive) Geographical Information Systems were the norm for working with and visualizing geospatial data. Open source tools, where they were available, were obscure and hard to use. What is more, everything ran on the desktop—the concept of working with geospatial data across the Internet was no more than a distant dream.

In 2005, Google released two products that completely changed the face of geospatial development. **Google Maps** and **Google Earth** made it possible for anyone with a web browser or a desktop computer to view and work with geospatial data. Instead of requiring expert knowledge and years of practice, even a four-year old could instantly view and manipulate interactive maps of the world.

Google's products are not perfect: the map projections are deliberately simplified, leading to errors and problems with displaying overlays; these products are only free for non-commercial use; and they include almost no ability to perform geospatial analysis. Despite these limitations, they have had a huge effect on the field of geospatial development. People became aware of what was possible, and the use of maps and their underlying geospatial data has become so prevalent that even cell phones now commonly include built-in mapping tools.

The **Global Positioning System (GPS)** has also had a major influence on geospatial development. Geospatial data for streets and other man-made and natural features used to be an expensive and tightly controlled resource, often created by scanning aerial photographs and then manually drawing an outline of a street or coastline over the top to digitize the required features. With the advent of cheap and readily-available portable GPS units, anyone who wishes to can now capture their own geospatial data. Indeed, many people have made a hobby of recording, editing, and improving the accuracy of street and topological data, which are then freely shared across the Internet. All this means that you're not limited to recording your own data, or purchasing data from a commercial organization; volunteered information is now often as accurate and useful as commercially-available data, and may well be suitable for your geospatial application.

The open source software movement has also had a major influence on geospatial development. Instead of relying on commercial toolsets, it is now possible to build complex geospatial applications entirely out of freely-available tools and libraries. Because the source code for these tools is often available, developers can improve and extend these toolkits, fixing problems and adding new features for the benefit of everyone. Tools such as PROJ.4, PostGIS, OGR, and GDAL are all excellent geospatial toolkits which are benefactors of the open source movement. We will be making use of all these tools throughout this book.

As well as standalone tools and libraries, a number of geospatial **Application Programming Interfaces** (**APIs**) have become available. Google have provided a number of APIs, which can be used to include maps and perform limited geospatial analysis within a website. Other services, such as the OpenStreetMap geocoder we used earlier, allow you to perform various geospatial tasks that would be difficult to do if you were limited to using your own data and programming resources.

As more and more geospatial data becomes available, from an increasing number of sources, and as the number of tools and systems which can work with this data also increases, it has become increasingly important to define standards for geospatial data. The **Open Geospatial Consortium**, often abbreviated to OGC (http://www.opengeospatial.org) is an international standards organization which aims to do precisely this: to provide a set of standard formats and protocols for sharing and storing geospatial data. These standards, including GML, KML, GeoRSS, WMS, WFS, and WCS, provide a shared "language" in which geospatial data can be expressed. Tools such as commercial and open source GIS systems, Google Earth, web-based APIs, and specialized geospatial toolkits such as OGR are all able to work with these standards. Indeed, an important aspect of a geospatial toolkit is the ability to understand and translate data between these various formats.

As GPS units have become more ubiquitous, it has become possible to record your location data as you are performing another task. **Geolocation**, the act of recording your location as you are doing something, is becoming increasingly common. The Twitter social networking service, for example, now allows you to record and display your current location as you enter a status update. As you approach your office, sophisticated To-do list software can now automatically hide any tasks which can't be done at that location. Your phone can also tell you which of your friends are nearby, and search results can be filtered to only show nearby businesses.

All of this is simply the continuation of a trend that started when GIS systems were housed on mainframe computers and operated by specialists who spent years learning about them.

Geospatial data and applications have been "democratized" over the years, making them available in more places, to more people. What was possible only in a large organization can now be done by anyone using a handheld device. As technology continues to improve, and the tools become more powerful, this trend is sure to continue.

Summary

In this chapter, we briefly introduced the Python programming language and the main concepts behind geospatial development. We have seen:

- That Python is a very high-level language eminently suited to the task of geospatial development.

- That there are a number of libraries which can be downloaded to make it easier to perform geospatial development work in Python.

- That the term "geospatial data" refers to information that is located on the earth's surface using coordinates.

- That the term "geospatial development" refers to the process of writing computer programs that can access, manipulate, and display geospatial data.

- That the process of accessing geospatial data is non-trivial, thanks to differing file formats and data standards.

- What types of questions can be answered by analyzing geospatial data.

- How geospatial data can be used for visualization.

- How mash-ups can be used to combine data (often geospatial data) in useful and interesting ways.

- How Google Maps, Google Earth, and the development of cheap and portable GPS units have "democratized" geospatial development.

- The influence the open source software movement has had on the availability of high quality, freely-available tools for geospatial development.

- How various standards organizations have defined formats and protocols for sharing and storing geospatial data.

- The increasing use of geolocation to capture and work with geospatial data in surprising and useful ways.

In the next chapter, we will look in more detail at traditional GIS, including a number of important concepts which you need to understand in order to work with geospatial data. Different geospatial formats will be examined, and we will finish by using Python to perform various calculations using geospatial data.

2
GIS

The term GIS generally refers to Geographical Information Systems, which are complex computer systems for storing, manipulating, and displaying geospatial data. GIS can also be used to refer to the more general Geographic Information Sciences, which is the science surrounding the use of GIS systems.

In this chapter we will look at:

- The central GIS concepts you will have to become familiar with: location, distance, units, projections, datums, coordinate systems, and shapes
- Some of the major data formats you are likely to encounter when working with geospatial data
- Some of the processes involved in working directly with geospatial data

Core GIS concepts

Working with geospatial data is complicated because you are dealing with mathematical models of the earth's surface. In many ways it is easy to think of the earth as a sphere on which you can place your data. That might be easy, but it isn't accurate—the earth is more like an oblate spheroid than a perfect sphere. This difference, as well as other mathematical complexities we won't get into here, means that representing points, lines, and areas on the surface of the earth is a rather complicated process.

Let's take a look at some of the key GIS concepts you will have to become familiar with as you work with geospatial data.

Location

Locations represent points on the surface of the earth. One of the most common ways to measure location is through the use of latitude and longitude coordinates. For example, my current location (as measured by a GPS receiver) is 38.167446 degrees south and 176.234436 degrees east. What do these numbers mean, and how are they useful?

Think of the earth as a hollow sphere with an axis drawn through the middle:

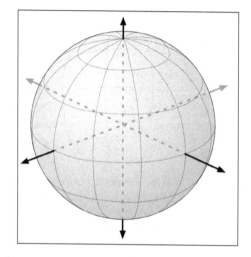

For any given point on the earth's surface, you can draw a line that connects that point with the centre of the earth, as shown in the following image:

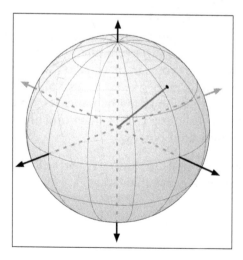

The point's latitude is the angle that this line makes in the north-south direction, relative to the equator:

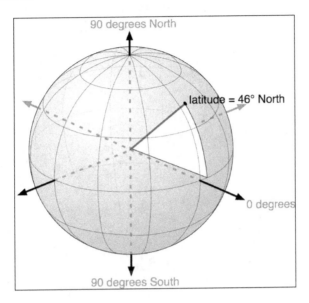

In the same way, the point's longitude is the angle that this line makes in the east-west direction, relative to an arbitrary starting point (typically the location of the Royal Observatory in Greenwich, England):

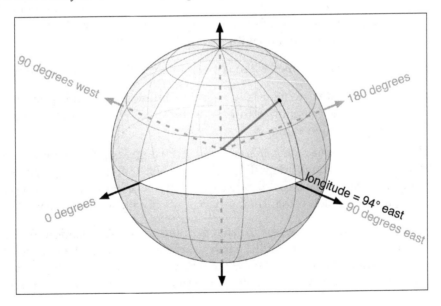

By convention, positive latitude values are in the northern hemisphere, while negative latitude values are in the southern hemisphere. Similarly, positive longitude values are east of Greenwich, and negative longitude values are west of Greenwich. Thus, latitudes and longitudes cover the entire earth as shown in the following image:

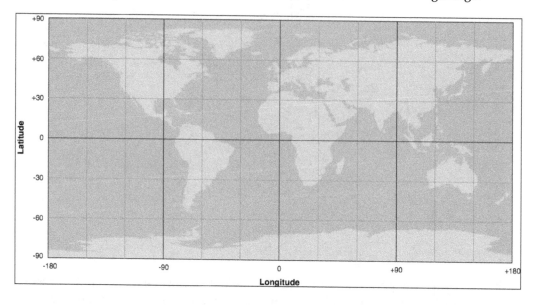

The horizontal lines, representing points of equal latitude, are called **parallels**, while the vertical lines, representing points of equal longitude, are called **meridians**. The meridian at zero longitude is often called the **prime meridian**. By definition, the parallel at zero latitude corresponds with the earth's equator.

There are two things to remember when working with latitude and longitude values:

1. Western longitudes are generally negative, but you may find situations (particularly when dealing with US-specific data) where western longitudes are given as positive values.

2. The longitude values *wrap around* at the ±180 degrees point. That is, as you travel east, your longitude will go 177, 178, 179, 180, -179, -178, -177, and so on. This can make basic distance calculations rather confusing if you are doing them yourself rather than relying on a library to do the work for you.

A latitude and longitude value refers to what is called a **geodetic location**. A geodetic location identifies a precise point on the earth's surface, regardless of what might be at that location. While much of the data we will be working with involves geodetic locations, there are other ways of describing a location which you may encounter.

For example, a **civic location** is simply a street address, which is another perfectly valid (though scientifically less precise) way of defining a location. Similarly, **jurisdictional locations** include information about which governmental boundary (such as an electoral ward, borough, or city) the location is within, as this information is important in some contexts.

Distance

The distance between two points on the earth's surface can be thought of in different ways. For example:

- **Angular distance**: This is the angle between two rays going out from the centre of the earth through the two points:

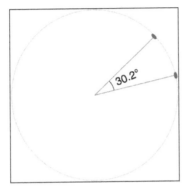

Angular distances are commonly used in seismology, and you may encounter them when working with geospatial data.

- **Linear distance**: This is what people typically mean when they talk of distance: how far apart two points on the earth's surface are:

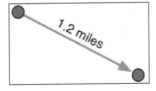

This is often described as an "as the crow flies" distance. We'll discuss this in more detail shortly, though be aware that linear distances aren't quite as simple as they might appear.

- **Traveling distance**: Linear ("as the crow flies") distances are all very well, but very few people can fly like crows. Another useful way of measuring distance is to measure how far you would actually have to travel to get from one point to another, typically following a road or other obvious route:

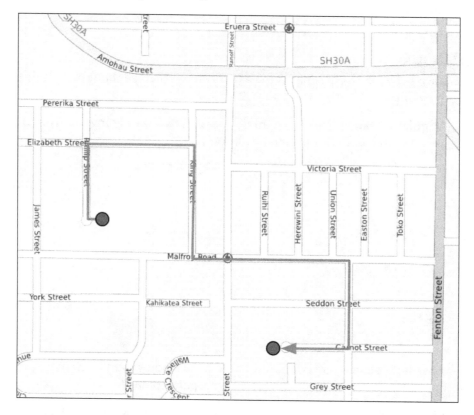

Most of the time, you will be dealing with linear distances. If the earth was flat, linear distances would be trivial to calculate — you simply measure the length of a line drawn between the two points. Of course, the earth is not flat, which means that actual distance calculations are rather more complicated:

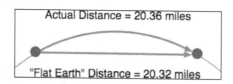

Because we are working with distances between points on the earth's surface, rather than points on a flat surface, we are actually using what is called the **great circle distance**. The great circle distance is the length of a semicircle between two points on the surface of the earth, where the semicircle is centered around the middle of the earth:

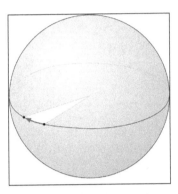

It is relatively straightforward to calculate the great circle distance between any two points if you assume that the earth is spherical; the **Haversine formula** is often used for this. More complicated techniques which more accurately represent the shape of the earth are available, though in many cases the Haversine formula is sufficient.

[We will learn more about the Haversine formula later in this chapter.]

Units

In September 1999, the Mars Climate Orbiter reached the outer edges of the Martian atmosphere, after having traveled through space for 286 days and costing a total of $327 million to create. As it approached its final orbit, a miscalculation caused it to fly too low, and the Orbiter was destroyed. The reason? The spacecraft's thrusters calculated force using imperial units, while the spacecraft's computer worked with metric units. The result was a disaster for NASA, and a pointed reminder of just how important it is to understand which units your data is in.

Geospatial data can come in a variety of different units. Distances can be measured in metric and imperial, of course, but there are actually a lot of different ways in which a given distance can be measured, including:

- Millimeters
- Centimeters

- Inches
- International feet
- U.S. Survey feet
- Meters
- Yards
- Kilometers
- International miles
- U.S. survey (statute) miles
- Nautical miles

Whenever you are working with distance data, it is important that you know which units those distances are in. You will also often find it necessary to convert data from one unit of measurement to another.

Angular measurements can also be in different units: degrees or radians. Once again, you will often have to convert from one to the other.

While these are not strictly speaking different units, you will often find yourself dealing with different ways of representing longitude and latitude values. Traditionally, longitude and latitude values have been written using degrees, minutes, and seconds notation, as follows:

```
176° 14' 4''
```

Another possible way of writing these numbers is to use degrees and decimal minutes notation:

```
176° 14.066'
```

Finally, there is the decimal degrees notation:

```
176.234436°
```

Decimal degrees are quite common now, mainly because these are simply floating-point numbers you can put directly into your programs, but you may well need to convert longitude and latitude values from other formats before you can use them.

Another possible issue with longitude and latitude values is that the **quadrant** (east, west, north, south) can sometimes be given as a separate value rather than using positive or negative values. For example:

```
176.234436° E
```

Fortunately, all these conversions are relatively straightforward. But it is important to know which units, and which format your data is in — your software may not crash a spacecraft, but it will produce some very strange and incomprehensible results if you aren't careful.

Projections

Creating a two-dimensional map from the three-dimensional shape of the earth is a process known as **projection**. A projection is a mathematical transformation that "unwraps" the three-dimensional shape of the earth and places it onto a two-dimensional plane.

Hundreds of different projections have been developed, but none of them are perfect. Indeed, it is mathematically impossible to represent the three-dimensional earth's surface on a two-dimensional plane without introducing some sort of distortion; the trick is to choose a projection where the distortion doesn't matter for your particular use. For example, some projections represent certain areas of the earth's surface accurately, while adding major distortion to other parts of the earth; these projections are useful for maps in the accurate portion of the earth, but not elsewhere. Other projections distort the shape of a country while maintaining its area, while yet other projections do the opposite.

There are three main groups of projections: cylindrical, conical, and azimuthal. Let's look at each of these briefly.

Cylindrical projections

An easy way to understand cylindrical projections is to imagine that the earth is like a spherical Chinese lantern, with a candle in the middle:

If you placed this lantern-earth inside a paper cylinder, the candle would "project" the surface of the earth onto the inside of the cylinder:

You can then "unwrap" this cylinder to obtain a two-dimensional image of the earth:

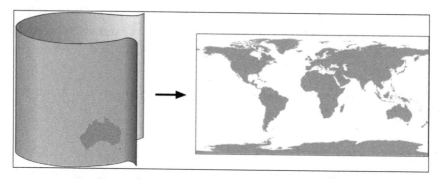

Of course, this is a simplification—in reality, map projections don't actually use light sources to project the earth's surface onto a plane, but instead use sophisticated mathematical transformations to achieve the same effect.

Some of the main types of cylindrical projections include the *Mercator Projection*, the *Equal-Area Cylindrical Projection*, and the *Universal Transverse Mercator Projection*. The following map, taken from Wikipedia, is an example of a Mercator projection:

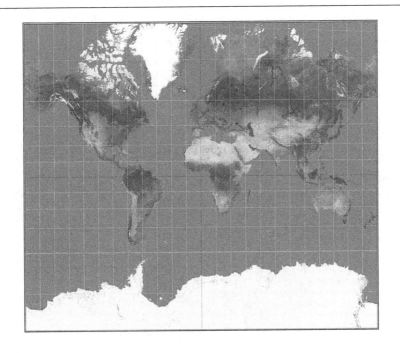

Conic projections

A conic projection is obtained by projecting the earth's surface onto a cone:

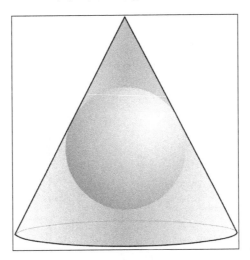

The cone is then "unwrapped" to produce the final map. Some of the more common types of conic projections include the *Albers Equal-Area Projection*, the *Lambert Conformal Conic Projection*, and the *Equidistant Projection*. The following is an example of a Lambert Conformal Conic Projection, again taken from Wikipedia:

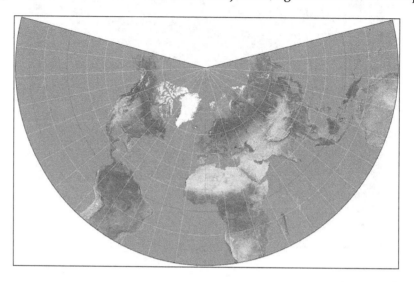

Polar-aligned conic projections are particularly useful when displaying areas that are wide but not very high, such as a map of Russia.

Azimuthal projections

An azimuthal projection involves projecting the earth's surface directly onto a flat surface:

Azimuthal projections are centered around a single point, and don't generally show the entire earth's surface. They do, however, emphasize the spherical nature of the earth. In many ways, azimuthal projections depict the earth as it would be seen from space.

Some of the main types of azimuthal projections include the *Gnomonic Projection*, the *Lambert Equal-Area Azimuthal Projection*, and the *Orthographic Projection*. The following example, taken from Wikipedia, shows a Gnomonic projection based around the north pole:

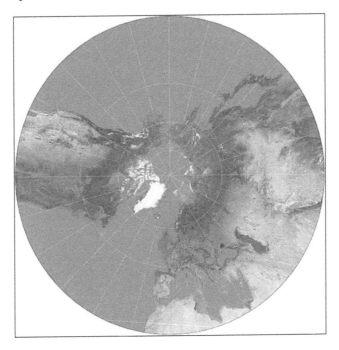

The nature of map projections

As mentioned earlier, there is no such thing as a perfect projection—every projection distorts the earth's surface in some way. Indeed, the mathematician Carl Gausse proved that it is mathematically impossible to project a three-dimensional shape such as a sphere onto a flat plane without introducing some sort of distortion. This is why there are so many different types of projections: some projections are more suited to a given purpose, but no projection can do everything.

Whenever you create or work with geospatial data, it is essential that you know which projection has been used to create that data. Without knowing the projection, you won't be able to plot data or perform accurate calculations.

Coordinate systems

Closely related to map projection is the concept of a **coordinate system**. There are two types of coordinate systems you will need to be familiar with: **projected coordinate systems**, and **unprojected coordinate systems**.

Latitude and longitude values are an example of an unprojected coordinate system. These are coordinates that refer directly to a point on the earth's surface:

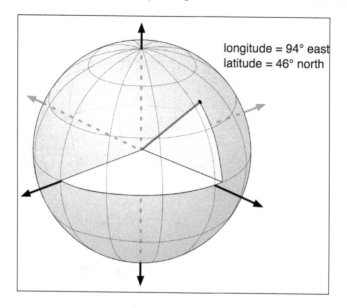

longitude = 94° east
latitude = 46° north

Unprojected coordinates are useful because they can accurately represent a desired point on the earth's surface, but they also make it quite difficult to perform distance and other geospatial calculations.

Projected coordinates, on the other hand, are coordinates which refer to a point on a two-dimensional map that *represents* the surface of the earth:

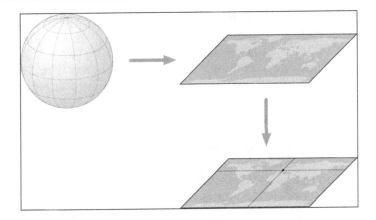

A projected coordinate system, as the name implies, makes use of a map projection to first convert the earth into a two-dimensional Cartesian plane, and then places points onto that plane. To work with a projected coordinate system, you need to know which projection was used to create the underlying map.

For both projected and unprojected coordinates, the coordinate system also implies a set of **reference points** that allow you to identify where a given point will be. For example, the unprojected lat/long coordinate system represents the longitude value of zero by a line running north-south through the Greenwich observatory in England. Similarly, a latitude value of zero represents a line running around the equator of the earth.

For projected coordinate systems, you typically define an origin and the map units. Some coordinate systems also use *false northing* and *false easting* values to adjust the position of the origin, as shown in the following image:

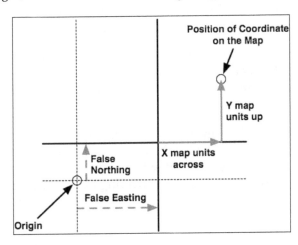

To give a concrete example, the **Universal Transverse Mercator (UTM)** coordinate system divides the world up into 60 different "zones", each zone using a different map projection to minimize projection errors. Within a given zone, the coordinates are measured as the number of meters away from the zone's origin, which is the intersection of the equator and the central meridian for that zone. False northing and false easting values are then added to the distance in meters away from this reference point to avoid having to deal with negative numbers.

As you can imagine, working with projected coordinate systems like this can get quite complicated. The big advantage of projected coordinates, however, is that it is easy to perform geospatial calculations using these coordinates. For example, to calculate the distance between two points that both use the same UTM coordinate system, you simply calculate the length of the line between them, which is the distance between the two points, in meters. This is ridiculously easy, compared with the work required to calculate distances using unprojected coordinates.

Of course, this assumes that the two points are both in the same coordinate system. Since projected coordinate systems are generally only accurate over a relatively small area, you can get into trouble if the two points aren't both in the same coordinate system (for example, if they are in two different UTM zones). This is where unprojected coordinate systems have a big advantage: they cover the entire earth.

Datums

Roughly speaking, a datum is a mathematical model of the earth used to describe locations on the earth's surface. A datum consists of a set of reference points, often combined with a model of the shape of the earth. The reference points are used to describe the location of other points on the earth's surface, while the model of the earth's shape is used when projecting the earth's surface onto a two-dimensional plane. Thus, datums are used by both map projections and coordinate systems.

While there are hundreds of different datums in use throughout the world, most of these only apply to a localized area. There are three main **reference datums** which cover larger areas, and which you are likely to encounter when working with geospatial data:

- **NAD 27**: This is the North American Datum of 1927. It includes a definition of the earth's shape (using a model called the Clarke Spheroid of 1866), and a set of reference points centered around Meades Ranch in Kansas. NAD 27 can be thought of as a local datum covering North America.

- **NAD 83**: The North American Datum of 1983. This datum makes use of a more complex model of the earth's shape (the **1980 Geodetic Reference System, GRS 80**). NAD 83 can be thought of as a local datum covering the United States, Canada, Mexico, and Central America.

- **WGS 84**: The World Geodetic System of 1984. This is a global datum covering the entire earth. It makes use of yet another model of the earth's shape (the **Earth Gravitational Model of 1996, EGM 96**) and uses reference points based on the IERS International Reference Meridian. WGS 84 is a very popular datum. When dealing with geospatial data covering the United States, WGS 84 is basically identical to NAD 83. WGS 84 also has the distinction of being used by Global Positioning System satellites, so all data captured by GPS units will use this datum.

While WGS 84 is the most common datum in use today, a lot of geospatial data makes use of other datums. Whenever you are dealing with a coordinate value, it is important to know which datum was used to calculate that coordinate. A given point in NAD 27, for example, may be several hundred feet away from that same coordinate expressed in WGS 84. Thus, it is vital that you know which datum is being used for a given set of geospatial data, and convert to a different datum where necessary.

Shapes

Geospatial data often represents **shapes** in the form of points, paths, and outlines:

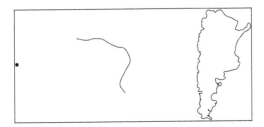

A **point**, of course, is simply a coordinate, described by two or more numbers within a projected or unprojected coordinate system.

Downloading the example code

You can download the example code files for all Packt books you have purchased from your account at http://www.packtpub.com. If you purchased this book elsewhere, you can visit http://www.packtpub.com/support and register to have the files e-mailed directly to you

A path is generally described using what is called a **linestring**:

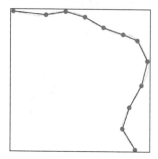

A linestring represents a path as a connected series of line segments. A linestring is a deliberate simplification of a path, a way of approximating the curving path without having to deal with the complex maths required to draw and manipulate curves. Linestrings are often used in geospatial data to represent roads, rivers, contour lines, and so on.

 Linestrings are also sometimes referred to as **polylines**. When a linestring is *closed* (that is, the last line segment finishes at the point where the first line segment starts), the linestring is often referred to as a **linear ring**.

An outline is often represented in geospatial data using a **polygon**:

Polygons are commonly used in geospatial data to describe the outline of countries, lakes, cities, and so on. A polygon has an *exterior ring*, defined by a closed linestring, and may optionally have one or more *interior rings* within it, each also defined by a closed linestring. The exterior ring represents the polygon's outline, while the interior rings (if any) represent "holes" within the polygon:

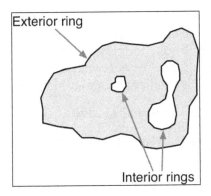

These holes are often used to depict interior features such as islands within a lake.

GIS data formats

A GIS data format specifies how geospatial data is stored in a file (or multiple files) on disk. The format describes the logical structure used to store geospatial data within the file(s).

> While we talk about storing information on disk, data formats can also be used to *transmit* geospatial information between computer systems. For example, a web service might provide map data on request, transmitting that data in a particular format.

A GIS data format will typically support:

- Geospatial data describing geographical features.
- Additional metadata describing this data, including the datum and projection used, the coordinate system and units that the data is in, the date this file was last updated, and so on.
- Attributes providing additional information about the geographical features that are being described. For example, a city feature may have attributes such as "name", "population", "average temperature", and others.
- Display information such as the color or line style to use when a feature is displayed.

There are two main types of GIS data: **raster format data**, and **vector format data**. Raster formats are generally used to store bitmapped images, such as scanned paper maps or aerial photographs. Vector formats, on the other hand, represent spatial data using points, lines, and polygons. Vector formats are the most common type used by GIS applications as the data is smaller and easier to manipulate.

Some of the more common raster formats include:

- **Digital Raster Graphic (DRG)**: This format is used to store digital scans of paper maps

- **Digital Elevation Model (DEM)**: Used by the US Geological Survey to record elevation data

- **Band Interleaved by Line, Band Interleaved by Pixel, Band Sequential (BIL, BIP, BSQ)**: These data formats are typically used by remote sensing systems

Some of the more common vector formats include:

- **Shapefile**: An open specification, developed by ESRI, for storing and exchanging GIS data. A Shapefile actually consists of a collection of files, all with the same base name, for example, `hawaii.shp`, `hawaii.shx`, `hawaii.dbf`, and so on.

- **Simple features**: An OpenGIS standard for storing geographical data (points, lines, polygons) along with associated attributes.

- **TIGER/Line**: A text-based format previously used by the US Census Bureau to describe geographic features such as roads, buildings, rivers, and coastlines. More recent data comes in the Shapefile format, so the TIGER/Line format is only used for earlier Census Bureau datasets.

- **Coverage**: A proprietary data format used by ESRI's ARC/INFO system.

In addition to these "major" data formats, there are also so-called "micro-formats" which are often used to represent individual pieces of geospatial data. These are often used to represent shapes within a running program, or to transfer shapes from one program to another, but aren't generally used to store data permanently. As you work with geospatial data, you are likely to encounter the following micro-formats:

- **Well-known Text (WKT)**: This is a simple text-based format for representing a single geographic feature such as a polygon or linestring

- **Well-known Binary (WKB)**: This alternative to WKT uses binary data rather than text to represent a single geographic feature

- **GeoJSON**: An open format for encoding geographic data structures, based on the JSON data interchange format
- **Geography Markup Language** (**GML**): An XML-based open standard for exchanging GIS data

Whenever you work with geospatial data, you need to know which format the data is in, so that you can extract the information you need from the file(s), and, where necessary, transform the data from one format to another.

Working with GIS data manually

Let's take a brief look at the process of working with GIS data manually. Before we can begin, there are two things you need to do:

- Obtain some GIS data
- Install the GDAL Python library so that you can read the necessary data files

Let's use the US Census Bureau's website to download a set of vector maps for the various US states. The main site for obtaining GIS data from the US Census Bureau can be found at:

```
http://www.census.gov/geo/www/tiger
```

To make things simpler though, let's bypass the website and directly download the file we need from the following link:

```
http://www2.census.gov/geo/tiger/TIGER2012/STATE/tl_2012_us_state.zip
```

The resulting file, `tl_2009_us_state.zip`, should be a ZIP-format archive. After uncompressing the archive, you should have the following files:

- `tl_2012_us_state.dbf`
- `tl_2012_us_state.prj`
- `tl_2012_us_state.shp`
- `tl_2012_us_state.shp.xml`
- `tl_2012_us_state.shx`

These files make up a **Shapefile** containing the outlines of all the US states. Place these files together in a convenient directory.

We next have to download the GDAL Python library. The main website for GDAL can be found at:

```
http://gdal.org
```

The easiest way to install GDAL onto a Windows or Unix machine is to use the **FWTools installer**, which can be downloaded from the following site:

```
http://fwtools.maptools.org
```

If you are running Mac OS X, you can find a complete installer for GDAL at:

```
http://www.kyngchaos.com/software/frameworks
```

After installing GDAL, you can check that it works by typing `import osgeo` into the Python command prompt; if the Python command prompt reappears with no error message, GDAL was successfully installed and you are all set to go:

```
>>> import osgeo
>>>
```

Now that we have some data to work with, let's take a look at it. You can either type the following directly into the command prompt, or else save it as a Python script so that you can run it whenever you wish (let's call this `analyze.py`):

```python
import osgeo.ogr

shapefile = osgeo.ogr.Open("tl_2012_us_state.shp")
numLayers = shapefile.GetLayerCount()

print "Shapefile contains %d layers" % numLayers
print

for layerNum in range(numLayers):
    layer = shapefile.GetLayer(layerNum)
    spatialRef = layer.GetSpatialRef().ExportToProj4()
    numFeatures = layer.GetFeatureCount()
    print "Layer %d has spatial reference %s" % (layerNum, spatialRef)
    print "Layer %d has %d features:" % (layerNum, numFeatures)
    print

    for featureNum in range(numFeatures):
        feature = layer.GetFeature(featureNum)
```

```
featureName = feature.GetField("NAME")

print "Feature %d has name %s" % (featureNum, featureName)
```

 The previous example assumes you've placed this script in the same directory as the `tl_2012_us_state.shp` file. If you've put it in a different directory, change the `osgeo.ogr.Open()` command to include the path to your Shapefile. If you are running MS Windows, don't forget to use double backslash characters (\ \) as directory separators.

This gives us a quick summary of how the Shapefile's data is structured:

```
Shapefile contains 1 layers

Layer 0 has spatial reference +proj=longlat +datum=NAD83 +no_defs
Layer 0 has 56 features:

Feature 0 has name Hawaii
Feature 1 has name Arkansas
Feature 2 has name New Mexico
Feature 3 has name Montana
. . .
Feature 53 has name Arizona
Feature 54 has name Nevada
Feature 55 has name California
```

This shows us that the data we downloaded consists of one layer, with 56 individual features corresponding to the various states and protectorates in the USA. It also tells us the "spatial reference" for this layer, which tells us that the coordinates are projected as latitude and longitude values using the NAD 83 datum.

As you can see from the previous example, using GDAL to extract data from Shapefiles is quite straightforward. Let's continue with another example. This time, we'll look at the details for Feature 2, New Mexico:

```
import osgeo.ogr

shapefile = osgeo.ogr.Open("tl_2012_us_state.shp")
```

```
layer = shapefile.GetLayer(0)
feature = layer.GetFeature(2)

print "Feature 2 has the following attributes:"
print

attributes = feature.items()

for key,value in attributes.items():
    print "  %s = %s" % (key, value)

geometry = feature.GetGeometryRef()
geometryName = geometry.GetGeometryName()

print
print "Feature's geometry data consists of a %s" % geometryName
```

Running this produces the following:

```
Feature 2 has the following attributes:

    DIVISION = 8
    INTPTLAT = +34.4346843
    NAME = New Mexico
    STUSPS = NM
    FUNCSTAT = A
    REGION = 4
    LSAD = 00
    INTPTLON = -106.1316181
    AWATER = 756438507.0
    STATENS = 00897535
    MTFCC = G4000
    STATEFP = 35
    ALAND = 3.14161109357e+11


Feature's geometry data consists of a POLYGON
```

The meaning of the various attributes is described on the US Census Bureau's website, but what interests us right now is the feature's geometry. A geometry object is a complex structure that holds some geospatial data, often using nested geometry objects to reflect the way the geospatial data is organized. So far, we've discovered that New Mexico's geometry consists of a polygon. Let's now take a closer look at this polygon:

```python
import osgeo.ogr

def analyzeGeometry(geometry, indent=0):
    s = []
    s.append("   " * indent)
    s.append(geometry.GetGeometryName())
    if geometry.GetPointCount() > 0:
        s.append(" with %d data points" % geometry.GetPointCount())
    if geometry.GetGeometryCount() > 0:
        s.append(" containing:")

    print "".join(s)

    for i in range(geometry.GetGeometryCount()):
        analyzeGeometry(geometry.GetGeometryRef(i), indent+1)

shapefile = osgeo.ogr.Open("tl_2012_us_state.shp")
layer = shapefile.GetLayer(0)
feature = layer.GetFeature(2)
geometry = feature.GetGeometryRef()

analyzeGeometry(geometry)
```

The `analyzeGeometry()` function gives a useful idea of how the geometry has been structured:

```
POLYGON containing:
  LINEARRING with 7550 data points
```

In GDAL (or more specifically the OGR Simple Feature library we are using here), polygons are defined as a single outer "ring" with optional inner rings that define "holes" in the polygon (for example, to show the outline of a lake).

New Mexico is a relatively simple feature in that it consists of only one polygon. If we ran the same program over California (feature 55 in our Shapefile), the output would be somewhat more complicated:

```
MULTIPOLYGON containing:
  POLYGON containing:
    LINEARRING with 10105 data points
  POLYGON containing:
    LINEARRING with 392 data points
  POLYGON containing:
    LINEARRING with 152 data points
  POLYGON containing:
    LINEARRING with 191 data points
  POLYGON containing:
    LINEARRING with 121 data points
  POLYGON containing:
    LINEARRING with 93 data points
  POLYGON containing:
    LINEARRING with 77 data points
```

As you can see, California is made up of seven distinct polygons, each defined by a single linear ring. This is because California is on the coast, and includes six outlying islands as well as the main inland body of the state.

Let's finish this analysis of the US state Shapefile by answering a simple question: what is the distance from the northernmost point to the southernmost point in California? There are various ways we could answer this question, but for now we'll do it by hand. Let's start by identifying the northernmost and southernmost points in California:

```
import osgeo.ogr

def findPoints(geometry, results):
    for i in range(geometry.GetPointCount()):
        x,y,z = geometry.GetPoint(i)
        if results['north'] == None or results['north'][1] < y:
            results['north'] = (x,y)
        if results['south'] == None or results['south'][1] > y:
            results['south'] = (x,y)
```

```
     for i in range(geometry.GetGeometryCount()):
       findPoints(geometry.GetGeometryRef(i), results)

shapefile = osgeo.ogr.Open("tl_2012_us_state.shp")
layer = shapefile.GetLayer(0)
feature = layer.GetFeature(55)
geometry = feature.GetGeometryRef()

results = {'north' : None,
           'south' : None}

findPoints(geometry, results)

print "Northernmost point is (%0.4f, %0.4f)" % results['north']
print "Southernmost point is (%0.4f, %0.4f)" % results['south']
```

The `findPoints()` function recursively scans through a geometry, extracting the individual points and identifying the points with the highest and lowest y (latitude) values, which are then stored in the `results` dictionary so that the main program can use it.

As you can see, GDAL makes it easy to work with the complex geometry data structure. The code does require recursion, but is still trivial compared with trying to read the data directly. If you run the previous program, the following will be displayed:

Northernmost point is (-122.3782, 42.0095)

Southernmost point is (-117.2049, 32.5288)

Now that we have these two points, we next want to calculate the distance between them. As described earlier, we have to use a **great circle distance** calculation here to allow for the curvature of the earth's surface. We'll do this manually, using the Haversine formula:

```
import math

lat1 = 42.0095
long1 = -122.3782

lat2 = 32.5288
long2 = -117.2049

rLat1 = math.radians(lat1)
```

```
rLong1 = math.radians(long1)
rLat2 = math.radians(lat2)
rLong2 = math.radians(long2)

dLat = rLat2 - rLat1
dLong = rLong2 - rLong1
a = math.sin(dLat/2)**2 + math.cos(rLat1) * math.cos(rLat2) \
                        * math.sin(dLong/2)**2
c = 2 * math.atan2(math.sqrt(a), math.sqrt(1-a))
distance = 6371 * c

print "Great circle distance is %0.0f kilometres" % distance
```

Don't worry about the complex maths involved here; basically, we are converting the latitude and longitude values to radians, calculating the difference in latitude/longitude values between the two points, and then passing the results through some trigonometric functions to obtain the great circle distance. The value of 6371 is the radius of the earth, in kilometers.

More details about the Haversine formula and how it is used in the previous example can be found at http://mathforum.org/library/drmath/view/51879.html.

If you run the previous program, your computer will tell you the distance from the northernmost point to the southernmost point in California:

```
Great circle distance is 1149 kilometres
```

There are, of course, other ways of calculating this. You wouldn't normally type the Haversine formula directly into your program, as there are libraries which will do this for you. But we deliberately did the calculation this way to show just how it can be done.

If you would like to explore this further, you might like to try writing programs to calculate the following:

- The easternmost and westernmost points in California.
- The midpoint in California. Hint: you can calculate the midpoint's longitude by taking the average of the easternmost and westernmost longitude.
- The midpoint in Arizona.
- The distance between the middle of California and the middle of Arizona.

As you can see, working with GIS data manually isn't too onerous. While the data structures and maths involved can be rather complex, using tools such as GDAL makes your data accessible and easy to work with.

Summary

In this chapter, we discussed many of the core concepts that underlie GIS development, looked briefly at the history of GIS, examined some of the more common GIS data formats, and got our hands dirty exploring US state maps downloaded from the US Census Bureau website. We have learned the following:

- Locations are often, but not always, represented using coordinates
- Calculating the distance between two points requires you to take into account the curvature of the earth's surface
- You must be aware of the units used in geospatial data
- Map projections represent the three-dimensional shape of the earth's surface as a two-dimensional map
- There are three main classes of map projections: cylindrical, conic and azimuthal
- Datums are mathematical models of the earth's shape
- The three most common datums in use are called NAD 27, NAD 83, and WGS 84
- Coordinate systems describe how coordinates relate to a given point on the earth's surface
- Unprojected coordinate systems directly represent points on the earth's surface
- Projected coordinate systems use a map projection to represent the earth as a two-dimensional Cartesian plane, onto which coordinates are then placed
- Geospatial data can represent shapes in the form of points, linestrings, and polygons
- There are a number of standard GIS data formats you might encounter. Some data formats work with raster data, while others use vector data
- Using Python to manually perform various geospatial calculations on Shapefile data

In the next chapter, we will look in more detail at the various Python libraries which can be used for working with geospatial data.

3
Python Libraries for Geospatial Development

This chapter examines a number of libraries and other tools which can be used for geospatial development in Python.

More specifically, we will cover:

- Python libraries for reading and writing geospatial data
- Python libraries for dealing with map projections
- Libraries for analyzing and manipulating geospatial data directly within your Python programs
- Tools for visualizing geospatial data

Note that there are two types of geospatial tools which are not discussed in this chapter: geospatial databases and geospatial web toolkits. Both of these will be examined in detail later in this book.

Reading and writing geospatial data

While you could in theory write your own parser to read a particular geospatial data format, it is much easier to use an existing Python library to do this. We will look at two popular libraries for reading and writing geospatial data: GDAL and OGR.

GDAL/OGR

Unfortunately, the naming of these two libraries is rather confusing. **Geospatial Data Abstraction Library (GDAL)**, was originally just a library for working with raster geospatial data, while the separate OGR library was intended to work with vector data. However, the two libraries are now partially merged, and are generally downloaded and installed together under the combined name of "GDAL". To avoid confusion, we will call this combined library **GDAL/OGR** and use "GDAL" to refer to just the raster translation library.

A default installation of GDAL supports reading 116 different raster file formats, and writing to 58 different formats. OGR by default supports reading 56 different vector file formats, and writing to 30 formats. This makes GDAL/OGR one of the most powerful geospatial data translators available, and certainly the most useful freely-available library for reading and writing geospatial data.

GDAL design

GDAL uses the following data model for describing raster geospatial data:

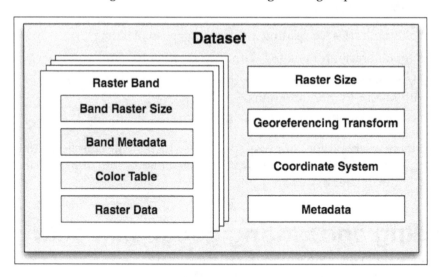

Let's take a look at the various parts of this model:

- A **dataset** holds all the raster data, in the form of a collection of raster "bands", along with information that is common to all these bands. A dataset normally represents the contents of a single file.

- A **raster band** represents a band, channel, or layer within the image. For example, RGB image data would normally have separate bands for the red, green, and blue components of the image.

- The **raster size** specifies the overall width and height of the image, in pixels.

- The **georeferencing transform** converts from (x, y) raster coordinates into georeferenced coordinates — that is, coordinates on the surface of the earth. There are two types of georeferencing transforms supported by GDAL: affine transformations and ground control points.

   ○ An **affine transformation** is a mathematical formula allowing the following operations to be applied to the raster data:

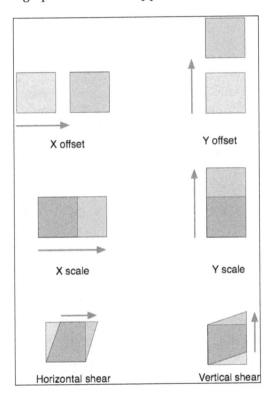

More than one of these operations can be applied at once; this allows you to perform sophisticated transforms such as rotations.

 Affine transformations are sometimes referred to as *linear transformations*.

- ○ **Ground Control Points (GCPs)** relate one or more positions within the raster to their equivalent georeferenced coordinates, as shown in the following figure:

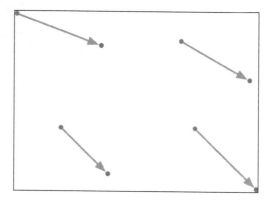

  Note that GDAL does not translate coordinates using GCPs — that is left up to the application, and generally involves complex mathematical functions to perform the transformation.

- The **coordinate system** describes the georeferenced coordinates produced by the georeferencing transform. The coordinate system includes the projection and datum, as well as the units and scale used by the raster data.

- The **metadata** contains additional information about the dataset as a whole.

Each raster band contains the following (among other things):

- The **band raster size**: This is the size (number of pixels across and number of lines high) for the data within the band. This may be the same as the raster size for the overall dataset, in which case the dataset is at full resolution, or the band's data may need to be scaled to match the dataset.

- Some **band metadata** providing extra information specific to this band.

- A **color table** describing how pixel values are translated into colors.

- The **raster data** itself.

GDAL provides a number of **drivers** which allow you to read (and sometimes write) various types of raster geospatial data. When reading a file, GDAL selects a suitable driver automatically based on the type of data; when writing, you first select the driver and then tell the driver to create the new dataset you want to write to.

GDAL example code

A **Digital Elevation Model (DEM)** file contains height values. In the following example program, we use GDAL to calculate the average of the height values contained in a sample DEM file. In this case, we use a DEM file downloaded from the GLOBE elevation dataset:

```
from osgeo import gdal,gdalconst
import struct

dataset = gdal.Open("data/e10g")
band = dataset.GetRasterBand(1)

fmt = "<" + ("h" * band.XSize)

totHeight = 0

for y in range(band.YSize):
    scanline = band.ReadRaster(0, y, band.XSize, 1,
                               band.XSize, 1,
                               band.DataType)
    values = struct.unpack(fmt, scanline)

    for value in values:
        if value == -500:
            # Special height value for the sea -> ignore.
            continue

        totHeight = totHeight + value

average = totHeight / (band.XSize * band.YSize)
print "Average height =", average
```

 Please refer to *Chapter 4, Sources of Geospatial Data,* for more information on the GLOBE dataset and how to download the data used in this example.

As you can see, this program obtains the single raster band from the DEM file, and then reads through it one scanline at a time. We then use the `struct` standard Python library module to read the individual height values out of the scanline. Because the GLOBE dataset uses a special height value of -500 to represent the ocean, we exclude these values from our calculations. Finally, we use the remaining height values to calculate the average height, in meters, over the entire DEM data file.

OGR design

OGR uses the following model for working with vector-based geospatial data:

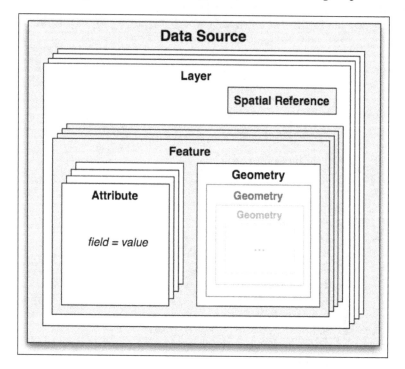

Let's take a look at this design in more detail:

- The **data source** represents the file you are working with—though it doesn't have to be a file. It could just as easily be a URL or some other source of data.

- The data source has one or more **layers**, representing sets of related data. For example, a single data source representing a country may contain a "terrain" layer, a "contour lines" layer, a "roads" later, and a "city boundaries" layer. Other data sources may consist of just one layer. Each layer has a spatial reference and a list of features.

- The **spatial reference** specifies the projection and datum used by the layer's data.

- A **feature** corresponds to some significant element within the layer. For example, a feature might represent a state, a city, a road, an island, and so on. Each feature has a list of attributes and a geometry.

- The **attributes** provide additional meta-information about the feature. For example, an attribute might provide the name for a city's feature, its population, or the feature's unique ID used to retrieve additional information about the feature from an external database.

- Finally, the **geometry** describes the physical shape or location of the feature. Geometries are recursive data structures that can themselves contain sub-geometries — for example, a "country" feature might consist of a geometry that encompasses several islands, each represented by a subgeometry within the main "country" geometry.

  The geometry design within OGR is based on the Open Geospatial Consortium's "Simple Features" model for representing geospatial geometries. For more information, see `http://www.opengeospatial.org/standards/sfa`.

Like GDAL, OGR also provides a number of drivers which allow you to read (and sometimes write) various types of vector-based geospatial data. When reading a file, OGR selects a suitable driver automatically; when writing, you first select the driver and then tell the driver to create the new data source to write to.

OGR example code

The following example program uses OGR to read through the contents of a shapefile, printing out the value of the NAME attribute for each feature along with the geometry type:

```python
from osgeo import ogr

shapefile = ogr.Open("TM_WORLD_BORDERS-0.3.shp")
layer = shapefile.GetLayer(0)

for i in range(layer.GetFeatureCount()):
    feature = layer.GetFeature(i)
    name = feature.GetField("NAME")
    geometry = feature.GetGeometryRef()
    print i, name, geometry.GetGeometryName()
```

Documentation

GDAL and OGR are well documented, but with a catch for Python programmers. The GDAL/OGR library and associated command-line tools are all written in C and C++. Bindings are available which allow access from a variety of other languages, including Python, but the documentation is all written for the C++ version of the libraries. This can make reading the documentation rather challenging—not only are all the method signatures written in C++, but the Python bindings have changed many of the method and class names to make them more "pythonic".

Fortunately, the Python libraries are largely self-documenting, thanks to all the docstrings embedded in the Python bindings themselves. This means you can explore the documentation using tools such as Python's built-in `pydoc` utility, which can be run from the command line like this:

```
% pydoc -g osgeo
```

This will open up a GUI window allowing you to read the documentation using a web browser. Alternatively, if you want to find out about a single method or class, you can use Python's built-in `help()` command from the Python command line, like this:

```
>>> import osgeo.ogr
>>> help(osgeo.ogr.DataSource.CopyLayer)
```

Not all the methods are documented, so you may need to refer to the C++ docs on the GDAL website for more information, and some of the docstrings are copied directly from the C++ documentation—but in general the documentation for GDAL/OGR is excellent, and should allow you to quickly come up to speed using this library.

Availability

GDAL/OGR runs on modern Unix machines, including Linux and Mac OS X, as well as most versions of Microsoft Windows. The main website for GDAL can be found at:

```
http://gdal.org
```

The main website for OGR is at:

```
http://gdal.org/ogr
```

To download GDAL/OGR, follow the **Downloads** link on the main GDAL website. Windows users may find the FWTools package useful, as it provides a wide range of geospatial software for win32 machines, including GDAL/OGR and its Python bindings. FWTools can be found at:

`http://fwtools.maptools.org`

For those running Mac OS X, prebuilt binaries can be obtained from:

`http://www.kyngchaos.com/software/frameworks`

 Make sure that you install GDAL Version 1.9 or later, as you will need this version to work through the examples in this book.

Being an open source package, the complete source code for GDAL/OGR is available from the website, so you can compile it yourself. Most people, however, will simply want to use a prebuilt binary version.

Dealing with projections

One of the challenges of working with geospatial data is that geodetic locations (points on the Earth's surface) are mapped into a two-dimensional Cartesian plane using a cartographic projection. We looked at projections in the previous chapter: whenever you have some geospatial data, you need to know which projection that data uses. You also need to know the datum (model of the Earth's shape) assumed by the data.

A common challenge when dealing with geospatial data is that you have to convert data from one projection/datum to another. Fortunately, there is a Python library pyproj which makes this task easy.

pyproj

pyproj is a Python "wrapper" around another library called PROJ.4. "PROJ.4" is an abbreviation for Version 4 of the PROJ library. PROJ was originally written by the US Geological Survey for dealing with map projections, and has been widely used in geospatial software for many years. The pyproj library makes it possible to access the functionality of PROJ.4 from within your Python programs.

Design

The `pyproj` library consists of the following pieces:

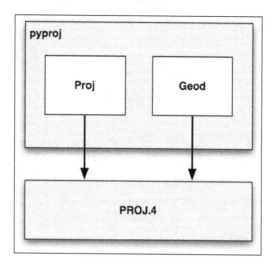

`pyproj` consists of just two classes: **Proj** and **Geod**. `Proj` converts from longitude and latitude values to native map (x, y) coordinates, and vice versa. `Geod` performs various Great Circle distance and angle calculations. Both are built on top of the `PROJ.4` library. Let's take a closer look at these two classes.

Proj

`Proj` is a cartographic transformation class, allowing you to convert geographic coordinates (that is, latitude and longitude values) into cartographic coordinates (x, y values, by default in meters) and vice versa.

When you create a new `Proj` instance, you specify the projection, datum, and other values used to describe how the projection is to be done. For example, to use the Transverse Mercator projection and the WGS84 ellipsoid, you would do the following:

```
projection = pyproj.Proj(proj='tmerc', ellps='WGS84')
```

Once you have created a `Proj` instance, you can use it to convert a latitude and longitude to an (x, y) coordinate using the given projection. You can also use it to do an inverse projection—that is, converting from an (x, y) coordinate back into a latitude and longitude value again.

The helpful `transform()` function can be used to directly convert coordinates from one projection to another. You simply provide the starting coordinates, the `Proj` object that describes the starting coordinates' projection, and the desired ending projection. This can be very useful when converting coordinates, either singly or en masse.

Geod

`Geod` is a geodetic computation class, which allows you to perform various Great Circle calculations. We looked at Great Circle calculations earlier, when considering how to accurately calculate the distance between two points on the Earth's surface. The `Geod` class, however, can do more than this:

- The `fwd()` method takes a starting point, an azimuth (angular direction) and a distance, and returns the ending point and the back azimuth (the angle from the end point back to the start point again):

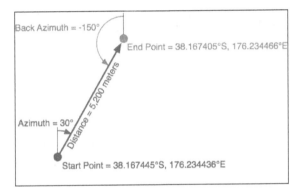

- The `inv()` method takes two coordinates and returns the forward and back azimuth as well as the distance between them:

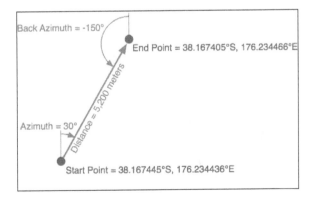

- The `npts()` method calculates the coordinates of a number of points spaced equidistantly along a geodesic line running from the start to the end point:

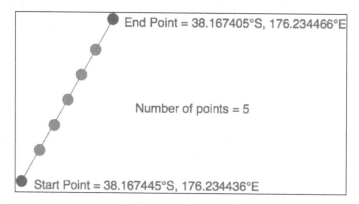

When you create a new `Geod` object, you specify the ellipsoid to use when performing the geodetic calculations. The ellipsoid can be selected from a number of predefined ellipsoids, or you can enter the parameters for the ellipsoid (equatorial radius, polar radius, and so on) directly.

Example code

The following example starts with a location specified using UTM zone 17 coordinates. Using two `Proj` objects to define the UTM Zone 17 and lat/long projections, it translates this location's coordinates into latitude and longitude values:

```
import pyproj

UTM_X = 565718.5235
UTM_Y = 3980998.9244

srcProj = pyproj.Proj(proj="utm", zone="11", ellps="clrk66",
units="m")
dstProj = pyproj.Proj(proj="longlat", ellps="WGS84", datum="WGS84")

long,lat = pyproj.transform(srcProj, dstProj, UTM_X, UTM_Y)

print "UTM zone 11 coordinate (%0.4f, %0.4f) = %0.4f, %0.4f" \
    % (UTM_X, UTM_Y, lat, long)
```

Continuing on with this example, let's take the calculated lat/long values and, using a Geod object, calculate another point 10 kilometers northeast of that location:

```
angle    = 315 # 315 degrees = northeast.
distance = 10000

geod = pyproj.Geod(ellps="WGS84")
long2,lat2,invAngle = geod.fwd(long, lat, angle, distance)

print "%0.4f, %0.4f is 10km northeast of %0.4f, %0.4f" \
    % (lat2, long2, lat, long)
```

Documentation

The documentation available on the pyproj website, and in the docs directory provided with the source code, is excellent as far as it goes. It describes how to use the various classes and methods, what they do and what parameters are required. However, the documentation is rather sparse when it comes to the parameters used when creating a new Proj object. As the documentation says:

> *A Proj class instance is initialized with proj map projection control parameter key/value pairs. The key/value pairs can either be passed in a dictionary, or as keyword arguments, or as a proj4 string (compatible with the proj command).*

The documentation does provide a link to a website listing a number of standard map projections and their associated parameters, but understanding what these parameters mean generally requires you to delve into the PROJ documentation itself. The documentation for PROJ is dense and confusing, even more so because the main manual is written for PROJ Version 3, with addendums for later versions. Attempting to make sense of all this can be quite challenging.

Fortunately, in most cases you won't need to refer to the PROJ documentation at all. When working with geospatial data using GDAL or OGR, you can easily extract the projection as a "proj4 string" which can be passed directly to the Proj initializer. If you want to hardwire the projection, you can generally choose a projection and ellipsoid using the proj="..." and ellps="..." parameters, respectively. If you want to do more than this, though, you will need to refer to the PROJ documentation for more details.

 To find out more about PROJ, and to read the original documentation, you can find everything you need at: http://trac.osgeo.org/proj

Availability

Prebuild versions of `pyproj` are available for MS Windows, with source code distributions for other platforms. The main web page for `pyproj` can be found at:

`http://code.google.com/p/pyproj`

How you go about installing it depends on which operating system you are running.

 Make sure that you install Version 4.8.0 or later of the PROJ framework, and Version 1.9.2 or later of the `pyproj` library. These versions are required to follow the examples in this book.

- **MS Windows**

    For computers running MS Windows, installation is easy: just go to the downloads page at the website mentioned earlier and and choose the appropriate installer for your version of Python. The installer includes everything you need, including the PROJ framework.

- **Linux**

    For computers running Linux, you have to download and install the PROJ framework separately, before installing `pyproj`. For Linux machines, you can generally obtain PROJ.4 as an RPM or source tarball which you can then compile yourself. Once this has been done, you can download the `pyproj` source code from the above website, and compile and install it in the usual way:

    ```
    python setup.py build
    python setup.py install
    ```

- **Macintosh**

    If your computer runs Mac OS X, you will also have to download and install PROJ separately. You can install a compiled version of the PROJ framework either as part of a "GDAL Complete" installation, or by just installing the PROJ framework by itself. Either are available at:

    `http://www.kyngchaos.com/software/frameworks`

Once you have installed PROJ.4, you will have to download and build your own copy of the `pyproj` library. Before you can compile `pyproj`, you will need to have Apple's developer tools installed. Doing this is a two-step process:

1. Download and install the latest version of **XCode**. XCode is available for free from the App store, or if you are running an older version of OS X you can download it from:

    `https://developer.apple.com/xcode`

2. Run XCode, and choose the **Preferences** command. Within the **Downloads** tab, click on the **Install** button beside the **Command Line Tools** item:

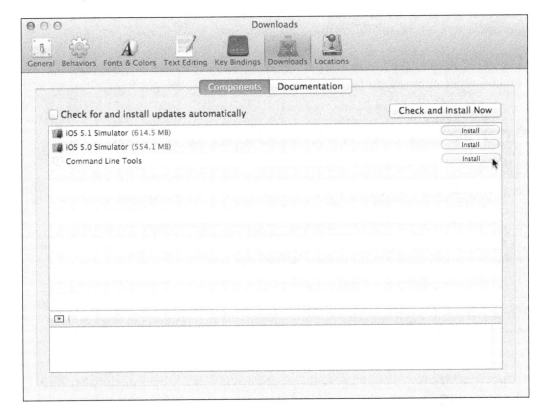

This installs the command-line tools you will need to compile `pyproj`.

Once you have the developer tools installed, download the source code to `pyproj` from the website mentioned earlier. Then open up a Terminal window and `cd` into the main source code directory, then type the following commands:

```
python setup.py build
sudo python.setup.py install
```

 The `sudo` command allows `pyproj` to install itself inside your Python installation's `site-packages` directory. You'll be asked to enter your password before this is done.

Once this has finished, you can check that it worked by running the Python interpreter and typing the following command:

```
import pyproj
```

The Python prompt should reappear without any error messages being shown.

Analyzing and manipulating geospatial data

Because geospatial data works with geometrical features such as points, lines, and polygons, you often need to perform various calculations using these geometrical features. Fortunately, there are some very powerful tools for doing exactly this. For reasons we will describe shortly, the library of choice for performing this type of computational geometry in Python is **Shapely**.

Shapely

Shapely is a Python package for the manipulation and analysis of two-dimensional geospatial geometries. Shapely is based on the GEOS library, which implements a wide range of geospatial data manipulations in C++. GEOS is itself based on a library called the Java Topology Suite, which provides the same functionality for Java programmers. Shapely provides a Pythonic interface to GEOS which makes it easy to use these manipulations directly from your Python programs.

Design

The Shapely library is organized as follows:

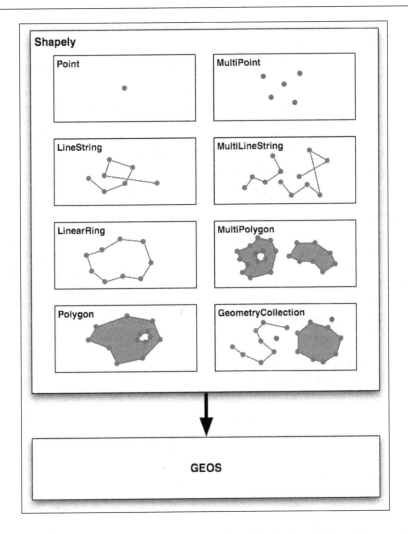

All of Shapely's functionality is built on top of GEOS. Indeed, Shapely requires GEOS to be installed before it can run.

Shapely itself consists of eight major classes, representing different types of geometrical shapes:

- The **Point** class represents a single point in space. Points can be two-dimensional (x, y), or three-dimensional (x, y, z).

- The **LineString** class represents a sequence of points joined together to form a line. LineStrings can be *simple* (no crossing line segments) or *complex* (where two line segments within the LineString cross).

- The **LinearRing** class represents a line string which finishes at the starting point. The line segments within a LinearRing cannot cross or touch.

- The **Polygon** class represents a filled area, optionally with one or more "holes" inside it.

- The **MultiPoint** class represents a collection of Points.

- The **MultiLineString** class represents a collection of LineStrings.

- The **MultiPolygon** class represents a collection of Polygons.

- The **GeometryCollection** class represents a collection of any combination of Points, LineStrings, LinearRings, and Polygons.

As well as being able to represent these various types of geometries, Shapely provides a number of methods and attributes for manipulating and analyzing these geometries. For example, the LineString class provides a `length` attribute that equals the length of all the line segments that make up the LineString, and a `crosses()` method that returns true if two LineStrings cross. Other methods allow you to calculate the intersection of two polygons, dilate or erode geometries, simplify a geometry, calculate the distance between two geometries, and build a polygon that encloses all the points within a given list of geometries (called the `convex_hull` attribute).

Note that Shapely is a *spatial* manipulation library rather than a *geospatial* manipulation library. It has no concept of geographical coordinates. Instead, it assumes that the geospatial data has been projected onto a two-dimensional Cartesian plane before it is manipulated, and the results can then be converted back into geographic coordinates if desired.

Example code

The following program creates two Shapely geometry objects, a circle and a square, and calculates their intersection:

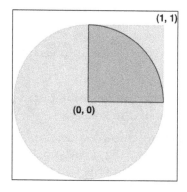

The intersection will be a polygon in the shape of a quarter circle , as indicated by the dark grey portion of the preceding image:

```
import shapely.geometry

pt = shapely.geometry.Point(0, 0)
circle = pt.buffer(1.0)

square = shapely.geometry.Polygon([(0, 0), (1, 0),
                                   (1, 1), (0, 1),
                                   (0, 0)])

intersect = circle.intersection(square)

for x,y in intersect.exterior.coords:
    print x,y
```

Notice how the circle is constructed by taking a Point geometry and using the `buffer()` method to create a Polygon representing the outline of a circle.

Documentation

Shapely comes with excellent documentation, with detailed descriptions, extended code samples, and many illustrations that clearly show how the various classes, methods, and attributes work.

The Shapely documentation is entirely self-contained; there is no need to refer to the GEOS documentation, or to the Java Topology Suite it is based on, unless you particularly want to see how things are done in these libraries. The only exception is that you may need to refer to the GEOS documentation if you are compiling GEOS from source and are having problems getting it to work.

Availability

Shapely will run on all major operating systems, including MS Windows, Mac OS X, and Linux. Shapely's main website can be found at:

`http://pypi.python.org/pypi/Shapely`

The website has everything you need, including the documentation and downloads for the Shapely library, in both source code form and prebuilt binaries for MS Windows.

If you are installing Shapely on a Windows computer, the prebuilt binaries include the GEOS library built-in. Otherwise, you will be responsible for installing GEOS before you can use Shapely.

 Make sure that you install Shapely Version 1.2 or later; you will need this version to work through the examples in this book.

The GEOS library's website is at:

`http://trac.osgeo.org/geos`

To install GEOS in a Unix-based computer, you can either download the source code from the GEOS website and compile it yourself, or you can install a suitable RPM or APT package which includes GEOS. If you are running Mac OS X, you can either try to download and build GEOS yourself, or you can install the prebuild GEOS framework, which is available from the following website:

`http://www.kyngchaos.com/software/frameworks`

 If you've installed the "GDAL Complete" package from the above website, you'll already have GEOS installed on your Mac OS X computer.

After installing GEOS, you need to download, compile, and install the Shapely library. This can be slightly tricky on a Mac OS X computer, so you may find the following blog post useful:

`http://tumblr.pauladamsmith.com/post/17663153373`

Visualizing geospatial data

It's very hard, if not impossible, to understand geospatial data unless it is turned into a visual form—that is, until it is rendered as an image of some sort. Converting geospatial data into images requires a suitable toolkit. While there are several such toolkits available, we will look at one in particular: Mapnik.

Mapnik

Mapnik is a freely-available toolkit for building mapping applications. It takes geospatial data from a PostGIS database, shapefile, or any other format supported by GDAL/OGR, and turns it into clearly-rendered, good-looking images.

There are a lot of complex issues involved in rendering maps well, and Mapnik does a good job of allowing the application developer to control the rendering process. Rules control which features should appear on the map, while "symbolizers" control the visual appearance of these features.

Mapnik allows developers to create XML stylesheets that control the map-creation process. Just as with CSS stylesheets, Mapnik's stylesheets allow you complete control over the way geospatial data is rendered. Alternatively, you can create your styles by hand if you prefer.

Mapnik itself is written in C++, though bindings are included which allow access to almost all of the Mapnik functionality via Python. Because these bindings are included in the main code base rather than being added by a third party developer, support for Python is built right into Mapnik. This makes Python eminently suited to developing Mapnik-based applications.

Mapnik is heavily used by OpenStreetMap (`http://openstreetmap.org`), EveryBlock (`http://everyblock.com`), among others. Since the output of Mapnik is simply an image, it is easy to include Mapnik as part of a web-based application, or you can display the output directly in a window as part of a desktop-based application. Mapnik works equally well on the desktop and on the web.

Design

When using Mapnik, the main object you are dealing with is called the **Map**. A Map object has the following parts:

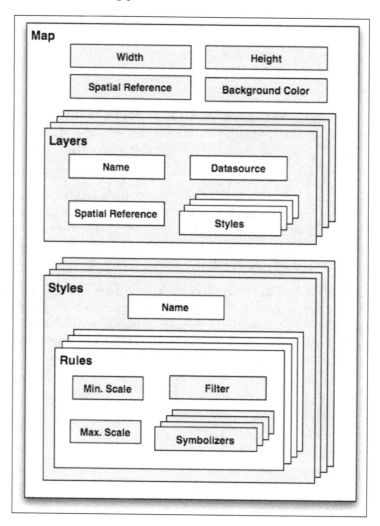

When creating a Map object, you assign values for the following:

- The overall **width** and **height** of the map, in pixels.
- The **spatial reference** to use for the map.
- The **background color** to draw behind the contents of the map.

You then define one or more **Layers** which hold the map's contents. Each Layer has the following:

- A **name**.

- A **Datasource** object defining where to get the data for this layer from. The Datasource can be a reference to a database, or it can be a shapefile or other GDAL/OGR data source.

- A **spatial reference** to use for this layer. This can be different from the spatial reference used by the map as a whole, if appropriate.

- A list of **styles** to apply to this layer. Each style is referred to by name, since the styles are actually defined elsewhere (often in an XML stylesheet).

Finally, you define one or more **Styles**, which tell Mapnik how to draw the various layers. Each Style has a **name** and of a list of `Rules`, which make up the main part of the style's definition. Each `Rule` has:

- A **minimum scale** and **maximum scale** value (called the "scale denominator"). The `Rule` will only apply if the map's scale is within this range.

- A **filter** expression. The `Rule` will only apply to those features which match this filter expression.

- A list of **Symbolizers**. These define how the matching features will be drawn onto the map.

There are a number of different types of Symbolizers implemented by Mapnik:

- `LineSymbolizer` is used to draw a "stroke" along a line, a linear ring, or around the outside of a polygon.

- `LinePatternSymbolizer` uses the contents of an image file (specified by name) to draw the "stroke" along a line, a linear ring, or around the outside of a polygon.

- `PolygonSymbolizer` is used to draw the interior of a polygon.

- `PolygonPatternSymbolizer` uses the contents of an image file (again specified by name) to draw the interior of a polygon.

- `PointSymbolizer` uses the contents of an image file (specified by name) to draw an image at a point.

- `TextSymbolizer` draws a feature's text. The text to be drawn is taken from one of the feature's attributes, and there are numerous options to control how the text is to be drawn.

- `RasterSymbolizer` is used to draw raster data taken from any GDAL dataset.

- `ShieldSymbolizer` draws a textual label and a point together. This is similar to the use of a `PointSymbolizer` to draw the image and a `TextSymbolizer` to draw the label, except that it ensures that both the text and the image are drawn together.

- `BuildingSymbolizer` uses a pseudo-3D effect to draw a polygon, to make it appear that the polygon is a three-dimensional building.

- `MarkersSymbolizer` draws blue directional arrows or SVG markers following the direction of polygon and line geometries.

When you instantiate a Symbolizer and add it to a style (either directly in code, or via an XML stylesheet), you provide a number of parameters which define how the Symbolizer should work. For example, when using the `PolygonSymbolizer`, you can specify the fill color, the opacity, and a "gamma" value that helps draw adjacent polygons of the same color without the boundary being shown:

```
p = mapnik.PolygonSymbolizer(mapnik.Color(127, 127, 0))
p.fill_opacity = 0.8
p.gamma = 0.65
```

If the `Rule` that uses this Symbolizer matches one or more polygons, those polygons will be drawn using the given color, opacity, and gamma value.

Different rules can, of course, have different Symbolizers, as well as different filter values. For example, you might set up rules which draw countries in different colors depending on their population.

Example code

The following example program displays a simple world map using Mapnik:

```
import mapnik

symbolizer = mapnik.PolygonSymbolizer(
                         mapnik.Color("darkgreen"))

rule = mapnik.Rule()
rule.symbols.append(symbolizer)

style = mapnik.Style()
style.rules.append(rule)
```

```
layer = mapnik.Layer("mapLayer")
layer.datasource = mapnik.Shapefile(file="TM_WORLD_BORDERS-0.3.shp")
layer.styles.append("mapStyle")

map = mapnik.Map(800, 400)
map.background = mapnik.Color("steelblue")
map.append_style("mapStyle", style)
map.layers.append(layer)

map.zoom_all()
mapnik.render_to_file(map, "map.png", "png")
```

 If you are running Mapnik Version 2.0, you should replace the import mapnik statement in the first line of this program with import mapnik2 as mapnik.

Notice that this program creates a PolygonSymbolizer to display the country polygons, and then attaches the symbolizer to a Mapnik Rule object. The Rule then becomes part of a Mapnik Style object. We then create a Mapnik Layer object, reading the layer's map data from a shapefile data source. Finally, a Mapnik Map object is created, the layer is attached, and the resulting map is rendered to a PNG-format image file:

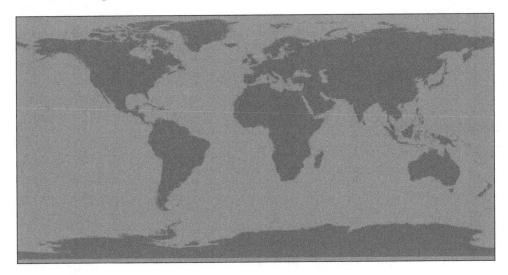

Documentation

Mapnik's has reasonable documentation for an open source project: there are good installation guides and some excellent tutorials, but the API documentation is often confusing. The Python documentation is derived from the C++ documentation, and concentrates on describing how the Python bindings are implemented rather than how an end user would work with Mapnik using Python—there's a lot of technical details that aren't relevant to the Python programmer, and many Python-specific descriptions are missing.

The best way to get started with Mapnik is to follow the installation instructions, and then to work your way through the supplied Python-specific tutorial. You can then check out the *Learning Mapnik* page on the Mapnik Wiki:

```
http://trac.mapnik.org/wiki/LearningMapnik
```

It is well worth spending some time reading through the Mapnik Wiki, even though not all of it is Python-specific. It is also a good idea to look at the Python API documentation, despite its limitations. The main page lists the various classes, which are available and a number of useful functions, many of which are documented. The classes themselves list the methods and properties (attributes) you can access, and even though many of these lack Python-specific documentation, you can generally guess what they do.

 Chapter 8, Using Python and Mapnik to Produce Maps, of this book includes a comprehensive description of Mapnik and how to use it from Python; you may find this more useful than the Python API documentation on the Mapnik website.

Availability

Mapnik runs on all major operating systems, including MS Windows, Mac OS X, and Linux. The main Mapnik website can be found at:

```
http://mapnik.org
```

Download links are provided for downloading the Mapnik source code, which can be readily compiled if you are running on a Unix machine, and you can also download prebuilt binaries for Windows and Mac OS X.

 Make sure that you install Mapnik Version 2.0 or later; you will need to use this version as you work through the examples in this book.

Summary

In this chapter, we looked at a number of important libraries for developing geospatial applications using Python. We learned the following:

- **GDAL** is a C++ library for reading (and sometimes writing) raster-based geospatial data.

- **OGR** is a C++ library for reading (and sometimes writing) vector-based geospatial data.

- GDAL and OGR include Python bindings that are easy to use, and support a large number of data formats.

- The **PROJ.4** library, and its Pythonic `pyproj` wrapper, allow you to convert between geographic coordinates (points on the Earth's surface) and cartographic coordinates (x,y coordinates on a two-dimensional plane) using any desired map projection and ellipsoid.

- The `pyproj` Geod class allows you to perform various geodetic calculations based on points on the Earth's surface, a given distance, and a given angle (azimuth).

- A geospatial data manipulation library called the Java Topology Suite was originally developed for Java. This was then rewritten in C++ under the name GEOS, and there is now a Python interface to GEOS called **Shapely**.

- Shapely makes it easy to represent geospatial data in the form of Points, LineStrings, LinearRings, Polygons, MultiPoints, MultiLineStrings, MultiPolygons, and GeometryCollections.

- As well as representing geospatial data, these classes allow you to perform a variety of geospatial calculations.

- **Mapnik** is a tool for producing good-looking maps based on geospatial data.

- Mapnik can use an XML stylesheet to control the elements that appear on the map, and how they are formatted. Styles can also be created by hand if you prefer.

- Each Mapnik style has a list of **Rules** which are used to identify features to draw onto the map.

- Each Mapnik rule has a list of **Symbolizers** that control how the selected features are drawn.

While these tools are very powerful, you can't do anything with them until you have some geospatial data to work with. Unless you are lucky enough to have access to your own source of data, or are willing to pay large sums to purchase data commercially, your only choice is to make use of the geospatial data which is freely available on the Internet. These freely-available sources of geospatial data are the topic of the next chapter.

4
Sources of Geospatial Data

When creating a geospatial application, the data you use will be just as important as the code you write. High-quality geospatial data, and in particular base maps and imagery, will be the cornerstone of your application. If your maps don't look good, then your application will be treated as the work of an amateur, no matter how well you write the rest of your program.

Traditionally, geospatial data has been treated as a valuable and scarce resource, being sold commercially for many thousands of dollars and with strict licensing constraints. Fortunately, as with the trend towards "democratizing" geospatial tools, geospatial data is now becoming increasingly available for free and with little or no restriction on its use. There are still situations where you may have to pay for data, for example, to guarantee the quality of the data, or if you need something that isn't available elsewhere, but it is now usually just a case of downloading the data you need, for free, from a suitable server.

This chapter provides an overview of some of these major sources of freely-available geospatial data. This is not intended to be an exhaustive list, but rather to provide information on the sources which are likely to be most useful to the Python geospatial developer.

In this chapter, we will cover:

- Some of the major freely-available sources of vector-format geospatial data
- Some of the main freely-available sources of raster geospatial data
- Sources of other types of freely-available geospatial data, concentrating on databases of city and other place names

Sources of geospatial data in vector format

Vector-based geospatial data represents physical features as collections of points, lines, and polygons. Often, these features will have metadata associated with them. In this section, we will look at some of the major sources of free vector-format geospatial data.

OpenStreetMap

OpenStreetMap (`http://openstreetmap.org`) is a website where people can collaborate to create and edit geospatial data. It describes itself as a "free editable map of the whole world made by people like you."

The following screenshot shows a portion of a street map for Onchan, Isle of Man, based on data from OpenStreetMap:

Data format

OpenStreetMap does not use a standard format such as shapefiles to store its data. Instead, it has developed its own XML-based format for representing geospatial data in the form of **nodes** (single points), **ways** (sequences of points that define a line), **areas** (closed ways that represent polygons), and **relations** (collections of other elements). Any element (node, way, or relation) can have a number of **tags** associated with it that provide additional information about the element.

Following is an example of how the OpenStreetMap XML data looks:

```
<osm>
  <node id="603279517" lat="-38.1456457"
   lon="176.2441646".../>
  <node id="603279518" lat="-38.1456583"
   lon="176.2406726".../>
  <node id="603279519" lat="-38.1456540"
   lon="176.2380553".../>
  ...
  <way id="47390936"...>
    <nd ref="603279517"/>
    <nd ref="603279518"/>
    <nd ref="603279519"/>
    <tag k="highway" v="residential"/>
    <tag k="name" v="York Street"/>
  </way>
  ...
  <relation id="126207"...>
    <member type="way" ref="22930719" role=""/>
    <member type="way" ref="23963573" role=""/>
    <member type="way" ref="28562757" role=""/>
    <member type="way" ref="23963609" role=""/>
    <member type="way" ref="47475844" role=""/>
    <tag k="name" v="State Highway 30A"/>
    <tag k="ref" v="30A"/>
    <tag k="route" v="road"/>
    <tag k="type" v="route"/>
  </relation>
</osm>
```

Obtaining and using OpenStreetMap data

You can obtain geospatial data from OpenStreetMap in one of following three ways:

- You can use the OpenStreetMap API to download a subset of the data you are interested in.

- You can download the entire OpenStreetMap database, called `Planet.osm`, and process it locally. Note that this is a multi-gigabyte download.

- You can make use of one of the mirror sites that provide OpenStreetMap data nicely packaged into smaller chunks and converted into other data formats. For example, you can download the data for North America on a state-by-state basis, in one of several available formats, including shapefiles.

Let's take a closer look at each of these three options.

The OpenStreetMap API

Using the OpenStreetMap API (`http://wiki.openstreetmap.org/wiki/API`), you can download selected data from the OpenStreetMap database in one of following three ways:

- You can specify a **bounding** box defining the minimum and maximum longitude and latitude values, as shown in the following screenshot:

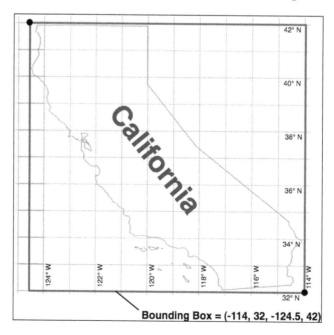

Bounding Box = (-114, 32, -124.5, 42)

The API will return all of the elements (nodes, ways, and relations), which are completely or partially inside the specified bounding box.

- You can ask for a set of **changesets** which have been applied to the map. This returns all the changes made over a given time period, either for the entire map or just for the elements within a given bounding box.

- You can download a specific element by ID, or all the elements which are associated with a specified element (for example, all elements belonging to a given relation).

OpenStreetMap provides a Python module called `OsmApi`, which makes it easy to access the OpenStreetMap API. More information about this module can be found at `http://wiki.openstreetmap.org/wiki/PythonOsmApi`.

Planet.osm

If you choose to download the entire OpenStreetMap database for processing on your local computer, you will first need to download the entire `Planet.osm` database. This database is available in two formats: a compressed XML-format file containing all the nodes, ways, and relations in the OpenStreetMap database, or a special binary format called PBF that contains the same information but is smaller and faster to read.

 PBF is replacing XML as the preferred data format; libraries for reading and writing PBF files are available for various languages, including Python.

The `Planet.osm` database is currently 23 GB in size if you download it in XML format, or 18 GB if you download it in PBF format. Both formats can be downloaded from `http://planet.openstreetmap.org`.

The entire dump of the `Planet.osm` database is updated weekly, but regular "diffs" are produced which you can use to update your local copy of the `Planet.osm` database without having to download the entire database each time. The daily diffs are approximately 40 MB when they have been compressed.

Mirror sites and extracts

Because of the size of the downloads, Planet.osm recommends that you use a mirror site rather than downloading it directly from their servers. Extracts are also provided, which allow you to download the data for a given area rather than the entire world. These mirror sites and extracts are maintained by third parties; for a list of the URLs, see http://wiki.openstreetmap.org/wiki/Planet.osm.

Note that these extracts are often made available in alternative formats on the mirror sites, including shapefiles and direct database dumps.

Working with OpenStreetMap data

When you download Planet.osm, you will end up with an enormous file on your hard disk—currently it would be 250 GB if you downloaded the data in XML format. You have two main options for processing this file using Python:

- You could use a library such as imposm (http://dev.omniscale.net/imposm.parser) to read through the file and extract the information you want

- You could import the data into a database, and then access that database from Python

In most cases, you will want to import the data into a database before you attempt to work with it. To do this, use the excellent osm2pgsql tool, which is available at http://wiki.openstreetmap.org/wiki/Osm2pgsql. osm2pgsql was created to import the entire Planet.osm data into a PostgreSQL database, and so is highly optimized.

Once you have imported the Planet.osm data into your local database, you can use the psycopg2 library, as described in *Chapter 6, GIS in the Database*, to access the OpenStreetMap data from your Python programs.

TIGER

The United States Census Bureau have made available a large amount of geospatial data under the name **TIGER (Topologically Integrated Geographic Encoding and Referencing System)**. The TIGER data includes information on streets, railways, rivers, lakes, geographic boundaries, and legal and statistical areas such as school districts, and urban regions. Separate cartographic boundary and demographic files are also available for download.

The following screenshot shows state and urban area outlines for California, based on data downloaded from the TIGER website:

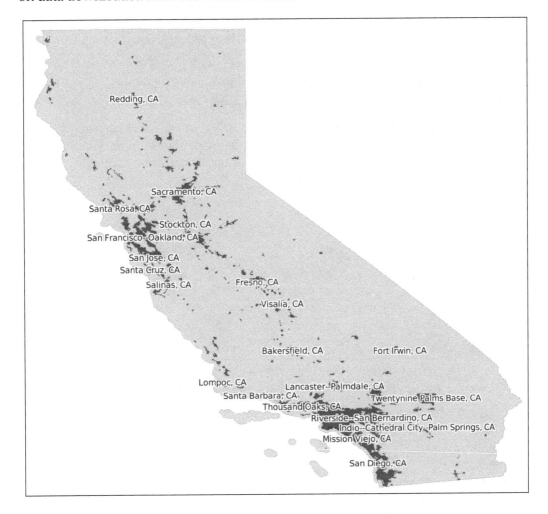

Because it is produced by the US government, TIGER only includes information for the United States and its protectorates (Puerto Rico, American Samoa, the Northern Mariana Islands, Guam, and the US Virgin Islands). For these areas, TIGER is an excellent source of geospatial data.

Data format

Up until 2006, the US Census Bureau provided the TIGER data in a custom text-based format called TIGER/Line. TIGER/Line files stored each type of record in a separate file, and required custom tools to process. Fortunately, OGR supports TIGER/Line files should you need to read them.

Since 2007, all TIGER data has been produced in the form of shapefiles, which are (somewhat confusingly) called TIGER/Line shapefiles.

You can download up-to-date shapefiles containing geospatial data such as street address ranges, landmarks, census blocks, metropolitan statistical areas, and school districts. For example, the "Core Based Statistical Area" shapefile contains the outline of each statistical area:

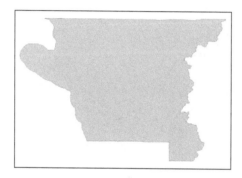

This particular feature has the following metadata associated with it:

```
ALAND 2606489666.0
AWATER 578526971.0
CBSAFP 18860
CSAFP None
FUNCSTAT S
INTPTLAT +41.7499033
INTPTLON -123.9809983
LSAD M2
MEMI 2
MTFCC G3110
NAME Crescent City, CA
NAMELSAD Crescent City, CA Micropolitan Statistical Area
PARTFLG N
```

Information on these various attributes can be found in the extensive documentation available at the TIGER website.

You can also download shapefiles which include demographic data such as population, number of houses, median age, and racial breakdown. For example, the following map tints each metropolitan area in California according to its total population:

Obtaining and using TIGER data

The TIGER datafiles can be downloaded from:

```
http://www.census.gov/geo/www/tiger/index.html
```

Make sure that you download the technical documentation, as it describes the various files you can download, and all of the attributes associated with each feature. For example, if you want to download a current set of urban areas for the US, the shapefile you are looking for is called `tl_2012_us_uac10.shp` and it includes information such as the city or town name and the size in square meters.

Natural Earth

Natural Earth (`http://www.naturalearthdata.com`) is a website that provides public domain vector and raster map data at high, medium, and low resolutions. Two types of vector map data are provided:

- **Cultural map data**: This includes polygons for country, state or province, urban area, and park outlines, as well as point and line data for populated places, roads, and railways:

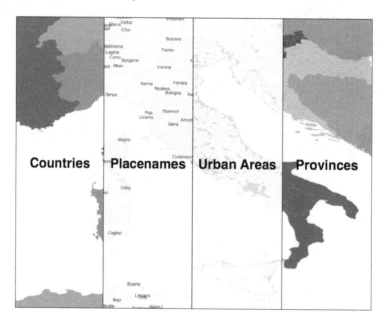

- **Physical map data**: This includes polygons and linestrings for land masses, coastlines, oceans, minor islands, reefs, rivers, lakes, and so on:

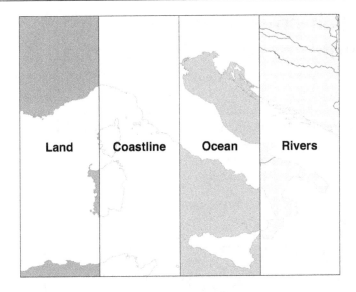

All of this can be downloaded and used freely in your geospatial programs, making the Natural Earth site an excellent source of data for your application.

Data format

All the vector-format data on the Natural Earth website is provided in the form of shapefiles. All the data is in geographic (latitude and longitude) coordinates, using the standard WGS84 datum, making it very easy to use these files in your own application.

Obtaining and using Natural Earth vector data

The Natural Earth site is uniformly excellent, and downloading the files you want is easy; simply click on the **Get the Data** link on the main page. You can then choose the resolution and the type of data you are looking for, and you can choose to download either a single shapefile, or a number of shapefiles bundled together. Once they are downloaded, you can use the Python libraries discussed in the previous chapter to work with the contents of these shapefiles.

The Natural Earth website is very comprehensive; it includes detailed information about the geospatial data you can download, and a forum where you can ask questions and discuss any problems you may have.

Global, self-consistent, hierarchical, high-resolution shoreline database (GSHHS)

The US National Geophysical Data Center (part of the NOAA) have been working on a project to produce high-quality vector shoreline data for the entire world. The resulting database, called the **Global self-consistent, hierarchical, high-resolution shoreline database (GSHHS)**, includes detailed vector data for shorelines, lakes, and rivers at five different resolutions. The data has been broken out into four different "levels": ocean boundaries, lake boundaries, island-in-lake boundaries, and pond-on-island-in-lake boundaries.

The following screenshot shows European shorelines, lakes, and islands, taken from the GSHHS database:

The GSHHS has been constructed out of two public-domain geospatial databases: the World Data Bank II includes data on coastlines, lakes, and rivers, while the World Vector Shoreline only provides coastline data. Because the World Vector Shoreline database has more accurate data, but lacks information on rivers and lakes, the two databases were combined to provide the most accurate information possible. After merging the databases, the author then manually edited the data to make it consistent and to remove a number of errors. The result is a high-quality database of land and water boundaries worldwide.

More information about the process used to create the GSHHS database can be found at: http://www.soest.hawaii.edu/pwessel/papers/1996/JGR_96/jgr_96.html

Data format

The GSHHS database is available in two different formats: a binary data format specific to the Generic Mapping Tools (http://gmt.soest.hawaii.edu), and as a series of shapefiles.

 Generic Mapping Tools (**GMT**) is a collection of tools for working with geospatial data. Because they don't have Python bindings, we won't be working with GMT in this book.

If you download the data in shapefile format, you will end up with a total of twenty separate shapefiles, one for every combination of resolution and level:

- The resolution represents the amount of detail in the map:

Resolution Code	Resolution	Includes
c	Crude	Features greater than 500 sq.km.
l	Low	Features greater than 100 sq.km.
i	Intermediate	Features greater than 20 sq.km.
h	High	Features greater than 1 sq.km.
f	Full	Every feature

- The level indicates the type of boundaries that are included in the shapefile:

Level Code	Includes
1	Ocean boundaries
2	Lake boundaries
3	Island-in-lake boundaries
4	Pond-on-island-in-lake boundaries

The name of the shapefile tells you the resolution and level of the included data. For example, the shapefile for ocean boundaries at full resolution would be named `GSHHS_f_L1.shp`.

Each shapefile consists of a single layer containing the various polygon features making up the given type of boundary.

Obtaining the GSHHS database

The main GSHHS website can be found at:

`http://www.ngdc.noaa.gov/mgg/shorelines/gshhs.html`

The files are available in both GMT and shapefile format — unless you particularly want to use the Generic Mapping Tools, you will most likely want to download the shapefile version. Once you have downloaded the data, you can use OGR to read the files and extract the data from them in the usual way.

World Borders Dataset

Many of the data sources we have examined so far are rather complex. If all you are looking for is some simple vector data covering the entire world, the World Borders Dataset may be all you need. While some of the country borders are apparently disputed, the simplicity of the World Borders Dataset makes it an attractive choice for many basic geospatial applications.

The following map was generated using the World Borders Dataset:

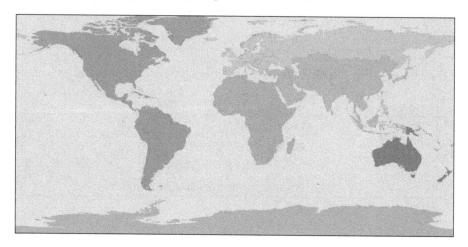

The World Borders Dataset will be used extensively throughout this book. Indeed, you have already seen an example program in *Chapter 3, Python Libraries for Geospatial Development*, where we used Mapnik to generate a world map using the World Borders Dataset shapefile.

Data format

The World Borders Dataset is available in the form of a shapefile with a single layer and one feature for each country. For each country, the feature has one or more polygons that define the country's boundary, along with useful attributes including the name of the country or area, various ISO, FIPS, and UN codes identifying the country, a region and subregion classification, the country's population, land area, and latitude/longitude.

The various codes make it easy to match the features against your own country-specific data, and you can also use information such as the population and area to highlight different countries on the map. For example, the preceding screenshot uses the "region" field to draw each geographic region using a different color.

Obtaining World Borders Dataset

The World Borders Dataset can be downloaded from:

```
http://thematicmapping.org/downloads/world_borders.php
```

This website also provides further details on the contents of the dataset, including links to the United Nations' website where the region and subregion codes are listed.

Sources of geospatial data in raster format

One of the most enthralling aspects of programs such as Google Earth is the ability to "see" the Earth as you appear to fly above it. This is achieved by displaying satellite and aerial photographs carefully stitched together to provide the illusion that you are viewing the Earth's surface from above.

While writing your own version of Google Earth would be an almost impossible task, it is possible to obtain free satellite imagery in the form of raster format geospatial data, which you can then use in your own geospatial applications.

Raster data is not just limited to images of the Earth's surface however; other useful information can be found in raster format—for example, **digital elevation maps (DEM)** contain the height of each point on the Earth's surface, which can then be used to calculate the elevation of any desired point. DEM data can also be used to generate two-dimensional images that represent different heights using different shades or colors, or to simulate the shading effect of hills using a technique called **shaded relief imagery**.

In this section, we will look at an extremely comprehensive source of satellite imagery, the raster-format data available on the Natural Earth site, and some freely-available sources of digital elevation data.

Landsat

Landsat is an ongoing effort to collect images of the Earth's surface. The name is derived from land and satellite. A group of dedicated satellites have been continuously gathering images since 1972. Landsat imagery includes black and white, traditional red/green/blue (RGB) color images, as well as infrared and thermal imaging. The color images are typically at a resolution of 30 meters per pixel, while the black and white images from Landsat 7 are at a resolution of 15 meters per pixel.

The following screenshot shows color-corrected Landsat satellite imagery for the city of Rotorua, New Zealand. The city itself is on the southern (bottom) edge of a lake:

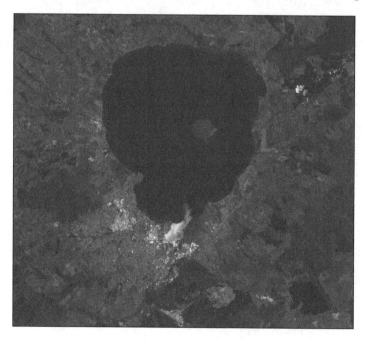

Data format

Landsat images are typically available in the form of GeoTIFF files. GeoTIFF is a geospatially tagged TIFF image file format, allowing images to be georeferenced onto the Earth's surface. Most GIS software and tools, including GDAL, are able to read GeoTIFF formatted files.

Because the images come directly from a satellite, the files you can download typically store separate bands of data in separate files. Depending on the satellite the data came from, there can be up to eight different bands of data—for example, Landsat 7 generates separate red, green, and blue bands, as well as three different infrared bands, a thermal band, and a high-resolution "panchromatic" (black-and-white) band.

To understand how this works, let's take a closer look at the process required to create the preceding screenshot. The raw satellite data consists of eight separate GeoTIFF files, one for each band. Band 1 contains the blue color data, band 2 contains the green color data, and band 3 contains the red color data. These separate files can then be combined using GDAL to produce a single color image as follows:

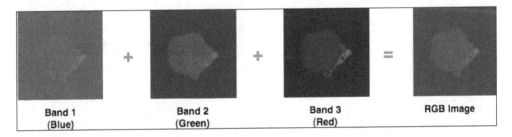

Another complication with the Landsat data is that the images produced by the satellites are distorted by various factors, including the ellipsoid shape of the Earth, the elevation of the terrain being photographed, and the orientation of the satellite as the image is taken. The raw data is therefore not a completely accurate representation of the features being photographed. Fortunately a process known as **orthorectification** can be used to correct these distortions. In most cases, orthorectified versions of the satellite images can be downloaded directly.

Obtaining Landsat imagery

The easiest way to access Landsat imagery is to make use of the University of Maryland's *Global Land Cover Facility* website:

```
http://glcf.umiacs.umd.edu/data/landsat
```

Click on the **Download via Search and Preview Tool** link, and then click on **Map Search**. Select **ETM+** from the **Landsat Imagery** list, and if you zoom in on the desired part of the Earth you will see the areas covered by various Landsat images:

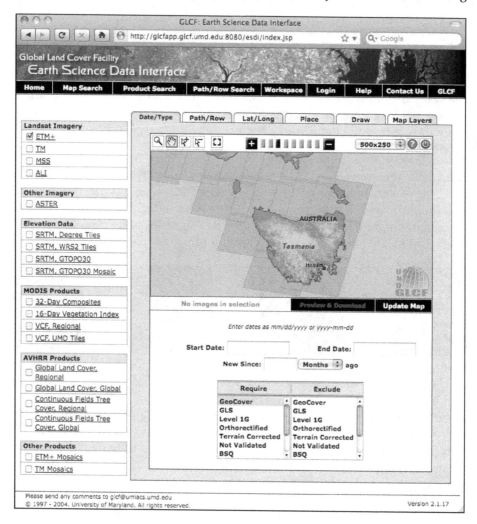

If you choose the selection tool (⬚), you will be able to click on a desired area, then select **Preview & Download** to choose the image to download.

Alternatively, if you know the path and row number of the desired area of the earth, you can directly access the files via FTP. The path and row number (as well as the **world reference system (WRS)** used by the data) can be found on the **Preview & Download** page:

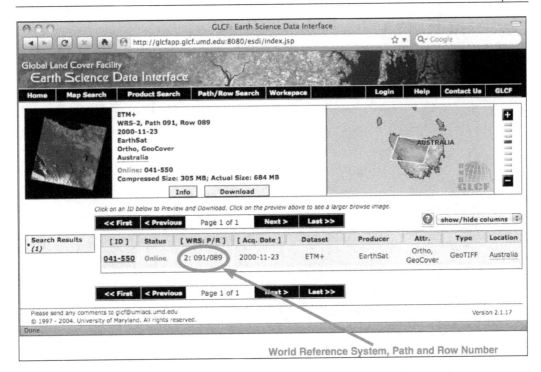

World Reference System, Path and Row Number

If you want to download the image files via FTP, the main FTP site is at:

```
ftp://ftp.glcf.umd.edu/glcf/Landsat
```

The directories and files have complex names which include the WRS, the path and row number, the satellite number, the date at which the image was taken, and the band number. For example, a file named `p091r089_7t20001123_z55_nn10.tif.gz` refers to path `091` and row `089`, which happens to be the portion of Tasmania highlighted in the preceding screenshot. The `7` refers to the number of the Landsat satellite that took the image, and `20001123` is a datestamp indicating when the image was taken. The final part of the filename, `nn10`, tells us that the file is for band 1.

By interpreting the filename in this way, you can download the correct files, and match the files against the desired bands. For more information on what all these different satellites and bands mean, refer to the documentation links in the upper right-hand corner of the Global Land Cover Facility website:

```
http://glcf.umiacs.umd.edu/data/landsat
```

Natural Earth

In addition to providing vector map data, the Natural Earth website (http://www.naturalearthdata.com) makes available five different types of raster maps at both 1:10 million and 1:50 million scale:

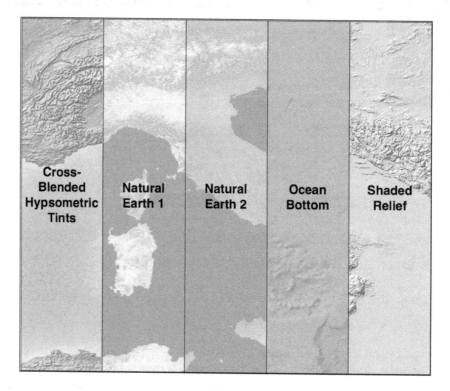

- The rather esoterically-named **Cross-Blended Hypsometric Tints** provide visualizations where the color is selected based on both elevation and climate. These images are then often combined with shaded relief images to make a realistic-looking view of the Earth's surface.

- **Natural Earth 1** and **Natural Earth 2** are more idealized views of the Earth's surface, using a light palette and softly-blended colors, providing an excellent backdrop for drawing your own geospatial data.

- The **Ocean Bottom** dataset uses a combination of shaded relief imagery and depth-based coloring to provide a visualization of the ocean floor.

- The **Shaded Relief** imagery uses greyscale to "shade" the surface of the Earth based on high-resolution elevation data.

One additional raster dataset is available that provides bathymetry (underwater depth) visualizations at 1:50 million scale. The following screenshot is an example of the bathymetry data for the oceans surrounding New Zealand:

Data format

Most of the raster-format data on the Natural Earth site is in the standard TIFF image format. The one exception is the bathymetry data, which is provided in the form of a layered Adobe Photoshop file with differing shades of blue associated with each depth band.

In all cases, the raster data is in geographic (latitude/longitude) projection, and uses the standard WGS84 datum, making it easy to translate between latitude and longitude coordinates and pixel coordinates within the raster image.

Obtaining and using Natural Earth raster data

As with the vector data, the raster-format data on the Natural Earth site is easy to download; simply go to the site and follow the **Get the Data** link to download the raster-format data. You can choose to download the data at either 1:10 million scale, or 1:50 million scale, and you can also choose to download the large or small size of each file.

Once you have downloaded the TIFF format data, you can open the file in an image editor, or use a standard command-line utility such as gdal_translate to manipulate the image. For the bathymetry data, you can open the file directly in Adobe Photoshop, or use a cheaper alternative such as the GIMP or Flying Meat's Acorn. Each depth band is a separate layer in the file, and by default is associated with a specific shade of blue. You can choose different colors if you prefer, and can select which layers to show or hide. When you are finished, you can then flatten the image and save it as a TIFF file for use in your programs.

Global Land One-kilometer Base Elevation (GLOBE)

GLOBE is an international effort to produce high-quality, medium-resolution digital elevation (DEM) data for the entire world. The result is a set of freely-available DEM files, which can be used for many types of geospatial analysis and development.

The following screenshot shows GLOBE DEM data for northern Chile, converted to a grayscale image:

Data format

Like all DEM data, GLOBE uses raster values to represent the elevation at a given point on the Earth's surface. In the case of GLOBE, this data consists of 32-bit signed integers representing the height above (or below) sea level, in meters. Each cell or "pixel" within the raster data represents the elevation of a square on the Earth's surface which is 30 arc-seconds of longitude wide, and 30 arc-seconds of latitude high:

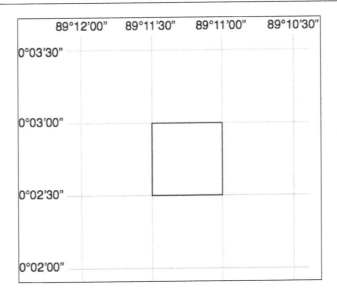

Note that 30 arc-seconds equals approximately 0.00833 degrees of latitude or longitude, which equates to a square roughly one kilometer wide and one kilometer high.

The raw GLOBE data is simply a long list of 32-bit integers in big-endian format, where the cells are read left-to-right and then top-to-bottom, like this:

x=0, y=0	x=1, y=0	...	x=10800, y=0
x=0, y=1	x=1, y=1	...	x=10800, y=1
...	...	...	...
x=0, y=6000	x=1, y=6000	...	x=10800,y=6000

A separate header (.hdr) file provides more detailed information about the DEM data, including the width and height and its georeferenced location. Tools such as GDAL are able to read the raw data as long as the header file is provided.

Obtaining and using GLOBE data

The main website for the GLOBE project can be found at:

```
http://www.ngdc.noaa.gov/mgg/topo/globe.html
```

For detailed documentation of the GLOBE data, you can follow the **Get Data Online** link to download precalculated sets of data or to choose a given area to download DEM data for.

If you download one of the premade tiles, you will need to also download the associated .hdr file so that the data can be georeferenced and processed using GDAL. If you choose a custom area to download, a suitable .hdr file will be created for you—just make sure you choose an export type of **ESRI ArcView** so that the header is created in the format expected by GDAL.

If you download a premade tile, the header files can be quite hard to find. Suitable header files in ESRI format can be downloaded from:

```
http://www.ngdc.noaa.gov/mgg/topo/elev/esri/hdr
```

Once you have downloaded the data, simply place the raw DEM file into the same directory as the .hdr file. You can then open the file directly using GDAL, like this:

```
import osgeo.gdal
dataset = osgeo.gdal.Open("j10g.bil")
```

The dataset will consist of a single band of raster data, which you can then translate, read or process using the GDAL library and related tools.

To see an example of using GDAL to process DEM data, please refer to the GDAL section in *Chapter 3, Python Libraries for Geospatial Development*.

National Elevation Dataset (NED)

The **National Elevation Dataset** (**NED**) is a high-resolution digital elevation dataset provided by the US Geological Survey. It covers the Continental United States, Alaska, Hawaii, and other US territories. Most of the United States is covered by elevation data at 30 meters/pixel or 10 meters/pixel resolution, with selected areas available at 3 meters/pixel. Alaska is generally only available at 60 meters/pixel resolution.

The following shaded relief screenshot was generated using NED elevation data for the Marin Headlands, San Francisco:

Data format

The NED data can be downloaded in various formats including GeoTIFF and ArcGRID, both of which can be processed using GDAL.

As with other DEM data, each "pixel" in the raster image represents the height of a given area on the Earth's surface. For NED data, the height is in meters above or below a reference height known as the *North American Vertical Datum of 1988*. This roughly equates to the height above or below sea level, allowing for tidal and other variations.

Obtaining and using NED data

The main website for the National Elevation Dataset can be found at:

`http://ned.usgs.gov`

This site describes the NED dataset; to download the data you'll have to use the National Map Viewer, which is available at:

`http://viewer.nationalmap.gov/viewer/`

To use the viewer, zoom in to the area you want, and then click on the **Download Data** option at the top of the page:

Click on this option to download by the current map extent, and select **Elevation** as the data you want to download. You can choose from a variety of data formats; GeoTIFF is a good option to use. A window then appears to show the various sets of elevation data you can download:

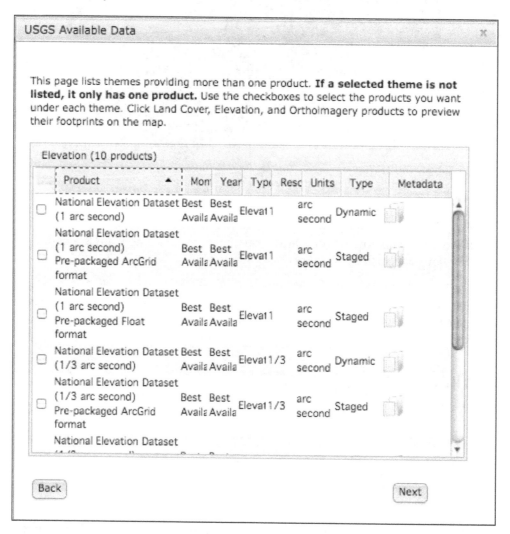

Downloading data from the National Map Viewer is a bit like buying something online: you add the desired item to your "cart", then you "checkout" your order and enter your e-mail address. Once you "place your order", you'll be sent an e-mail with links to where you can download the data you need.

Unfortunately, the National Map Viewer is quite slow to make the data available; expect to spend several minutes waiting for the data to start downloading.

You will receive a compressed .zip format file containing the data you want, along with a large number of metadata files and documentation about the National Elevation Dataset.

 Note that you might need to rename the files to remove the backslashes before you can open them; GDAL can get confused by filenames with backslashes.

Once you have downloaded the desired GeoTIFF files, you can open them in GDAL just as you would open any other raster dataset:

```
import osgeo.gdal
dataset = osgeo.gdal.Open("dem.tif")
```

Finally, if you are working with DEM data you might like to check out the gdaldem utility, which is included as part of the GDAL download. This program makes it easy to view and manipulate DEM raster data. The preceding shaded relief screenshot was created using this utility, like this:

```
gdaldem hillshade dem.tif image.tiff
```

Sources of other types of geospatial data

The vector and raster geospatial data we have looked at so far is generally used to provide images or information about the Earth itself. However, geospatial applications often have to place data onto the surface of the Earth—that is, georeference something such as a place or event. In this section, we will look at two additional sources of geospatial data; in this case databases that place cities, towns, natural features, and points of interest onto the surface of the Earth.

This data can be used in two important ways. First, it can be used to *label* features— for example, to place the label "London" onto a georeferenced image of southern England. Secondly, this data can be used to *locate* something by name, for example by allowing the user to choose a city from a drop-down list and then draw a map centered around that city.

GEOnet Names Server

The GEOnet Names Server provides a large database of place names. It is an official repository of non-American place names, as decided by the US Board on geographic names.

The following screenshot is an extract from the GEOnet Names Server database:

LAT	LONG	FC	DSG	ELEV	NT	FULL_NAME
-46.333333	168.716667	S	RSTN		N	Kamahi
-46.816667	168.25	T	ISL		N	North Island
-40.959722	175.6575	P	PPL		N	Masterton
-52.556111	169.136667	H	COVE		N	Camp Cove
-39.455556	173.858333	P	PPL		N	Opunake
-52.501389	169.120556	T	ISL	76	N	Gomez Island
-39.591667	174.283333	P	PPL		N	Hawera
-36.641944	175.360833	T	RKS		N	Motupotaka Rocks
-41.255833	173.263333	S	TOWR		N	Boulder Bank Lighthouse
-36.605278	174.9175	T	RK		N	Shearer Rock
-36.610556	174.705556	P	PPL		N	Red Beach
-46.5625	169.619444	T	ISL		N	Cosgrove Island
-42.133333	171.616667	T	MT		N	Mount McHardy
-39.266667	174.616667	T	MT		N	Turakirai
-37.433333	174.7	T	HLL		N	Nihonui
-44.033333	169.25	H	STM		N	Cowan Creek
-44.65	170.35	H	STM		N	Deep Creek
-40.966667	173.916667	H	BAY		V	Waitara Bay
-42.183333	173.466667	H	STM		N	Spray Stream
-39.45	173.833333	H	STM		N	Heimama Stream
-46.1	166.466667	H	CHNM		V	Eastern Entrance
-36.766667	174.4	T	BCH		N	Muriwai Beach
-38.983333	177.45	T	HLL		N	Ohinemaemae
-41.25	174.116667	H	BAY		N	Kahikatea Bay
-36.583333	174.6	P	PPL		N	Parakakau
-41.152222	173.438333	H	COVE		N	Pier Cove
-39.183333	177.85	H	STM		N	Mangatea Stream
-41.383333	172.583333	T	MT		N	Mount Gomorrah
-42.55	171.966667	H	STM		N	Waiheke River

As you can see from this example, this database includes longitude and latitude values, as well as codes indicating the type of place (populated place, administrative district, natural feature, and so on), the elevation (where relevant), and a code indicating the type of name (official, conventional, historical, and so on).

The GEOnet Names Server database contains approximately 5 million features, with 8 million names. It includes every country other than the US and Antarctica.

Data format

The GEOnet Names Server's data is provided as a simple tab-delimited text file, where the first row in the file contains the field names and the subsequent rows contains the various features, one per row. Importing this name data into a spreadsheet or database is trivial.

For more information on the supplied fields and what the various codes mean, please refer to:

`http://earth-info.nga.mil/gns/html/gis_countryfiles.html`

Obtaining and using GEOnet Names Server data

The main website for the GEOnet Names Server is:

`http://earth-info.nga.mil/gns/html`

The main interface to the GEOnet Names Server is through various search tools that provide filtered views onto the data. To download the data directly rather than through searching, go to:

`http://earth-info.nga.mil/gns/html/namefiles.htm`

Each country is listed; simply click on the hyperlink for the country you want data on and your browser will download a `.zip` file containing the tab-delimited text file containing all the features within that country. There is also an option to download all the countries in one file, which is a 370 MB download.

Once you have downloaded the file and decompressed it, you can load the file directly into a spreadsheet or database for further processing. By filtering on the **Feature Classification (FC)**, **Feature Designation Code (DSG)**, and other fields, you can select the particular set of place names you want, and then use this data directly in your application.

Geographic Names Information System (GNIS)

The **Geographic Names Information System (GNIS)** is the US equivalent of the GEOnet Names Server—it contains name information for the United States.

The following screenshot is an extract from the GNIS database:

FEATURE_NAME	FEATURE_CLASS	STATE_ALPHA	PRIM_LAT_DEC	PRIM_LONG_DEC	ELEVATION
Abbott Ranch	Locale	CA	36.2305176	-121.4657686	250
Abbott Reservoir	Reservoir	CA	40.9060035	-120.8613504	1760
Abbott Spring	Spring	CA	40.9093369	-120.8535725	1794
Abbotts Lagoon	Lake	CA	38.1174233	-122.9533306	0
Abbotts Peak	Summit	CA	37.9763136	-120.6224262	471
Abbotts Upper Cabin	Building	CA	41.4295777	-123.1875457	1477
ABC Camp Rustic Campsite	Locale	CA	36.0232958	-121.4299341	756
ABC-TV Heliport	Airport	CA	34.1033427	-118.2834088	129
Abel Canyon	Valley	CA	34.8233155	-119.8643049	524
Abel Canyon Campground	Locale	CA	34.82276	-119.8626382	524
Abel Canyon Spring	Spring	CA	34.8710918	-119.816803	1190
Abel Square Shopping Center	Locale	CA	37.427717	-121.9080126	5
Abelardo Cabin	Locale	CA	36.3102401	-120.7585092	1146
Abelian Group Math School	School	CA	37.8685219	-122.2876776	23
Abels Apple Acres	Locale	CA	38.7465695	-120.748544	797
Aberdeen	Populated Place	CA	36.9779897	-118.2534321	1193
Aberdeen Bypass Ditch	Canal	CA	36.9616004	-118.2362091	1173
Aberdeen Canyon	Valley	CA	34.1155644	-118.2889647	196
Aberdeen Ditch	Canal	CA	36.9646558	-118.225931	1174
Aberdeen-Inverness Residence Hall	Building	CA	33.978349	-117.3253209	331
Abernathy Meadow	Flat	CA	37.8752015	-119.8993467	1292
Abestos Number 1 Prospect	Mine	CA	36.8940982	-118.069813	2033
Abilene	Populated Place	CA	36.145507	-119.053714	124
Able Spring	Spring	CA	39.1473909	-122.6310973	924
Ables Drain	Canal	CA	37.4274355	-120.9690959	19
Abney Butte	Summit	CA	41.9759586	-123.1603266	1269
Abolitos Park	Park	CA	32.9833782	-117.0600321	175
Abraham Lincoln Continuation High School	School	CA	33.9711265	-117.3661556	275
Abraham Lincoln Elementary School	School	CA	33.6100221	-117.8606119	89

GNIS includes natural, physical, and cultural features, though it does not include road or highway names.

As with the GEOnames database, the GNIS database contains the official names used by the US Government, as decided by the US Board on Geographic Names. GEOnames is run by the US Geological Survey, and currently contains over 2.2 million features.

Data format

GNIS names are available for download as "pipe-delimited" compressed text files. This format uses the "pipe" character (|) to separate the various fields:

```
FEATURE_ID|FEATURE_NAME|FEATURE_CLASS|...
1397658|Ester|Populated Place|...
1397926|Afognak|Populated Place|...
```

The first line contains the field names, and subsequent lines contain the various features. The available information includes the name of the feature, its type, elevation, the county and state the feature is in, the latitude/longitude coordinate of the feature itself, and the latitude/longitude coordinate for the "source" of the feature (for streams, valleys, and so on).

Obtaining and using GNIS Data

The main GNIS website can be found at:

```
http://geonames.usgs.gov/domestic
```

Click on the **Download Domestic Names** hyperlink, and you will be given options to download all the GNIS data on a state-by-state basis, or all the features in a single large download. You can also download "topical gazetteers" that include selected subsets of the data—all populated places, all historical places, and so on.

If you click on one of the file format hyperlinks, a pop-up window will appear describing the structure of the files in more detail.

Once you have downloaded the data you want, you can simply import the file into a database or spreadsheet. To import into a spreadsheet, use the "Delimited" format and enter | as the custom delimiter character. You can then sort or filter the data in whatever way you want so that you can use it in your application.

Choosing your geospatial data source

If you need to obtain map data, images, elevations, or place names for use in your geospatial applications, the sources we have covered should give you everything you need. Of course, this is not an exhaustive list—other sources of data are available, and can be found online using a search engine or sites such as `http://freegis.org`.

The following table lists the various requirements you may have for geospatial data in your application development, and which data source(s) may be most appropriate in each case:

Requirement	Suitable data sources
Simple base map	World Borders Dataset
Shaded relief (pseudo-3D) maps	GLOBE or NED data processed using `gdaldem`; Natural Earth raster images
Street map	OpenStreetMap
City outlines	TIGER (US); Natural Earth urban areas
Detailed country outlines	GSHHS Level 1
Photorealistic images of the Earth	Landsat
City and place names	GNIS (US) or Geonet Names Server (elsewhere)

Summary

In this chapter, we have surveyed a number of sources of freely-available geospatial data. We have learned that:

- OpenStreetMap is a collaborative website where people can create and edit vector maps worldwide.

- TIGER is a service of the US Geological Survey providing geospatial data on streets, railways, rivers, lakes, geographic boundaries, and legal and statistical entities such as school districts and urban regions.

- Natural Earth Data is an excellent source for physical and cultural boundaries in vector format, as well as various raster-format visualizations of the Earth.

- GSHHS is a high-resolution shoreline database containing detailed vector data for shorelines, lakes, and rivers worldwide.

- The World Borders Dataset is a simple vector data source containing country borders and related data for the entire world bundled into one convenient package.

- Landsat provides detailed raster satellite imagery of all land masses on the Earth.

- GLOBE provides medium-resolution digital elevation (DEM) data for the entire world.

- The National Elevation Dataset includes high-resolution digital elevation (DEM) data for the Continental United States, Alaska, Hawaii, and other US territories.

- The GEOnet Names Server provides information on official place names for every country other than the US and Antarctica.

- GNIS provides official place names for the United States.

In the next chapter, we will use the Python toolkits described in *Chapter 3, Python Libraries for Geospatial Development*, to work with some of this geospatial data in interesting and useful ways.

5
Working with Geospatial Data in Python

In this chapter, we combine the Python libraries and geospatial data covered earlier to accomplish a variety of tasks. These tasks have been chosen to demonstrate various techniques for working with geospatial data in your Python programs; while in some cases there are quicker and easier ways to achieve these results (for example, using command-line utilities), we will create these solutions in Python so you can learn how to work with geospatial data in your own Python programs.

This chapter will cover:

- Reading and writing geospatial data in both vector and raster format
- Changing the datums and projections used by geospatial data
- Representing and storing geospatial data within your Python programs
- Performing geospatial calculations on points, lines, and polygons
- Converting and standardizing units of geometry and distance

This chapter is formatted like a cookbook, detailing various real-world tasks you might want to perform and providing "recipes" for accomplishing them.

Pre-requisites

If you want to follow through the examples in this chapter, make sure you have the following Python libraries installed on your computer:

- GDAL/OGR Version 1.9 or later (http://gdal.org)
- pyproj Version 1.9.2 or later (http://code.google.com/p/pyproj)

- Shapely Version 1.2 or later (`http://trac.gispython.org/lab/wiki/Shapely`)

For more information about these libraries and how to use them, including references to the API documentation for each library, please refer to *Chapter 3, Python Libraries for Geospatial Development*.

Reading and writing geospatial data

In this section, we will look at some examples of tasks you might want to perform which involve reading and writing geospatial data in both vector and raster format.

Task – calculate the bounding box for each country in the world

In this slightly contrived example, we will make use of a shapefile to calculate the minimum and maximum latitude/longitude values for each country in the world. This "bounding box" can be used, among other things, to generate a map of a particular country. For example, the bounding box for Turkey would look like this:

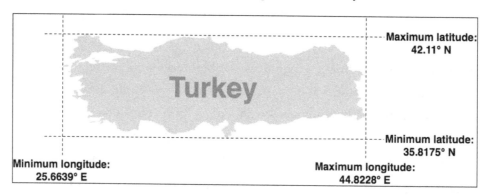

Start by downloading the World Borders Dataset from:

`http://thematicmapping.org/downloads/world_borders.php`

Decompress the `.zip` archive and place the various files that make up the shapefile (the `.dbf`, `.prj`, `.shp`, and `.shx` files) together in a suitable directory.

Next, we need to create a Python program which can read the borders for each country. Fortunately, using OGR to read through the contents of a shapefile is trivial:

```
from osgeo import ogr

shapefile = ogr.Open("TM_WORLD_BORDERS-0.3.shp")
layer = shapefile.GetLayer(0)

for i in range(layer.GetFeatureCount()):
    feature = layer.GetFeature(i)
```

The feature consists of a **geometry** and a set of **fields**. For this data, the geometry is a polygon that defines the outline of the country, while the fields contain various pieces of information about the country. According to the Readme.txt file, the fields in this shapefile include the ISO-3166 three-letter code for the country (in a field named ISO3) as well as the name for the country (in a field named NAME). This allows us to obtain the country code and name like this:

```
countryCode = feature.GetField("ISO3")
countryName = feature.GetField("NAME")
```

We can also obtain the country's border polygon using:

```
geometry = feature.GetGeometryRef()
```

There are all sorts of things we can do with this geometry. For example, we could calculate the geometry's centroid, test if a point lies within the polygon, or convert the polygon to WKT format. In this case, however, we want to obtain the bounding box or **envelope** for the polygon. We can do this in the following way:

```
minLong,maxLong,minLat,maxLat = geometry.GetEnvelope()
```

Let's put all this together into a complete working program:

```
# calcBoundingBoxes.py

from osgeo import ogr

shapefile = ogr.Open("TM_WORLD_BORDERS-0.3.shp")
layer = shapefile.GetLayer(0)

countries = [] # List of (code,name,minLat,maxLat,
               #          minLong,maxLong) tuples.
```

```
for i in range(layer.GetFeatureCount()):
    feature = layer.GetFeature(i)
    countryCode = feature.GetField("ISO3")
    countryName = feature.GetField("NAME")
    geometry = feature.GetGeometryRef()
    minLong,maxLong,minLat,maxLat = geometry.GetEnvelope()

    countries.append((countryName, countryCode,
                        minLat, maxLat, minLong, maxLong))

countries.sort()

for name,code,minLat,maxLat,minLong,maxLong in countries:
    print "%s (%s) lat=%0.4f..%0.4f, long=%0.4f..%0.4f" \
        % (name, code,minLat, maxLat,minLong, maxLong)
```

> If you aren't storing the TM_WORLD_BORDERS-0.3.shp shapefile in
> the same directory as the script itself, you will need to add the directory
> where the shapefile is stored to your ogr.Open() call. You can also
> store the boundingBoxes.shp shapefile in a different directory if you
> prefer, by changing the path where this shapefile is created.

Running this program produces the following output:

```
% python calcBoundingBoxes.py
Afghanistan (AFG) lat=29.4061..38.4721, long=60.5042..74.9157
Albania (ALB) lat=39.6447..42.6619, long=19.2825..21.0542
Algeria (DZA) lat=18.9764..37.0914, long=-8.6672..11.9865
```

Task – save the country bounding boxes into a shapefile

While the previous example simply printed out the latitude and longitude values, it might be more useful to draw the bounding boxes onto a map. To do this, we have to convert the bounding boxes into polygons, and save these polygons into a shapefile.

Creating a shapefile involves the following steps:

1. Define the **spatial reference** used by the shapefile's data. In this case, we'll use the WGS84 datum and unprojected geographic coordinates (that is latitude and longitude values). You can define this spatial reference using OGR in the following way:

```
from osgeo import osr

spatialReference = osr.SpatialReference()
spatialReference.SetWellKnownGeogCS('WGS84')
```

2. We can now create the shapefile itself using this spatial reference:

```
from osgeo import ogr

driver = ogr.GetDriverByName("ESRI Shapefile")
dstFile = driver.CreateDataSource("boundingBoxes.shp"))
dstLayer = dstFile.CreateLayer("layer", spatialReference)
```

3. After creating the shapefile, you next define the various fields which will hold the metadata for each feature. In this case, let's add two fields, to store the country name and ISO-3166 code for each country:

```
fieldDef = ogr.FieldDefn("COUNTRY", ogr.OFTString)
fieldDef.SetWidth(50)
dstLayer.CreateField(fieldDef)

fieldDef = ogr.FieldDefn("CODE", ogr.OFTString)
fieldDef.SetWidth(3)
dstLayer.CreateField(fieldDef)
```

4. We now need to create the geometry for each feature—in this case, a polygon defining the country's bounding box. A polygon consists of one or more **linear rings**; the first linear ring defines the exterior of the polygon, while additional rings define "holes" inside the polygon. In this case, we want a simple polygon with a rectangular exterior and no holes:

```
linearRing = ogr.Geometry(ogr.wkbLinearRing)
linearRing.AddPoint(minLong, minLat)
linearRing.AddPoint(maxLong, minLat)
linearRing.AddPoint(maxLong, maxLat)
linearRing.AddPoint(minLong, maxLat)
linearRing.AddPoint(minLong, minLat)

polygon = ogr.Geometry(ogr.wkbPolygon)
polygon.AddGeometry(linearRing)
```

You may have noticed that the coordinate (minLong, minLat) was added to the linear ring twice. This is because we are defining line segments rather than just points — the first call to AddPoint() defines the starting point, and each subsequent call to AddPoint() adds a new line segment to the linear ring. In this case, we start in the lower-left corner and move counter-clockwise around the bounding box until we reach the lower-left corner again:

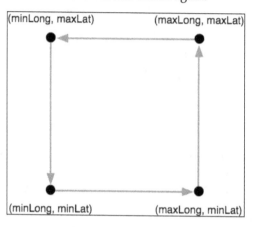

5. Once we have the polygon, we can use it to create a feature:

```
feature = ogr.Feature(dstLayer.GetLayerDefn())
feature.SetGeometry(polygon)
feature.SetField("COUNTRY", countryName)
feature.SetField("CODE", countryCode)
dstLayer.CreateFeature(feature)
feature.Destroy()
```

Notice how we use the setField() method to store the feature's metadata. We also have to call the Destroy() method to close the feature once we have finished with it; this ensures that the feature is saved into the shapefile.

6. Finally, we call the output shapefile's Destroy() method to close the file:

```
dstFile.Destroy()
```

Putting all this together, and combining it with the code from the previous recipe to calculate the bounding boxes for each country in the World Borders Dataset shapefile, we end up with the following complete program:

```
# boundingBoxesToShapefile.py

import os, os.path, shutil

from osgeo import ogr
from osgeo import osr

# Open the source shapefile.

srcFile = ogr.Open("TM_WORLD_BORDERS-0.3.shp")
srcLayer = srcFile.GetLayer(0)

# Open the output shapefile.

if os.path.exists("bounding-boxes"):
    shutil.rmtree("bounding-boxes")
os.mkdir("bounding-boxes")

spatialReference = osr.SpatialReference()
spatialReference.SetWellKnownGeogCS('WGS84')

driver = ogr.GetDriverByName("ESRI Shapefile")
dstPath = os.path.join("bounding-boxes", "boundingBoxes.shp")
dstFile = driver.CreateDataSource(dstPath)
dstLayer = dstFile.CreateLayer("layer", spatialReference)

fieldDef = ogr.FieldDefn("COUNTRY", ogr.OFTString)
fieldDef.SetWidth(50)
dstLayer.CreateField(fieldDef)

fieldDef = ogr.FieldDefn("CODE", ogr.OFTString)
fieldDef.SetWidth(3)
dstLayer.CreateField(fieldDef)

# Read the country features from the source shapefile.

for i in range(srcLayer.GetFeatureCount()):
    feature = srcLayer.GetFeature(i)
```

```
countryCode = feature.GetField("ISO3")
countryName = feature.GetField("NAME")
geometry = feature.GetGeometryRef()
minLong,maxLong,minLat,maxLat = geometry.GetEnvelope()

# Save the bounding box as a feature in the output
# shapefile.

linearRing = ogr.Geometry(ogr.wkbLinearRing)
linearRing.AddPoint(minLong, minLat)
linearRing.AddPoint(maxLong, minLat)
linearRing.AddPoint(maxLong, maxLat)
linearRing.AddPoint(minLong, maxLat)
linearRing.AddPoint(minLong, minLat)

polygon = ogr.Geometry(ogr.wkbPolygon)
polygon.AddGeometry(linearRing)

feature = ogr.Feature(dstLayer.GetLayerDefn())
feature.SetGeometry(polygon)
feature.SetField("COUNTRY", countryName)
feature.SetField("CODE", countryCode)
dstLayer.CreateFeature(feature)
feature.Destroy()

# All done.

srcFile.Destroy()
dstFile.Destroy()
```

The only unexpected twist in this program is the use of a subdirectory called bounding-boxes that is used to store the output shapefile. Because a shapefile is actually made up of multiple files on disk (a .dbf file, a .prj file, a .shp file, and a .shx file), it is easier to place these together in a subdirectory. We use the Python Standard Library module shutil to delete the previous contents of this directory, and then os.mkdir() to create it again.

Running this program creates the bounding box shapefile, which we can then draw onto a map. For example, here is the outline of Thailand along with a bounding box taken from the boundingBox.shp shapefile:

We will be looking at how to draw maps like this in *Chapter 8, Using Python and Mapnik to Generate Maps.*

Task – analyze height data using a digital elevation map

A **Digital Elevation Map (DEM)** is a raster geospatial data format where each pixel value represents the height of a point on the Earth's surface. We encountered DEM files in the previous chapter, where we saw two examples of data sources that supply this type of information: the National Elevation Dataset covering the United States, and GLOBE which provides DEM files covering the entire Earth.

Because a DEM file contains height data, it can be interesting to analyze the height values for a given area. For example, we could draw a histogram showing how much of a country's area is at a certain elevation. Let's take some DEM data from the GLOBE dataset, and calculate a height histogram using that data.

To keep things simple, we will choose a small country surrounded by ocean: New Zealand.

> We're using a small country so that we don't have too much data to work with, and we're using a country surrounded by ocean so that we can check all the points within a bounding box, rather than having to use a polygon to exclude points outside of the country's boundaries.

To download the DEM data, go to the GLOBE website (`http://www.ngdc.noaa.gov/mgg/topo/globe.html`) and click on the **Get Data Online** hyperlink. We're going to use the data already calculated for this area of the world, so click on the **Any or all 16 "tiles"** hyperlink. New Zealand is in tile **L**, so click on the hyperlink for this tile to download it.

The file you download will be called `110g.zip` (or `110g.gz` if you chose to download the tile in GZIP format). If you decompress it, you will end up with a single file called `110g` containing the raw elevation data.

By itself, this file isn't very useful—it needs to be georeferenced onto the Earth's surface so that you can match up each height value with its position on the Earth. To do this, you need to download the associated header file. Unfortunately, the GLOBE website makes this rather difficult; the header files for the premade tiles can be found at:

`http://www.ngdc.noaa.gov/mgg/topo/elev/esri/hdr`

Download the file named `110g.hdr` and place it into the same directory as the `110g` file you downloaded earlier. You can then read the DEM file using GDAL:

```
from osgeo import gdal

dataset = gdal.Open("110g")
```

As you must have noticed when you downloaded the `110g` tile that this tile covers much more than just New Zealand—all of Australia is included, as well as Malaysia, Papua New Guinea, and several other East-Asian countries. To work with the height data for just New Zealand, we have to be able to identify the relevant portion of the raster DEM—that is, the range of x and y coordinates which cover New Zealand. We start by looking at a map and identifying the minimum and maximum latitude/longitude values which enclose all of New Zealand, but no other country:

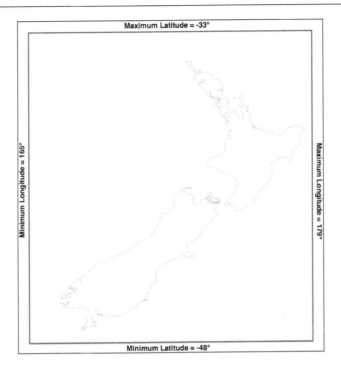

Rounded to the nearest whole degree, we get a longitude/latitude bounding box of (165, -48)…(179, -33). This is the area we want to scan to cover all of New Zealand.

There is, however, a problem: the raster data consists of pixels or "cells" identified by x and y coordinates, not longitude and latitude values. We have to convert from longitudes and latitudes into x and y coordinates. To do this, we need to make use of the raster DEM's **affine transformation**.

If you remember, back in Chapter 3, *Python Libraries for Geospatial Development*, we discussed that an affine transformation is a complex system for mapping geographic coordinates (latitude and longitude values) into raster (x, y) coordinates. Fortunately we don't have to deal with these formulas directly, as GDAL will do it for us. We start by obtaining our dataset's affine transformation:

```
t = dataset.GetGeoTransform()
```

Using this transformation, we can convert an (x, y) coordinate into its associated latitude and longitude value. In this case, however, we want to do the opposite — we want to take a latitude and longitude, and calculate the associated x and y coordinate.

To do this, we have to *invert* the affine transformation. Once again, GDAL will do this for us:

```
success,tInverse = gdal.InvGeoTransform(t)
if not success:
    print "Failed!"
    sys.exit(1)
```

 There are some cases where an affine transformation can't be inverted. This is why gdal.InvGeoTransform() returns a success flag as well as the inverted transformation. With this particular set of DEM data, however, the affine transformation should always be invertible.

Now that we have the inverse affine transformation, it is possible to convert from a latitude and longitude into an x and y coordinate, like this:

```
x,y = gdal.ApplyGeoTransform(tInverse, longitude, latitude)
```

Using this, we can finally identify the minimum and maximum (x, y) coordinates that cover the area we are interested in:

```
x1,y1 = gdal.ApplyGeoTransform(tInverse, minLong, minLat)
x2,y2 = gdal.ApplyGeoTransform(tInverse, maxLong, maxLat)

minX = int(min(x1, x2))
maxX = int(max(x1, x2))
minY = int(min(y1, y2))
maxY = int(max(y1, y2))
```

Now that we know the x and y coordinates for the portion of the DEM that we're interested in, we can use GDAL to read in the individual height values. We start by obtaining the raster band that contains the DEM data:

```
band = dataset.GetRasterBand(1)
```

 GDAL band numbers start at one. There is only one raster band in the DEM data we're using.

Now that we have the raster band, we can use the band.ReadRaster() method to read the raw DEM data. This is what the ReadRaster() method looks like:

```
band.ReadRaster(x, y, width, height, dWidth, dHeight, pixelType)
```

This method takes the following parameters:

- `x` is the number of pixels from the left-hand side of the raster band to the left-hand side of the portion of the band to read from
- `y` is the number of pixels from the top of the raster band to the top of the portion of the band to read from
- `width` is the number of pixels across to read
- `height` is the number of pixels down to read
- `dWidth` is the width of the resulting data
- `dHeight` is the height of the resulting data
- `pixelType` is a constant defining how many bytes of data there are for each pixel value, and how that data is to be interpreted

 Normally, you would set dWidth and dHeight to the same value as width and height; if you don't do this, the raster data will be scaled up or down when it is read.

The `ReadRaster()` method returns a string containing the raster data as a raw sequence of bytes. You can then read the individual integer height values from this string using the `struct` standard library module:

```
values = struct.unpack("<" + ("h" * width), data)
```

 Notice that we use the h format code to read through the data, treating each pair of bytes as a signed 16-bit integer. The < format code forces the use of little-endian byte order. This matches the format used by the DEM file.

Putting all this together, we can use GDAL to open the raster data file and read all the pixel values within the bounding box surrounding New Zealand:

```
# histogram.py

import sys, struct
from osgeo import gdal
from osgeo import gdalconst

minLat  = -48
maxLat  = -33
```

```
minLong = 165
maxLong = 179

dataset = gdal.Open("110g")
band = dataset.GetRasterBand(1)

t = dataset.GetGeoTransform()
success,tInverse = gdal.InvGeoTransform(t)
if not success:
    print "Failed!"
    sys.exit(1)

x1,y1 = gdal.ApplyGeoTransform(tInverse, minLong, minLat)
x2,y2 = gdal.ApplyGeoTransform(tInverse, maxLong, maxLat)

minX = int(min(x1, x2))
maxX = int(max(x1, x2))
minY = int(min(y1, y2))
maxY = int(max(y1, y2))

width = (maxX - minX) + 1
fmt = "<" + ("h" * width)

for y in range(minY, maxY+1):
    scanline = band.ReadRaster(minX, y,width, 1,
                               width, 1,
                               gdalconst.GDT_Int16)
    values = struct.unpack(fmt, scanline)

    for value in values:
```

 Don't forget to add a directory path to the gdal.Open() statement if you placed the 110g file in a different directory.

Let's finish this example by using these height values to calculate a histogram:

```
width = (maxX - minX) + 1
fmt = "<" + ("h" * width)

histogram = {} # Maps height to # pixels with that height.
```

```
for y in range(minY, maxY+1):
    scanline = band.ReadRaster(minX, y,width, 1,
                               width, 1,
                               gdalconst.GDT_Int16)
    values = struct.unpack(fmt, scanline)

    for value in values:
        try:
            histogram[value] += 1
        except KeyError:
            histogram[value] = 1

for height in sorted(histogram.keys()):
    print height,histogram[height]
```

If you run this, you will see a list of heights (in meters) and how many pixels there are at that height:

```
-500 2607581
1 6641
2 909
3 1628
...
3097 1
3119 2
3173 1
```

This reveals one final problem: there are a large number of pixels with a value of -500. What is going on here? Clearly -500 is not a valid height value. The GLOBE documentation explains this as follows:

> "*Every tile contains values of -500 for oceans, with no values between -500 and the minimum value for land noted here.*"

So all those points with a value of -500 represents pixels over the ocean. Fortunately, it is easy to exclude these; every raster file includes the concept of a **no data value**, which is used for pixels without valid data. GDAL includes the GetNoDataValue() method that allows us to exclude these pixels:

```
for value in values:
    if value != band.GetNoDataValue():
        try:
            histogram[value] += 1
        except KeyError:
            histogram[value] = 1
```

This finally gives us a histogram of the heights across New Zealand. You could create a graph using this data if you wished. For example, the following chart shows the total number of pixels at or below a given height:

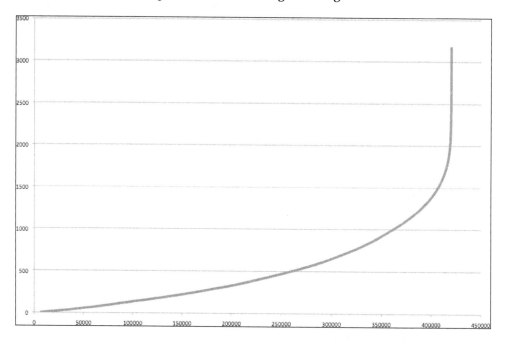

Changing datums and projections

If you remember, in *Chapter 2*, *GIS*, we discussed that a **datum** is a mathematical model of the Earth's shape, while a **projection** is a way of translating points on the Earth's surface into points on a two-dimensional map. There are a large number of available datums and projections—whenever you are working with geospatial data, you must know which datum and which projection (if any) your data uses. If you are combining data from multiple sources, you will often have to change your geospatial data from one datum to another, or from one projection to another.

Task – change projections to combine shapefiles using geographic and UTM coordinates

In this recipe, we will work with two shapefiles that have different projections. We haven't yet encountered any geospatial data that uses a projection—all the data we've seen so far uses geographic (unprojected) latitude and longitude values. So let's start by downloading some geospatial data in **Universal Transverse Mercator (UTM)** projection.

The WebGIS website (`http://webgis.com`) provides shapefiles describing land-use and land-cover, called LULC datafiles. For this example, we will download a shapefile for southern Florida (Dade County, to be exact), which uses the Universal Transverse Mercator projection.

You can download this shapefile from the following URL:

`http://webgis.com/MAPS/fl/lulcutm/miami.zip`

The decompressed directory contains the shapefile, called `miami.shp`, along with a `datum_reference.txt` file describing the shapefile's coordinate system. This file tells us the following:

```
The LULC shape file was generated from the original USGS GIRAS LULC
file by Lakes Environmental Software.
Datum: NAD83
Projection: UTM
Zone: 17
Data collection date by U.S.G.S.: 1972
Reference: http://edcwww.cr.usgs.gov/products/landcover/lulc.html
```

So this particular shapefile uses UTM Zone 17 projection, and a datum of NAD83.

Let's take a second shapefile, this time in geographic coordinates. We'll use the GSHHS shoreline database, which uses the WGS84 datum and geographic (latitude/longitude) coordinates.

You don't need to download the GSHHS database for this example; while we will display a map overlaying the LULC data on top of the GSHHS data, you only need the LULC shapefile to complete this recipe. Drawing maps such as the one shown in this recipe will be covered in *Chapter 8, Using Python and Mapnik to Produce Maps*.

We can't directly compare the coordinates in these two shapefiles; the LULC shapefile has coordinates measured in UTM (that is, in meters from a given reference line), while the GSHHS shapefile has coordinates in latitude and longitude values (in decimal degrees):

```
LULC:   x=485719.47, y=2783420.62
        x=485779.49, y=2783380.63
        x=486129.65, y=2783010.66
        . . .


GSHHS: x=180.0000, y=68.9938
       x=180.0000, y=65.0338
       x=179.9984, y=65.0337
```

Before we can combine these two shapefiles, we first have to convert them to use the same projection. We'll do this by converting the LULC shapefile from UTM-17 to geographic (latitude/longitude) coordinates. Doing this requires us to define a **coordinate transformation** and then apply that transformation to each of the features in the shapefile.

Here is how you can define a coordinate transformation using OGR:

```
from osgeo import osr

srcProjection = osr.SpatialReference()
srcProjection.SetUTM(17)

dstProjection = osr.SpatialReference()
dstProjection.SetWellKnownGeogCS('WGS84') # Lat/long.

transform = osr.CoordinateTransformation(srcProjection,
                                         dstProjection)
```

Using this transformation, we can transform each of the features in the shapefile from UTM projection back into geographic coordinates:

```
for i in range(layer.GetFeatureCount()):
    feature = layer.GetFeature(i)
    geometry = feature.GetGeometryRef()
    geometry.Transform(transform)
```

Putting all this together with the techniques we explored earlier for copying the features from one shapefile to another, we end up with the following complete program:

```
# changeProjection.py

import os, os.path, shutil
from osgeo import ogr
from osgeo import osr
from osgeo import gdal

# Define the source and destination projections, and a
# transformation object to convert from one to the other.

srcProjection = osr.SpatialReference()
srcProjection.SetUTM(17)

dstProjection = osr.SpatialReference()
dstProjection.SetWellKnownGeogCS('WGS84') # Lat/long.

transform = osr.CoordinateTransformation(srcProjection,
                                         dstProjection)

# Open the source shapefile.

srcFile = ogr.Open("miami/miami.shp")
srcLayer = srcFile.GetLayer(0)

# Create the dest shapefile, and give it the new projection.

if os.path.exists("miami-reprojected"):
    shutil.rmtree("miami-reprojected")
os.mkdir("miami-reprojected")

driver = ogr.GetDriverByName("ESRI Shapefile")
dstPath = os.path.join("miami-reprojected", "miami.shp")
dstFile = driver.CreateDataSource(dstPath)
dstLayer = dstFile.CreateLayer("layer", dstProjection)

# Reproject each feature in turn.

for i in range(srcLayer.GetFeatureCount()):
```

```
        feature = srcLayer.GetFeature(i)
        geometry = feature.GetGeometryRef()

        newGeometry = geometry.Clone()
        newGeometry.Transform(transform)

        feature = ogr.Feature(dstLayer.GetLayerDefn())
        feature.SetGeometry(newGeometry)
        dstLayer.CreateFeature(feature)
        feature.Destroy()

    # All done.

    srcFile.Destroy()
    dstFile.Destroy()
```

 Note that this example doesn't copy field values into the new shapefile; if your shapefile has metadata, you will want to copy the fields across as you create each new feature. Also, the preceding code assumes that the `miami.shp` shapefile has been placed into a `miami` sub-directory; you'll need to change the `ogr.Open()` statement to use the appropriate path name if you've stored this shapefile in a different place.

After running this program over the `miami.shp` shapefile, the coordinates for all the features in the shapefile will have been converted from UTM-17 into geographic coordinates:

```
Before reprojection:   x=485719.47, y=2783420.62
                       x=485779.49, y=2783380.63
                       x=486129.65, y=2783010.66
                       ...

 After reprojection:  x=-81.1417, y=25.1668
                      x=-81.1411, y=25.1664
                      x=-81.1376, y=25.1631
```

To see whether this worked, let's draw a map showing the reprojected LULC data overlaid on the GSHHS shoreline data:

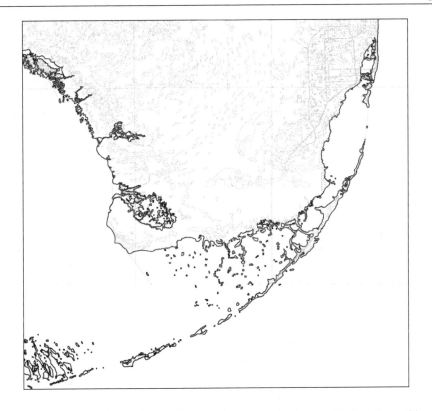

The light gray outlines show the various polygons within the LULC shapefile, while the black outline shows the shoreline as defined by the GLOBE shapefile. Both of these shapefiles now use geographic coordinates, and as you can see the coastlines match exactly.

 If you have been watching closely, you may have noticed that the LULC data is using the NAD83 datum, while the GSHHS data and our reprojected version of the LULC data both use the WGS84 datum. We can do this without error because the two datums are identical for points within North America.

Task – change datums to allow older and newer TIGER data to be combined

For this example, we will need to obtain some geospatial data that uses the NAD27 datum. This datum dates back to 1927, and was commonly used for North American geospatial analysis up until the 1980s when it was replaced by NAD83.

ESRI makes available a set of TIGER/Line files from the 2000 US census, converted into shapefile format. These files can be downloaded from:

`http://esri.com/data/download/census2000-tigerline/index.html`

For the 2000 census data, the TIGER/Line files were all in NAD83, with the exception of Alaska which used the older NAD27 datum. So we can use the preceding site to download a shapefile containing features in NAD27. Go to the site, click on the **Preview and Download** hyperlink, and then choose **Alaska** from the drop-down menu. Select the **Line Features - Roads** layer, then click on the **Submit Selection** button.

This data is divided up into individual counties. Click on the checkbox beside **Anchorage**, then click on the **Proceed to Download** button to download the shapefile containing road details in Anchorage. The resulting shapefile will be named `tgr02020lkA.shp`, and will be in a directory called `lkA02020`.

As described on the website, this data uses the NAD27 datum. If we were to assume this shapefile used the WSG83 datum, all the features would be in the wrong place:

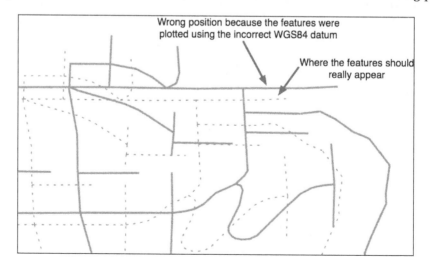

To make the features appear in the correct place, and to be able to combine these features with other data that uses the WGS84 datum, we need to convert the shapefile to use WGS84. Changing a shapefile from one datum to another requires the same basic process we used earlier to change a shapefile from one projection to another: first you choose the source and destination datums, and define a coordinate transformation to convert from one to the other:

```
srcDatum = osr.SpatialReference()
srcDatum.SetWellKnownGeogCS('NAD27')

dstDatum = osr.SpatialReference()
dstDatum.SetWellKnownGeogCS('WGS84')

transform = osr.CoordinateTransformation(srcDatum, dstDatum)
```

You then process each feature in the shapefile, transforming the feature's geometry using the coordinate transformation:

```
for i in range(srcLayer.GetFeatureCount()):
    feature = srcLayer.GetFeature(i)
    geometry = feature.GetGeometryRef()
    geometry.Transform(transform)
```

Here is the complete Python program to convert the 1kA02020 shapefile from the NAD27 datum to WGS84:

```
# changeDatum.py

import os, os.path, shutil
from osgeo import ogr
from osgeo import osr
from osgeo import gdal

# Define the source and destination datums, and a
# transformation object to convert from one to the other.

srcDatum = osr.SpatialReference()
srcDatum.SetWellKnownGeogCS('NAD27')

dstDatum = osr.SpatialReference()
dstDatum.SetWellKnownGeogCS('WGS84')
```

```python
transform = osr.CoordinateTransformation(srcDatum, dstDatum)

# Open the source shapefile.

srcFile = ogr.Open("lkA02020/tgr02020lkA.shp")
srcLayer = srcFile.GetLayer(0)

# Create the dest shapefile, and give it the new projection.

if os.path.exists("lkA-reprojected"):
    shutil.rmtree("lkA-reprojected")
os.mkdir("lkA-reprojected")

driver = ogr.GetDriverByName("ESRI Shapefile")
dstPath = os.path.join("lkA-reprojected", "lkA02020.shp")
dstFile = driver.CreateDataSource(dstPath)
dstLayer = dstFile.CreateLayer("layer", dstDatum)

# Reproject each feature in turn.

for i in range(srcLayer.GetFeatureCount()):
    feature = srcLayer.GetFeature(i)
    geometry = feature.GetGeometryRef()

    newGeometry = geometry.Clone()
    newGeometry.Transform(transform)

    feature = ogr.Feature(dstLayer.GetLayerDefn())
    feature.SetGeometry(newGeometry)
    dstLayer.CreateFeature(feature)
    feature.Destroy()

# All done.

srcFile.Destroy()
dstFile.Destroy()
```

The preceding code assumes that the lkA02020 folder is in the same directory as the Python script itself. If you've placed this folder somewhere else, you'll need to change the ogr.Open() statement to use the appropriate directory path.

If we now plot the reprojected features using the WGS84 datum, the features will appear in the correct place:

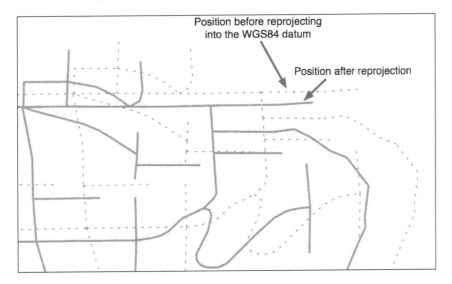

Representing and storing geospatial data

While geospatial data is often supplied in the form of vector-format files such as shapefiles, there are situations where shapefiles are unsuitable or inefficient. One such situation is where you need to take geospatial data from one library and use it in a different library. For example, imagine that you have read a set of geometries out of a shapefile and want to store them in a database, or work with them using the `shapely` library. Because all the different Python libraries use their own private classes to represent geospatial data, you can't just take an OGR `Geometry` object and pass it to `shapely`, or use a GDAL `SpatialReference` object to define the datum and projection to use for data stored in a database.

In these situations, you need to have an independent format for representing and storing geospatial data that isn't limited to just one particular Python library. This format, the *lingua franca* for vector-format geospatial data, is called **Well-Known Text (WKT)**.

WKT is a compact text-based description of a geospatial object such as a point, a line or a polygon. For example, here is the geometry defining the boundary of the Vatican City in the World Borders Dataset, converted into a WKT string:

```
POLYGON ((12.445090330888604 41.90311752178485,
12.451653339580503 41.907989033391232,
12.456660170953796 41.901426024699163,
12.445090330888604 41.90311752178485))
```

As you can see, the WKT string contain a straightforward textual description of a geometry—in this case, a polygon consisting of four x and y coordinates. Obviously, WKT text strings can be far more complex than this, containing many thousands of points and storing multipolygons and collections of different geometries. No matter how complex the geometry is, however, it can still be represented as a simple text string.

 There is an equivalent binary format called **Well-Known Binary** (**WKB**), which stores the same information as binary data. WKB is often used to store geospatial data within a database.

WKT strings can also be used to represent a **spatial reference** encompassing a projection, a datum and/or a coordinate system. For example, here is an `osr.SpatialReference` object representing a geographic coordinate system using the WGS84 datum, converted into a WKT string:

```
GEOGCS["WGS 84",DATUM["WGS_1984",SPHEROID["WGS
84",6378137,298.257223563,AUTHORITY["EPSG","7030"]],TOWGS84[0,0,0,0,
0,0,0],AUTHORITY["EPSG","6326"]],PRIMEM["Greenwich",0,AUTHORITY["EP
SG","8901"]],UNIT["degree",0.0174532925199433,AUTHORITY["EPSG","9108"]
],AUTHORITY["EPSG","4326"]]
```

As with geometry representations, spatial references in WKT format can be used to pass a spatial reference from one Python library to another.

Task – define the border between Thailand and Myanmar

In this recipe, we will make use of the World Borders Dataset to obtain polygons defining the borders of Thailand and Myanmar. We will then transfer these polygons into Shapely, and use Shapely's capabilities to calculate the common border between these two countries.

If you haven't already done so, download the World Borders Dataset from the Thematic Mapping website:

```
http://thematicmapping.org/downloads/world_borders.php
```

The World Borders Dataset conveniently includes ISO 3166 two-character country codes for each feature, so we can identify the features corresponding to Thailand and Myanmar as we read through the shapefile:

```
from osgeo import ogr

shapefile = ogr.Open("TM_WORLD_BORDERS-0.3.shp")
layer = shapefile.GetLayer(0)

for i in range(layer.GetFeatureCount()):
    feature = layer.GetFeature(i)
    if feature.GetField("ISO2") == "TH":
        ...
    elif feature.GetField("ISO2") == "MM":
...
```

 As usual, this code assumes that you have placed the TM_WORLD_BORDERS-0.3.shp shapefile in the same directory as the Python script. If you've placed it into a different directory, you'll need to adjust the ogr.Open() statement to match.

Once we have identified the features we want, it is easy to extract the features' geometries as WKT strings:

```
geometry = feature.GetGeometryRef()
wkt = geometry.ExportToWkt()
```

We can then convert these to Shapely geometry objects using the shapely.wkt module:

```
import shapely.wkt
...
border = shapely.wkt.loads(wkt)
```

Now that we have the country outlines in Shapely, we can use Shapely's computational geometry capabilities to calculate the common border between these two countries:

```
commonBorder = thailandBorder.intersection(myanmarBorder)
```

The result will be a LineString (or a MultiLineString if the border is broken up into more than one part). If we wanted to, we could then convert this Shapely object back into a OGR geometry, and save it into a shapefile again:

```
wkt = shapely.wkt.dumps(commonBorder)

feature = ogr.Feature(dstLayer.GetLayerDefn())
feature.SetGeometry(ogr.CreateGeometryFromWkt(wkt))
dstLayer.CreateFeature(feature)
feature.Destroy()
```

With the common border saved into a shapefile, we can finally display the results as a map:

The contents of the `common-border/border.shp` shapefile is represented by the heavy line along the countries' common border.

Here is the entire program used to calculate this common border:

```
# calcCommonBorders.py

import os,os.path,shutil
```

```
from osgeo import ogr
import shapely.wkt

# Load the thai and myanmar polygons from the world borders
# dataset.

shapefile = ogr.Open("TM_WORLD_BORDERS-0.3.shp")
layer = shapefile.GetLayer(0)

thailand = None
myanmar = None

for i in range(layer.GetFeatureCount()):
    feature = layer.GetFeature(i)
    if feature.GetField("ISO2") == "TH":
        geometry = feature.GetGeometryRef()
        thailand = shapely.wkt.loads(geometry.ExportToWkt())
    elif feature.GetField("ISO2") == "MM":
        geometry = feature.GetGeometryRef()
        myanmar = shapely.wkt.loads(geometry.ExportToWkt())

# Calculate the common border.

commonBorder = thailand.intersection(myanmar)

# Save the common border into a new shapefile.

if os.path.exists("common-border"):
    shutil.rmtree("common-border")
os.mkdir("common-border")

spatialReference = osr.SpatialReference()
spatialReference.SetWellKnownGeogCS('WGS84')

driver = ogr.GetDriverByName("ESRI Shapefile")
dstPath = os.path.join("common-border", "border.shp")
dstFile = driver.CreateDataSource(dstPath)
dstLayer = dstFile.CreateLayer("layer", spatialReference)

wkt = shapely.wkt.dumps(commonBorder)
```

```
feature = ogr.Feature(dstLayer.GetLayerDefn())
feature.SetGeometry(ogr.CreateGeometryFromWkt(wkt))
dstLayer.CreateFeature(feature)
feature.Destroy()

dstFile.Destroy()
```

 If you've placed your TM_WORLD_BORDERS-0.3.shp shapefile into a different directory, change the ogr.Open() statement to include the correct directory path.

We will use this shapefile later in this chapter to calculate the length of the Thailand – Myanmar border, so make sure you generate and keep a copy of the common-borders/border.shp shapefile.

Task – save geometries into a text file

WKT is not only useful for transferring geometries from one Python library to another. It can also be a useful way of *storing* geospatial data without having to deal with the complexity and constraints imposed by using shapefiles.

In this example, we will read a set of polygons from the World Borders Dataset, convert them to WKT format, and save them as text files:

```
# saveAsText.py

import os,os.path,shutil

from osgeo import ogr

if os.path.exists("country-wkt-files"):
    shutil.rmtree("country-wkt-files")
os.mkdir("country-wkt-files")

shapefile = ogr.Open("TM_WORLD_BORDERS-0.3.shp")
layer = shapefile.GetLayer(0)

for i in range(layer.GetFeatureCount()):
    feature = layer.GetFeature(i)
    name = feature.GetField("NAME")
    geometry = feature.GetGeometryRef()
```

```
f = file(os.path.join("country-wkt-files",
                      name + ".txt"), "w")
f.write(geometry.ExportToWkt())
f.close()
```

As usual, you'll need to change the `ogr.Open()` statement to include a directory path if you've stored the shapefile in a different directory.

You might be wondering why you want to do this, rather than creating a shapefile to store your geospatial data. Well, shapefiles are limited, in that all the features in a single shapefile must have the same geometry type. Also, the complexity of setting up metadata and saving geometries can be overkill for some applications. Sometimes, dealing with plain text is just easier.

Performing geospatial calculations

Shapely is a very capable library for performing various calculations on geospatial data. Let's put it through its paces with a complex, real-world problem.

Task – identify parks in or near urban areas

The US Census Bureau make available a shapefile containing something called **Core Based Statistical Areas** (**CBSAs**), which are polygons defining urban areas with a population of 10,000 or more. At the same time, the GNIS website provides lists of place names and other details. Using these two data sources, we will identify any parks within or close to an urban area.

Because of the volume of data we are dealing with, we will limit our search to California. It would take a very long time to check all the CBSA polygon/place name combinations for the entire United States; it's possible to optimize the program to do this quickly, but this would make the example too complex for our current purposes.

Let's start by downloading the necessary data. Go to the TIGER website:

```
http://census.gov/geo/www/tiger
```

Click on the **TIGER/Line Shapefiles** link, then follow the **Download** option for the latest version of the TIGER/Link shapefiles (as of this writing, this is the 2012 version). Select the **Web Interface** option, and choose **Core Based Statistical Areas** from the pop-up menu. The shapefile you want is called **Metropolitan/Micropolitan Statistical Area**; click on this button to download the CBSA data for the entire USA.

The file you download will have a name similar to `tl_XXXX_us_cbsa.zip`, where XXXX is the year of the data you've downloaded. Once the file has downloaded, decompress it and place the resulting shapefile into a convenient location so that you can work with it.

You now need to download the GNIS place name data. Go to the GNIS website:

`http://geonames.usgs.gov/domestic`

Click on the **Download Domestic Names** hyperlink, and then choose the option **download all national features in one .zip file**. The resulting file will be named `NationalFile_XXX.zip`, where XXX is a date stamp. Decompress the ZIP archive, and place the resulting .txt file in a convenient place.

We're now ready to write the code. Let's start by reading through the CBSA urban area shapefile and extracting the polygons that define the boundary of each urban area:

```
shapefile = ogr.Open("tl_2009_06_cbsa.shp")
layer = shapefile.GetLayer(0)

for i in range(layer.GetFeatureCount()):
    feature = layer.GetFeature(i)
    geometry = feature.GetGeometryRef()
```

Using what we learned in the previous section, we can convert this geometry into a `Shapely` object so that we can work with it:

```
wkt = geometry.ExportToWkt()
shape = shapely.wkt.loads(wkt)
```

Next, we need to scan through the `NationalFile_XXX.txt` file to identify the features marked as a park. As we mentioned earlier, this file is too large for us to process in its entirety; instead we'll just extract the features for California. For each of these features, we want to extract the name of the feature and its associated latitude and longitude. Here's how we might do this:

```
f = file("NationalFile_XXX.txt", "r")
for line in f.readlines():
    chunks = line.rstrip().split("|")
    if chunks[2] == "Park" and chunks[3] == "CA":
        name = chunks[1]
        latitude = float(chunks[9])
        longitude = float(chunks[10])
```

Remember that the GNIS place name database is a "pipe-delimited" text file. That's why we have to split the line up using `line.rstrip().split("|")`.

Now comes the fun part: we need to figure out which parks are within or close to each urban area. There are two ways we could do this, either of which will work:

- We could use the `shape.distance()` method to calculate the distance between the shape and a `Point` object representing the park's location:

- We could *dilate* the polygon using the `shape.buffer()` method, and then see if the resulting polygon contained the desired point:

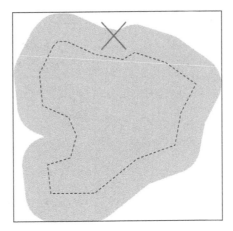

The second option is faster when dealing with a large number of points, as we can precalculate the dilated polygons and then use them to compare against each point in turn. Let's take this option:

```python
# findNearbyParks.py

from osgeo import ogr
import shapely.geometry
import shapely.wkt

MAX_DISTANCE = 0.1 # Angular distance; approx 10 km.

print "Loading urban areas..."

urbanAreas = {} # Maps area name to Shapely polygon.

shapefile = ogr.Open("tl_2012_us_cbsa.shp")
layer = shapefile.GetLayer(0)

for i in range(layer.GetFeatureCount()):
    feature = layer.GetFeature(i)
    name = feature.GetField("NAME")
    geometry = feature.GetGeometryRef()
    shape = shapely.wkt.loads(geometry.ExportToWkt())
    dilatedShape = shape.buffer(MAX_DISTANCE)
    urbanAreas[name] = dilatedShape

print "Checking parks..."

f = file("NationalFile_XXX.txt", "r")
for line in f.readlines():
    chunks = line.rstrip().split("|")
    if chunks[2] == "Park" and chunks[3] == "CA":
        parkName = chunks[1]
        latitude = float(chunks[9])
        longitude = float(chunks[10])

        pt = shapely.geometry.Point(longitude, latitude)

        for urbanName,urbanArea in urbanAreas.items():
            if urbanArea.contains(pt):
                print parkName + " is in or near " + urbanName
f.close()
```

Don't forget to change the name of the `NationalFile_XXX.txt` file to match the actual name of the file you downloaded. You may also add a path of the references to `tl_2012_us_cbsa.shp` and `NationalFile_XXX.txt` in your program if you placed these in a different directory.

If you run this program, you will get a complete list of all the parks that are in or close to an urban area:

```
% python findNearbyParks.py
Loading urban areas...
Checking parks...
Imperial National Wildlife Refuge is in or near El Centro, CA
TwinLakesStateBeach is in or near Santa Cruz-Watsonville, CA
AdmiralWilliamStandleyState Recreation Area is in or near Ukiah, CA
Agate Beach County Park is in or near San Francisco-Oakland-Fremont,
CA
```

Note that our program uses **angular distances** to decide if a park is in or near a given urban area. As we mentioned in *Chapter 2, GIS*, an angular distance is the angle between two lines going out from the center of the Earth to the Earth's surface:

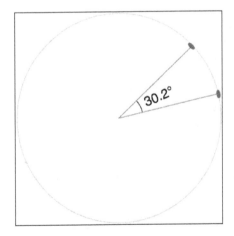

Because we are dealing with data for California, where one degree of angular measurement roughly equals 100 kilometers on the Earth's surface, an angular measurement of 0.1 roughly equals a real distance of 10 km.

Using angular measurements makes the distance calculation easy and quick to calculate, though it doesn't give an exact distance on the Earth's surface. If your application requires exact distances, you could start by using an angular distance to filter out the features obviously too far away, and then obtain an exact result for the remaining features by calculating the point on the polygon's boundary that is closest to the desired point, and then calculating the linear distance between the two points. You would then discard the points that exceed your desired exact linear distance. Implementing this would be an interesting challenge, though not one we will examine in this book.

Converting and standardizing units of geometry and distance

Imagine that you have two points on the Earth's surface, with a straight line drawn between them:

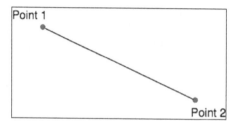

Each of these points can be described as a coordinate using some arbitrary coordinate system (for example, using latitude and longitude values), while the length of the straight line could be described as the "distance" between the two points.

 Of course, because the Earth's surface is not flat, we aren't really dealing with straight lines at all. Rather, we are calculating geodetic or **Great Circle** distances across the surface of the Earth.

Given any two coordinates, it is possible to calculate the distance between them. Conversely, you can start with one coordinate, a desired distance and a direction, and then calculate the coordinates for the other point.

The `pyproj` Python library allows you to perform these types of calculations for any given datum. You can also use `pyproj` to convert from projected coordinates back to geographic coordinates, and vice versa, allowing you to perform these sorts of calculations for any desired datum, coordinate system and projection.

Ultimately, a geometry such as a line or a polygon consists of nothing more than a list of connected points. This means that, using the process mentioned earlier, you can calculate the geodetic distance between each of the points in any polygon and total the results to get the actual length for any geometry. Let's use this knowledge to solve a real-world problem.

Task – calculate the length of the Thai-Myanmar border

To solve this problem, we will make use of the `common-border/border.shp` shapefile we created earlier. This shapefile contains a single feature, which is a LineString defining the border between the two countries. Let's start by taking a look at the individual line segments that make up this feature's geometry:

```python
import os.path
from osgeo import ogr

def getLineSegmentsFromGeometry(geometry):
    segments = []
    if geometry.GetPointCount() > 0:
        segment = []
        for i in range(geometry.GetPointCount()):
            segment.append(geometry.GetPoint_2D(i))
        segments.append(segment)
    for i in range(geometry.GetGeometryCount()):
        subGeometry = geometry.GetGeometryRef(i)
        segments.extend(
            getLineSegmentsFromGeometry(subGeometry))
    return segments

filename = os.path.join("common-border", "border.shp")
shapefile = ogr.Open(filename)
layer = shapefile.GetLayer(0)
feature = layer.GetFeature(0)
geometry = feature.GetGeometryRef()

segments = getLineSegmentsFromGeometry(geometry)

print segments
```

 Don't forget to change the `os.path.join()` statement to match the location of your `border.shp` shapefile.

Note that we use a recursive function, `getLineSegmentsFromGeometry()`, to pull the individual coordinates for each line segment out of the geometry. Because geometries are recursive data structures, we have to pull out the individual line segments before we can work with them.

Running this program produces a long list of points that make up the various line segments defining the border between these two countries:

```
% python calcBorderLength.py
[[(100.08132200000006, 20.348840999999936),
(100.08943199999999, 20.347217999999941)],
[(100.08943199999999, 20.347217999999941),
(100.0913700000001, 20.348606000000075)], ...]
```

Each line segment consists of a list of points — in this case, you'll notice that each segment has only two points — and if you look closely you will notice that each segment starts at the same point as the previous segment ended. There are a total of 459 segments defining the border between Thailand and Myanmar — that is, 459 point pairs that we can calculate the geodetic distance for.

 Remember that a geodetic distance is a distance measured on the surface of the Earth.

Let's see how we can use `pyproj` to calculate the geodetic distance between any two points. We first create a `Geod` instance:

```
geod = pyproj.Geod(ellps='WGS84')
```

`Geod` is the `pyproj` class that performs geodetic calculations. Note that we have to provide it with details of the datum used to describe the shape of the Earth. Once our `Geod` instance has been set up, we can calculate the geodetic distance between any two points by calling `geod.inv()`, the "inverse geodetic transformation" method:

```
angle1,angle2,distance = geod.inv(long1, lat1, long2, lat2)
```

`angle1` will be the angle from the first point to the second, measured in decimal degrees, `angle2` will be the angle from the second point back to the first (again in degrees), and `distance` will be the Great Circle distance between the two points, in meters.

Using this, we can iterate over the line segments, calculate the distance from one point to another, and total up all the distances to obtain the total length of the border:

```python
geod = pyproj.Geod(ellps='WGS84')

totLength = 0.0
for segment in segments:
    for i in range(len(segment)-1):
        pt1 = segment[i]
        pt2 = segment[i+1]

long1,lat1 = pt1
    long2,lat2 = pt2

    angle1,angle2,distance = geod.inv(long1, lat1,
long2, lat2)
    totLength += distance
```

Upon completion, `totLength` will be the total length of the border, in meters.

Putting all this together, we end up with a complete Python program to read the `border.shp` shapefile, calculate and then display the total length of the common border:

```python
# calcBorderLength.py

import os.path
from osgeo import ogr
import pyproj

def getLineSegmentsFromGeometry(geometry):
    segments = []
    if geometry.GetPointCount() > 0:
        segment = []
        for i in range(geometry.GetPointCount()):
            segment.append(geometry.GetPoint_2D(i))
        segments.append(segment)
    for i in range(geometry.GetGeometryCount()):
        subGeometry = geometry.GetGeometryRef(i)
        segments.extend(
            getLineSegmentsFromGeometry(subGeometry))
    return segments
```

```
filename = os.path.join("common-border", "border.shp")
shapefile = ogr.Open(filename)
layer = shapefile.GetLayer(0)
feature = layer.GetFeature(0)
geometry = feature.GetGeometryRef()
segments = getLineSegmentsFromGeometry(geometry)

geod = pyproj.Geod(ellps='WGS84')

totLength = 0.0
for segment in segments:
    for i in range(len(segment)-1):
        pt1 = segment[i]
        pt2 = segment[i+1]

        long1,lat1 = pt1
        long2,lat2 = pt2

        angle1,angle2,distance = geod.inv(long1, lat1,
                                          long2, lat2)
        totLength += distance

print "Total border length = %0.2f km" % (totLength/1000)
```

Running this program tells us the total calculated length of the Thai-Myanmar border:

```
% python calcBorderLength.py
Total border length = 1730.55 km
```

In this program, we have assumed that the shapefile is in geographic coordinates using the WGS84 ellipsoid, and only contains a single feature. Let's extend our program to deal with any supplied projection and datum, and at the same time process all the features in the shapefile rather than just the first. This will make our program more flexible, and allow it to work with any arbitrary shapefile rather than just the common-border shapefile we created earlier.

Let's deal with the projection and datum first. We could change the projection and datum for our shapefile before we process it, just as we did with the LULC and 1kA02020 shapefiles earlier in this chapter. That would work, but it would require us to create a temporary shapefile just to calculate the length, which isn't very efficient. Instead, let's make use of pyproj directly to reproject the shapefile back into geographic coordinates if necessary. We can do this by querying the shapefile's spatial reference:

```
shapefile = ogr.Open(filename)
layer = shapefile.GetLayer(0)
spatialRef = layer.GetSpatialRef()
if spatialRef == None:
    print "Shapefile has no spatial reference, using WGS84."
    spatialRef = osr.SpatialReference()
    spatialRef.SetWellKnownGeogCS('WGS84')
```

Once we have the spatial reference, we can see if the spatial reference is projected, and if so use `pyproj` to turn the projected coordinates back into lat/long values again, like this:

```
if spatialRef.IsProjected():
    # Convert projected coordinates back to lat/long values.
    srcProj = pyproj.Proj(spatialRef.ExportToProj4())
    dstProj = pyproj.Proj(proj='longlat', ellps='WGS84',
    datum='WGS84')
...
long,lat = pyproj.transform(srcProj, dstProj, x, y)
```

Using this, we can rewrite our program to accept data using any projection and datum. At the same time, we'll change it to calculate the overall length of every feature in the file, rather than just the first, and also to accept the name of the shapefile from the command line. Finally, we'll add some error-checking. Let's call our new program `calcFeatureLengths.py`.

We'll start by copying the `getLineSegmentsFromGeometry()` function we used earlier:

```
import sys
from osgeo import ogr, osr
import pyproj

def getLineSegmentsFromGeometry(geometry):
    segments = []
    if geometry.GetPointCount() > 0:
        segment = []
        for i in range(geometry.GetPointCount()):
            segment.append(geometry.GetPoint_2D(i))
        segments.append(segment)
    for i in range(geometry.GetGeometryCount()):
        subGeometry = geometry.GetGeometryRef(i)
        segments.extend(
```

```
          getLineSegmentsFromGeometry(subGeometry))
    return segments
```

Next, we'll get the name of the shapefile to open from the command line:

```
if len(sys.argv) != 2:
    print "Usage: calcFeatureLengths.py <shapefile>"
    sys.exit(1)


filename = sys.argv[1]
```

We'll then open the shapefile and obtain its spatial reference, using the code we wrote earlier:

```
shapefile = ogr.Open(filename)
layer = shapefile.GetLayer(0)
spatialRef = layer.GetSpatialRef()
if spatialRef == None:
    print "Shapefile lacks a spatial reference, using WGS84."
    spatialRef = osr.SpatialReference()
    spatialRef.SetWellKnownGeogCS('WGS84')
```

We'll then get the source and destination projections, again using the code we wrote earlier. Note that we only need to do this if we're using projected coordinates:

```
if spatialRef.IsProjected():
    srcProj = pyproj.Proj(spatialRef.ExportToProj4())
    dstProj = pyproj.Proj(proj='longlat', ellps='WGS84',
                          datum='WGS84')
```

We are now ready to start processing the shapefile's features:

```
for i in range(layer.GetFeatureCount()):
    feature = layer.GetFeature(i)
```

Now that we have the feature, we can borrow the code we used earlier to calculate the total length of that feature's line segments:

```
        geometry = feature.GetGeometryRef()
        segments = getLineSegmentsFromGeometry(geometry)

        geod = pyproj.Geod(ellps='WGS84')

        totLength = 0.0
        for segment in segments:
```

```
for j in range(len(segment)-1):
    pt1 = segment[j]
    pt2 = segment[j+1]

    long1,lat1 = pt1
    long2,lat2 = pt2
```

The only difference is that we need to transform the coordinates back to WGS84 if we are using a projected coordinate system:

```
if spatialRef.IsProjected():
    long1,lat1 = pyproj.transform(srcProj,
                                  dstProj,
                                  long1, lat1)
    long2,lat2 = pyproj.transform(srcProj,
                                  dstProj,
                                  long2, lat2)
```

We can then use `pyproj` to calculate the distance between the two points, as we did in our earlier example. This time, though, we'll wrap it in a `try...except` statement so that any failure to calculate the distance won't crash the program:

```
try:
    angle1,angle2,distance = geod.inv(long1, lat1,
                                      long2, lat2)
except ValueError:
    print "Unable to calculate distance from " \
        + "%0.4f,%0.4f to %0.4f,%0.4f" \
        % (long1, lat1, long2, lat2)
    distance = 0.0
totLength += distance
```

 The `geod.inv()` call can raise a `ValueError` if the two coordinates are in a place where an angle can't be calculated — for example if the two points are at the poles.

And finally, we can print out the feature's total length, in kilometers:

```
print "Total length of feature %d is %0.2f km" \
    % (i, totLength/1000)
```

This program can be run over any shapefile, regardless of the projection and datum. For example, you could use it to calculate the border length for every country in the world by running it over the World Borders Dataset:

```
% python calcFeatureLengths.py TM_WORLD_BORDERS-0.3.shp
Total length of feature 0 is 127.28 km
Total length of feature 1 is 7264.69 km
Total length of feature 2 is 2514.76 km
Total length of feature 3 is 968.86 km
Total length of feature 4 is 1158.92 km
Total length of feature 5 is 6549.53 km
Total length of feature 6 is 119.27 km
```

This program is an example of converting geometry coordinates into distances. Let's take a look at the inverse calculation: using distances to calculate new geometry coordinates.

Task – find a point 132.7 kilometers west of Soshone, California

Using the `NationalFile_XXX.txt` file we downloaded earlier, it is possible to find the latitude and longitude of Shoshone, a small town in California east of Las Vegas:

```
f = file("NationalFile_XXXX.txt", "r")
for line in f.readlines():
    chunks = line.rstrip().split("|")
    if chunks[1] == "Shoshone" and \
       chunks[2] == "Populated Place" and \
       chunks[3] == "CA":
        latitude = float(chunks[9])
        longitude = float(chunks[10])
```

Given this coordinate, we can use `pyproj` to calculate the coordinate of a point a given distance away, at a given angle:

```
geod = pyproj.Geod(ellps="WGS84")
newLong,newLat,invAngle = geod.fwd(latitude, longitude,
                                   angle, distance)
```

For this task, we are given the desired distance and we know that the angle we want is "due west". `pyproj` uses azimuth angles, which are measured clockwise from North. Thus, due west would correspond to an angle of 270 degrees.

Putting all this together, we can calculate the coordinates of the desired point:

```
# findShoshone.py

import pyproj

distance = 132.7 * 1000
angle    = 270.0

f = file("NationalFile_XXX.txt", "r")
for line in f.readlines():
    chunks = line.rstrip().split("|")
    if chunks[1] == "Shoshone" and \
       chunks[2] == "Populated Place" and \
       chunks[3] == "CA":
        latitude = float(chunks[9])
        longitude = float(chunks[10])

        geod = pyproj.Geod(ellps='WGS84')
        newLong,newLat,invAngle = geod.fwd(longitude,
                                           latitude,
                                           angle, distance)

        print "Shoshone is at %0.4f,%0.4f" % (latitude,
                                              longitude)
        print "The point %0.2f km west of Shoshone " \
            % (distance/1000.0) \
            + "is at %0.4f, %0.4f" % (newLat, newLong)

f.close()
```

Running this program gives us the answer we want:

```
% python findShoshone.py
Shoshone is at 35.9730,-116.2711
The point 132.70 km west of Shoshone is at 35.9640,
-117.7423
```

Exercises

If you are interested in exploring the techniques used in this chapter further, you might like to challenge yourself with the following tasks:

- Change the "Calculate Bounding Box" calculation to exclude outlying islands.

    Hint

    You can split each country's MultiPolygon into individual Polygon objects, and then check the area of each polygon to exclude those which are smaller than a given total value.

- Use the World Borders Dataset to create a new shapefile, where each country is represented by a single "Point" geometry containing the geographical center of each country.

    Hint

    You can start with the country bounding boxes we calculated earlier, and then calculate the midpoint using:

    ```
    midLat = (minLat + maxLat) / 2
    midLong = (minLong + maxLong) / 2
    ```

    For an extra challenge, you could use Shapely's centroid() method to calculate a more accurate representation of each country's center. To do this, you would have to convert the country's outline into a Shapely geometry, calculate the centroid, and then convert the centroid back into an OGR geometry before saving it into the output shapefile.

- Extend the preceding histogram example to only include height values that fall inside a selected country's outline.

    Hint

    Implementing this in an efficient way can be difficult. A good approach would be to identify the bounding box for each of the polygons that make up the country's outline, and then iterate over the DEM coordinates within that bounding box. You could then check to see if a given coordinate is actually inside the country's outline using polygon.contains(point), and only add the height to the histogram if the point is indeed within the country's outline.

- Optimize the "identify nearby parks" example given earlier so that it can work quickly with larger data sets.

Hint

One possibility might be to calculate the rectangular bounding box around each urban area, and then expand that bounding box north, south, east, and west by the desired angular distance. You could then quickly exclude all the points which aren't in that bounding box before making the time-consuming call to `polygon.contains(point)`.

- Calculate the total length of the coastline of the United Kingdom.

Hint

Remember that a country outline is a MultiPolygon, where each Polygon in the MultiPolygon represents a single island. You will need to extract the exterior ring from each of these individual island polygons, and calculate the total length of the line segments within that exterior ring. You can then total the length of each individual island to get the length of the entire country's coastline.

- Design your own reusable library of geospatial functions which build on OGR, GDAL, Shapely, and pyproj to perform common operations such as those discussed in this chapter.

Hint

Writing your own reusable library modules is a common programming tactic. Think about the various tasks we have solved in this chapter, and how they can be turned into generic library functions. For example, you might like to write a function named `calcLineStringLength()` which takes a LineString and returns the total length of the LineString's segments, optionally transforming the LineString's coordinates into lat/long values before calling `geod.inv()`.

You could then write a `calcPolygonOutlineLength()` function which uses `calcLineStringLength()` to calculate the length of a polygon's outer ring.

Summary

In this chapter we have looked at various techniques for using OGR, GDAL, Shapely, and `pyproj` within Python programs to solve real-world problems. We have learned the following:

- Reading and writing to vector-format geospatial data in shapefiles
- Reading and analyzing raster-format geospatial data
- Changing the datum and projection used by a shapefile
- Using the Well-Known Text (WKT) format to represent geospatial features and spatial references in plain text
- Using WKT to transfer geospatial data from one Python library to another
- Using WKT to store geospatial data in plain text format
- Using the Shapely library to perform various geospatial calculations on geometries, including distance calculations, dilation, and intersections.
- Using the `pyproj.Proj` class to convert coordinates from one projection and datum to another
- Using the `pyproj.Geod` class to convert from geometry coordinates to distances, and vice versa

Up to now, we have written programs that work directly with shapefiles and other data sources to load and then process geospatial data. In the next chapter, we will look at ways in which databases can be used to store and work with geospatial data. This is much faster and more scalable than storing geospatial data in files which have to be imported each time they are used.

6

GIS in the Database

This chapter examines the various open source options for storing geospatial data in a database. More specifically, we will cover:

- The concept of a spatially-enabled database
- Spatial indexes and how they work
- A summary of the major open-source spatial databases
- Recommended best practices for storing spatial data in a database
- Working with geospatial databases using Python

This chapter is intended to be an introduction to using databases in a geospatial application; *Chapter 7, Working with Spatial Data*, will build on this to perform powerful spatial queries that are not possible using shapefiles and other geospatial data files.

Spatially-enabled databases

In a sense, almost any database can be used to store geospatial data: simply convert a geometry to WKT format and store the results in a `text` column. But while this would allow you to store geospatial data in a database, it wouldn't let you query it in any useful way. All you could do is retrieve the raw WKT text and convert it back to a geometry object, one record at a time.

A spatially-enabled database, on the other hand, is aware of the notion of *space*, and allows you to work with spatial objects and concepts directly. In particular, a spatially-enabled database allows you to do the following:

- Store **spatial datatypes** (points, lines, polygons, and so on) directly in the database, in the form of a `geometry` column.

- Perform **spatial queries** on your data. For example:

  ```
  select all landmarks within 10 km of the city named "San Francisco"
  ```

- Perform **spatial joins** on your data. For example:

  ```
  select all cities and their associated countries by joining cities
  and countries on (city inside country).
  ```

- Create new spatial objects using various **spatial functions**. For example:

  ```
  set "danger_zone" to the intersection of the "flooded_area" and
  "urban_area" polygons.
  ```

As you can imagine, a spatially-enabled database is an extremely powerful tool for working with geospatial data. By using **spatial indexes** and other optimizations, spatial databases can quickly perform these types of operations, and can scale to support vast amounts of data simply not feasible using other data-storage schemes.

Spatial indexes

One of the defining characteristics of a spatial database is the ability to create special **spatial indexes** to speed up geometry-based searches. These indexes are used to perform spatial operations such as identifying all the features that lie within a given bounding box, identifying all the features within a certain distance of a given point, or identifying all the features that intersect with a given polygon.

A spatial index is defined in the same way as you define an ordinary database index, except that you add the SPATIAL keyword to identify the index as a spatial index. For example:

```
CREATE TABLE cities (
    id   INTEGER AUTO_INCREMENT PRIMARY KEY,
    name CHAR(255),
    geom POLYGON NOT NULL,

    INDEX (name),
    SPATIAL INDEX (geom))
```

All three open source spatial databases we will examine in this chapter implement spatial indexes using **R-Tree** data structures.

 PostGIS implements R-Trees using PostgreSQL's **Generalized Search Tree (GiST)** index type. Even though you define your spatial indexes in PostGIS using the GIST type, they are still implemented as R-Trees internally.

R-Tree indexes are one of the most powerful features of spatial databases, and it is worth spending a moment becoming familiar with how they work. R-Trees use the **minimum bounding rectangle** for each geometry to allow the database to quickly search through the geometries using their position in space:

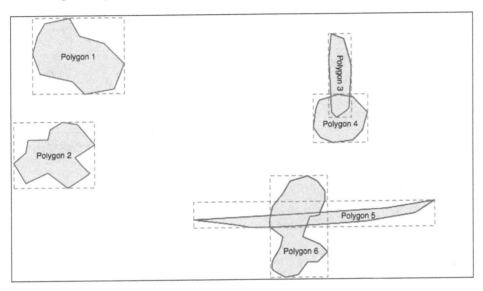

These bounding boxes are grouped into a nested hierarchy based on how close together they are:

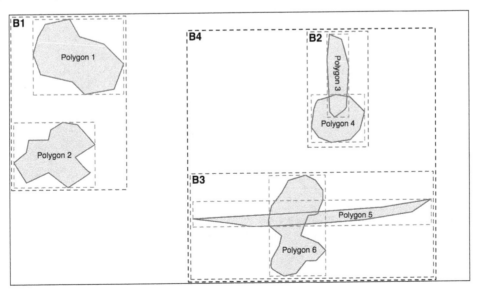

This hierarchy of nested bounding boxes is then represented using a tree-like data structure:

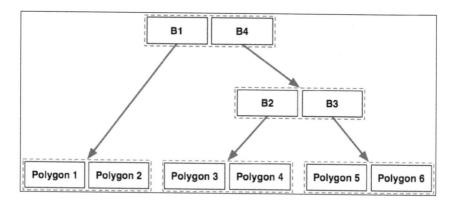

The computer can quickly scan through this tree to find a particular geometry, or to compare the positions or sizes of the various geometries. For example, imagine that we want to find the polygon that intersects the following point:

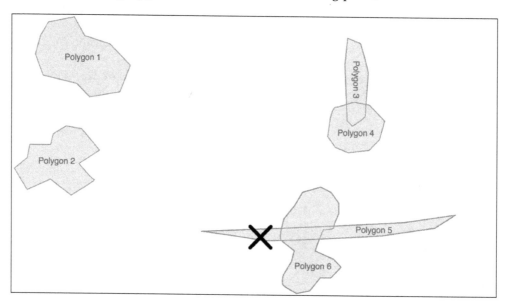

The database can quickly find this geometry by traversing the tree and comparing the bounding boxes at each level. The R-Tree will be searched in the following manner:

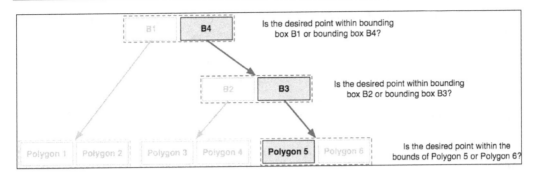

Using the R-Tree index, it took just three comparisons to find the desired polygon.

Because of the hierarchical nature of the tree structure, R-Tree indexes scale extremely well, and can search through many tens of thousands of features using only a handful of bounding box comparisons. And because every geometry is reduced to a simple bounding box, R-Trees can support any type of geometry, not just polygons.

R-Tree indexes are not limited to only searching for enclosed coordinates; they can be used for all sorts of spatial comparisons, and for spatial joins. We will be working with spatial indexes extensively in the next chapter.

Open source spatially-enabled databases

If you wish to use an open source database for your geospatial development work, you currently have three main options: **MySQL**, **PostGIS** and **SpatiaLite**. Each has its own advantages and disadvantages, and no one database is the ideal choice in every situation. Let's take a closer look at each of these spatially-enabled databases.

MySQL

MySQL is the world's most popular open source database, and is generally an extremely capable database. It is also spatially-enabled, though with some limitations, which we will get to in a moment.

The MySQL database server can be downloaded from `http://mysql.com/downloads` for a variety of operating systems, including MS Windows, Mac OS X, and Linux. Click on the MySQL Community Server link to download the server.

Once downloaded, running the installer will set up everything you need, and you can access MySQL directly from the command line:

```
% mysql
Welcome to the MySQL monitor.  Commands end with ; or \g.
Your MySQL connection id is 14
Server version: 5.5.28 MySQL Community Server (GPL)

Copyright (c) 2000,2012, Oracle and/or its affiliates. All rights
reserved.

Oracle is a registered trademark of Oracle Corporation and/or its
affiliates. Other names may be trademarks of their respective owners.

Type 'help;' or '\h' for help. Type '\c' to clear the current input
statement.

mysql>
```

To access MySQL from your Python programs, you need the MySQL-Python driver, which is available from `http://sourceforge.net/projects/mysql-python`. You can download the driver in source code format for Mac OS X and Linux, as well as MS Windows installers for Python version 2.7. If you need MS Windows installers for earlier versions of Python, these are available at `http://www.codegood.com`.

The MySQL-Python driver acts as an interface between MySQL and your Python programs:

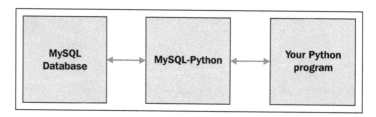

Once you have installed the MySQL-Python driver, it will be available as a module named `MySQLdb`. Here is an example of how you might use this module from within your Python programs:

```
import MySQLdb

connection = MySQLdb.connect(user="...", passwd="...")
```

```
cursor = connection.cursor()
cursor.execute("USE myDatabase")
```

The `cursor.execute()` method lets you execute any MySQL command, just as if you were using the MySQL command-line client. `MySQLdb` is also completely compatible with the **Python Database API** specification (`http://www.python.org/dev/peps/pep-0249`) and allows you to access all of MySQL's features from within your Python programs.

Learning how to use databases within Python is beyond the scope of this book. If you haven't used a DB-API compatible database from Python before, you may want to check out one of the many available tutorials on the subject, for example: `http://tutorialspoint.com/python/python_database_access.htm`. Also, the Python Database Programming Wiki page (`http://wiki.python.org/moin/DatabaseProgramming`) and the users guide for MySQLdb (`http://mysql-python.sourceforge.net/MySQLdb.html`) have useful information.

MySQL comes with spatial capabilities built in. For example, the following MySQL command creates a new database table that contains a polygon:

```
CREATE TABLE cities (
    id      INTEGER AUTO_INCREMENT PRIMARY KEY,
    name    CHAR(255),
    outline POLYGON NOT NULL,

    INDEX (name),
    SPATIAL INDEX (outline)) ENGINE=MyISAM
```

 Note that you have to specify the `MyISAM` storage engine if you want to use spatial indexes. As of MySQL Version 5.5, the default storage engine changed from `MyISAM` to `InnoDB`, so you now need to specify the engine when creating your spatial database table.

Notice that `POLYGON` is a valid column type, and that you can directly create a spatial index on a geometry. This allows you to issue queries such as:

```
SELECT name FROM cities WHERE MBRContains(outline, myLocation)
```

The preceding query will return all the cities where the `MBRContains()` function determines that the given location is within the city's outline.

This brings us to the first big disadvantage with using MySQL as a spatial database: the "MBR" at the start of the MBRContains() function stands for **Minimum Bounding Rectangle**. The MBRContains() function doesn't actually determine if the point is inside the polygon; rather, it determines if the point is inside the polygon's minimum bounding rectangle:

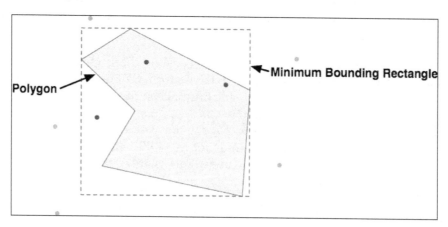

As you can see, the dark points are inside the minimum bounding rectangle, while the lighter points are outside this rectangle. This means that the MBRContains() function returns *false positives*; that is, points that are inside the bounding rectangle, but outside the polygon itself.

MySQL Version 5.6 will remove this limitation, though as of this writing Version 5.5 is the current stable release and Version 5.6 (and its associated Python drivers) may not be available for some time.

Now, before you give up on MySQL completely, consider what this bounding-rectangle calculation gives you. If you have a million points and need to quickly determine which points are within a given polygon, the MBRContains() function will reduce that down to the small number of points that might be inside the polygon, by virtue of being in the polygon's bounding rectangle. You can then extract the polygon from the database and use another function such as Shapely's polygon.contains(point) method to do the final calculation on these few remaining points, like this:

```
# Fetch the polygon we want to compare against:

cursor.execute("SELECT AsText(outline) FROM cities WHERE...")
wkt = cursor.fetchone()[0]
```

```
polygon = shapely.wkt.loads(wkt)
pointsInPolygon = []

# Search for coordinates within the polygon's bounding rectangle:

cursor.execute("SELECT X(coord),Y(coord) FROM coordinates " +
               "WHERE MBRContains(GEOMFromText(%s), coord)",
               (wkt,))
for x,y in cursor:

    # See if the polygon actually contains this coordinate.

    point = shapely.geometry.Point(x, y)
    if polygon.contains(point):
        pointsInPolygon.append(point)
```

As you can see, we first ask the database to find all points within the polygon's minimum bounding rectangle, and then check each returned point to see if it is actually inside the polygon. This approach is a bit more work, but it gets the job done and (for typical polygon shapes) will be extremely efficient and scalable.

MySQL has other disadvantages as well—the range of spatial functions is more limited, and performance can sometimes be a problem—but it does have two major advantages which make it a serious contender for geospatial development:

- MySQL is extremely popular, so if you are using a hosted server or have a computer set up for you, chances are that MySQL will already be installed. Hosting providers in particular may be very reluctant to install a different database server for you to use.

- MySQL is the easiest database to install, set up, and administer. Other databases (in particular PostgreSQL) are often much more difficult to set up and use correctly.

PostGIS

PostGIS is an extension to the **PostgreSQL** database, allowing geospatial data to be stored in a PostgreSQL database. To use PostGIS from a Python application, you first have to install PostgreSQL, followed by the PostGIS extension, and finally the **Psycopg** database adapter so you can access PostgreSQL from Python. All this can get rather confusing:

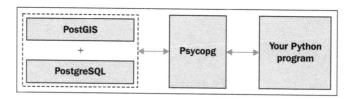

Installing and configuring PostGIS

Let's take a look at what is required to use PostGIS on your computer:

1. Install PostgreSQL:

   You first have to download and install the PostgreSQL database server. For MS Windows and Linux, installers can be found at:

   `http://postgresql.org/download`

   For Mac OS X, you should use the installer available at:

   `http://kyngchaos.com/software/postgres`

   Be warned that installing PostgreSQL can be complicated, and you may well need to configure or debug the server before it will work. The PostgreSQL documentation (`http://postgresql.org/docs`) can help, and remember that Google is your friend if you encounter any problems.

    Take note of where PostgreSQL has been installed on your computer. You will need to refer to files in the `pgsql` directory when you set up your spatially-enabled database.

2. Install the PostGIS extension:

   The PostGIS spatial extension to PostgreSQL, along with full documentation, can be downloaded from:

   `http://postgis.refractions.net`

Make sure you install the correct version of PostGIS to match the version of PostgreSQL you are using.

 For Mac OS X, use the PostGIS installer available from the KyngChaos site.

3. Install Psycopg:

Psycopg allows you to access PostgreSQL (and PostGIS) databases from Python. The `Psycopg` database adapter can be found at:

```
http://initd.org/psycopg
```

Make sure you use Version 2 and not the outdated Version 1 of Psycopg. For Windows, you can download a prebuilt version of Psycopg; for Linux and Mac OS X, you need to download the source code and build it yourself in the usual way:

```
% cd psycopg2
% python setup.py build
% python setup.py install
```

 Mac OS X users: If you are building `Psycopg` to run with the Kyngchaos version of PostgreSQL, type the following into the terminal window before you attempt to build Psycopg:

```
% export PATH="/usr/local/pgsql/bin:$PATH"
% export ARCHFLAGS="-arch i386"
```

4. Setting up a New PostgreSQL user and database:

Before you can use PostgreSQL, you need to have a **user** (sometimes called a "role" in the PostgreSQL manuals) that owns the database you create. While you might have a user account on your computer that you use for logging in and out, the PostgreSQL user is completely separate from this account, and is used only within PostgreSQL. You can set up a PostgreSQL user with the same name as your computer username, or you can give it a different name if you prefer.

To create a new PostgreSQL user, type the following command:

```
% pgsql/bin/createuser -s <username>
```

Obviously, replace <username> with whatever name you want to use for your new user. You may also need to change the path to the createuser command, if your PostgreSQL's bin directory isn't on your path. Finally, if you're running on a Mac, add -U postgres to the end of this command.

Once you have set up a new PostgreSQL user, you can create a new database to work with:

```
% pgsql/bin/createdb -U <username> <dbname>
```

 Once again, replace <username> and <dbname> with the appropriate names for the user and database you wish to set up, and change the path to the createdb command if necessary.

Note that we are keeping this as simple as possible. Setting up and administering a properly-configured PostgreSQL database is a major undertaking, and is way beyond the scope of this book. The preceding commands, however, should be enough to get you up and running.

5. Spatially enable your new database:

So far you have created a plain-vanilla PostgreSQL database. To turn this into a spatially-enabled database, you will need to configure the database to use PostGIS. Doing this is straightforward:

```
% pgsql/bin/psql -d <dbname> -c "CREATE EXTENSION postgis;"
```

After following these steps, you will have your own spatially-enabled PostGIS database. Let's now see how you can access this database from your Python programs.

Using PostGIS

Once you have installed the various pieces of software, and have set up a spatially-enabled database, you can use the Psycopg database adapter in the same way to how you would use MySQLdb to access a MySQL database:

```
import psycopg2

connection = psycopg2.connect("dbname=... user=...")
```

```
cursor = connection.cursor()
cursor.execute("SELECT id,name FROM cities WHERE pop>100000")
for row in cursor:
  print row[0],row[1]
```

Because `Psycopg` conforms to Python's DB-API specification, using PostgreSQL from Python is relatively straightforward, especially if you have used databases from Python before.

Here is how you might create a new spatially-enabled table using PostGIS:

```
import psycopg2

connection = psycopg2.connect("dbname=... user=...")
cursor = connection.cursor()

cursor.execute("DROP TABLE IF EXISTS cities")
cursor.execute("CREATE TABLE cities (id INTEGER," +
               "name VARCHAR(255), PRIMARY KEY (id))")
cursor.execute("SELECT AddGeometryColumn('cities', 'geom', " +
               "-1, 'POLYGON', 2)")
cursor.execute("CREATE INDEX cityIndex ON cities " +
               "USING GIST (geom)")
connection.commit()
```

Let's take a look at each of these steps in more detail. We first get a `cursor` object to access the database, and then create the nonspatial parts of our table using standard SQL statements:

```
connection = psycopg2.connect("dbname=... user=...")
cursor = connection.cursor()

cursor.execute("DROP TABLE IF EXISTS cities")
cursor.execute("CREATE TABLE cities (id INTEGER," +
               "name VARCHAR(255), PRIMARY KEY (id))")
```

Once the table itself has been created, we have to use a separate PostGIS function called `AddGeometryColumn()` to define the spatial columns within our table:

```
cursor.execute("SELECT AddGeometryColumn('cities', 'geom', " +
               "-1, 'POLYGON', 2)")
```

Recent versions of PostGIS support two distinct types of geospatial data, called **geometries** and **geographies**. The geometry type (which we are using here) uses Cartesian coordinates to place features onto a plane, and all calculations are done using Cartesian (x, y) coordinates. The geography type, on the other hand, identifies geospatial features using angular coordinates (latitude and longitude values) positioning the features onto a spheroid model of the Earth.

The geography type is relatively new, much slower to use, and doesn't yet support all the functions that are available for the geometry type. Despite having the advantages of being able to accurately calculate distances which cover a large portion of the Earth and not requiring knowledge of projections and spatial references, we will not be using the geography type in this book.

Finally, we create a spatial index so that we can efficiently search using the new geometry column:

```
cursor.execute("CREATE INDEX cityIndex ON cities " +
               "USING GIST (geom)")
```

Once you have created your database, you can insert geometry features into it using the ST_GeomFromText() function, like this:

```
cursor.execute("INSERT INTO cities (name,geom) VALUES " +
               "(%s, ST_GeomFromText(%s)", (cityName, wkt))
```

Conversely, you can retrieve a geometry from the database in WKT format using the ST_AsText() function:

```
cursor.execute("select name,ST_AsText(geom) FROM cities")
for name,wkt in cursor:
```

Documentation

Because PostGIS is an extension to PostgreSQL, and you use Psycopg to access it, there are three separate sets of documentation that you will need to refer to:

- The PostgreSQL manual: http://postgresql.org/docs
- The PostGIS manual: http://postgis.refractions.net/docs
- The Psycopg documentation: http://initd.org/psycopg/docs

Of these, the PostGIS manual is probably going to be the most useful, and you will also need to refer to the Psycopg documentation to find out the details of using PostGIS from Python. You will probably also need to refer to the PostgreSQL manual to learn the nonspatial aspects of using PostGIS, though be aware that this manual is huge and extremely complex, and reflects the complexity of PostgreSQL itself.

Advanced PostGIS features

PostGIS supports the following features that not available with MySQL:

- On-the-fly transformations of geometries from one spatial reference to another.
- The ability to edit geometries by adding, changing, and removing points, and by rotating, scaling, and shifting entire geometries.
- The ability to read and write geometries in GeoJSON, GML, KML, and SVG formats, in addition to WKT and WKB.
- A complete range of bounding-box comparisons, including `A overlaps B`, `A contains B`, `A is to the left of B`, and so on. These comparison operators make use of spatial indexes to identify matching features extremely quickly.
- Proper spatial comparisons between geometries, including intersection, containment, crossing, equality, overlap, touching, and so on. These comparisons are done using the true geometry rather than just their bounding boxes.
- Spatial functions to calculate information such as the area, centroid, closest point, distance, length, perimeter, shortest connecting line, and so on. These functions take into account the geometry's spatial reference, if known.
- Support for both vector and raster format geospatial data.
- An optional **geocoder** based on TIGER/Line data, allowing you to convert from street addresses to a list of matching locations (US addresses only).

PostGIS has a reputation for being a geospatial powerhouse. While it is not the only option for storing geospatial data, and is certainly the most complex database discussed in this book, it is worth considering if you are looking for a powerful spatially-enabled database to use from within your Python geospatial programs and can deal with the complexity of setting up and administering a PostgreSQL database.

SpatiaLite

As the name suggests, SpatiaLite is a "lightweight" spatial database, though the performance is surprisingly good and it doesn't skimp on features. Just like PostGIS is a spatial extension to PostgreSQL, SpatiaLite is a spatial extension to the serverless SQLite database engine. To access SQLite (and SpatiaLite) from Python, you need to use the `pysqlite` database adapter:

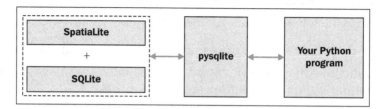

Installing SpatiaLite

Before you can use SpatiaLite in your Python programs, you need to install SQLite, SpatiaLite, and `pysqlite`. How you do this depends on which operating system your computer is running.

- **Mac OS X**

  If you're using a Mac OS X-based system, you're in luck. The framework build of `sqlite3` can be downloaded from:

  `http://www.kyngchaos.com/software/frameworks`

  This will install everything you need, and you won't have to deal with any configuration issues at all.

- **MS Windows**

  For MS Windows based systems, you can download binary installers from the following site:

  `http://gaia-gis.it/gaia-sins`

  Near the bottom of this page is the MS Windows Binaries section, where you can download the appropriate installer.

- **Linux**

  For Linux, you can download the source code to `libspatialite` from the SpatiaLite website:

  `https://www.gaia-gis.it/fossil/libspatialite/index`

  You can then follow the build instructions to compile `libspatialite` yourself.

Installing pysqlite

After installing the `libspatialite` library and its dependencies, you'll need to make sure you have a workable version of `pysqlite`, the Python database adapter for SQLite.

 Mac users are once again in luck; the `sqlite3` framework you downloaded already includes a suitable version of `pysqlite`, so you can ignore this section.

A version of `pysqlite` comes bundled with Python Version 2.5 and later, in the form of a standard library module named `sqlite3`. This standard library module, however, may not work with SpatiaLite. Because SpatiaLite is an *extension* to SQLite, the `pysqlite` library must be able to load extensions—a feature that was only introduced in `pysqlite` Version 2.5, and is often disabled by default. To see if your version of Python includes a usable version of `sqlite3`, type the following into the Python command line:

```
>>> import sqlite3
>>> conn = sqlite3.connect(":memory:")
>>> conn.enable_load_extension(True)
```

If you get an `AttributeError`, your built-in version of `sqlite3` does not support loading extensions, and you will have to download and install a different version.

The main website for `pysqlite` is:

```
http://code.google.com/p/pysqlite
```

You can download binary versions for MS Windows, and source code packages for Linux, which you can compile yourself.

Accessing SpatiaLite from Python

Now that you have all the libraries installed, you are ready to start using `pysqlite` to access and work with SpatiaLite databases. There is, however, one final thing to be aware of; because `pysqlite` is a database adapter for SQLite rather than SpatiaLite, you will need to load the `libspatialite` extension before you can use any of the SpatiaLite functionality in your Python program.

> Mac users don't need to do this, because the version of sqlite3 you downloaded comes with the libspatialite extension built in.
>
> If you are running on MS Windows, you may need to copy the SpatiaLite DLLs into the SYSTEM32 folder, or add the folder containing the SpatiaLite DLLs to the system path.

To load the libspatialite extension, add the following highlighted statements to your Python program:

```
from pysqlite2 import dbapi as sqlite

conn = sqlite.connect("...")
conn.enable_load_extension(True)
conn.execute('SELECT load_extension("libspatialite-2.dll")')
curs = conn.cursor()
```

For Linux users, make sure you use the correct name for the libspatialite extension. You may also need to change the name of the pysqlite2 module you're importing depending on which version you downloaded.

Documentation

With all these different packages, it can be quite confusing knowing where to look for more information. First off, you can learn more about the SQL syntax supported by SQLite (and SpatiaLite) by looking at the *SQL as Understood by SQLite* page:

```
http://sqlite.org/lang.html
```

Then, to learn more about SpatiaLite itself, check out the main SpatiaLite web page:

```
https://www.gaia-gis.it/fossil/libspatialite/index
```

You can access the SpatiaLite online documentation, as well as read through various tutorials, though these aren't Python-specific.

Finally, to learn more about using pysqlite to access SQLite and SpatiaLite from Python, see:

```
http://pysqlite.googlecode.com/svn/doc/sqlite3.html
```

Using SpatiaLite

In many ways, SpatiaLite has been modeled after PostGIS. Before using SpatiaLite for your database, you need to initialize SpatiaLite's internal metadata tables. You also need to explicitly define your spatial columns by calling the AddGeometryColumn() function, just like you do in PostGIS. Let's see how all this works by creating a SpatiaLite database and creating an example database table.

As described earlier, the first step in using SpatiaLite is to connect to the database and load the SpatiaLite extension, like this:

```
from pysqlite2 import dbapi2 as sqlite

db = sqlite.connect("myDatabase.db")
db.enable_load_extension(True)
db.execute('SELECT load_extension("libspatialite.dll")')
cursor = db.cursor()
```

Note that because SQLite is a serverless database, the myDatabase.db database is simply a file on your hard disk. Also, if you are running on Mac OS X, you can skip the enable_load_extension/SELECT load_extension dance and remove or comment out these two lines.

You next need to initialize the SpatiaLite metadata tables in your database. In previous versions of SpatiaLite, you had to import these tables by hand. It's now much easier—simply execute the following within your Python script:

```
cursor.execute('SELECT InitSpatialMetaData()')
```

> If the metadata tables already exist, InitSpatialMetaData() will do nothing. This means you can safely call this function whenever you open the database, regardless of whether or not the database has already been initialized.

After initializing the metadata, you can create your own database table to hold your geospatial data. As with PostGIS, this is a two-step process; you first create the nonspatial parts of your table using standard SQL statements:

```
cursor.execute("DROP TABLE IF EXISTS cities")
cursor.execute("CREATE TABLE cities (" +
            "id INTEGER PRIMARY KEY AUTOINCREMENT, " +
            "name CHAR(255))")
```

You then use the SpatiaLite function `AddGeometryColumn()` to define the spatial column(s) in your table:

```
cursor.execute("SELECT AddGeometryColumn('cities', 'geom', " +
               "4326, 'POLYGON', 2)")
```

> The number `4326` is the spatial reference ID (SRID) used to identify the spatial reference this column's features will use. The SRID number `4326` refers to a spatial reference using latitude and longitude values and the WGS84 datum; we will look at SRID values in more detail in the *Recommended Best Practices* section.

You can then create a spatial index on your geometries using the `CreateSpatialIndex()` function, like this:

```
cursor.execute("SELECT CreateSpatialIndex('cities', 'geom')")
```

Now that you have set up your database table, you can insert geometry features into it using the `GeomFromText()` function:

```
cursor.execute("INSERT INTO cities (name, geom)" +
               " VALUES (?, GeomFromText(?, 4326))",
               (city, wkt))
```

And you can retrieve geometries from the database in WKT format using the `AsText()` function:

```
cursor.execute("SELECT name,AsText(geom) FROM cities")
for name,wkt in cursor:
```

SpatiaLite capabilities

Some highlights of SpatiaLite include:

- The ability to handle all the major geometry types, including **Point, LineString, Polygon, MultiPoint, MultiLineString, MultiPolygon** and **GeometryCollection**.

- Experimental support for topology-based datatypes (nodes, edges, faces, and so on) as an alternative to the above geometry types.

- Every geometry feature has a spatial reference identifier (SRID) which tells you the spatial reference used by this feature.

- Geometry columns are constrained to a particular type of geometry and a particular SRID. This prevents you from accidentally storing the wrong type of geometry, or a geometry with the wrong spatial reference, in a database table.

- Support for translating geometries to and from various microformats, including WKT, WKB , GML, KML, and GeoJSON.

- Support for geometry functions to do things such as calculate the area of a polygon, to simplify polygons and linestrings, to calculate the distance between two geometries, to calculate intersections, differences, and buffers.

- Functions to transform geometries from one spatial reference to another, and to shift, scale, and rotate geometries.

- Support for fast spatial relationship calculations using minimum bounding rectangles.

- Support for complete spatial relationship calculations (equals, touches, intersects, and so on) using the geometry itself rather than just the bounding rectangle.

- The use of R-Tree indexes, which can (if you use them correctly) produce impressive results when performing spatial queries. Calculating the intersection of 500,000 linestrings with 380,000 polygons took just nine seconds, according to one researcher.

- An alternative way of implementing spatial indexes, using in-memory MBR caching. This can be an extremely fast way of indexing features using minimum bounding rectangles, though it is limited by the amount of available RAM and so isn't suitable for extremely large datasets.

While SpatiaLite is considered to be a lightweight database, it is indeed surprisingly capable. Depending on your application, SpatiaLite may well be an excellent choice for your Python geospatial programming needs.

Commercial Spatially-enabled databases

While we will be concentrating on the use of open source databases in this book, it is worth spending a moment exploring the commercial alternatives. There are two major commercial databases which support spatial operations: Oracle and Microsoft's SQL Server.

Oracle

Oracle provides one of the world's most powerful and popular commercial database systems. Spatial extensions to the Oracle database are available in two flavors. **Oracle Spatial** provides a large range of geospatial database features, including spatial data types, spatial indexes, the ability to perform spatial queries and joins, and a range of spatial functions. Oracle Spatial also supports linear referencing systems, spatial analysis, and data-mining functions, geocoding, and support for raster-format data.

While Oracle Spatial is only available for the Enterprise edition of the Oracle database, it is one of the most powerful spatially-enabled databases available anywhere.

A subset of the Oracle Spatial functionality, called **Oracle Locator**, is available for the Standard edition of the Oracle database. Oracle Locator does not support common operations such as unions and buffers, intersections, area and length calculations. It also excludes support for more advanced features such as linear referencing systems, spatial analysis functions, geocoding, and raster format data.

While being extremely capable, Oracle does have the disadvantage of using a somewhat non-standard syntax compared with other SQL databases. It also uses non-standard function names for its spatial extensions, making it difficult to switch database engines or use examples written for other databases.

MS SQL Server

Microsoft's SQL Server is another widely-used and powerful commercial database system. SQL Server supports a full range of geospatial operations, including support for both geometry and geography data types, and all of the standard geospatial functions and operators.

Because Microsoft has followed the Open Geospatial Consortium's standards, the data types and function names used by SQL Server match those used by the open source databases we have already examined. The only difference stems from SQL Server's own internal object oriented nature; for example, rather than `ST_Intersects(geom, pt)`, SQL Server uses `geom.STIntersects(pt)`.

Unlike Oracle, all of Microsoft's spatial extensions are included in every edition of the SQL Server; there is no need to obtain the Enterprise edition to get the full range of spatial capabilities.

There are two limitations with MS SQL Server that may limit its usefulness as a spatially-enabled database. Firstly, SQL Server only runs on Microsoft Windows based computers. This limits the range of servers it can be installed on. Also, SQL Server does not support transforming data from one spatial reference system to another.

Recommended best practices

In this section, we will look at a number of practical things you can do to ensure your geospatial databases work as efficiently and effectively as possible.

Using the database to keep track of spatial references

As we've seen in earlier chapters, different sets of geospatial data use different coordinate systems, datums, and projections. Consider, for example, the following two geometry objects:

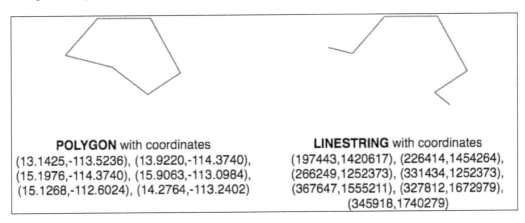

POLYGON with coordinates
(13.1425,-113.5236), (13.9220,-114.3740),
(15.1976,-114.3740), (15.9063,-113.0984),
(15.1268,-112.6024), (14.2764,-113.2402)

LINESTRING with coordinates
(197443,1420617), (226414,1454264),
(266249,1252373), (331434,1252373),
(367647,1555211), (327812,1672979),
(345918,1740279)

The geometries are represented as a series of coordinates, which are nothing more than numbers. By themselves, these numbers aren't particularly useful—you need to position these coordinates onto the Earth's surface by identifying the **spatial reference** (coordinate system, datum and projection) used by the geometry.

In this case, the POLYGON is using unprojected lat/long coordinates in the WGS84 datum, while the LINESTRING is using coordinates defined in meters using the UTM Zone 12N projection. Once you know the spatial reference, you can place the two geometries onto the Earth's surface. This reveals that the two geometries actually overlap:

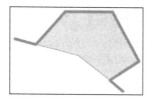

In all but the most trivial databases, it is recommended that you store the spatial reference for each feature directly in the database itself. This makes it easy to keep track of which spatial reference is used by each feature. It also allows the queries and database commands you write to be aware of the spatial reference, and enables you to transform geometries from one spatial reference to another as necessary in your spatial queries.

Spatial references are generally referred to using a simple integer value called a **Spatial Reference Identifier (SRID)**. While you could choose arbitrary SRID values to represent various spatial references, it is strongly recommended that you use the **European Petroleum Survey Group (EPSG)** numbers as standard SRID values. Using this internationally-recognized standard makes your data interchangeable with other databases, and allows tools such as OGR and Mapnik to identify the spatial reference used by your data.

To learn more about EPSG numbers, and SRID values in general, please refer to:

http://epsg-registry.org

You have seen SRID values before. For example, in the *Using SpatiaLite* section of this chapter, we encountered the following SQL statement:

```
SELECT AddGeometryColumn('cities','geom',4326,'POLYGON',2)
```

The value 4326 is the SRID used to identify a particular spatial reference, in this case the WGS84 Long Lat reference (unprojected lat/long coordinates using the WGS84 datum).

Both PostGIS and SpatiaLite add a special table to your spatially-enabled database called `spatial_ref_sys`. This table comes preloaded with a list of over 3,000 commonly-used spatial references, all identified by EPSG number. Because the SRID value is the primary key into this table, tools that access the database can refer to this table to perform on-the-fly coordinate transformations using the PROJ.4 library. Even if you are using MySQL, which doesn't provide a `spatial_ref_sys` table or other direct support for coordinate transformations, you should be using standard EPSG numbers for your spatial references.

Note that all three open source spatial databases allow you to associate an SRID value with a geometry when importing from WKT:

- MySQL: `GeometryFromText(wkt, [srid])`
- PostGIS: `ST_GeometryFromText(wkt, [srid])`
- SpatiaLite: `GeometryFromText(wkt, [srid])`

While the SRID value is optional, you should use this wherever possible to tell the database which spatial reference your geometry is using. In fact, both PostGIS and SpatiaLite require you to use the correct SRID value if a column has been set up to use a particular SRID. This prevents you from using mixing spatial references within a table.

Using the appropriate spatial reference for your data

When you import spatial data into your database, it will be in a particular spatial reference. This doesn't mean, though, that it has to stay in that spatial reference. In many cases, it will be more efficient and accurate to transform your data into the most appropriate spatial reference for your particular needs. Of course, "appropriate" depends on what you want to achieve.

With the exception of PostGIS and its new geography type, all three spatial databases assume that coordinates exist on a Cartesian plane — that is, that you are using projected coordinates. If you store unprojected coordinates (latitude and longitude values) in the database, you will be limited in what you can do. Certainly, you can use unprojected geographic coordinates in a database to compare two features (for example, to see if one feature intersects with another), and you will be able to store and retrieve geospatial data quickly. However, any calculation that involves area or distance will be all but meaningless.

Consider, for example, what would happen if you asked MySQL to calculate the length of a LINESTRING geometry:

```
mysql> SELECT GLength(geom) FROM roads WHERE id=9513;
+--------------------+
| GLength(geom)      |
+--------------------+
| 192.3644911426572  |
+--------------------+
```

If your data was in unprojected lat/long coordinates, the resulting "length" would be a number in decimal degrees. Unfortunately, this number is not particularly useful. You can't assume a simple relationship between the decimal degree "length" and the actual length on the Earth's surface, for example multiplying by some constant to yield the true length in meters. The only thing is that this so-called "length" value could be used for is to give a very rough estimate of the true length, as we did in the previous chapter to filter out features obviously too far away from a desired point.

If you do need to perform length and area calculations on your geospatial data (and it is likely that you will need to do this at some stage), you have three options:

- Using a database that supports unprojected coordinates
- Transform the features into projected coordinates before performing the length or distance calculation
- Store your geometries in projected coordinates from the outset

Let's consider each of these options in more detail.

Option 1 – using a database that supports geographies

Of the open source databases we are considering, only PostGIS has the ability to work directly with unprojected coordinates, through the use of the relatively-new geography type. Unfortunately, the geography type has some major limitations which make this a less than ideal solution:

- Performing calculations on unprojected coordinates takes approximately an order of magnitude longer than performing the same calculations using projected (Cartesian) coordinates
- The geography type only supports lat/long values on the WGS84 datum (SRID 4326)
- Many of the functions available for projected coordinates are not yet supported by the geography type

For these reasons, as well as the fact that they are only supported by PostGIS, we will not be using geography columns in this book.

Option 2 – transforming features as required

Another possibility is to store your data in unprojected lat/long coordinates, and transform the coordinates into a projected coordinate system before you calculate the distance or area. While this will work, and will give you accurate results, you should beware of doing this because (a) you may well forget to transform into a projected coordinate system before making the calculation, and (b) performing on-the-fly transformations of large numbers of geometries is very time-consuming.

Despite these problems, there are situations where storing unprojected coordinates makes sense. We will look at this shortly.

Option 3 – transforming features from the outset

Because transforming features from one spatial reference to another is rather time-consuming, it often makes sense to do this once, at the time you import your data, and store it in the database already converted to a projected coordinate system.

Doing this, you will be able to perform your desired spatial calculations quickly and accurately. However, there are situations where this is not the best option, as we will see in the next section.

When to use unprojected coordinates

As we saw in *Chapter 2, GIS*, projecting features from the three-dimensional surface of the Earth onto a two-dimensional Cartesian plane can never be done perfectly. It is a mathematical truism that there will always be errors in any projection.

Different map projections are generally chosen to preserve values such as distance or area for a particular portion of the Earth's surface. For example, the Mercator projection is accurate at the tropics but distorts features closer to the poles.

Because of this inevitable distortion, projected coordinates work best when your geospatial data only covers a part of the Earth's surface. If you are only dealing with data for Austria, then a projected coordinate system will work very well indeed. But if your data includes features in both Austria and Australia, then using the same projected coordinates for both sets of features will once again produce inaccurate results.

For this reason, it is generally best to use a projected coordinate system for data that covers only part of the Earth's surface, but unprojected coordinates will work best if you need to store data covering large parts of the Earth.

Of course, using unprojected coordinates leads to problems of its own, as discussed earlier. This is why it is recommended that you use the appropriate spatial reference for your particular needs; what is appropriate for you depends on what data you need to store and how you intend to use it.

The best way to find out what is appropriate would be to experiment; try importing your data in both spatial references, and write some test programs to work with the imported data. This will tell you which is the fastest and easiest spatial reference to work with, rather than having to guess.

Avoiding on-the-fly transformations within a query

Imagine that you have a `cities` table with a `geom` column containing POLYGON geometries in UTM 12N projection (EPSG number 32612). Being a competent geospatial developer, you have set up a spatial index on this column.

Now, imagine that you have a variable named `pt` that holds a POINT geometry in unprojected WGS84 coordinates (EPSG number 4326). You might want to find the city that contains this point, so you would issue the following reasonable-looking query:

```
SELECT * FROM cities WHERE
            Contains(Transform(geom, 4326), pt);
```

This would give you the right answer, but would take an extremely long time. Why is it that? Because the `Transform(geom, 4326)` expression is converting *every* geometry in the table from UTM 12N to WGS84 coordinates before the database can check to see if the point is inside the geometry. The spatial index is completely ignored, as it is in the wrong coordinate system.

Compare this with the following query:

```
SELECT * FROM cities WHERE
            Contains(geom, Transform(pt, 32612));
```

A very minor change, but a dramatically different result. Instead of taking hours, the answer should come back almost immediately. Can you see why? The transformation is being done on a variable that does not change from one record to the next, so the `Transform(pt, 32612)` expression is being called just once, and the `Contains()` call can make use of your spatial index to quickly find the matching city.

The lesson here is simple: be aware of what you are asking the database to do, and make sure you structure your queries to avoid on-the-fly transformations of large numbers of geometries.

Don't create geometries within a query

While we are discussing database queries that can cause the database to perform a huge amount of work, consider the following (where `poly` is a polygon):

```
SELECT * FROM cities WHERE
    NOT ST_IsEmpty(ST_Intersection(outline, poly));
```

In a sense this is perfectly reasonable: identify all cities which have a nonempty intersection between the city's outline and the given polygon. And the database will indeed be able to answer this query—it will just take an extremely long time to do so. Hopefully you can see why; the `ST_Intersection()` function creates a new geometry out of two existing geometries. This means that for every row in the database table, a new geometry is created, and is then passed to `ST_IsEmpty()`. As you can imagine, these types of operations are extremely inefficient. To avoid creating a new geometry each time, you can rephrase your query like this:

```
SELECT * FROM cities WHERE ST_Intersects(outline, poly);
```

While this example may seem obvious, there are many cases where spatial developers have forgotten this rule, and have wondered why their queries were taking so long to complete. A common example is to use the `ST_Buffer()` function to see if a point is within a given distance of a polygon, like this:

```
SELECT * FROM cities WHERE
    ST_Contains(ST_Buffer(outline, 100), pt);
```

Once again, this query will work, but will be painfully slow. A much better approach would be to use the `ST_DWithin()` function:

```
SELECT * FROM cities WHERE ST_DWithin(outline, pt, 100);
```

As a general rule, remember that you *never* want to call any function which returns a `Geometry` object (or one of its subclasses) within the `WHERE` portion of a `SELECT` statement.

Using spatial indexes appropriately

Just as ordinary database indexes can make an immense difference to the speed and efficiency of your database, spatial indexes are also a very powerful tool for speeding up your database queries. Like all powerful tools, though, they have their limits:

- If you don't explicitly define a spatial index, the database can't use it. Conversely, if you have too many spatial indexes, the database will slow down because each index needs to be updated every time a record is added, updated or deleted. Thus, it is crucial that you define the *right* set of spatial indexes: index the information you are going to search on, and nothing more.

- Because spatial indexes work on the geometries' bounding boxes, the index itself can only tell you which bounding boxes actually overlap or intersect; they can't tell you if the underlying points, lines, or polygons have this relationship. Thus, they are really only the first step in searching for the information you want. With PostGIS and SpatiaLite, the database itself can further refine the search by comparing the individual geometries for you; with MySQL, you have to do this yourself, as we saw earlier.

- Spatial indexes are most efficient when dealing with lots of relatively small geometries. If your polygons cover a large area, the polygon bounding boxes are going to be so large that they will intersect with many other geometries, and the database will have to revert to doing full polygon calculations rather than just the bounding box. Furthermore, if your geometries consist of many thousands of vertices, these calculations can be very slow indeed — the entire polygon will have to be loaded into memory and processed one vertex at a time. If you have polygons that are both large and complex, your spatial queries will be slow. If possible, it is generally better to split large and complex polygons (and multipolygons) into smaller pieces so that the spatial index can work with them more efficiently.

 We will revisit this issue in *Chapter 7, Working with Spatial Data*, where we'll split large polygons into smaller ones to speed up our program.

Knowing the limits of your database's query optimizer

When you send a query to the database, it automatically attempts to *optimize* the query to avoid unnecessary calculations and to make use of any available indexes. For example, if you issued the following (nonspatial) query:

```
SELECT * FROM people WHERE name=Concat("John ","Doe");
```

The database would know that `Concat("John ","Doe")` yields a constant, and so would only calculate it once before issuing the query. It would also look for a database index on the `name` column, and use it to speed up the operation.

This type of query optimization is very powerful, and the logic behind it is extremely complex. In a similar way, spatial databases have a **spatial query optimizer** that looks for ways to precalculate values and make use of spatial indexes to speed up the query. For example, consider this spatial query from the previous section:

```
select * from cities where ST_DWithin(outline, pt, 12.5);
```

In this case, the PostGIS function `ST_DWithin()` is given one geometry taken from a table (`outline`), and a second geometry that is specified as a fixed value (`pt`), along with a desired distance (12.5 "units", whatever that means in the geometry's spatial reference). The query optimizer knows how to handle this efficiently, by first precalculating the bounding box for the fixed geometry plus the desired distance (`pt ±12.5`), and then using a spatial index to quickly identify the records which may have their `outline` geometry within that extended bounding box.

While there are times when the database's query optimizer seems to be capable of magic, there are many other times when it is incredibly stupid. Part of the art of being a good database developer is to have a keen sense of how your database's query optimizer works, when it doesn't—and what to do about it.

Let's see how you can find out more about the query optimization process in each of our three spatial databases.

MySQL

MySQL provides a command, `EXPLAIN SELECT`, that tells you how the query optimizer will process your query. For example:

```
mysql> EXPLAIN SELECT * FROM cities
          WHERE MBRContains(geom,
                       GeomFromText(pt))\G
```

```
********************** 1. row **********************
           id: 1
  select_type: SIMPLE
        table: cities
         type: range
possible_keys: geom
          key: geom
      key_len: 34
          ref: NULL
         rows: 1
        Extra: Using where
1 row in set (0.00 sec)
```

 Don't worry about the \G at the end of the command; this just formats the output in a way which makes it easier to read.

This command tells you that this query involves a simple search against the cities table, searching for a range of records using the geom spatial index to speed up the results. The rows:1 tells you that the query optimizer thinks it only needs to read a single row from the table to find the results.

This is good. Compare it with the following:

```
mysql> EXPLAIN SELECT * FROM cities
           WHERE MBRContains(Envelope(geom),
                             GeomFromText(pt))\G

********************** 1. row **********************
           id: 1
  select_type: SIMPLE
        table: cities
         type: ALL
possible_keys: NULL
          key: NULL
      key_len: NULL
          ref: NULL
```

```
      rows: 34916
     Extra: Using where
1 row in set (0.00 sec)
```

This query uses the `Envelope()` function to create a new geometry, which is then checked to see if it contains the given point. As explained in the *Don't Create Geometries Within a Query* section, the database has to create a new geometry for every row in the table. In this case the query optimizer cannot use an index, as shown by the `NULL` value for `possible_keys` and `key`. It also tells you that it would have to scan through 34,916 records to find the matching points—not exactly an efficient query. Indeed, running this query could take several minutes to complete.

PostGIS

MySQL uses a theoretical approach to query optimization, looking only at the query itself to see how it could be optimized. PostGIS, on the other hand, takes into account the amount of information in the database and how it is distributed. In order to work well, the PostGIS query optimizer needs to have up-to-date statistics on the database's contents. It then uses a sophisticated *genetic algorithm* to determine the most effective way to run a particular query.

Because of this approach, you need to regularly run the `VACUUM ANALYZE` command, which gather statistics on the database so that the query optimizer can work as effectively as possible. If you don't run `VACUUM ANALYZE`, the optimizer simply won't be able to work.

Here is how you can run the `VACUUM ANALYZE` command from Python:

```python
import psycopg2

connection = psycopg2.connect("dbname=... user=...")
cursor = connection.cursor()

old_level = connection.isolation_level
connection.set_isolation_level(0)
cursor.execute("VACUUM ANALYZE")
connection.set_isolation_level(old_level)
```

Don't worry about the `isolation_level` logic here; that just allows you to run the `VACUUM ANALYZE` command from Python using the transaction-based `psycopg2` adapter.

It is possible to set up an *autovacuum daemon* that runs automatically after a given period of time, or after a table's contents has changed enough to warrant another vacuum. Setting up an autovacuum daemon is beyond the scope of this book.

Once you have run the VACUUM ANALYZE command, the query optimizer will be able to start optimizing your queries. As with MySQL, you can see how the query optimizer works using the EXPLAIN SELECT command:

```
psql> EXPLAIN SELECT * FROM cities
          WHERE ST_Contains(geom,pt);


                     QUERY PLAN
---------------------------------------------------------
 Seq Scan on cities   (cost=0.00..7.51 rows=1 width=2619)
    Filter: ((geom &&
'0101000000000000000000000000000000000000000'::geometry) AND _st_
contains(geom, '0101000000000000000000000000000000000000000'::geometry))
(2 rows)
```

Don't worry about the Seq Scan part; there are only a few records in this table, so PostGIS knows that it can scan the entire table faster than it can read through an index. When the database gets bigger, it will automatically start using the index to quickly identify the desired records.

The cost= part is an indication of how much this query will "cost", measured in arbitrary units that by default are relative to how long it takes to read a page of data from disk. The two numbers represent the "start up cost" (how long it takes before the first row can be processed), and the estimated total cost (how long it would take to process every record in the table). Since reading a page of data from disk is quite fast, a total cost of 7.51 is very quick indeed.

The most interesting part of this explanation is the Filter. Let's take a closer look at what the EXPLAIN SELECT command tells us about how PostGIS will filter this query. The first part is given here:

```
(geom && '0101000000000000000000000000000000000000000'::geometry)
```

This makes use of the `&&` operator, which searches for matching records using the bounding box defined in the spatial index. The second part of the filter condition is:

```
_st_contains(geom,
'0101000000000000000000000000000000000000000'::geometry)
```

This uses the `ST_Contains()` function to identify the exact geometries which actually contain the desired point. This two-step process (first filtering by bounding box, then by the geometry itself) is exactly what we had to implement manually when using MySQL. As you can see, PostGIS does this for us automatically, resulting in a quick and accurate search for geometries that contain a given point.

SpatiaLite

One of the disadvantages of using a lightweight database such as SpatiaLite is that the query optimizer is rather naive. In particular, the SpatiaLite query optimizer will only make use of B*Tree indexes; you can create a spatial R-Tree index, but it won't be used unless you explicitly include it in your query.

For example, consider the following SQL statements:

```
CREATE TABLE cities (id INTEGER PRIMARY KEY AUTOINCREMENT,
                     name CHAR(255));
SELECT AddGeometryColumn('cities','geom',4326,'POLYGON',2);
INSERT INTO cities (name,geom)
       VALUES ('London', GeomFromText(wkt, 4326);
```

This creates a `cities` table, defines a spatial index and inserts a record into the table. Because SpatiaLite uses **triggers** to automatically update the spatial index as records are added, updated, or deleted, the preceding statements would correctly create the spatial index and update it as the new record is inserted. However, if we then issue the following query:

```
SELECT * FROM cities WHERE Contains(geom, pt);
```

The SpatiaLite query optimizer won't know about the spatial index, and so will ignore it. We can confirm this using the `EXPLAIN QUERY PLAN` command, which shows the indexes used by the query:

```
sqlite> EXPLAIN QUERY PLAN SELECT * FROM cities
             WHERE id < 100;
```

```
0|0|0|SEARCH TABLE cities USING INTEGER PRIMARY KEY (rowid<?) (~250000
rows)

sqlite> EXPLAIN QUERY PLAN SELECT * FROM cities
            WHERE Contains(geom, pt);

0|0|0|SCAN TABLE cities
```

The first query (WHERE id < 100) makes use of a B*Tree index, and so the query optimizer knows to use the primary key to index the query. The second query (WHERE Contains(geom, pt)) uses the spatial index which the query optimizer doesn't know about. In this case, the cities table will be scanned sequentially, without any index at all. This will be acceptable for small numbers of records, but for large databases this will be very slow indeed.

To use the spatial index, we have to include it directly in the query:

```
SELECT * FROM cities WHERE id IN
    (SELECT pkid FROM idx_cities_geom WHERE xmin <= X(pt)
    AND X(pt) <= xmax AND ymin <= Y(pt) AND Y(pt) <= ymax);
```

The EXPLAIN QUERY PLAN command tells us that this query would indeed use the database indexes to speed up the query:

```
sqlite> EXPLAIN QUERY PLAN SELECT * FROM cities
            WHERE id IN (SELECT pkid FROM idx_cities_geom
                WHERE xmin <= X(pt) AND X(pt) <= xmax
                AND ymin <= Y(pt) AND Y(pt) <= ymax);

0|0|0|SEARCH TABLE cities USING INTEGER PRIMARY KEY (rowid=?) (~25
rows)
0|0|0|EXECUTE LIST SUBQUERY 1
1|0|0|SCAN TABLE idx_cities_geom VIRTUAL TABLE INDEX 2:BaDbBcDd (~0
rows)
```

This is an unfortunate consequence of using SpatiaLite: you have to include the indexes explicitly in every spatial query you make, or they won't be used at all. This can make creating your spatial queries more complicated, though the performance of the end result will be excellent.

Working with geospatial databases using python

In this section, we will build on what we've learned so far by writing a short program to (i) create a geospatial database, (ii) import data from a shapefile, (iii) perform a spatial query on that data, and (iv) save the results in WKT format. We will write the same program using each of the three databases we have explored in this chapter, so that you can see the differences and issues involved with using each particular database.

Prerequisites

Before you can run these examples, you will need to do the following:

1. If you haven't already done so, follow the instructions given earlier in this chapter to install MySQL, PostGIS, and SpatiaLite onto your computer.

2. We will be working with the GSHHS shoreline dataset from *Chapter 4, Sources of Geospatial Data*. If you haven't already downloaded this dataset, you can download the shapefiles from:

    `http://www.ngdc.noaa.gov/mgg/shorelines/gshhs.html`

3. Take a copy of the `l` (low-resolution) shapefiles from the GSHHS shoreline dataset and place them in a convenient directory (we will call this directory `GSHHS_l` in the code samples shown here).

 We will use the low-resolution shapefiles to keep the amount of data manageable, and to avoid problems with large polygons triggering a "Got a packet bigger than `max_allowed_packet` bytes" error in MySQL. Large polygons are certainly supported by MySQL (by increasing the `max_allowed_packet` setting), but doing so is beyond the scope of this chapter. We'll learn more about this setting in the next chapter.

Working with MySQL

We have already seen how to connect to MySQL and create a database table:

```
import MySQLdb
connection = MySQLdb.connect(user="..." passwd="...")
```

```
cursor = connection.cursor()

cursor.execute("DROP DATABASE IF EXISTS spatialTest")
cursor.execute("CREATE DATABASE spatialTest")
cursor.execute("USE spatialTest")

cursor.execute("""CREATE TABLE gshhs (
                id        INTEGER AUTO_INCREMENT,
                level     INTEGER,
                geom      POLYGON NOT NULL,

                PRIMARY KEY (id)
                INDEX (level),
                SPATIAL INDEX (geom)) ENGINE=MyISAM
            """)
connection.commit()
```

We next need to read the features from the GSHHS shapefiles and insert them into the database:

```
import os.path
from osgeo import ogr

for level in [1, 2, 3, 4]:
    fName = os.path.join("GSHHS_l",
                        "GSHHS_l_L"+str(level)+".shp")
    shapefile = ogr.Open(fName)
    layer = shapefile.GetLayer(0)
    for i in range(layer.GetFeatureCount()):
        feature = layer.GetFeature(i)
        geometry = feature.GetGeometryRef()
        wkt = geometry.ExportToWkt()

        cursor.execute("INSERT INTO gshhs (level, geom) " +
                    "VALUES (%s, GeomFromText(%s, 4326))",
                    (level, wkt))
connection.commit()
```

 Note that we are assigning an SRID value (4326) to the features as we import them into the database. Even though we don't have a spatial_ref_sys table in MySQL, we are following the best practices by storing SRID values in the database.

We now want to query the database to find the shoreline information we want. In this case, we'll take the coordinate for London and search for a level 1 (ocean boundary) polygon that contains this point. This will give us the shoreline for the United Kingdom:

```
import shapely.wkt

LONDON = 'POINT(-0.1263 51.4980)'

cursor.execute("SELECT id,AsText(geom) FROM gshhs " +
               "WHERE (level=%s) AND " +
               "(MBRContains(geom, GeomFromText(%s, 4326)))",
               (1, LONDON))

shoreline = None
for id,wkt in cursor:
    polygon = shapely.wkt.loads(wkt)
    point   = shapely.wkt.loads(LONDON)
    if polygon.contains(point):
        shoreline = wkt
```

 Remember that MySQL only supports bounding-rectangle queries, so we have to use Shapely to identify if the point is actually within the polygon, rather than just within its minimum bounding rectangle.

To check that this query can be run efficiently, we will follow the recommended best practice of asking the MySQL Query Optimizer what it will do with the query:

```
% /usr/local/mysql/bin/mysql
mysql> use myDatabase;
mysql> EXPLAIN SELECT id,AsText(geom) FROM gshhs
       WHERE (level=1) AND (MBRContains(geom,
       GeomFromText('POINT(-0.1263 51.4980)',
       4326)))\G

********************** 1. row **********************
          id: 1
  select_type: SIMPLE
       table: gshhs
```

```
         type: range
possible_keys: level,geom
          key: geom
      key_len: 34
          ref: NULL
         rows: 1
        Extra: Using where
1 row in set (0.00 sec)
```

As you can see, we simply retyped the query, adding the word EXPLAIN to the front and filling in the parameters to make a valid SQL statement. The result tells us that the SELECT query is indeed using the indexed geom column, allowing it to quickly find the desired feature.

Now that we have a working program that can quickly retrieve the desired geometry, let's save the UK shoreline polygon to a text file:

```
f = file("uk-shoreline.wkt", "w")
f.write(shoreline)
f.close()
```

Running this program saves a low-resolution outline of the United Kingdom's shoreline into the uk-shoreline.wkt file:

Working with PostGIS

Let's rewrite this program to use PostGIS. The first part, where we open the database and define our gshhs table, is almost identical:

```
import psycopg2

connection = psycopg2.connect("dbname=... user=...")
cursor = connection.cursor()

cursor.execute("DROP TABLE IF EXISTS gshhs")
cursor.execute("""CREATE TABLE gshhs (
                    id      SERIAL,
                    level   INTEGER,

                    PRIMARY KEY (id))
            """)
cursor.execute("CREATE INDEX levelIndex ON gshhs(level)")
cursor.execute("SELECT AddGeometryColumn('gshhs', " +
                    "'geom', 4326, 'POLYGON', 2)")
cursor.execute("CREATE INDEX geomIndex ON gshhs " +
                "USING GIST (geom)")
connection.commit()
```

The only difference is that we have to use the psycopg2 database adapter, and the fact that we have to create the geometry column (and spatial index) separately from the CREATE TABLE statement itself.

The second part of this program where we import the data from the shapefile into the database is once again almost identical to the MySQL version:

```
import os.path
from osgeo import ogr

for level in [1, 2, 3, 4]:
    fName = os.path.join("GSHHS_l",
                        "GSHHS_l_L"+str(level)+".shp")
    shapefile = ogr.Open(fName)
    layer = shapefile.GetLayer(0)
    for i in range(layer.GetFeatureCount()):
        feature = layer.GetFeature(i)
        geometry = feature.GetGeometryRef()
        wkt = geometry.ExportToWkt()
```

```
cursor.execute("INSERT INTO gshhs (level, geom) " +
               "VALUES (%s, ST_GeomFromText(%s, " +
               "4326))", (level, wkt))
connection.commit()
```

Now that we have brought the shapefile's contents into the database, we need to do something in PostGIS that isn't necessary with MySQL or SpatiaLite: we need to run a VACUUM ANALYZE command so that PostGIS can gather statistics to help it optimize our database queries:

```
old_level = connection.isolation_level
connection.set_isolation_level(0)
cursor.execute("VACUUM ANALYZE")
connection.set_isolation_level(old_level)
```

We next want to search for the UK shoreline based upon the coordinate for London. This code is simpler than the MySQL version, thanks to the fact that PostGIS automatically does the bounding box check followed by the full polygon check, so we don't have to do this by hand:

```
LONDON = 'POINT(-0.1263 51.4980)'

cursor.execute("SELECT id,ST_AsText(geom) FROM gshhs " +
               "WHERE (level=%s) AND " +
               "(ST_Contains(geom, ST_GeomFromText(%s, 4326)))",
               (1, LONDON))

shoreline = None
for id,wkt in cursor:
    shoreline = wkt
```

Following the recommended best practices, we will ask PostGIS to tell us how it thinks this query will be performed:

```
% usr/local/pgsql/bin/psql -U userName -d dbName
psql> EXPLAIN SELECT id,ST_AsText(geom) FROM gshhs
        WHERE (level=2) AND (ST_Contains(geom,
        ST_GeomFromText('POINT(-0.1263 51.4980)', 4326)));

                        QUERY PLAN
------------------------------------------------------------
 Index Scan using geomindex on gshhs (cost=0.00..8.53 rows=1
width=673)
```

```
    Index Cond: (geom && '0101000020E6100000ED0DBE30992AC0BF39B4C876BEB
F4940'::geometry)
    Filter: ((level = 2) AND _st_contains(geom, '0101000020E6100000ED0D
BE30992AC0BF39B4C876BEBF4940'::geometry))
(3 rows)
```

This tells us that PostGIS will answer this query by scanning through the `geomindex` spatial index, first filtering by bounding box (using the `&&` operator), and then calling `ST_Contains()` to see if the polygon actually contains the desired point.

This is exactly what we were hoping to see; the database is processing this query as quickly as possible while still giving us completely accurate results.

Now that we have the desired shoreline polygon, let's finish our program by saving the polygon's WKT representation to disk:

```
f = file("uk-shoreline.wkt", "w")
f.write(shoreline)
f.close()
```

As with the MySQL version, running this program will create the `uk-shoreline.wkt` file containing the same low-resolution outline of the United Kingdom's shoreline.

Working with SpatiaLite

Let's rewrite this program once more, this time to use SpatiaLite. As discussed earlier, we will create a database file and then call the `InitSpatialMetaData()` function. This will create and set up our spatial database.

```
import os, os.path
from pysqlite2 import dbapi2 as sqlite

if os.path.exists("gshhs-spatialite.db"):
    os.remove("gshhs-spatialite.db")

db = sqlite.connect("gshhs-spatialite.db")
db.enable_load_extension(True)
db.execute('SELECT load_extension("libspatialite.dll")')
cursor = db.cursor()

cursor.execute("SELECT InitSpatialMetaData()")
```

If you are running on Mac OS X, you can skip the `db.enable_load_extension(...)` and `db.execute('SELECT load_extension(...)')` statements.

We next need to create our database table. This is done in almost exactly the same way as our PostGIS version:

```
cursor.execute("DROP TABLE IF EXISTS gshhs")
cursor.execute("CREATE TABLE gshhs (" +
                "id INTEGER PRIMARY KEY AUTOINCREMENT, " +
                "level INTEGER)")
cursor.execute("CREATE INDEX gshhs_level on gshhs(level)")
cursor.execute("SELECT AddGeometryColumn('gshhs', 'geom', " +
                "4326, 'POLYGON', 2)")
cursor.execute("SELECT CreateSpatialIndex('gshhs', 'geom')")
db.commit()
```

Loading the contents of the shapefile into the database is almost the same as the other versions of our program:

```
import os.path
from osgeo import ogr

for level in [1, 2, 3, 4]:
    fName = os.path.join("GSHHS_l",
                        "GSHHS_l_L"+str(level)+".shp")
    shapefile = ogr.Open(fName)
    layer = shapefile.GetLayer(0)
    for i in range(layer.GetFeatureCount()):
        feature = layer.GetFeature(i)
        geometry = feature.GetGeometryRef()
        wkt = geometry.ExportToWkt()

        cursor.execute("INSERT INTO gshhs (level, geom) " +
                        "VALUES (?, GeomFromText(?, 4326))",
                        (level, wkt))
    db.commit()
```

We've now reached the point where we want to search through the database for the desired polygon. Here is how we can do this in SpatiaLite:

```
import shapely.wkt

LONDON = 'POINT(-0.1263 51.4980)'
```

```
pt = shapely.wkt.loads(LONDON)

cursor.execute("SELECT id,level,AsText(geom) " +
               "FROM gshhs WHERE id IN " +
               "(SELECT pkid FROM idx_gshhs_geom" +
               " WHERE xmin <= ? AND ? <= xmax" +
               " AND ymin <= ? and ? <= ymax) " +
               "AND Contains(geom, GeomFromText(?, 4326))",
               (pt.x, pt.x, pt.y, pt.y, LONDON))

shoreline = None
for id,level,wkt in cursor:
    if level == 1:
        shoreline = wkt
```

Because SpatiaLite's query optimizer doesn't use spatial indexes by default, we have to explicitly included the `idx_gshhs_geom` index in our query. Notice, however, that this time we aren't using Shapely to extract the polygon to see if the point is within it. Instead, we are using SpatiaLite's `Contains()` function directly to do the full polygon check directly within the query itself, after doing the bounding-box check using the spatial index.

This query is complex, but in theory should produce a fast and accurate result. Following the recommended best practice, we want to check our query by asking SpatiaLite's query optimizer how the query will be processed. This will tell us if we have written the query correctly.

Unfortunately, depending on how your copy of SpatiaLite was installed, you may not have access to the SQLite command line. So instead, let's call the EXPLAIN QUERY PLAN command from Python:

```
cursor.execute("EXPLAIN QUERY PLAN " +
               "SELECT id,level,AsText(geom) " +
               "FROM gshhs WHERE id IN " +
               "(SELECT pkid FROM idx_gshhs_geom" +
               " WHERE xmin <= ? AND ? <= xmax" +
               " AND ymin <= ? and ? <= ymax) " +
               "AND Contains(geom, GeomFromText(?, 4326))",
               (pt.x, pt.x, pt.y, pt.y, LONDON))
for row in cursor:
    print row
```

Running this tells us that the SpatiaLite query optimizer will use the spatial index (along with the table's primary key) to quickly identify the features that match by bounding box:

```
(0, 0, 0, 'SEARCH TABLE gshhs USING PRIMARY KEY (rowid=?) (~12 rows)')
(0, 0, 0, 'EXECUTE LIST SUBQUERY 1')
(1, 0, 0, 'SCAN TABLE idx_gshhs_geom VIRTUAL TABLE INDEX 2:BaDbBcDd (~0
rows)')
```

> Note that there is a bug in SpatiaLite that prevents it from using both a spatial index and an ordinary B*Tree index in the same query. This is why our Python program asks SpatiaLite to return the `level` value, and then checks for the level explicitly before identifying the shoreline, rather than simply embedding `AND (level=1)` in the query itself.

Now that we have the shoreline, saving it to a text file is again trivial:

```
f = file("uk-shoreline.wkt", "w")
f.write(shoreline)
f.close()
```

Comparing the databases

Now that we have seen how our program is implemented using each of the three open source spatial databases, we can start to draw some conclusions about these databases:

- MySQL is easy to set up and use, is widely deployed, and can be used as a capable spatial database, though it does suffer from some limitations which require work-arounds.

- PostGIS is the workhorse of open-source geospatial databases. It is fast and scales well, and has more capabilities than any of the other databases we have examined. At the same time, PostGIS has a reputation for being hard to set up and administer, and may be overkill for some applications.

- SpatiaLite is fast and capable, though it is tricky to use well and has its fair share of quirks and bugs.

Which database you choose to use, of course, depends on what you are trying to achieve, as well as factors such as which tools you have access to on your particular server, and your personal preference for which of these databases you want to work with. Whichever database you choose, you can be confident that it is more than capable of meeting your spatial database needs.

Summary

In this chapter, we have taken an in-depth look at the concept of storing spatial data in a database, and examined three of the principal open source spatial databases. We have seen the following:

- Spatial databases differ from ordinary relational databases as they directly support spatial data types, spatial queries, and spatial joins

- Spatial indexes generally make use of R-Tree data structures to represent nested hierarchies of bounding boxes

- Spatial indexes can be used to quickly find geometries based on their position in space, as well as for performing spatial comparisons between geometries based on their bounding boxes

- MySQL, the world's most popular open source database, has spatial capabilities built in, though with some limitations

- PostGIS is considered to be the powerhouse of spatial databases, built on top of the PostgreSQL open source database engine

- SpatiaLite is an extension to the SQLite serverless database, with a large number of spatial capabilities built in

- Each database has a set of best practices for working with geospatial data

- MySQL is an adequate though limited spatial database, PostGIS is a complex workhorse that scales well, and SpatiaLite is surprisingly capable but is quirky and suffers from bugs

- All three spatial databases are powerful enough to use in complex, real-world geospatial applications, and that the choice of which database to use often comes down to personal preference and availability

In the next chapter, we will look at how we can use spatial databases to solve a variety of geospatial problems while building a sophisticated geospatial application.

7

Working with Spatial Data

In this chapter we will apply and build on the knowledge we have gained in previous chapters to create a hypothetical web application called DISTAL (**Distance-based Identification of Shorelines, Towns And Lakes**). In the process of building this application, we will learn the following:

- Working with substantial amounts of geospatial data stored in a database

- Performing complex spatial database queries

- Dealing with accurate distance-based calculations and limiting queries by distance

- Reviewing and improving a geospatial application's design and implementation

- Handling usability, quality, and performance issues

About DISTAL

The DISTAL application will have the following basic workflow:

1. The user starts by selecting the country they wish to work with:

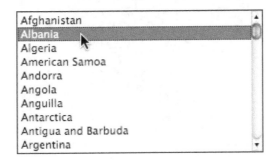

2. A simple map of the country is displayed:

3. The user selects a desired radius in miles, and clicks on a point within the country:

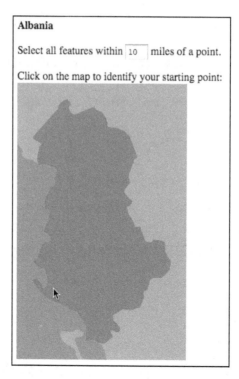

4. The system identifies all of the cities and towns within the given radius of that point:

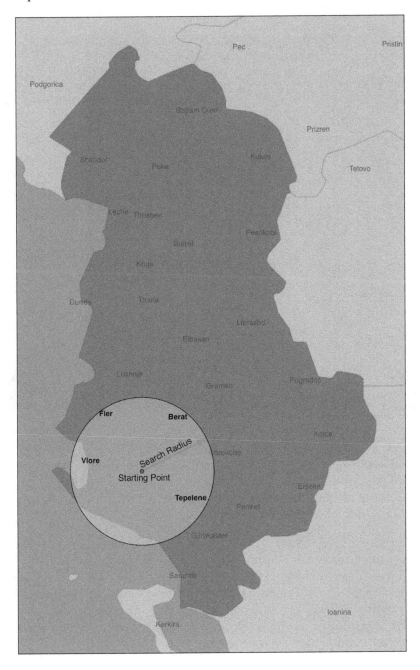

5. Finally, the resulting features are displayed at a higher resolution for the user to view or print:

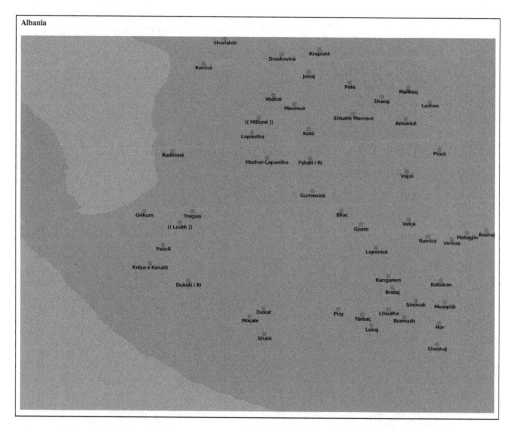

While we haven't yet looked at the map-rendering and user-interface aspects of geospatial applications, we do know enough to proceed with a very simple implementation of the DISTAL system. In this implementation, we will make use of basic CGI scripts and a "black box" map-generator module, while focusing on the data storage and manipulation aspects of the DISTAL application.

Note that *Chapter 8, Using Python and Mapnik to Produce Maps*, will look at the details of generating maps using the Mapnik map-rendering toolkit, while *Chapter 9, Putting It All Together – a Complete Mapping System*, will look at the user-interface aspects of building a sophisticated web-based geospatial application. If you wanted to, you could rewrite the DISTAL implementation using the information in the next two chapters to produce a more robust and fully-functional version of the DISTAL application that could be deployed on the Internet.

Designing and building the database

Let's start our design of the DISTAL application by thinking about the various pieces of data it will require:

- A list of all the countries. Each country needs to include a simple boundary map which can be displayed to the user.
- Detailed shoreline and lake boundaries worldwide.
- A list of all major cities and towns worldwide. For each city/town, we need to have the name of the city/town and a point representing the location of that town or city.

Fortunately, this data is readily available:

- The list of countries and their outlines are included in the World Borders Dataset.
- Shoreline and lake boundaries (as well as other land-water boundaries such as islands within lakes) are readily available using the GSHHS shoreline database.

  City and town data can be found in two places: The GNIS Database (http://geonames.usgs.gov/domestic) provides official place-name data for the United States, while the GEOnet Names Server (http://earth-info.nga.mil/gns/html) provides similar data for the rest of the world.

Looking at these data sources, we can start to design the database schema for the DISTAL system:

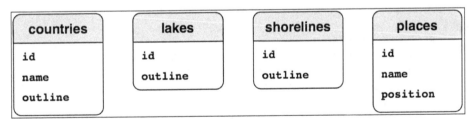

 The level field in the shorelines table corresponds to the level value in the GSHHS database: a value of 1 represents a coastline, 2 represents a lake, 3 represents an island within a lake, and 4 represents a pond on an island in a lake.

While this is very simple, it's enough to get us started. Let's use this schema to create our database, firstly in MySQL:

```
import MySQLdb

connection = MySQLdb.connect(user="...", passwd="...")
cursor = connection.cursor()

cursor.execute("DROP DATABASE IF EXISTS distal")
cursor.execute("CREATE DATABASE distal")
cursor.execute("USE distal")

cursor.execute("""
    CREATE TABLE countries (
        id      INTEGER AUTO_INCREMENT PRIMARY KEY,
        name    CHAR(255) CHARACTER SET utf8 NOT NULL,
        outline GEOMETRY NOT NULL,

        SPATIAL INDEX (outline)) ENGINE=MyISAM
""")

cursor.execute("""
    CREATE TABLE shorelines (
        id      INTEGER AUTO_INCREMENT PRIMARY KEY,
        level   INTEGER NOT NULL,
        outline GEOMETRY NOT NULL,

        SPATIAL INDEX (outline)) ENGINE=MyISAM
""")

cursor.execute("""
    CREATE TABLE places (
        id INTEGER AUTO_INCREMENT PRIMARY KEY,
        name CHAR(255) CHARACTER SET utf8 NOT NULL,
        position POINT NOT NULL,

        SPATIAL INDEX (position)) ENGINE=MyISAM
""")

connection.commit()
```

 Note that we define the countries and places name fields to use UTF-8 character encoding. This allows us to store non-English names into these fields.

The same code in PostGIS would look like this:

```
import psycopg2

connection = psycopg2.connect("dbname=... user=...")
cursor = connection.cursor()

cursor.execute("DROP TABLE IF EXISTS countries")
cursor.execute("""
    CREATE TABLE countries (
        id    SERIAL,
        name VARCHAR(255),

        PRIMARY KEY (id))
""")
cursor.execute("""
    SELECT AddGeometryColumn('countries', 'outline',
                                4326, 'GEOMETRY', 2)
""")
cursor.execute("""
    CREATE INDEX countryIndex ON countries
        USING GIST(outline)
""")

cursor.execute("DROP TABLE IF EXISTS shorelines")
cursor.execute("""
    CREATE TABLE shorelines (
        id    SERIAL,
        level INTEGER,

        PRIMARY KEY (id))
""")
cursor.execute("""
    SELECT AddGeometryColumn('shorelines', 'outline',
                                4326, 'GEOMETRY', 2)
""")
cursor.execute("""
    CREATE INDEX shorelineIndex ON shorelines
        USING GIST(outline)
""")

cursor.execute("DROP TABLE IF EXISTS places")
```

```
cursor.execute("""
    CREATE TABLE places (
        id    SERIAL,
        name VARCHAR(255),

        PRIMARY KEY (id))
""")
cursor.execute("""
    SELECT AddGeometryColumn('places', 'position',
                            4326, 'POINT', 2)
""")
cursor.execute("""
    CREATE INDEX placeIndex ON places
        USING GIST(position)
""")

connection.commit()
```

 Note how the PostGIS version allows us to specify the SRID value for the geometry columns. We'll be using the WG84 datum and unprojected lat/long coordinates for all our spatial data, which is why we specified SRID 4326 when we created our geometries.

And finally, using SpatiaLite:

```
import os, os.path
from pysqlite2 import dbapi2 as sqlite

if os.path.exists("distal.db"):
    os.remove("distal.db")

db = sqlite.connect("distal.db")
db.enable_load_extension(True)
db.execute('SELECT load_extension("...")')
cursor = db.cursor()

# Initialize the SpatiaLite meta-tables.

cursor.execute('SELECT InitSpatialMetaData()')

# Create the database tables.
```

```
cursor.execute("DROP TABLE IF EXISTS countries")
cursor.execute("""
    CREATE TABLE countries (
        id    INTEGER PRIMARY KEY AUTOINCREMENT,
        name CHAR(255))
""")
cursor.execute("""
    SELECT AddGeometryColumn('countries', 'outline',
                            4326, 'GEOMETRY', 2)
""")
cursor.execute("""
    SELECT CreateSpatialIndex('countries', 'outline')
""")

cursor.execute("DROP TABLE IF EXISTS shorelines")
cursor.execute("""
    CREATE TABLE shorelines (
        id    INTEGER PRIMARY KEY AUTOINCREMENT,
        level INTEGER)
""")
cursor.execute("""
    SELECT AddGeometryColumn('shorelines', 'outline',
                            4326, 'GEOMETRY', 2)
""")
cursor.execute("""
    SELECT CreateSpatialIndex('shorelines', 'outline')
""")

cursor.execute("DROP TABLE IF EXISTS places")
cursor.execute("""
    CREATE TABLE places (
        id    INTEGER PRIMARY KEY AUTOINCREMENT,
        name CHAR(255))
""")
cursor.execute("""
    SELECT AddGeometryColumn('places', 'position',
                            4326, 'POINT', 2)
""")
cursor.execute("""
    SELECT CreateSpatialIndex('places', 'position')
""")

db.commit()
```

Now that we've set up our database, let's get the data we need for the DISTAL application.

Downloading the data

As mentioned in the previous section, the DISTAL application will make use of four separate sets of freely-available geospatial data:

- The World Borders Dataset
- The high-resolution GSHHS shoreline database
- The GNIS Database of US place names
- The GEONet Names Server's list of non-US place names

 For more information on these sources of data, please refer to *Chapter 4, Sources of Geospatial Data*

To keep track of the data as we download it, create a directory named something similar to DISTAL-data. Then it's time to download the information we need.

World Borders Dataset

If you haven't already done so, download the World Borders Dataset from:

http://thematicmapping.org/downloads/world_borders.php

When you decompress the TM_WORLD_BORDERS-0.3.zip archive, you will end up with a folder containing the World Borders Dataset in shapefile format. Move this folder into your DISTAL-data directory.

GSHHS

We next need to download the GSHHS shoreline database in shapefile format. If you haven't already downloaded it, the database can be found at:

http://www.ngdc.noaa.gov/mgg/shorelines/gshhs.html

Decompress the .zip format archive and move the resulting GSHHS_shp folder (which itself contains twenty separate shapefiles) into your DISTAL-data directory.

GNIS

For the database of US place names, go to:

http://geonames.usgs.gov/domestic

Click on the **Download Domestic Names** hyperlink, and choose the **Download all national features in one .zip file** option. This will download a file named `NationalFile_YYYYMMDD.zip`, where `YYYYMMDD` is the datestamp identifying when the file was last updated. Once again, decompress the resulting `.zip` format archive and move the `NationalFile_YYYYMMDD.txt` file into your `DISTAL-data` directory.

GEOnet Names Server

Finally, to download the database of non-US place names, go to:

`http://earth-info.nga.mil/gns/html/namefiles.htm`

Click on the option to download a single compressed ZIP file that contains the entire country files dataset. This is a large download (370 MB compressed) that contains all the place name information we need worldwide. The resulting file will be named `geonames_dd_dms_date_YYYYMMDD.zip`, where once again `YYYMMDD` is the datestamp identifying when the file was last updated.

 Don't get fooled by the confusing names here: we go to the Geonames website to download a file named `NationalFile`, and to the GEOnet Names Server to download a file named `geonames`. From now on, we'll refer to the name of the file rather than the website it came from.

Decompress the `.zip` format archive, and move the resulting `geonames_dd_dms_date_YYYYMMDD.txt` file into the `DISTAL-data` directory.

Importing the data

We are now ready to import our four sets of data into the DISTAL database. We will be using the techniques discussed in *Chapter 3, Python Libraries for Geospatial Development*, and *Chapter 5, Working with Geospatial Data in Python*, to read the data from these data sets, and then insert them into the database using the techniques we discussed in *Chapter 6, GIS in the Database*.

Let's work through each of the files in turn.

World Borders Dataset

The World Borders Dataset consists of a shapefile containing the outline of each country along with a variety of metadata, including the country's name in Latin-1 character encoding. We can import this directly into our `countries` table using the following Python code for MySQL:

```
import os.path
import MySQLdb
import osgeo.ogr

connection = MySQLdb.connect(user="...", passwd="...")
cursor = connection.cursor()

cursor.execute("USE distal")
cursor.execute("DELETE FROM countries")
cursor.execute("SET GLOBAL max_allowed_packet=52428800")

srcFile = os.path.join("DISTAL-data", "TM_WORLD_BORDERS-0.3",
                       "TM_WORLD_BORDERS-0.3.shp")
shapefile = osgeo.ogr.Open(srcFile)
layer = shapefile.GetLayer(0)

for i in range(layer.GetFeatureCount()):
    feature = layer.GetFeature(i)
    name = feature.GetField("NAME").decode("Latin-1")
    wkt = feature.GetGeometryRef().ExportToWkt()

    cursor.execute("INSERT INTO countries (name,outline) " +
                   "VALUES (%s, GeometryFromText(%s, 4326))",
                   (name.encode("utf8"), wkt))

connection.commit()
```

The only unusual thing here is the SET GLOBAL max_allowed_packet instruction. This command (which works with MySQL Versions 5.1 and later) allows us to insert larger geometries into the database. If you are using an earlier version of MySQL, you will have to edit the my.cnf file and set this variable manually before running the program.

 Note that you must set max_allowed_packet to be a multiple of 1,024 bytes. In this example, we have set it to 50 megabytes (50 x 1,024 x 1,024 = 52,428,800).

Note that we are following the recommended best practice of associating the spatial reference with the polygon. In most cases we will be dealing with unprojected coordinates on the WGS84 datum (SRID 4326), although stating this explicitly can save us some trouble when we come to dealing with data that uses other spatial references.

Here is what the equivalent code would look like for PostGIS:

```
import os.path
import psycopg2
import osgeo.ogr

connection = psycopg2.connect("dbname=... user=...")
cursor = connection.cursor()

cursor.execute("DELETE FROM countries")

srcFile = os.path.join("DISTAL-data", "TM_WORLD_BORDERS-0.3",
                       "TM_WORLD_BORDERS-0.3.shp")
shapefile = osgeo.ogr.Open(srcFile)
layer = shapefile.GetLayer(0)

for i in range(layer.GetFeatureCount()):
    feature = layer.GetFeature(i)
    name = feature.GetField("NAME").decode("Latin-1")
    wkt = feature.GetGeometryRef().ExportToWkt()

cursor.execute("INSERT INTO countries (name,outline) " +
               "VALUES (%s, ST_GeometryFromText(%s, " +
               "4326))", (name.encode("utf8"), wkt))

connection.commit()
```

The equivalent code for SpatiaLite would look like this:

```
import os, os.path
from pysqlite2 import dbapi2 as sqlite
import osgeo.ogr

db = sqlite.connect("distal.db")
db.enable_load_extension(True)
db.execute('SELECT load_extension("...")')
cursor = db.cursor()
```

```
cursor.execute("DELETE FROM countries")

srcFile = os.path.join("DISTAL-data", "TM_WORLD_BORDERS-0.3",
                       "TM_WORLD_BORDERS-0.3.shp")
shapefile = osgeo.ogr.Open(srcFile)
layer = shapefile.GetLayer(0)

for i in range(layer.GetFeatureCount()):
    feature = layer.GetFeature(i)
    name = feature.GetField("NAME").decode("Latin-1")
    wkt = feature.GetGeometryRef().ExportToWkt()

    cursor.execute("INSERT INTO countries (name,outline) " +
                   "VALUES (?, ST_GeometryFromText(?, " +
                   "4326))", (name, wkt))

db.commit()
```

> SpatiaLite doesn't know about UTF-8 encoding, so in this case we store the country names directly as Unicode strings.

GSHHS

The GSHHS shoreline database consists of five separate shapefiles defining the land/water boundary at five different resolutions. For the DISTAL application, we want to import the four levels of GSHHS data (coastline, lake, island-in-lake, and pond-in-island-in-lake) at full resolution. We can directly import these shapefiles into the `shorelines` table within our DISTAL database.

For MySQL, we use the following code:

```
import os.path
import MySQLdb
import osgeo.ogr

connection = MySQLdb.connect(user="...", passwd="...")
cursor = connection.cursor()

cursor.execute("USE distal")
cursor.execute("DELETE FROM shorelines")
cursor.execute("SET GLOBAL max_allowed_packet=52428800")
```

```
for level in [1, 2, 3, 4]:
    srcFile = os.path.join("DISTAL-data", "GSHHS_shp", "f",
                           "GSHHS_f_L" + str(level) + ".shp")
    shapefile = osgeo.ogr.Open(srcFile)
    layer = shapefile.GetLayer(0)

    for i in range(layer.GetFeatureCount()):
        feature = layer.GetFeature(i)
        wkt = feature.GetGeometryRef().ExportToWkt()

        cursor.execute("INSERT INTO shorelines " +
                       "(level,outline) VALUES " +
                       "(%s, GeometryFromText(%s, 4326))",
                       (level, wkt))

    connection.commit()
```

Note that this might take a minute or two to complete, as we are importing more than 180,000 polygons into the database.

The equivalent code for PostGIS would look like this:

```
import os.path
import psycopg2
import osgeo.ogr

connection = psycopg2.connect("dbname=... user=...")
cursor = connection.cursor()

cursor.execute("DELETE FROM shorelines")

for level in [1, 2, 3, 4]:
    srcFile = os.path.join("DISTAL-data", "GSHHS_shp", "f",
                           "GSHHS_f_L" + str(level) + ".shp")
    shapefile = osgeo.ogr.Open(srcFile)
    layer = shapefile.GetLayer(0)

    for i in range(layer.GetFeatureCount()):
        feature = layer.GetFeature(i)
        wkt = feature.GetGeometryRef().ExportToWkt()

        cursor.execute("INSERT INTO shorelines " +
                       "(level,outline) VALUES " +
```

```
                          "(%s, ST_GeometryFromText(%s, 4326))",
                          (level, wkt))

        connection.commit()
```

The equivalent code using SpatiaLite would look like this:

```
    import os.path
    from pysqlite2 import dbapi2 as sqlite
    import osgeo.ogr

    db = sqlite.connect("distal.db")
    db.enable_load_extension(True)
    db.execute('SELECT load_extension("...")')
    cursor = db.cursor()

    cursor.execute("DELETE FROM shorelines")

    for level in [1, 2, 3, 4]:
        srcFile = os.path.join("DISTAL-data", "GSHHS_shp", "f",
                               "GSHHS_f_L" + str(level) + ".shp")
        shapefile = osgeo.ogr.Open(srcFile)
        layer = shapefile.GetLayer(0)

        for i in range(layer.GetFeatureCount()):
            feature = layer.GetFeature(i)
            wkt = feature.GetGeometryRef().ExportToWkt()

            cursor.execute("INSERT INTO shorelines " +
                           "(level,outline) VALUES " +
                           "(?, ST_GeometryFromText(?, 4326))",
                           (level, wkt))

        db.commit()
```

US place name data

The list of US place names is stored in the large text file you downloaded named `NationalFile_YYYYMMDD.txt` (where `YYYYMMDD` is a timestamp). This is a *pipe-delimited* file, meaning that each column is separated by a | character like this:

```
    FEATURE_ID|FEATURE_NAME|FEATURE_CLASS|...|DATE_EDITED
    399|Agua Sal Creek|Stream|AZ|...|02/08/1980
    400|Agua Sal Wash|Valley|AZ|...|02/08/1980
```

The first line contains the names of the various fields. While there are a lot of fields in the file, there are four fields that we are particularly interested in:

- The FEATURE_NAME field contains the name of the location. Note that this field uses UTF-8 character encoding.

- The FEATURE_CLASS field tells us what type of feature we are dealing with, in this case a Stream or a Valley. There are a lot of features we don't need for the DISTAL application, for example the names of bays, beaches, bridges, oilfields, and so on. In fact, there is only one feature class we are interested in: Populated Place.

- The PRIM_LONG_DEC and PRIM_LAT_DEC fields contain the longitude and latitude of the location, in decimal degrees. According to the documentation, these coordinates use the NAD83 datum rather than the WGS84 datum used by the other data we are importing. Unprojected lat/long coordinates in the NAD83 datum have an SRID value of 4269.

One way of approaching all this would be to create a temporary database table, import the entire NationalFile_YYYYMMDD.txt file into it, extract the features with our desired feature classes, translate them from NAD83 to WGS84, and finally insert the features into our places table. However, this approach has two disadvantages:

- It would take a long time to insert more than two million features into the database, when we only want a small percentage of these features in our places table.

- MySQL doesn't support on-the-fly transformation of geometries, so we would have to read the geometry from the database, convert it into an OGR Geometry object, transform the geometry using OGR, and then convert it back to WKT format for adding back into the database.

To avoid all this, we'll take a slightly different approach:

- Extract all the features from the file
- Ignore features with the wrong feature class
- Use pyproj to convert from NAD83 to WGS84
- Insert the resulting features directly into the places table

With the exception of this final step, this approach is completely independent of the database. This means that the same code can be used regardless of the database you are using:

```python
import os.path
import pyproj

srcProj = pyproj.Proj(proj='longlat', ellps='GRS80',
                      datum='NAD83')
dstProj = pyproj.Proj(proj='longlat', ellps='WGS84',
                      datum='WGS84')

f = file(os.path.join("DISTAL-data",
                      "NationalFile_YYYYMMDD.txt"), "r")
heading = f.readline() # Ignore field names.
for line in f.readlines():
    parts = line.rstrip().split("|")
    featureName = parts[1]
    featureClass = parts[2]
    lat = float(parts[9])
    long = float(parts[10])

    if featureClass == "Populated Place":
        long,lat = pyproj.transform(srcProj, dstProj,
                                    long, lat)
    ...
f.close()
```

Make sure you use the correct name for the `NationalFile_YYYYMMDD.txt` file you downloaded, allowing for the datestamp on the downloaded file.

Strictly speaking, the preceding code is being somewhat pedantic. We are using `pyproj` to transform coordinates from NAD83 to WGS84. However, the data we are importing is all within the United States, and these two datums happen to be identical for points within the United States. Because of this, `pyproj` won't actually change the coordinates at all. But we will do this anyway, following the recommended practice of knowing the spatial reference for our data and transforming when necessary—even if that transformation is a no-op at times.

We can now add the database-specific code to add the feature into our `places` table. For MySQL, add the following code to the start of your program:

```
import MySQLdb

connection = MySQLdb.connect(user="USERNAME", passwd="PASSWORD")
cursor = connection.cursor()
cursor.execute("USE distal")
cursor.execute("DELETE FROM places")

num_inserted = 0
```

Next, replace the . . . in the previous example with the following:

```
cursor.execute("INSERT INTO places " +
               "(name, position) VALUES (%s, " +
               "GeomFromWKB(Point(%s, %s), 4326))",
               (featureName, long, lat))

num_inserted += 1
if num_inserted % 1000 == 0:
    connection.commit()
```

Finally, add the following line to the end:

```
connection.commit()
```

 Note that we regularly call `connection.commit()` to commit our changes to the database. This helps to speed up our program when inserting many thousands of records.

As you can see, our `INSERT` statement creates a new `Point` object out of the translated latitude and longitude values, and then uses `GeomFromWKB()` to assign an SRID value to the geometry. The result is stored into the `position` column within the `places` table.

The same code using PostGIS would look like this:

```
import psycopg2
connection = psycopg2.connect("dbname=DATABASE user=USER")
cursor = connection.cursor()
cursor.execute("SET NAMES 'utf8'")
cursor.execute("DELETE FROM places")
```

```
num_inserted = 0
...
        cursor.execute("INSERT INTO places " +
                     "(name, position) VALUES (%s, " +
                     "ST_SetSRID(" +
                     "ST_MakePoint(%s,%s), 4326))",
                     (featureName, long, lat))

        num_inserted += 1
        if num_inserted % 1000 == 0:
            connection.commit()
...
connection.commit()
```

 As with the MySQL example, place the first chunk of code at the top of your program, the second replaces . . ., and the commit() statement goes at the end.

As with the MySQL example, we are creating a Point geometry and then assigning an SRID value to it, all within the SQL INSERT statement.

Finally, the SpatiaLite version would look like this:

```
from pysqlite2 import dbapi2 as sqlite
db = sqlite.connect("distal.db")
db.enable_load_extension(True)
db.execute('SELECT load_extension("...")')
cursor = db.cursor()
cursor.execute("DELETE FROM places")

num_inserted = 0
...
cursor.execute("INSERT INTO places " +
                     "(name, position) VALUES "
                     "(?, MakePoint(?, ?, 4326))",
                     (featureName.decode("utf-8"),
                      long, lat))

        num_inserted += 1
        if num_inserted % 1000 == 0:
            db.commit()
...
db.commit()
```

Because SpatiaLite doesn't know about UTF-8 character encoding, we convert the place name to a Unicode string and store that directly into the database.

Worldwide place name data

The list of non-US place names is stored in the `geonames_dd_dms_date_YYYYMMDD` file you downloaded earlier. This is a tab-delimited text file in UTF-8 character encoding, and will look something like this:

```
RC  UFI      ...  FULL_NAME_ND_RG  NOTE       MODIFY_DATE
1   -1307834 ...  Pavia                       1993-12-21
1   -1307889 ...  Santa Anna       gjgscript  1993-12-21
```

As with the US places' name data, there are many more features here than we need for the DISTAL application. Since we are only interested in the official names for towns and cities, we need to filter this data in the following way:

- The **FC (Feature Classification)** field tells us what type of feature we are dealing with. We want features with an FC value of "P" (populated place).

- The **NT (Name Type)** field tells us the status of this feature's name. We want names with an NT value of "N" (approved name).

- The **DSG (Feature Designation Code)** field tells us the type of feature, in more detail than the FC field. A full list of all the feature designation codes can be found at `http://geonames.nga.mil/ggmagaz/feadesgsearchhtml.asp`. We are interested in features with a DSG value of "PPL" (populated place), "PPLA" (administrative capital), or "PPLC" (capital city).

There are also several different versions of each place name; we want the full name in normal reading order, which is in the field named FULL_NAME_RO. Knowing this, we can write some Python code to extract the features we want from the file:

```python
import os.path

f = file(os.path.join("DISTAL-data",
                      "geonames_dd_dms_date_YYYYMMDD.txt"),
         "r")

heading = f.readline() # Ignore field names.

for line in f.readlines():
    parts = line.rstrip().split("\t")
```

```
lat = float(parts[3])
long = float(parts[4])
featureClass = parts[9]
featureDesignation = parts[10]
nameType = parts[17]
featureName = parts[22]

if (featureClass == "P" and nameType == "N" and
    featureDesignation in ["PPL", "PPLA", "PPLC"]):
    ...
```

```
f.close()
```

Now that we have the name, latitude, and longitude for each of the features we want, we can re-use the code from the previous section to insert these features into the database. For example, for MySQL we would add the following to the start of our program:

```
import MySQLdb
connection = MySQLdb.connect(user="...", passwd="...")
cursor = connection.cursor()
cursor.execute("USE distal")

num_inserted = 0
```

We would then replace the ... with the following:

```
cursor.execute("INSERT INTO places " +
               "(name, position) VALUES (%s, " +
               "GeomFromWKB(Point(%s, %s), 4326))",
               (featureName, long, lat))

num_inserted += 1
if num_inserted % 1000 == 0:
    connection.commit()
```

And finally, we would add the following code line to the end:

```
connection.commit()
```

 Because we are dealing with worldwide data here, the lat/long values already use the WGS84 datum, so there is no need to translate the coordinates before adding them to the database.

If you are using PostGIS or SpatiaLite, simply copy the equivalent code from the previous section. Note that, because there are over two million features we want to add to the database, it can take a while for this program to complete.

Implementing the DISTAL application

Now that we have the data, we can start to implement the DISTAL application itself. To keep things simple, we will use CGI scripts to implement the user interface.

 CGI scripts aren't the only way we could implement the DISTAL application. Other possible approaches include using web application frameworks such as TurboGears or Django, using AJAX to write your own dynamic web application, using CherryPy (http://cherrypy.org) or even using tools such as Pyjamas (http://pyjs.org) to compile Python code into JavaScript. All of these approaches, however, are more complicated than CGI, and we will be making use of CGI scripts in this chapter to keep the code as straightforward as possible.

Let's take a look at how our CGI scripts will implement the DISTAL application's workflow:

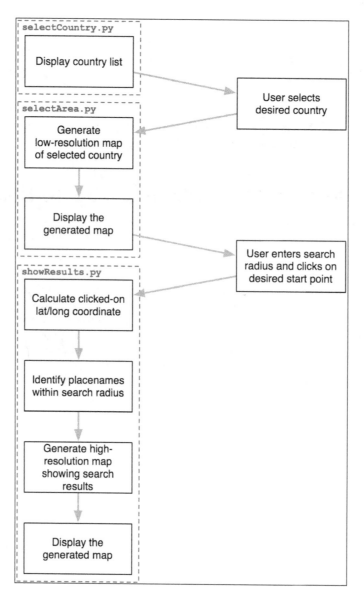

As you can see, there are three separate CGI scripts, selectCountry.py, selectArea.py, and showResults.py, each implementing a distinct part of the DISTAL application.

What is a CGI Script?

While the details of writing CGI scripts are beyond the scope of this book, the basic concept is to print the raw HTML output to `stdout`, and to process the incoming CGI parameters from the browser using the built-in `cgi` module.

To run a Python program as a CGI script, you have to do two things: first, you have to add a "shebang" line to the start of the script, like this:

```
#!/usr/bin/python
```

For MS Windows, add the following line:

```
#!C:\Python27\python.exe -U
```

The exact path you use will depend on where you have Python installed on your computer.

The second thing you need to do, at least on Unix-like systems, is make your script executable. For example:

```
chmod +x selectCountry.py
```

For more information, see one of the CGI tutorials commonly available on the Internet, for example: `http://wiki.python.org/moin/CgiScripts`.

Let's start by creating a simple web server capable of running our CGI scripts. With Python this is easy; simply create the following program, which we will call `webServer.py`:

```
import BaseHTTPServer
import CGIHTTPServer

address = ('', 8000)
handler = CGIHTTPServer.CGIHTTPRequestHandler
server = BaseHTTPServer.HTTPServer(address, handler)
server.serve_forever()
```

Next, create a subdirectory named `cgi-bin` within the same directory as your `webServer.py` program. This subdirectory will hold the various CGI scripts you create.

Running `webServer.py` will set up a web server at `http://127.0.0.1:8000`, which will execute any CGI scripts you place into the `cgi-bin` subdirectory. So, for example, to access the `selectCountry.py` script, you would enter the following URL into your web browser:

```
http://127.0.0.1:8000/cgi-bin/selectCountry.py
```

The shared "database" module

To make things easier, we'll put all the database-specific code into a separate module, which we'll call database.py. Here is the basic structure for this module, along with the implementation of the database.open() function, which we'll use
in our CGI scripts to open a connection to the database:

```
# database.py

import os.path
import pyproj
from shapely.geometry import Polygon
import shapely.wkt

###############################################################
# Edit these constants as necessary to match your setup.

MYSQL_DBNAME    = "distal"
MYSQL_USERNAME  = "XXX"
MYSQL_PASSWORD  = "XXX"

POSTGIS_DBNAME    = "distal"
POSTGIS_USERNAME  = "XXX"
POSTGIS_PASSWORD  = "XXX"

SPATIALITE_DB_PATH = os.path.join(os.path.dirname(__file__),
                                  "..", "distal.db")

DB_TYPE = "XXX"

###############################################################

def open():
    global _connection, _cursor

    if DB_TYPE == "MySQL":
        import MySQLdb
        _connection = MySQLdb.connect(user=MYSQL_USERNAME,
                                      passwd=MYSQL_PASSWORD)
        _cursor = _connection.cursor()
        _cursor.execute("USE "+MYSQL_DBNAME)
    elif DB_TYPE == "PostGIS":
        import psycopg2
```

```
        params = []
        params.append("dbname=" + POSTGIS_DBNAME)
        if POSTGIS_USERNAME != None:
            params.append("user=" + POSTGIS_USERNAME)
        if POSTGIS_PASSWORD != None:
            params.append("password=" + POSTGIS_PASSWORD)
        _connection = psycopg2.connect(" ".join(params))
        _cursor = _connection.cursor()
    elif DB_TYPE == "SpatiaLite":
        from pysqlite2 import dbapi2 as sqlite
        _connection = sqlite.connect(SPATIALITE_DBNAME)
        _connection.enable_load_extension(True)
        _connection.execute('SELECT load_extension("...")')
        _cursor = _connection.cursor()
    else:
        raise RuntimeError("Unknown database type: " +
                           db_type)
```

Make sure you place this `database.py` module into the same directory as your CGI scripts.

Don't forget to edit the constants at the top of the module to match your particular setup, entering the appropriate database names, usernames and passwords, and so on.

 The `SPATIALITE_DB_PATH` constant is set to the absolute path to our `distal.db` file. We use the Python's built-in `__file__` global to avoid having to hardwire paths into our module.

Note that we use private global variables (prefixed with an underscore character) to store the database connection and cursor. This lets us access these variables later on, as we add more functions to this module.

The "select country" script

The task of the `selectCountry.py` script is to display a list of countries to the user, so that the user can choose a desired country which is then passed to the `selectArea.py` script for further processing.

Here is what the `selectCountry.py` script's output will look like:

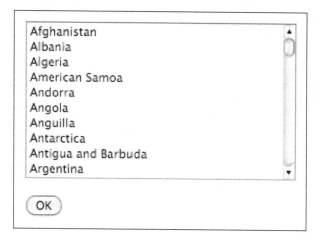

This CGI script is very basic: we simply print out the contents of the HTML page which lets the user choose a country from a list of country names:

```
#!/usr/bin/python

import database
database.open()

print 'Content-Type: text/html; charset=UTF-8\n\n'
print '<html>'
print '<head><title>Select Country</title></head>'
print '<body>'
print '<form method="POST" action="selectArea.py">'
print '<select name="countryID" size="10">'

for id,name in database.list_countries():
    print '<option value="'+str(id)+'">'+name+'</option>'

print '</select>'
print '<p>'
print '<input type="submit" value="OK">'
print '</form>'
print '</body>'
print '</html>'
```

Understanding HTML Forms

If you haven't used HTML forms before, don't panic. They are quite straightforward, and if you want you can just copy the code from the examples given here. To learn more about HTML forms, check out one of the many tutorials available online. A good example can be found at http://www.pagetutor.com/form_tutor.

As you can see, we call the `list_countries()` function within the `database` module to return a list of country record IDs and their associated names. The implementation of this function is straightforward; simply add the following code to your `database.py` module:

```
def list_countries():
    global _cursor
    results = []
    _cursor.execute("SELECT id,name FROM countries " +
                    "ORDER BY name")
    for id,name in _cursor:
        results.append((id, name))
    return results
```

Unfortunately, there is a problem with this code: because SpatiaLite can't handle UTF-8 character encoding, we have to manually convert the country name from Unicode to UTF-8 before returning it. We can do this by adding the following highlighted lines to our function:

```
    . . .
    for id,name in _cursor:
        if DB_TYPE == "SpatiaLite":
            name = name.encode("utf-8")
        results.append((id, name))
    . . .
```

This completes the "select country" script. You should now be able to run it by typing the following URL in your web browser:

```
http://127.0.0.1:8000/cgi-bin/selectCountry.py
```

All going well, you should see the list of countries and be able to select one. If you click on the **OK** button, you should see a 404 error, indicating that the `selectArea.py` script doesn't exist yet—which is perfectly correct, as we haven't implemented it yet.

The "select area" script

The next part of the DISTAL application is `selectArea.py`. This script generates a web page that displays a simple map of the selected country. The user can enter a desired search radius and click on the map to identify the starting point for the DISTAL search:

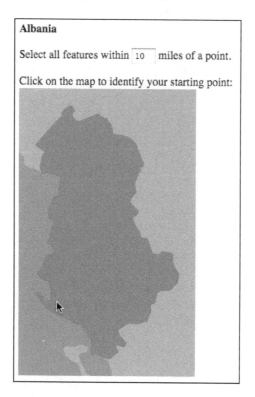

For this script to work, we're going to need some way of generating a map. Map generation using the Mapnik toolkit will be covered in detail in *Chapter 8, Using Python and Mapnik to Generate Maps*; for now, we are going to create a standalone `mapGenerator.py` module, which does the map rendering for us so that we can focus on the other aspects of the DISTAL application.

Here is the full source code for the `mapGenerator.py` module, which should be placed in your `cgi-bin` directory:

```
# mapGenerator.py

import os, os.path, sys, tempfile
```

```python
import mapnik

def generateMap(datasource, minX, minY, maxX, maxY,
                mapWidth, mapHeight,
                hiliteExpr=None, background="#8080a0",
                hiliteLine="#000000", hiliteFill="#408000",
                normalLine="#404040", normalFill="#a0a0a0",
                points=None):
    srcType = datasource['type']
    del datasource['type']

    if srcType == "OGR":
        source = mapnik.Ogr(**datasource)
    elif srcType == "PostGIS":
        source = mapnik.PostGIS(**datasource)
    elif srcType == "SQLite":
        source = mapnik.SQLite(**datasource)

    layer = mapnik.Layer("Layer")
    layer.datasource = source

    map = mapnik.Map(mapWidth, mapHeight,
                     '+proj=longlat +datum=WGS84')
    map.background = mapnik.Color(background)

    style = mapnik.Style()

    rule = mapnik.Rule()
    if hiliteExpr != None:
        rule.filter = mapnik.Filter(hiliteExpr)

    rule.symbols.append(mapnik.PolygonSymbolizer(
        mapnik.Color(hiliteFill)))
    rule.symbols.append(mapnik.LineSymbolizer(
        mapnik.Stroke(mapnik.Color(hiliteLine), 0.1)))

    style.rules.append(rule)

    rule = mapnik.Rule()
    rule.set_else(True)

    rule.symbols.append(mapnik.PolygonSymbolizer(
        mapnik.Color(normalFill)))
```

```python
rule.symbols.append(mapnik.LineSymbolizer(
    mapnik.Stroke(mapnik.Color(normalLine), 0.1)))

style.rules.append(rule)

map.append_style("Map Style", style)
layer.styles.append("Map Style")
map.layers.append(layer)

if points != None:
    memoryDatasource = mapnik.MemoryDatasource()
    context = mapnik.Context()
    context.push("name")
    next_id = 1
    for long,lat,name in points:
        wkt = "POINT (%0.8f %0.8f)" % (long,lat)
        feature = mapnik.Feature(context, next_id)
        feature['name'] = name
        feature.add_geometries_from_wkt(wkt)
        next_id = next_id + 1
        memoryDatasource.add_feature(feature)

    layer = mapnik.Layer("Points")
    layer.datasource = memoryDatasource

    style = mapnik.Style()
    rule = mapnik.Rule()

    pointImgFile = os.path.join(os.path.dirname(__file__),
                                "point.png")

    shield = mapnik.ShieldSymbolizer(
            mapnik.Expression('[name]'),
            "DejaVu Sans Bold", 10,
            mapnik.Color("#000000"),
            mapnik.PathExpression(pointImgFile))
    shield.displacement(0, 7)
    shield.unlock_image = True
    rule.symbols.append(shield)

    style.rules.append(rule)
```

```
        map.append_style("Point Style", style)
        layer.styles.append("Point Style")

        map.layers.append(layer)

    map.zoom_to_box(mapnik.Envelope(minX, minY, maxX, maxY))

    scriptDir = os.path.dirname(__file__)
    cacheDir = os.path.join(scriptDir, "..", "mapCache")
    if not os.path.exists(cacheDir):
        os.mkdir(cacheDir)
    fd,filename = tempfile.mkstemp(".png", dir=cacheDir)
    os.close(fd)

    mapnik.render_to_file(map, filename, "png")

    return "../mapCache/" + os.path.basename(filename)
```

Don't worry too much about the details of this module; everything will be explained in *Chapter 8, Using Python and Mapnik to Generate Maps*. In the meantime, just use this module as written. There are just two things to be aware of:

- You need to have Mapnik installed on your computer for this module to work. The Mapnik toolkit can be found at http://mapnik.org.

- This module requires a small image file that is used to mark place names on the map. This 9 x 9 pixel image looks like this:

  This preceding image is available as part of the example source code that comes with this book. If you don't have access to the example code, you can create or search for an image that looks like this; make sure the image is named point.png and is placed into the same directory as the mapGenerator.py module itself.

We're now ready to start looking at the selectArea.py script itself. We'll start with our shebang line and import the various modules we'll need:

```
#!/usr/bin/python

import cgi, os.path, sys
import shapely.wkt
```

```
import database
import mapGenerator
```

Next, we define some useful constants:

```
HEADER = "Content-Type: text/html; charset=UTF-8\n\n" \
       + "<html><head><title>Select Area</title>" \
       + "</head><body>"

FOOTER = "</body></html>"

MAX_WIDTH = 600
MAX_HEIGHT = 400
```

Then we open up the database:

```
database.open()
```

Our next task is to extract the ID of the country the user clicked on:

```
form = cgi.FieldStorage()
if not form.has_key("countryID"):
    print HEADER
    print '<b>Please select a country</b>'
    print FOOTER
    sys.exit(0)

countryID = int(form['countryID'].value)
```

Now that we have the ID of the selected country, we're ready to start generating the map. Doing this is a four-step process:

- Calculate the bounding box that defines the portion of the world to be displayed
- Calculate the map's dimensions
- Set up the data source
- Render the map image

Let's look at each of these in turn.

Calculating the bounding box

Before we can show the selected country on a map, we need to calculate the bounding box for that country — that is, the minimum and maximum latitude and longitude values. Knowing the bounding box allows us to draw a map centered over the desired country. If we didn't do this, the map would cover the entire world.

Let's start by adding a function to our `database` module to extract the information we need about the selected country:

```python
def get_country_details(country_id):
    global _cursor

    if DB_TYPE == "MySQL":
        _cursor.execute("SELECT name," +
                        "AsText(Envelope(outline)) " +
                        "FROM countries WHERE id=%s",
                        (country_id,))
    elif DB_TYPE == "PostGIS":
        _cursor.execute("SELECT name," +
                        "ST_AsText(ST_Envelope(outline)) " +
                        "FROM countries WHERE id=%s",
                        (country_id,))
    elif DB_TYPE == "SpatiaLite":
        _cursor.execute("SELECT name," +
                        "ST_AsText(ST_Envelope(outline)) " +
                        "FROM countries WHERE id=?",
                        (country_id,))

    row = _cursor.fetchone()
    if row != None:
        return {'name'       : row[0],
                'bounds_wkt' : row[1]}
    else:
        return None
```

This function returns the given country's name and its bounding box as a WKT-format string. Note how we first calculate the envelope (or bounding box) for the country's outline, and then convert that envelope into a WKT string using the `AsText` function.

With this function in place, we can now add the necessary code to our `selectArea.py` script to calculate the area of the world to display on our map; simply add the following to the end of your CGI script:

```
details = database.get_country_details(countryID)

envelope = shapely.wkt.loads(details['bounds_wkt'])
minLong,minLat,maxLong,maxLat = envelope.bounds
minLong = minLong - 0.2
minLat = minLat - 0.2
maxLong = maxLong + 0.2
maxLat = maxLat + 0.2
```

As you can see, we use Shapely to extract the minimum and maximum latitude and longitude values, and then increase these bounds slightly so that the country won't butt up against the edge of the map.

There's just one problem with our code: if an invalid country ID was specified, our program will crash. To get around this, add the following error-handling code to the script, immediately below the call to `database.get_country_details()`:

```
if details == None:
    print HEADER
    print '<b>Missing Country ' + repr(countryID) + '</b>'
    print FOOTER
    sys.exit(0)
```

Calculating the map's dimensions

The bounding box isn't useful only to zoom in on the desired part of the map: it also helps us to correctly define the map's dimensions. Note that the preceding map of Albania shows the country as being taller than it is wide. If you were to naively draw this map as a square image, Albania would end up looking like this:

Even worse, Chile would look like this:

Rather than this:

 This is a slight simplification; the mapping toolkits generally do try to preserve the aspect ratio for a map, but their behavior is unpredictable and means that you can't identify the lat/long coordinates for a clicked-on point.

To display the country correctly, we need to calculate the country's **aspect ratio** (its width as a proportion of its height) and then calculate the size of the map image based on this aspect ratio, while limiting the overall size of the image so that it can fit within a web page. Here's the necessary code, which you should add to the end of your `selectArea.py` script:

```
width = float(maxLong - minLong)
height = float(maxLat - minLat)
aspectRatio = width/height

mapWidth = MAX_WIDTH
mapHeight = int(mapWidth / aspectRatio)

if mapHeight > MAX_HEIGHT:
    # Scale the map to fit.
    scaleFactor = float(MAX_HEIGHT) / float(mapHeight)
    mapWidth = int(mapWidth * scaleFactor)
    mapHeight = int(mapHeight * scaleFactor)
```

Doing this means that the map is correctly sized to reflect the dimensions of the country we are displaying.

Setting up the data source

The **data source** tells the map generator how to access the underlying map data. How data sources work is beyond the scope of this chapter; for now, we are simply going to set up the required `datasource` dictionary and related files so that we can generate our map. Note that the contents of this dictionary will vary depending on which database you are using, as well as which table you are trying to access; in this case, we are trying to display selected features from the `countries` table. To handle this, we'll create a new function within our `database` module to set up the data source for our particular database:

```
def get_country_datasource():
    if DB_TYPE == "MySQL":
        vrtFile = os.path.join(os.path.dirname(__file__),
                               "countries.vrt")
        f = file(vrtFile, "w")
        f.write('<OGRVRTDataSource>\n')
        f.write('  <OGRVRTLayer name="countries">\n')
        f.write('    <SrcDataSource>MySQL:' + MYSQL_DBNAME)
        if MYSQL_USERNAME != None:
            f.write(",user=" + MYSQL_USERNAME)
        if MYSQL_PASSWORD != None:
            f.write(",passwd=" + MYSQL_PASSWORD)
    f.write('</SrcDataSource>\n')
    f.write('    <SrcSQL>SELECT id,outline ' +
            'FROM countries</SrcSQL>\n')
        f.write('  </OGRVRTLayer>\n')
        f.write('</OGRVRTDataSource>\n')
        f.close()

        return {'type'  : "OGR",
                'file'  : vrtFile,
                'layer' : "countries"}
    elif DB_TYPE == "PostGIS":
        return {'type'     : "PostGIS",
                'dbname'   : "distal",
                'table'    : "countries",
                'user'     : POSTGIS_USERNAME,
                'password' : POSTGIS_PASSWORD}
```

```
    elif DB_TYPE == "SpatiaLite":
        return {'type'            : "SQLite",
                'file'            : SPATIALITE_DBNAME,
                'table'           : "countries",
                'geometry_field'  : "outline",
                'key_field'       : "id"}
```

MySQL uses what is called a "virtual datasource", which is a special file that tells Mapnik how to access the data. We create this file as we need it, storing the username and other details into the file as required.

> Note that we are storing the `countries.vrt` file in the same directory as our CGI scripts. This makes it easier to access this file from Mapnik.

Now that we have written the `get_datasource()` function, it's time to use it. Add the following line to the end of your `selectArea.py` script:

```
datasource = database.get_country_datasource()
```

Rendering the map image

With the bounding box, the map's dimensions and the data source all set up, we are finally ready to render the map into an image file. This is done using a single function call as follows:

```
imgFile = mapGenerator.generateMap(datasource,
                                   minLong, minLat,
                                   maxLong, maxLat,
                                   mapWidth, mapHeight,
                                   "[id] = "+str(countryID))
```

Note that our `datasource` has been set up to display features from the `countries` table, and that the `"[id] = "+str(countryID)` is a "highlight expression" is used to visually highlight the country with the given ID.

The `mapGenerator.generateMap()` function returns a reference to a PNG-format image file containing the generated map. This image file is stored in a temporary directory, and the file's relative pathname is returned to the caller. This allows us to use the returned `imgFile` directly within our CGI script, like this:

```
print 'Content-Type: text/html; charset=UTF-8\n\n'
print '<html>'
```

```
print '<head><title>Select Area</title></head>'
print '<body>'
print '<b>' + name + '</b>'
print '<p>'
print '<form method="POST" action="showResults.py">'
print 'Select all features within'
print '<input type="text" name="radius" value="10" size="2">'
print 'miles of a point.'
print '<p>'
print 'Click on the map to identify your starting point:'
print '<br>'
print '<input type="image" src="' + imgFile + '" ismap>'
print '<input type="hidden" name="countryID"'
print '        value="' + str(countryID) + '">'
print '<input type="hidden" name="mapWidth"'
print '        value="' + str(mapWidth) + '">'
print '<input type="hidden" name="mapHeight"'
print '        value="' + str(mapHeight) + '">'
print '</form>'
print '</body></html>'
```

 The <input type="hidden"> lines define "hidden form fields" that pass information on to the next CGI script. We'll discuss how this information is used in the next section.

The use of <input type="image" src="..." ismap> in this CGI script has the interesting effect of making the map clickable: when the user clicks on the image, the enclosing HTML form will be submitted with two extra parameters named x and y. These contain the coordinate within the image that the user clicked on.

This completes the selectArea.py CGI script. Make sure you added an appropriate "shebang" line to the start of your program and made it executable, as described earlier, so that it can run as a CGI script.

All going well, you should be able to point your web browser to:

http://127.0.0.1:8000/cgi-bin/selectCountry.py

Choose a country, and see a map of that country displayed within your web browser. If you click within the map, you'll get a 404 error, indicating that the final CGI script hasn't been written yet.

The "show results" script

The final CGI script is where the real work is done. Start by creating your `showResults.py` file, and type the following into this file:

```python
#!/usr/bin/env python

import cgi
import pyproj

import database
import mapGenerator

#############################################################

MAX_WIDTH = 1000
MAX_HEIGHT = 800

METERS_PER_MILE = 1609.344

#############################################################

database.open()
```

 Don't forget to mark this file as executable so that it can be run as a CGI script. You can do this using the chmod command, as described in the *What is a CGI script?* section earlier in this chapter.

In this script, we will take the (x, y) coordinate the user clicked on, along with the entered search radius, convert the (x, y) coordinate into a longitude and latitude, and identify all the place names within that search radius. We then generate a high-resolution map showing the shorelines and place names within the search radius, and display that map to the user.

 Remember that x corresponds to a longitude value, and y to a latitude value.

(x, y) equals (longitude, latitude), not (latitude, longitude).

Let's examine each of these steps in turn.

Identifying the clicked-on point

The `selectArea.py` script generates an HTML form that is submitted when the user clicks on the low-resolution country map. The `showResults.py` script receives the form parameters, including the x and y coordinates of the point the user clicked on.

By itself, this coordinate isn't very useful. It's simply the x and y offset, measured in pixels, of the point the user clicked on. We need to translate the submitted (x, y) pixel coordinate into a latitude and longitude value corresponding to the clicked-on point on the Earth's surface.

To do this, we need to have the following information:

- The map's bounding box in geographic coordinates: `minLong`, `minLat`, `maxLong`, and `maxLat`
- The map's size in pixels: `mapWidth` and `mapHeight`

These variables were all calculated in the previous section and passed to us using hidden form variables, along with the country ID, the desired search radius, and the (x, y) coordinate of the clicked on point. We can retrieve all of these using the `cgi` module; add the following code to the end of your `showResults.py` file:

```
form = cgi.FieldStorage()

countryID = int(form['countryID'].value)
radius    = int(form['radius'].value)
x         = int(form['x'].value)
y         = int(form['y'].value)
mapWidth  = int(form['mapWidth'].value)
mapHeight = int(form['mapHeight'].value)
```

With this information, we can now calculate the latitude and longitude that the user clicked on. To do this, we first have to calculate the bounds that were used to generate the map that the user clicked on. Add the following code to the end of your `showResults.py` file:

```
details = database.get_country_details(countryID)
envelope = shapely.wkt.loads(details['bounds_wkt'])

minLong, minLat, maxLong, maxLat = envelope.bounds
minLong = minLong - 0.2
minLat = minLat - 0.2
maxLong = maxLong + 0.2
maxLat = maxLat + 0.2
```

We can now calculate the exact latitude and longitude the user clicked on. We start by calculating how far across the image the user clicked, as a number in the range from 0 to 1:

```
xFract = float(x)/float(mapWidth)
```

An `xFract` value of 0.0 corresponds to the left side of the image, while an `xFract` value of 1.0 corresponds to the right side of the image. We then combine this with the minimum and maximum longitude values to calculate the longitude of the clicked-on point:

```
longitude = minLong + xFract * (maxLong-minLong)
```

We then do the same to convert the Y coordinate into a latitude value:

```
yFract = float(y)/float(mapHeight)
latitude = minLat + (1-yFract) * (maxLat-minLat)
```

Note that we are using `(1-yFract)` rather than `yFract` in the preceding calculation. This is because the `minLat` value refers to the latitude of the *bottom* of the image, while a `yFract` value of 0.0 corresponds to the *top* of the image. By using `(1-yFract)`, we flip the values vertically so that the latitude is calculated correctly.

Identifying features by distance

Let's review what we have achieved so far. The user has selected a country, viewed a simple map of the country's outline, entered a desired search radius, and clicked on a point on the map to identify the origin for the search. We have then converted this clicked-on point into a latitude and longitude value.

All of this provides us with three numbers: the desired search radius, and the lat/long coordinates for the point at which to start the search. Our task now is to identify which features are within the given search radius of the clicked-on point:

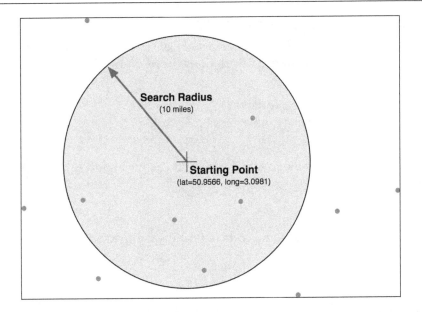

Because the search radius is specified as an actual distance in miles, we need to be able to calculate distances accurately. We looked at an approach to solving this problem in *Chapter 2, GIS*, where we considered the concept of a **great circle distance**:

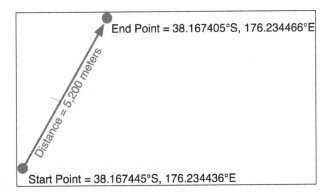

Given a start and end point, the great circle distance calculation tells us the distance along the Earth's surface between the two points.

In order to identify the matching features, we need to somehow find all the matching place names which have a great circle distance less than or equal to the desired search radius. Let's look at some ways in which we could possibly identify these features.

Calculating distances manually

As we saw in *Chapter 5, Working with Geospatial Data in Python,* `pyproj` allows us to do accurate great circle distance calculations based on two lat/long coordinates, like this:

```
geod = pyproj.Geod(ellps='WGS84')
angle1,angle2,distance = geod.inv(long1, lat1,
                                  long2, lat2)
```

The resulting distance is in meters, and we could easily convert this to miles as follows:

```
miles = distance / 1609.344
```

Based on this, we could write some code to find the features within the desired search radius:

```
geod = pyproj.Geod(ellps="WGS84")

cursor.execute("select id,X(position),Y(position) " +
               "from places")
for id,long,lat in cursor:
    angle1,angle2,distance = geod.inv(startLong, startLat,
                                      long, lat)
    if distance / 1609.344 <= searchRadius:
        ...
```

This would certainly work, and would return an accurate list of all features within the given search radius. The problem is speed; because there are more than four million features in our `places` table, this program would take several minutes to identify all the matching place names. Obviously this isn't a very practical solution.

Using angular distances

We saw an alternative way of identifying features by distance in *Chapter 5, Working with Geospatial Data in Python,* where we looked for all parks in or near an urban area. In that chapter, we used an **angular distance** to estimate how far apart two points were. An angular distance is a distance measured in degrees — technically, it is the angle between two rays going out from the center of the Earth through the two desired points on the Earth's surface. Because latitude and longitude values are angular measurements, we can easily calculate an angular distance based on two lat/long values like this:

```
distance = math.sqrt((long2-long1)**2) + (lat2-lat1)**2)
```

This is a simple Cartesian distance calculation. We are naively treating lat/long values as if they were Cartesian coordinates. This isn't right, but it does give us a distance measurement of sorts.

So what does this angular distance measurement give us? We know that the bigger the angular distance, the bigger the real (great circle) distance will be. In *Chapter 5, Working with Geospatial Data in Python*, we used this to identify all parks in California which where approximately within ten kilometers of an urban area. However, we could get away with this in that chapter because we were only dealing with data for California. In reality, the angular distance varies greatly depending on which latitude you are dealing with; looking for points within ±1 degree of longitude of your current location will include all points within 111 km if you are at the equator, 100 km if you are at ±30 degree latitude, 55 km at ±60 degree, and zero km at the poles:

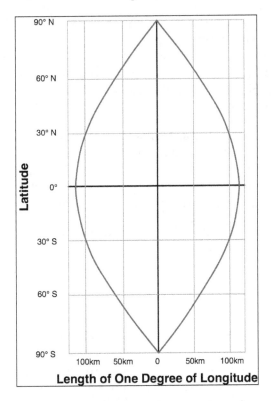

Because DISTAL includes data for the entire world, angular measurements would be all but useless — we can't assume that a given difference in latitude and longitude values would equal a given distance across the Earth's surface in any way which would help us do the distance-based searching.

Using projected coordinates

Another way of finding all points within a given distance is to use a projected coordinate system that accurately represents distance as differences between coordinate values. For example, the Universal Transverse Mercator projection defines Y coordinates as a number of meters north or south of the equator, and X coordinates as a number of meters east or west of a given reference point. Using the UTM projection, it would be easy to identify all points within a given distance by using the Cartesian distance formula:

```
distance = math.sqrt((long2-long1)**2) + (lat2-lat1)**2)
if distance < searchRadius:
    ......
```

Unfortunately, projected coordinate systems such as UTM are only accurate for data that covers a small portion of the Earth's surface. The UTM coordinate system is actually a large number of different projections, dividing the world up into sixty separate "zones" each six degrees of longitude wide. You need to use the correct UTM zone for your particular data: California's coordinates belong in UTM zone 10, and attempting to project them into UTM zone 20 would cause your distance measurements to be very inaccurate.

If you had data that covered only a small area of the Earth's surface, using a projected coordinate system would have great advantages. Not only could you calculate distances using Cartesian coordinates, you could also make use of database functions such as PostGIS's ST_DWithin() function to quickly find all points within a given physical distance of a central point.

Unfortunately, the DISTAL application makes use of data covering the entire Earth. For this reason, we can't use projected coordinates for this application, and have to find some other way of solving this problem.

 Of course, the DISTAL application was *deliberately* designed to include world-wide data, for precisely this reason. Being able to use a single UTM zone for all the data would be too convenient.

Actually, there is a way in which DISTAL could use projected UTM coordinates, but it's rather complicated. Because every feature in a given database table has to have the same spatial reference, it isn't possible to have different features in a table belonging to different UTM zones—the only way we could store worldwide data in UTM projections would be to have a separate database table for each UTM zone.

This would require sixty separate database tables! To identify the points within a given distance, you would first have to figure out which UTM zone the starting point was in, and then check the features within that database table. You would also have to deal with searches that extend out beyond the edge of a single UTM zone.

Needless to say, this approach is far too complex for us. It would work (and would scale better than any of the alternatives) but we won't consider it because of its complexity.

A hybrid approach

In *Chapter 6, GIS in the Database*, we looked at the process of identifying all points within a given polygon. Because MySQL only handles bounding-box intersection tests, we ended up having to write a program which asked the database to identify all points within the bounding box, and then manually checked each point to see if it was actually inside the polygon:

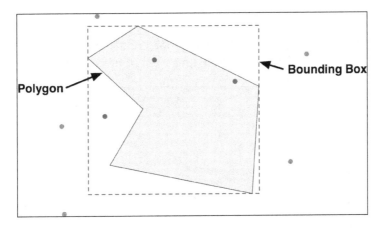

This suggests a way in which we can solve the distance-based-selection problem for DISTAL: we can calculate a bounding box which encloses the desired search radius, ask the database to identify all points within that bounding box, and then calculate the great circle distance for all the returned points, selecting just those points that are actually inside the search radius. Because a relatively small number of points will be inside the bounding box, calculating the great circle distance for just these points will be quick, allowing us to accurately find the matching points without a large performance penalty.

Let's start by calculating the bounding box. We already know the coordinates for the starting point and the desired search radius:

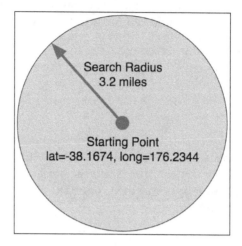

Using `pyproj`, we can calculate the lat/long coordinates for four points by traveling `radius` meters directly north, south, east, and west of the starting point:

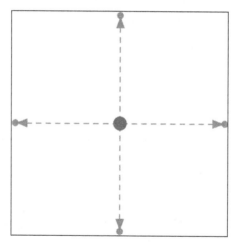

We then use these four points to define the bounding box that encloses the desired search radius:

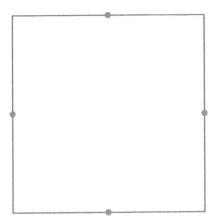

We're going to create a new function within our database module, which performs a spatial search using this bounding box. Let's start by adding the following to the end of your database.py module:

```
def find_places_within(startLat, startLong, searchRadius):
    global _cursor

    if DB_TYPE == "MySQL":
        . . .
    elif DB_TYPE == "PostGIS":
        . . .
    elif DB_TYPE == "SpatiaLite":
        . . .
```

Note that, because we're using pyproj to do a forward geodetic calculation, we can calculate the correct lat/long coordinates for the bounding box regardless of the latitude of the starting point. The only place this will fail is if startLat is within searchRadius meters of the North or South Pole—which is highly unlikely given that we're searching for cities (and we could always add error-checking code to catch this).

When it's finished, our find_places_within() function will return a list of all the places within the given bounding box, as well as the calculated bounding box. Because the spatial queries are different for each database, we'll look at each one individually.

For MySQL, we'll create a Polygon out of the supplied bounding box, and then use the `MBRContains()` function to search for places within that Polygon. To do this, replace the first . . . with the following code:

```
p = Polygon([(minLong, minLat), (maxLong, minLat),
             (maxLong, maxLat), (minLong, maxLat),
             (minLong, minLat)])
wkt = shapely.wkt.dumps(p)
_cursor.execute("SELECT name," +
                "X(position),Y(position) " +
                "FROM places WHERE MBRContains(" +
                "GeomFromText(%s), position)", (wkt,))
```

PostGIS uses a similar approach, creating a Polygon and then using the `ST_CONTAINS()` function to identify the matching places:

```
p = Polygon([(minLong, minLat), (maxLong, minLat),
             (maxLong, maxLat), (minLong, maxLat),
             (minLong, minLat)])
wkt = shapely.wkt.dumps(p)
_cursor.execute("SELECT name," +
                "ST_X(position),ST_Y(position) " +
                "FROM places WHERE ST_CONTAINS(" +
                "ST_GeomFromText(%s, 4326), " +
          "position)", (wkt,))
```

You might be wondering why we don't use PostGIS's `ST_DWITHIN()` function to identify the matching places. The problem is that we are using unprojected coordinates, which means that the "distance" supplied to `ST_DWITHIN()` would have to be in measured in degrees rather than meters. This is possible, but there are some tricky calculations required to convert from meters to degrees. To keep things simple, we'll use the `ST_CONTAINS()` function instead.

Finally, for SpatiaLite we have to do a bit more work. Remember that SpatiaLite doesn't automatically use a spatial index for queries. To make this code efficient in SpatiaLite, we have to check the spatial index directly:

```
_cursor.execute("SELECT name," +
                "X(position),Y(position) " +
                "FROM places WHERE id in " +
                "(SELECT pkid " +
```

```
                    "FROM idx_places_position " +
                    "WHERE xmin >= ? AND xmax <= ? " +
                    "AND ymin >= ? and ymax <= ?)",
                    (minLong, maxLong, minLat, maxLat))
```

Now that we have executed an SQL query to identify all the points within the bounding box, we can check the great circle distance and discard those points, which are inside the bounding box, but outside the search radius. To do this, add the following to the end of your find_places_within() function:

```
places = [] # List of (long, lat, name) tuples.

geod = pyproj.Geod(ellps="WGS84")

for row in _cursor:
    name,long,lat = row
    angle1,angle2,distance = geod.inv(startLong, startLat,
                                      long, lat)
    if distance > searchRadius: continue

    places.append([long, lat, name])

return {'places'  : places,
        'minLat'  : minLat,
        'minLong' : minLong,
        'maxLat'  : maxLat,
        'maxLong' : maxLong}
```

As you can see, we return the list of matching places, along with the minimum and maximum latitude and longitude values we calculated.

This completes our find_places_within() function, which achieves a 100 percent accurate distance-based lookup on place names, with the results taking only a fraction of a second to calculate.

Displaying the results

Now that we have calculated the list of place names within the desired search radius, we can use the mapGenerator.py module to display them. Before we do so, though, we'll have to set up a data source to display the high-resolution shorelines. Let's add another function to our database.py module, which does this:

```
def get_shoreline_datasource():
    if DB_TYPE == "MySQL":
```

```
        vrtFile = os.path.join(os.path.dirname(__file__),
                               "shorelines.vrt")
        f = file(vrtFile, "w")
        f.write('<OGRVRTDataSource>\n')
        f.write('  <OGRVRTLayer name="shorelines">\n')
        f.write('    <SrcDataSource>MYSQL:' + MYSQL_DBNAME)
        if MYSQL_USERNAME not in ["", None]:
            f.write(",user=" + MYSQL_USERNAME)
        if MYSQL_PASSWORD not in ["", None]:
            f.write(",passwd=" + MYSQL_PASSWORD)
        f.write(',tables=shorelines</SrcDataSource>\n')
        f.write('    <SrcSQL>\n')
        f.write('      SELECT id,outline FROM shorelines ' +
                                    'WHERE level=1\n')
        f.write('    </SrcSQL>\n')
        f.write('  </OGRVRTLayer>\n')
        f.write('</OGRVRTDataSource>\n')
        f.close()

        return {'type'  : "OGR",
                'file'  : vrtFile,
                'layer' : "shorelines"}
    elif DB_TYPE == "PostGIS":
        return {'type'     : "PostGIS",
                'dbname'   : "distal",
                'table'    : "shorelines",
                'user'     : POSTGIS_USERNAME,
                'password' : POSTGIS_PASSWORD}
    elif DB_TYPE == "SpatiaLite":
        return {'type'           : "SQLite",
                'file'           : SPATIALITE_DBNAME,
                'table'          : "shorelines",
                'geometry_field' : "outline",
                'key_field'      : "id"}
```

As you can see, this is almost identical to our `get_country_datasource()` function, except that it accesses a different database table to display the high-resolution shoreline rather than the low-resolution country outlines.

Notice that the SrcSQL statement in our .VRT file only includes shoreline data where level is equal 1. This means that we're only displaying the coastlines, and not the lakes, islands-on-lakes, and so on. Because the mapGenerator.py module doesn't support multiple data sources, we aren't able to draw lakes in this version of the DISTAL system. Extending mapGenerator.py to support multiple data sources is possible, but is too complicated for this chapter. For now we'll just have to live with this limitation.

With this in place, we can finally return to our showResults.py file and use it to display our results:

```
results = database.find_places_within(latitude, longitude,
                                       radius)

imgFile = mapGenerator.generateMap(datasource,
                                    minLong, minLat,
                                    maxLong, maxLat,
                                    600, 600,
                                    points=results['places'])
```

When we called the map generator previously, we used a filter expression to highlight particular features. In this case we don't need to highlight anything. Instead, we pass it the list of place names to display on the map in the keyword parameter named points.

The map generator creates a PNG-format file, and returns a reference to that file which we can then display to the user:

```
print 'Content-Type: text/html; charset=UTF-8\n\n'
print '<html>'
print '<head><title>Search Results</title></head>'
print '<body>'
print '<b>' + countryName + '</b>'
print '<p>'
print '<img src="' + imgFile + '">'
print '</body>'
print '</html>'
```

This completes our first version of the showResults.py CGI script.

Application review and improvements

At this stage, we have a complete implementation of the DISTAL system that works as advertised: a user can choose a country, enter a search radius in miles, click on a starting point, and see a high-resolution map showing all the place names within the desired search radius. We have solved the distance problem, and have all the data needed to search for place names anywhere in the world.

Of course, we aren't finished yet. There are several areas where our DISTAL application doesn't work as it should, including the following:

- Usability
- Quality
- Performance

Let's take a look at each of these issues, and see how we could improve our design and implementation of the DISTAL system.

Usability

If you explore the DISTAL application, you will soon discover a major usability problem with some of the countries. For example, if you click on the **United States** in the **Select Country** page, you will be presented with the following map to click on:

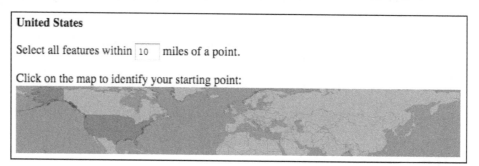

Accurately clicking on a desired point using this map would be almost impossible.

What has gone wrong? The problem here is twofold:

- The United States outline doesn't just cover the mainland US, but also includes the outlying states of Alaska and Hawaii. This increases the size of the map considerably.

- Alaska crosses the 180th meridian—the Alaska Peninsula extends beyond 180 degree west, and continues across the Aleutian Islands to finish at Attu Island with a longitude of 172 degree east. Because it crosses the 180th meridian, Alaska appears on both the left and right sides of the world map.

Because of this, the United States map goes from -180 degree to +180 degree longitude and +18 degree to +72 degree latitude. This map is far too big to be usable.

Even for countries which aren't split into separate outlying states, and which don't cross the 180th meridian, we can't be assured that the maps will be detailed enough to click on accurately. For example, here is the map for **Canada**:

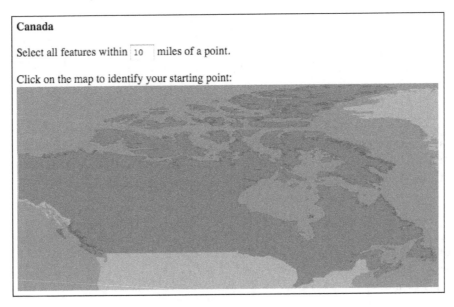

Because Canada is over 3,000 miles wide, accurately selecting a 10-mile search radius by clicking on a point on this map would be an exercise in frustration.

An obvious solution to these usability issues would be to let the user "zoom in" on a desired area of the large-scale map before clicking to select the starting point for the search. Thus, for these larger countries, the user would select the country, choose which portion of the country to search on, and then click on the desired starting point.

This doesn't solve the 180th meridian problem, which is somewhat more difficult. Ideally, you would identify those countries which cross the 180th meridian and reproject them into some other coordinate system that allows their polygons to be drawn contiguously.

Quality

As you use the DISTAL system, you will quickly notice some quality issues related to the underlying data that is being used. We are going to consider two such issues: problems with the name data, and problems with the place name lat/long coordinates.

Place name issues

If you look through the list of place names, you'll notice that some of the names have double parentheses around them, like this:

```
...
(( Shinavlash ))
(( Pilur ))
(( Kaçarat ))
(( Kaçaj ))
(( Goricë ))
(( Lilaj ))
...
```

These are names for places which are thought to no longer exist. Also, you will notice that some names have the word "historical" in them, surrounded by either square brackets or parentheses:

```
...
Fairbank (historical)
Kopiljača [historical]
Hardyville (historical)
Dorčol (historical)
Sotos Crossing (historical)
Dušanovac (historical)
...
```

Obviously, these should also be removed. Filtering out the names, which should be excluded from the DISTAL database is relatively straightforward, and could be added to our import logic as we read the `NationalFile` and `Geonames` files into the database.

Lat/Long coordinate problems

Consider the following DISTAL map, covering a part of Netherlands:

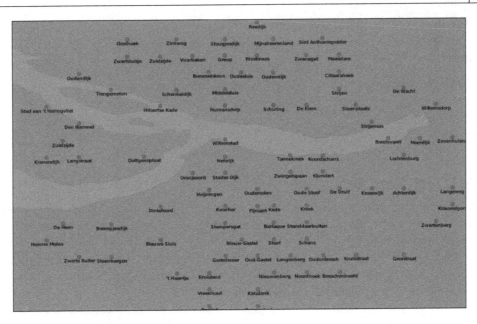

The placement of the cities look suspiciously regular, as if the cities are neatly stacked into rows and columns. Drawing a grid over this map confirms this suspicion:

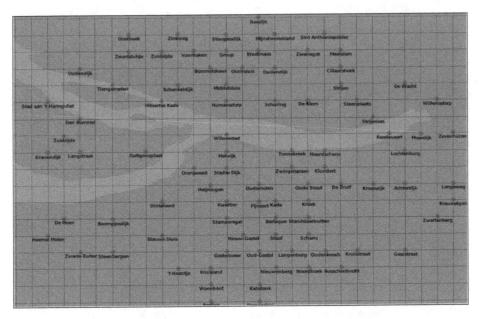

The towns and cities themselves aren't as regularly spaced as this, of course—the problem appears to be caused by inaccurately rounded lat/long coordinates within the international place name data.

This doesn't affect the operation of the DISTAL application, but users may be suspicious about the quality of the results when the place names are drawn so regularly onto the map. The only solution to this problem would be to find a source of more accurate coordinate data for international place names.

Performance

Our DISTAL application is certainly working, but its performance leaves something to be desired. While the `selectCountry.py` and `selectArea.py` scripts run quickly, it can take up to three seconds for `showResults.py` to complete. Clearly, this isn't good enough: a delay like this is annoying to the user, and would be disastrous for the server as soon as it receives more than twenty requests per minute, as it would be receiving more requests than it could process.

Finding the problem

Let's take a look at what is going on here. It's easy to add some basic timing code to `showResults.py`, like this:

```
import time
import logging
logger = logging.getLogger(...)

start_time = time.time()
...
end_time = time.time()
logger.debug("Operation took %0.4f seconds" % (end_time - start_time)
```

 Note that this uses the `logging` Python standard module to save the timing results. Because CGI scripts use `stdout` for the HTML output, we can't use the `print` statement to print out the results. If you want to time your own code, make sure you configure your logger (for example, to use a `logging.FileHandler`) first.

Running this code reveals where the script is taking most of its time:

```
Calculating lat/long coordinate took 0.0110 seconds
Identifying place names took 0.0088 seconds
```

```
Generating map took 3.0208 seconds
Building HTML page took 0.0000 seconds
```

Clearly the map-generation process is the bottleneck here. Since it only took a fraction of a second to generate a map within the `selectArea.py` script, there's nothing inherent in the map-generation process that causes this bottleneck. So what has changed?

It could be that displaying the place names takes a while, but that's unlikely. It's far more likely to be caused by the amount of map data that we are displaying: the `showResults.py` script is using high-resolution shoreline outlines taken from the GSHHS dataset, rather than the low-resolution country outline taken from the World Borders Dataset. To test this theory, we can change the map data being used to generate the map, altering `showResults.py` to use the low-resolution `countries` table instead of the high-resolution `shorelines` table.

The result is a dramatic improvement in speed:

```
Generating map took 0.1729 seconds
```

So how can we make the map generation in `showResults.py` faster? The answer lies in the nature of the shoreline data and how we are using it. Consider the situation where you are identifying points within 10 miles of Le Havre in France:

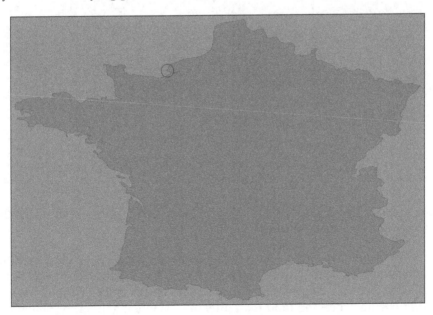

The high-resolution shoreline image would look like this:

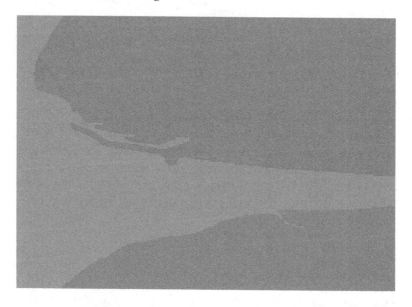

But this section of coastline is actually part of the following GSHHS shoreline feature:

This shoreline polygon is enormous, consisting of over 1.1 million points, and we're only displaying a very small part of it.

Because these shoreline polygons are so big, the map generator needs to read in the entire huge polygon and then discard 99 percent of it to get the desired section of shoreline. Also, because the polygon bounding boxes are so large, many irrelevant polygons are being processed (and then filtered out) when generating the map. This is why `showResults.py` is so slow.

Improving performance

It is certainly possible to improve the performance of the showResults.py script. As we mentioned in the *best practices* section of the previous chapter, spatial indexes work best when working with relatively small geometries—and our shoreline polygons are anything but small. However, because the DISTAL application only shows points within a certain distance, we can split these enormous polygons into "tiles" which are then precalculated and stored in the database.

Let's say that we're going to impose a limit of 100 miles to the search radius. We'll also arbitrarily define the tiles to be one whole degree of latitude high, and one whole degree of longitude wide:

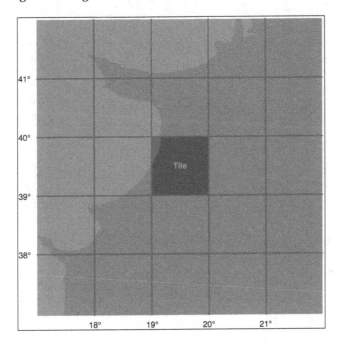

 Note that we could choose any tile size we like, but have selected whole degrees of longitude and latitude to make it easy to calculate which tile a given lat/long coordinate is inside. Each tile will be given an integer latitude and longitude value, which we'll call iLat and iLong. We can then calculate the tile to use for any given latitude and longitude like this:

```
iLat = int(round(latitude))

iLong = int(round(longitude))
```

We can then simply look up the tile with the given iLat and iLong value.

For each tile, we will use the same technique we used earlier to identify the bounding box of the search radius, to define a rectangle 100 miles north, east, west, and south of the tile:

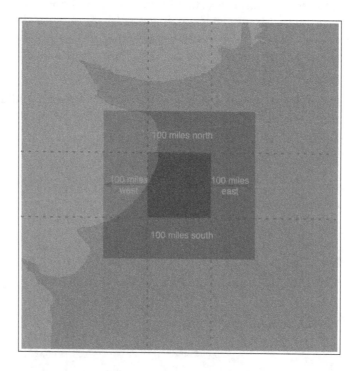

Using the bounding box, we can calculate the intersection of the shoreline data with this bounding box:

Any search done within the tile's boundary, up to a maximum of 100 miles in any direction, will only display shorelines within this bounding box. We simply store this intersected shoreline into the database, along with the lat/long coordinates for the tile, and tell the map generator to use the appropriate tile's outline to display the desired shoreline.

Calculating the tiled shorelines

Let's write the program that calculates these tiled shorelines. We'll store this program as `tileShorelines.py`. Start by entering the following into this file:

```
import math

import pyproj
from shapely.geometry import Polygon
from shapely.ops import cascaded_union
import shapely.wkt

import database

#############################################################

MAX_DISTANCE = 100000 # Maximum search radius, in meters.
```

 Note that we're importing the `database.py` module. Because `database.py` is within the `cgi-bin` directory, you should place your `tileShorelines.py` file in this directory.

We next need a function to calculate the tile bounding boxes. This function, `expandRect()`, should take a rectangle defined using lat/long coordinates, and expand it in each direction by a given number of meters. Using the techniques we have learned, this is straightforward: we can use `pyproj` to perform an inverse great circle calculation to calculate four points the given number of meters north, east, south, and west of the starting point. This will give us the desired bounding box. Here's what our function will look like:

```
def expandRect(minLat, minLong, maxLat, maxLong, distance):

    geod = pyproj.Geod(ellps="WGS84")
    midLat  = (minLat + maxLat) / 2.0
    midLong = (minLong + maxLong) / 2.0
```

```
    try:
        availDistance = geod.inv(midLong, maxLat, midLong,
                                 +90)[2]
        if availDistance >= distance:
            x,y,angle = geod.fwd(midLong, maxLat, 0, distance)
            maxLat = y
        else:
            maxLat = +90
    except:
        maxLat = +90 # Can't expand north.

    try:
        availDistance = geod.inv(maxLong, midLat, +180,
                                 midLat)[2]
        if availDistance >= distance:
            x,y,angle = geod.fwd(maxLong, midLat, 90,
                                 distance)
            maxLong = x
        else:
            maxLong = +180
    except:
        maxLong = +180 # Can't expand east.

    try:
        availDistance = geod.inv(midLong, minLat, midLong,
                                 -90)[2]
        if availDistance >= distance:
            x,y,angle = geod.fwd(midLong, minLat, 180,
                                 distance)
            minLat = y
        else:
            minLat = -90
    except:
        minLat = -90 # Can't expand south.

    try:
        availDistance = geod.inv(maxLong, midLat, -180,
                                 midLat)[2]
        if availDistance >= distance:
            x,y,angle = geod.fwd(minLong, midLat, 270,
                                 distance)
            minLong = x
```

```
    else:
        minLong = -180
except:
    minLong = -180 # Can't expand west.

return (minLat, minLong, maxLat, maxLong)
```

 Note that we've added error-checking here, to allow rectangles close to the north or south pole.

Using this function, we will be able to calculate the bounding rectangle for a given tile in the following way:

```
minLat,minLong,maxLat,maxLong = expandRect(iLat, iLong,
                                           iLat+1, iLong+1,
                                           MAX_DISTANCE)
```

Type the expandRect() function into your tileShorelines.py script, placing it immediately below the last import statement. With this in place, we're now ready to start creating the tiled shorelines.

As always, we'll be using the database.py module to handle the database-specific portions of our program. We'll start with a function to load the shoreline polygons into memory. Add the following to the end of your database.py module:

```
def load_shorelines():
    global _cursor

    shorelines = []

    if DB_TYPE == "MySQL":
        _cursor.execute("SELECT AsText(outline) " +
                        "FROM shorelines WHERE level=1")
    elif DB_TYPE == "PostGIS":
        _cursor.execute("SELECT ST_AsText(outline) " +
                        "FROM shorelines WHERE level=1")
    elif DB_TYPE == "SpatiaLite":
        _cursor.execute("SELECT ST_AsText(outline) " +
                        "FROM shorelines WHERE level=1")

    for row in _cursor:
        outline = shapely.wkt.loads(row[0])
```

```
shorelines.append(outline)

return shorelines
```

 This implementation of the shoreline tiling algorithm uses a lot of memory. If your computer has less than 2 gigabytes of RAM, you may need to store temporary results in the database. Doing this will of course slow down the tiling process, but it will still work.

We can now call this function from the `tileShorelines.py` script to load the shoreline polygons into memory. Add the following lines to the end of your program:

```
database.open()
shorelines = database.load_shorelines()
```

Now that we've loaded the shoreline polygons, we can start calculating the contents of each tile. Let's create a list-of-lists which will hold the (possibly clipped) polygons that appear within each tile; add the following to the end of your `tileShorelines.py` script:

```
tilePolys = []
for iLat in range(-90, +90):
    tilePolys.append([])
    for iLong in range(-180, +180):
        tilePolys[-1].append([])
```

For a given `iLat`/`iLong` combination, `tilePolys[iLat][iLong]` will contain a list of the shoreline polygons which appear inside that tile.

We now want to fill the `tilePolys` array with the portions of the shorelines that will appear within each tile. The obvious way to do this is to calculate the polygon intersections, like this:

```
shorelineInTile = shoreline.intersection(tileBounds)
```

Unfortunately, this approach would take a very long time to calculate—just as the map generation takes about 2-3 seconds to calculate the visible portion of a shoreline, it takes about 2-3 seconds to perform this intersection on a huge shoreline polygon. Because there are 360 x 180 = 64,800 tiles, it would take several days to complete this calculation using this naive approach.

A much faster solution would be to "divide and conquer" the large polygons. We first split the huge shoreline polygon into vertical strips, like this:

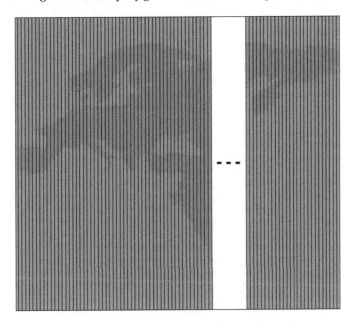

We then split each vertical strip horizontally to give us the individual parts of the polygon, which can be merged into the individual tiles:

By dividing the huge polygons into strips, and then further dividing each strip, the intersection process is much faster. Here is the code which performs this intersection; we start by iterating over each shoreline polygon and calculating the polygon's bounds:

For shoreline in shorelines:

```
minLong,minLat,maxLong,maxLat = shoreline.bounds
minLong = int(math.floor(minLong))
minLat  = int(math.floor(minLat))
maxLong = int(math.ceil(maxLong))
maxLat  = int(math.ceil(maxLat))
```

We then split the polygon into vertical strips:

```
vStrips = []
for iLong in range(minLong, maxLong+1):

    stripMinLat  = minLat
    stripMaxLat  = maxLat
    stripMinLong = iLong
    stripMaxLong = iLong + 1

    bMinLat,bMinLong,bMaxLat,bMaxLong = \
            expandRect(stripMinLat, stripMinLong,
                    stripMaxLat, stripMaxLong,
                    MAX_DISTANCE)

    bounds = Polygon([(bMinLong, bMinLat),
                    (bMinLong, bMaxLat),
                    (bMaxLong, bMaxLat),
                    (bMaxLong, bMinLat),
                    (bMinLong, bMinLat)])

    strip = shoreline.intersection(bounds)
    vStrips.append(strip)
```

Next, we process each vertical strip, splitting the strip into tile-sized blocks and storing it into `tilePolys`:

```
stripNum = 0
for iLong in range(minLong, maxLong+1):
    vStrip = vStrips[stripNum]
    stripNum = stripNum + 1

    for iLat in range(minLat, maxLat+1):
        bMinLat,bMinLong,bMaxLat,bMaxLong = \
            expandRect(iLat, iLong, iLat+1, iLong+1,
                    MAX_DISTANCE)
```

```
bounds = Polygon([(bMinLong, bMinLat),
                  (bMinLong, bMaxLat),
                  (bMaxLong, bMaxLat),
                  (bMaxLong, bMinLat),
                  (bMinLong, bMinLat)])

polygon = vStrip.intersection(bounds)
if not polygon.is_empty:
    tilePolys[iLat][iLong].append(polygon)
```

We're now ready to save the tiled shorelines back into the database. Before we can do that, we have to create the appropriate database tables. To do this, add the following function to your database.py module:

```
def create_tile_tables():
    global _cursor, _connection

    if DB_TYPE == "MySQL":
        _cursor.execute("""
            CREATE TABLE IF NOT EXISTS tiled_shorelines (
                intLat   INTEGER,
                intLong INTEGER,
                outline GEOMETRY,

                PRIMARY KEY (intLat, intLong))
        """)
    elif DB_TYPE == "PostGIS":
        _cursor.execute("DROP TABLE IF EXISTS " +
                        "tiled_shorelines")
        _cursor.execute("""
            CREATE TABLE tiled_shorelines (
                intLat   INTEGER,
                intLong INTEGER,

                PRIMARY KEY (intLat, intLong))
        """)
        _cursor.execute("""
            SELECT AddGeometryColumn('tiled_shorelines',
                                     'outline', 4326,
                                     'GEOMETRY', 2)
        """)
        _cursor.execute("""
```

```
                CREATE INDEX tiledShorelineIndex
                    ON tiled_shorelines
                    USING GIST(outline)
            """)
    elif DB_TYPE == "SpatiaLite":
        _cursor.execute("DROP TABLE IF EXISTS " +
                        "tiled_shorelines")
        _cursor.execute("""
            CREATE TABLE tiled_shorelines (
                intLat   INTEGER,
                intLong  INTEGER,
                PRIMARY KEY (intLat, intLong))
        """)
        _cursor.execute("""
            SELECT AddGeometryColumn('tiled_shorelines',
                                     'outline', 4326,
                                     'GEOMETRY', 2)
        """)
        _cursor.execute("""
            SELECT CreateSpatialIndex('tiled_shorelines',
                                      'outline')
        """)

    _connection.commit()
```

We're using the same technique we used earlier to create the `countries` and `shorelines` tables to create our new `tiled_shorelines` table. We can now call this from our `tileShorelines.py` program:

```
database.create_tile_tables()
```

Because we'll be storing geometries (Polygons or MultiPolygons) into this new table, we'll want to define a function to do this for each type of database. Add the following to the end of your `database.py` module:

```
def save_tiled_shoreline(iLat, iLong, outline_wkt):
    global _cursor, _connection

    if DB_TYPE == "MySQL":
        _cursor.execute("INSERT INTO tiled_shorelines " +
                        "(intLat, intLong, outline) " +
                        "VALUES (%s, %s, GeomFromText(%s))",
                        (iLat, iLong, outline_wkt))
    elif DB_TYPE == "PostGIS":
        _cursor.execute("INSERT INTO tiled_shorelines " +
                        "(intLat, intLong, outline) " +
                        "VALUES (%s, %s, " +
```

```
                         "ST_GeomFromText(%s, 4326))",
                         (iLat, iLong, outline_wkt))
        elif DB_TYPE == "SpatiaLite":
            _cursor.execute("INSERT INTO tiled_shorelines " +
                          "(intLat, intLong, outline) " +
                          "VALUES (?, ?, " +
                          "ST_GeomFromText(%s, 4326))",
                          (iLat, iLong, outline_wkt))

        _connection.commit()
```

Finally, we can combine the list of polygons within each tile into a single Geometry object, and save the results into the database. Add the following to the end of tileShorelines.py:

```
for iLat in range(-90, +90):
    for iLong in range(-180, +180):
        polygons = tilePolys[iLat][iLong]
        if len(polygons) == 0:
            outline = Polygon()
        else:
            outline = shapely.ops.cascaded_union(polygons)
        wkt = shapely.wkt.dumps(outline)

        database.save_tiled_shoreline(iLat, iLong, wkt)
```

This completes our program to tile the shorelines. You can run it by typing the following command from the command line:

python tileShorelines.py

Note that it may take an hour or more to complete, because of all the shoreline data that needs to be processed.

> The first time you run the program, you might want to replace this line:
>
> ```
> for shoreline in shorelines:
> ```
>
> with the following line:
>
> ```
> for shoreline in shorelines[1:2]:
> ```
>
> This will let the program finish in only a few minutes so you can make sure it's working, before removing the [1:2] and running it over the entire shoreline database.

Using tiled shorelines

All this gives us a new database table, tiled_shorelines, which holds the shoreline data split into partly-overlapping tiles:

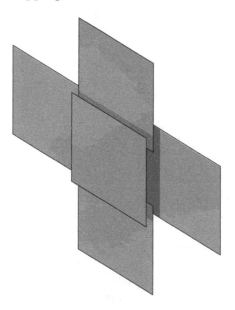

Since we can guarantee that all the shoreline data for a given set of search results will be within a single tiled_shoreline record, we can modify showResults.py (and database.py) to use the tiled shoreline rather than the raw shoreline data.

To do this, we'll need to modify our datasource dictionary so that Mapnik will know which of the shoreline tiles to use. Let's define a new version of the get_shoreline_datasource() function which returns a data source which can handle our tiled shorelines. Add the following to the end of your database.py module:

```
def get_tiled_shoreline_datasource(iLat, iLong):
    if DB_TYPE == "MySQL":
        vrtFile = os.path.join(os.path.dirname(__file__),
                               "shorelines.vrt")
        f = file(vrtFile, "w")
        f.write('<OGRVRTDataSource>\n')
        f.write('  <OGRVRTLayer name="shorelines">\n')
        f.write('    <SrcDataSource>MYSQL:' + MYSQL_DBNAME)
        if MYSQL_USERNAME not in ["", None]:
            f.write(",user=" + MYSQL_USERNAME)
```

```
            if MYSQL_PASSWORD not in ["", None]:
                f.write(",passwd=" + MYSQL_PASSWORD)
            f.write(',tables=tiled_shorelines</SrcDataSource>\n')
            f.write('    <SrcSQL>\n')
            f.write('        SELECT outline ' +
                         'FROM tiled_shorelines WHERE ' +
                         '(intLat=%d) AND (intlong=%d)' %
                         (iLat, iLong) + '\n')
            f.write('    </SrcSQL>\n')
            f.write('  </OGRVRTLayer>\n')
            f.write('</OGRVRTDataSource>\n')
            f.close()

            return {'type'  : "OGR",
                    'file'  : vrtFile,
                    'layer' : "shorelines"}
        elif DB_TYPE == "PostGIS":
            sql = "(SELECT outline FROM tiled_shorelines" \
                + " WHERE (intLat=%d) AND (intLong=%d)) " \
                % (iLat, iLong) + "AS shorelines"

            return {'type'                : "PostGIS",
                    'dbname'              : "distal",
                    'table'               : sql,
                    'extent_from_subquery' : True,
                    'user'                : POSTGIS_USERNAME,
                    'password'            : POSTGIS_PASSWORD}
        elif DB_TYPE == "SpatiaLite":
            sql = "(SELECT outline FROM tiled_shorelines" \
                + " WHERE (intLat=%d) AND (intLong=%d)) " \
                % (iLat, iLong) + "AS shorelines"

            return {'type'           : "SQLite",
                    'file'           : SPATIALITE_DBNAME,
                    'table'          : sql,
                    'geometry_field' : "outline",
                    'key_field'      : "id"}
```

We can now use this within our showResults.py script to use the tiled shorelines. To do this, replace the line that says:

```
datasource = database.get_shoreline_datasource()
```

with the following code:

```
iLat = int(round(latitude))
iLong = int(round(longitude))

datasource = database.get_tiled_shoreline_datasource(iLat, iLong)
```

With these changes, the `showResults.py` script will use the tiled shorelines rather than the full shoreline data downloaded from GSHHS. Let's now take a look at how much of a performance improvement these tiled shorelines give us.

Analyzing the performance improvement

As soon as you run this new version of the DISTAL application, you'll notice a huge improvement in speed: `showResults.py` now seems to return its results almost instantly. Where before the map generator was taking about 2-3 seconds to generate the high-resolution maps, it's now only taking a fraction of a second:

```
Generating map took 0.1074 seconds
```

That's a dramatic improvement in performance: the map generator is now 15-20 times faster than it was, and the total time taken by the `showResults.py` script is now less than a quarter of a second. That's not bad for a relatively simple change to our underlying map data.

Summary

In this chapter, we have implemented, tested, and made improvements to a simple web-based application which displays shorelines, towns, and lakes (DISTAL) within a given radius of a starting point. This application was the impetus for exploring a number of important concepts within geospatial application development, including the following:

- The creation of a simple but complete web-based geospatial application
- Using databases to store and work with large amounts of geospatial data
- Using a "black-box" map rendering module to create maps using spatial data selected from a database
- Examining the issues involved in identifying features based on their true distance rather than using a lat/long approximation
- Learning how to use spatial joins effectively

- Exploring usability issues in a prototype implementation
- Dealing with issues of data quality
- Learning how to precalculate data to improve performance

As a result of our development efforts, we have learned the following:

- Setting up a database and importing large quantities of data from shapefiles and other data sources
- Designing and structuring a simple web-based application to display maps and respond to user input
- There are three steps in displaying a map: calculating the lat/long bounding box, calculating the pixel size of the map image, and telling the map renderer which tables to get its data from
- Given the (x, y) coordinate of a point the user clicked on within a map, how to translate this point into equivalent latitude and longitude value
- Various ways in which true distance calculations, and selection of features by distance, can be performed
- Manually calculating distance for every point using the great circle distance formula is accurate but very slow
- Angular distances (that is, differences in lat/long coordinates) is an easy approximation of distance but doesn't relate in any useful way to true distances across the Earth's surface
- Using projected coordinates makes true distance calculations easy, but is limited to data covering only part of the Earth's surface
- Using a hybrid approach to accurately and quickly identify features by distance, by calculating a lat/long bounding box to identify potential features, and then doing a great circle distance calculation on these features to weed out the false positives
- Setting up a `datasource` to access and retrieve data from MySQL, PostGIS and SpatiaLite databases
- Displaying a country's outline and asking the user to click on a desired point works when the country is relatively small and compact, but breaks down for larger countries
- Learning how issues of data quality can affect the overall usefulness of your geospatial application

- Learning how you cannot assume that geospatial data comes in the best form for use in your application

- Very large polygons can degrade performance, and can often be split into smaller subpolygons, resulting in dramatic improvements in performance

- A divide-and-conquer approach to splitting large polygons is much faster than simply calculating the intersection using the full polygon each time

In the next chapter, we will explore the details of using the Mapnik library to convert raw geospatial data into map images.

8

Using Python and Mapnik to Generate Maps

Because geospatial data is almost impossible to understand until it is displayed, the creation of maps to visually represent spatial data is an extremely important topic. In this chapter we will look at Mapnik, a powerful Python library for generating maps out of geospatial data.

This chapter will cover the following:

- Underlying concepts used by Mapnik to generate maps
- Creating a simple map using the contents of a shapefile
- Different data sources that Mapnik supports
- Using rules, filters, and styles to control the map generation process
- Using "symbolizers" to draw lines, polygons, labels, points, and raster images onto your map
- Defining the colors used on a map
- Working with maps and layers
- Setting your options for rendering a map image
- The `mapGenerator.py` module, introduced in the previous chapter, uses Mapnik to generate maps
- Using map definition files to control and simplify the map-generation process

Introducing Mapnik

Mapnik is a powerful toolkit for using geospatial data to create maps. Mapnik can be downloaded from:

```
http://mapnik.org
```

Mapnik is a complex library with many different parts, and it is easy to get confused by the various names and concepts. Let's start our exploration of Mapnik by looking at a simple map:

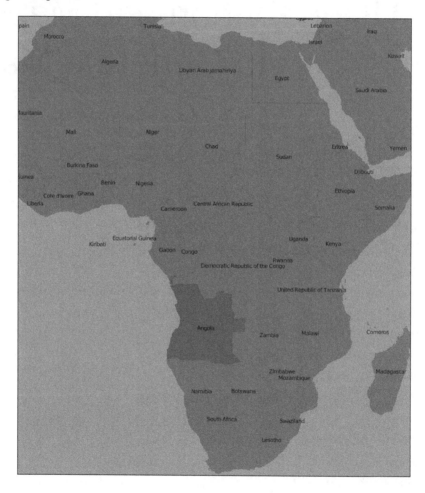

One thing that may not be immediately obvious is that the various elements within the map are *layered*, like this:

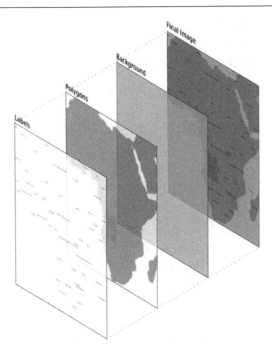

To generate this map, you have to tell Mapnik to initially draw the background, then the polygons, and finally the labels. This ensures that the polygons sit on top of the background, and the labels appear in front of both the polygons and the background.

> Strictly speaking, the background isn't a layer. It's simply a color or image that Mapnik draws onto the map before it starts drawing the first layer.

Mapnik allows you to control the order in which the map elements are drawn through the use of **Layer** objects. A simple map may consist of just one layer, but most maps have multiple layers. The layers are drawn in a strict back-to-front order, so the first layer you define will appear at the back. In the preceding example, the "Polygons" layer would be defined first, followed by the "Labels" layer, to ensure that the labels appear in front of the polygons. This layering approach is called the **painter's algorithm** because of its similarity to placing layers of paint onto an artist's canvas.

Each Layer has its own data source, which tells Mapnik where to load the data from. A data source can refer to a shapefile, a spatial database, a raster image file, or any number of other geospatial data sources. In most cases, setting up a Layer's data source is very easy.

Within each Layer, the visual display of the geospatial data is controlled through something called **Symbolizer**. While there are many different types of symbolizers available within Mapnik, three symbolizers are of interest to us here:

- The PolygonSymbolizer is used to draw filled polygons:

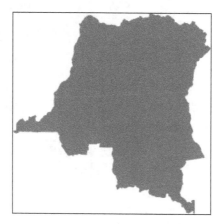

- The LineSymbolizer is used to draw the outline of polygons, as well as drawing LineStrings and other linear features, like this:

- The TextSymbolizer is used to draw labels and other text onto the map:

Democratic Republic of the Congo

In many cases, these three symbolizers are enough to draw an entire map. Indeed, almost all of the preceding example maps was produced using just one `PolygonSymbolizer`, one `LineSymbolizer`, and one `TextSymbolizer`:

"Polygon" Layer

> **PolygonSymbolizer**
>
> ```
> fill = mapnik.Color("#406040")
> ```

> **LineSymbolizer**
>
> ```
> stroke = mapnik.Stroke(mapnik.Color("#000000"), 0.1)
> ```

"Labels" Layer

> **TextSymbolizer**
>
> ```
> expression  =  "[NAME]"
> font        =  "DejaVu Sans Book"
> size        =  10
> color       =  mapnik.Color("#000000")
> ```

Within each layer, the symbolizers are processed using the same "painter's algorithm" described earlier. In this case, the `LineSymbolizer` would be drawn on top of the `PolygonSymbolizer`.

Note that the symbolizers aren't associated directly with a layer. Rather, there is an indirect association of symbolizers with a layer through the use of styles and rules. We'll look at styles in a minute, but for now let's take a closer look at the concept of a Mapnik rule.

A **rule** allows a set of symbolizers to apply only when a given condition is met. For example, the map at the start of this chapter displayed Angola in a different color. This was done by defining two rules within the "Polygons" layer:

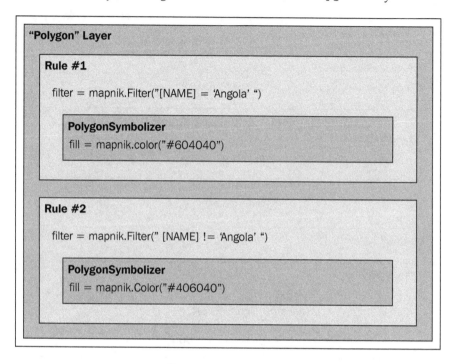

The first rule has a **filter** that only applies to features that have a NAME attribute equal to the string Angola. For features that match this filter condition, the rule's PolygonSymbolizer will be used to draw the feature in dark red.

The second rule has a similar filter, this time checking for features that don't have a NAME attribute equal to "Angola". These features are drawn using the second rule's PolygonSymbolizer, which draws the features in dark green.

Obviously, rules can be very powerful in selectively changing the way features are displayed on a map. We'll be looking at rules in much more detail in the *Rules, filters and styles* section of this chapter.

When you define your symbolizers, you place them into rules. The rules themselves are grouped into **styles**, which can be used to organize and keep track of your various rules. Each map layer itself has a list of the styles which apply to that particular layer.

While this complex relationship between layers, styles, rules, filters, and symbolizers can be confusing, it also provides much of Mapnik's power and flexibility. It is important that you understand how these various classes work together:

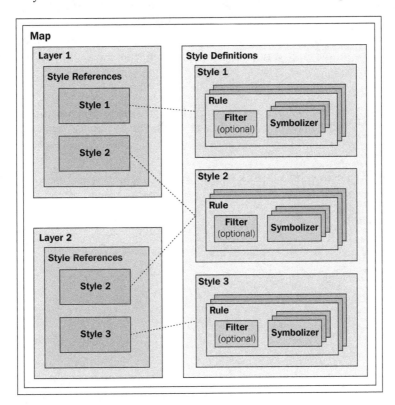

As you can see, you define the styles within the map itself, while the various layers refer to the styles that you have defined. This works in much the same way as a stylesheet in a word processing document, where you define styles and use them again and again. Note that the same style can be used in multiple layers.

Finally, instead of using Python code to create the various Mapnik objects by hand, you can choose to use a **Map Definition File**. This is an XML-format file, which defines all the symbolizers, filters, rules, styles, and layers within a map. Your Python code then simply creates a new `mapnik.Map` object and tells Mapnik to load the map's contents from the XML definition file. This allows you to define the contents of your map separately from the Python code that does the map generation, in much the same way as an HTML templating engine separates form and content within a web application.

Creating an example map

To better understand how the various parts of Mapnik work together, let's write a simple Python program, which generates the map shown at the start of this chapter. This map makes use of the World Borders Dataset, which you downloaded in an earlier chapter; copy the TM_WORLD_BORDERS-0.3 shapefile directory into a convenient place, and create a new Python script in the same place. We'll call this program createExampleMap.py.

 Obviously, if you've gotten this far without downloading and installing Mapnik, you need to do so now. Mapnik can be found at http://mapnik.org..

We'll start by importing the Mapnik toolkit and defining some constants, which the program will need:

```
import mapnik

MIN_LAT   = -35
MAX_LAT   = +35
MIN_LONG  = -12
MAX_LONG  = +50

MAP_WIDTH  = 700
MAP_HEIGHT = 800
```

The MIN_LAT, MAX_LAT, MIN_LONG, and MAX_LONG constants define the lat/long coordinates for the portion of the world to display on the map, while the MAP_WIDTH and MAP_HEIGHT constants define the size of the generated map image, in pixels. Obviously, you can change these if you want.

We're now ready to define the contents of the map. This map will have two layers, one for drawing the polygons and another for drawing the labels. We'll define a Mapnik Style object for each of these two layers. Let's start with the style for the "Polygons" layer:

```
polygonStyle = mapnik.Style()
```

As we discussed in the previous section, a filter object lets you choose which particular features a rule will apply to. In this case, we want to set up two rules, one to draw Angola in dark red, and another to draw all the other countries in dark green:

```
rule = mapnik.Rule()
rule.filter = mapnik.Filter("[NAME] = 'Angola'")
symbol = mapnik.PolygonSymbolizer(mapnik.Color("#604040"))
rule.symbols.append(symbol)

polygonStyle.rules.append(rule)

rule = mapnik.Rule()
rule.filter = mapnik.Filter("[NAME] != 'Angola'")
symbol = mapnik.PolygonSymbolizer(mapnik.Color("#406040"))
rule.symbols.append(symbol)

polygonStyle.rules.append(rule)
```

Note how we create a `PolygonSymbolizer` to fill the country polygon in an appropriate color, and then add this symbolizer to our current rule. As we define the rules, we add them to our polygon style.

Now that we've filled the country polygons, we'll define an additional rule to draw the polygon outlines:

```
rule = mapnik.Rule()
symbol = mapnik.LineSymbolizer(mapnik.Color("#000000"), 0.1)
rule.symbols.append(symbol)

polygonStyle.rules.append(rule)
```

This is all that's required to display the country polygons onto the map. Let's now go ahead and define a second Mapnik `Style` object for the "Labels" layer:

```
labelStyle = mapnik.Style()

rule = mapnik.Rule()
symbol = mapnik.TextSymbolizer(mapnik.Expression("[NAME]"),
                               "DejaVu Sans Book", 12,
                               mapnik.Color("#000000"))
rule.symbols.append(symbol)

labelStyle.rules.append(rule)
```

This style uses a `TextSymbolizer` to draw the labels onto the map. Note that we create an Expression object to define the text to be displayed—in this case, we use the attribute called NAME from the shapefile; this attribute contains the name of the country.

In this example, we are only using a single Mapnik style for each layer. When generating a more complex map, you will typically have a number of styles which can be applied to each layer, and styles may be shared between layers as appropriate. For this example, though, we are keeping the map definition as simple as possible.

Now that we have set up our styles, we can start to define our map's layers. Before we do this, though, we need to set up our data source:

```python
datasource = mapnik.Shapefile(file="TM_WORLD_BORDERS-0.3/" +
                              "TM_WORLD_BORDERS-0.3.shp")
```

We can then define the two layers used by our map:

```python
polygonLayer = mapnik.Layer("Polygons")
polygonLayer.datasource = datasource
polygonLayer.styles.append("PolygonStyle")

labelLayer = mapnik.Layer("Labels")
labelLayer.datasource = datasource
labelLayer.styles.append("LabelStyle")
```

 Note that we refer to styles by name, rather than inserting the style directly. This allows us to re-use styles, or to define styles in an XML definition file and then refer to them within our Python code. We'll add the styles definitions to our map shortly.

We can now finally create our Map object. A Mapnik Map object has a size and projection, a background color, a list of styles, and a list of the layers that make up the map:

```python
map = mapnik.Map(MAP_WIDTH, MAP_HEIGHT,
                 "+proj=longlat +datum=WGS84")
map.background = mapnik.Color("#8080a0")

map.append_style("PolygonStyle", polygonStyle)
map.append_style("LabelStyle", labelStyle)

map.layers.append(polygonLayer)
map.layers.append(labelLayer)
```

The last thing we have to do is tell Mapnik to zoom in on the desired area of the world, and then render the map into an image file:

```
map.zoom_to_box(mapnik.Box2d(MIN_LONG, MIN_LAT,
                             MAX_LONG, MAX_LAT))
mapnik.render_to_file(map, "map.png")
```

If you run this program and open the `map.png` file, you will see the map you have generated:

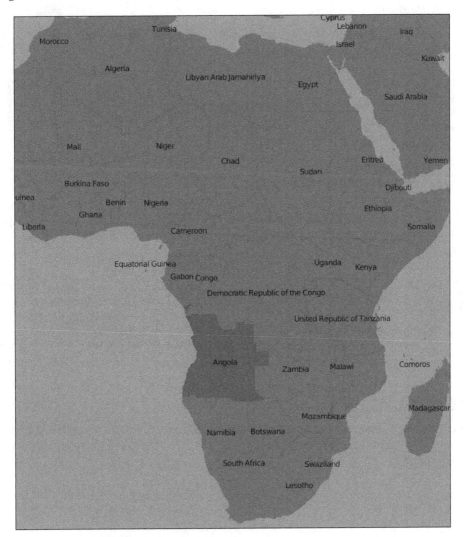

Obviously there's a lot more that you can do with Mapnik, but this example covers the main points and should be enough to let you started for generating your own maps. Make sure that you play with this example to become familiar with the way Mapnik works. Here are some things you might like to try:

- Adjust the MIN_LAT, MIN_LONG, MAX_LAT, and MAX_LONG constants at the start of the program to zoom in on the country where you reside

- Change the size of the generated image

- Alter the map's colors

- Add extra rules to display the country name in different font sizes and colors based on the country's population

Hint

To do this, you'll need to define filters that look like this:

mapnik.Filter("[POP2005] > 1000000 and [POP2005] <= 2000000")

Mapnik in depth

In this section, we will examine the Python interface of the Mapnik toolkit in much more detail. The Python documentation for Mapnik (http://media.mapnik.org/ api_docs/python) is confusing and incomplete, so you may find this section to be a useful reference guide while writing your own Mapnik-based programs.

The Mapnik toolkit is written in C++, and provides bindings to let you access it via Python. Not every feature implemented in Mapnik is available from Python; only those features that are available and relevant to the Python developer will be discussed here.

Data sources

Before you can access a given set of geospatial data within a map, you need to set up a Mapnik **Datasource** object. This acts as a "bridge" between Mapnik and your geospatial data:

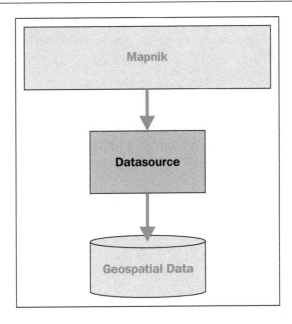

You typically create the data source using one of the convenience constructors described here. Then you add that data source to any Mapnik Layer objects, which will use that data:

```
layer.datasource = datasource
```

A single `Datasource` object can be shared by multiple layers, or it can be used by just one layer.

There are many different types of data sources supported by Mapnik, some of which are experimental or access data in commercial databases. Let's take a closer look at the types of data sources you are likely to find useful.

Shapefile

It is easy to use a shapefile as a Mapnik data source. All you need to do is supply the name and directory path for the desired shapefile to the `mapnik.Shapefile()` convenience constructor:

```
import mapnik
...
datasource = mapnik.Shapefile(file="shapefile.shp")
```

If the shapefile is in a different directory, you can use `os.path.join()` to define the full path. For example, you can open a shapefile in a directory relative to your Python program like this:

```
datasource = mapnik.Shapefile(file=os.path.join("..", "data",
                                                 "shapes.shp"))
```

When you open a shapefile data source, the shapefile's attributes can be used within a filter expression, and as fields to be displayed by a TextSymbolizer. By default, all text within the shapefile will be assumed to be in UTF-8 character encoding; if you need to use a different character encoding, you can use the `encoding` parameter, as follows:

```
datasource = mapnik.Shapefile(file="shapefile.shp",
                              encoding="latin1")
```

PostGIS

This data source allows you to use data from a PostGIS database on your map. The basic usage of the PostGIS data source is like this:

```
import mapnik
...
datasource = mapnik.PostGIS(user="..." password="...",
                            dbname="...", table="...")
```

You simply pass in the username and password used to access the PostGIS database, the name of the database, and the name of the table that contains the spatial data you want to include on your map. As with the shapefiles, the fields in the database table can be used inside a filter expression, and fields to be displayed using a TextSymbolizer.

There are some performance issues to be aware of when retrieving data from a PostGIS database. Imagine that we're accessing a large database table, and use the following to generate our map's layer:

```
datasource = mapnik.PostGIS(user="...", password="...",
                            dbname="...", table="myBigTable")

layer = mapnik.Layer("myLayer")
layer.datasource = datasource
layer.styles.append("myLayerStyle")

symbol = mapnik.PolygonSymbolizer(mapnik.Color("#406080"))
```

```
rule = mapnik.Rule()
rule.filter = mapnik.Filter("[level] = 1")
rule.symbols.append(symbol)

style = mapnik.Style()
style.rules.append(rule)

map.append_style("myLayerStyle", style)
```

Note how the data source refers to the `myBigTable` table within the PostGIS database, and we use a filter expression (`[level] = 1`) to select the particular records within that database table to be displayed using our `PolygonSymbolizer`.

When rendering this map layer, Mapnik will scan through every record in the table, apply the filter expression to each record in turn, and then use the PolygonSymbolizer to draw the record's polygon if and only if the record matches the filter expression. This is fine if there aren't many records in the table, or if most of the records will match the filter expression. But imagine that the `myBigTable` table contains a million records, with only 10,000 records having a `level` value of 1. In this case, Mapnik will scan through the entire table and discard 99 percent of the records. Only the remaining 1 percent will actually be drawn.

As you can imagine, this is extremely inefficient. Mapnik will waste a lot of time filtering the records in the database when PostGIS itself is much better suited to the task. In situations like this, you can make use of a **subselect query** so that the database itself will do the filtering before the data is received by Mapnik. We actually used a subselect query in the previous chapter, where we retrieved tiled shoreline data from our PostGIS database, though we didn't explain how it worked in any depth.

To use a subselect query, you replace the table name with an SQL `select` statement that does the filtering and returns the fields needed by Mapnik to generate the map's layer. Here is an updated version of the preceding example that uses a subselect query:

```
query = "(select geom from myBigTable where level=1) as data"
datasource = mapnik.PostGIS(user="...", password="...",
                            dbname="...", table=query)

layer = mapnik.Layer("myLayer")
layer.datasource = datasource
layer.styles.append("myLayerStyle")

symbol = mapnik.PolygonSymbolizer(mapnik.Color("#406080"))
```

```
rule = mapnik.Rule()
rule.symbols.append(symbol)

style = mapnik.Style()
style.rules.append(rule)

map.append_style("myLayerStyle", style)
```

We've replaced the table name with a PostGIS subselect statement that filters out all records with a `level` value not equal to 1 and returns just the `geom` field for the matching records back to Mapnik. We've also removed the `rule.filter` = line in our code, as the data source will only ever return records that already match the filter expression.

 Note that the subselect statement ends with ...as data. We have to give the results of the subselect statement a name, even though that name is ignored. In this case, we've called the results data, though you can use any name you like.

If you use a subselect, it is important that you include all the fields used by your filter expressions and symbolizers. If you don't include a field in the subselect statement, it won't be available for Mapnik to use.

Gdal

The Gdal data source allows you to include any GDAL-compatible raster image data file within your map. The Gdal data source is straightforward to use:

```
datasource = mapnik.Gdal(file="myRasterImage.tiff")
```

Once you have a Gdal data source, you need to use a RasterSymbolizer to draw it onto the map:

```
layer = mapnik.Layer("myLayer")
layer.datasource = datasource
layer.styles.append("myLayerStyle")

symbol = mapnik.RasterSymbolizer()

rule = mapnik.Rule()
rule.symbols.append(symbol)
```

```
style = mapnik.Style()
style.rules.append(rule)

map.append_style("myLayerStyle", style)
```

 Mapnik provides another way of reading TIFF-format raster images, using the Raster data source. In general, using the Gdal data source is more flexible and easier than using Raster.

Ogr

The Ogr data source lets you display any OGR-compatible vector data on your map. The convenience constructor for an Ogr data source requires at least two named parameters:

```
datasource = mapnik.Ogr(file="...", layer="...")
```

The `file` parameter is the name of an OGR-compatible data file, while `layer` is the name of the desired layer within that data file. You could use this, for example, to read a shapefile via the OGR driver:

```
datasource = mapnik.Ogr(file="shapefile.shp",
                        layer="shapefile")
```

More usefully, you can use this to load data from any vector-format data file supported by OGR. The various supported formats are listed on the following web page:

```
http://www.gdal.org/ogr/ogr_formats.html
```

The **Virtual Datasource (VRT)** format is of particular interest to us. The VRT format is an XML-formatted file that allows you to set up an OGR data source, which isn't stored in a simple file on disk. We saw in the previous chapter how this can be used to display data from a MySQL database on a map, despite the fact that Mapnik itself does not implement a MySQL data source.

The VRT file format is relatively complex, though it is explained fully on the OGR website. Here is an example of how you can use a VRT file to set up a MySQL virtual data source:

```
<OGRVRTDataSource>
  <OGRVRTLayer name="myLayer">
    <SrcDataSource>MYSQL:mydb,user=user,password=pass,
                 tables=myTable</SrcDataSource>
```

```
        <SrcSQL>
          SELECT name,geom FROM myTable
        </SrcSQL>
    </OGRVRTLayer>
</OGRVRTDataSource>
```

The `<SrcDataSource>` element contains a string that sets up the OGR MySQL data source. This string is of the following format:

```
MySQL:«dbName»,user=«username»,password=«pass»,tables=«tables»
```

You need to replace «dbName» with the name of your database, «username» and «pass» with the username and password used to access your MySQL database, and «tables» with a list of the database tables you want to retrieve your data from. If you are retrieving data from multiple tables, you need to separate the table names with a semicolon like this:

```
tables=lakes;rivers;coastlines
```

Note that all the text between `<SrcDataSource>` and `</SrcDataSource>` must be on a single line.

The text inside the `<SrcSQL>` element should be a MySQL `select` statement that retrieves the desired information from the database table(s). As with the PostGIS data source, you can use this to filter out unwanted records before they are passed to Mapnik, which will significantly improve performance.

The VRT file should be saved to disk. For example, the preceding virtual file definition might be saved to a file named `myLayer.vrt`. You would then use this file to define your Ogr data source like this:

```
datasource = mapnik.Ogr(file="myLayer.vrt", layer="myLayer")
```

SQLite

The SQLite data source allows you to include data from an SQLite (or SpatiaLite) database on a map. The `mapnik.SQLite()` convenience constructor accepts a number of keyword parameters; the ones most likely to be useful are:

- `file="..."`

  The name and optional path to the SQLite database file.

- `table="..."`

  The name of the desired table within this database.

- `geometry_field="..."`

   The name of a field within this table that holds the geometry to be displayed.

- `key_field="..."`

   The name of the primary key field within the table.

For example, to access a table named `countries` in a SpatiaLite database named `mapData.db`, you might use the following:

```
datasource = mapnik.SQLite(file="mapData.db",
                           table="countries",
                           geometry_field="outline",
                           key_field="id")
```

All of the fields within the `countries` table will be available for use in Mapnik filters and for display using a TextSymbolizer. The various symbolizers will use the geometry stored in the `outline` field for drawing lines, polygons, and so on.

OSM

The OSM data source allows you to include OpenStreetMap data onto a map. The OpenStreetMap data is stored in `.osm` format, which is an XML format containing the underlying nodes, ways and relations used by OpenStreetMap. The OpenStreetMap data format, and options for downloading `.osm` files, can be found at:

`http://wiki.openstreetmap.org/wiki/.osm`

If you have downloaded a `.osm` file and want to access it locally, you can set up your data source like this:

```
datasource = mapnik.OSM(file="myData.osm")
```

If you wish to use an OpenStreetMap API call to retrieve the OSM data on the fly, you can do this by supplying a URL to read the data from, along with a bounding box to identify which set of data you want to download. For example:

```
osmURL = "http://api.openstreetmap.org/api/0.6/map"
bounds = "176.193,-38.172,176.276,-38.108"
datasource = mapnik.OSM(url=osmURL, bbox=bounds)
```

The bounding box is a string containing the left, bottom, right, and top coordinates for the desired bounding box, respectively.

MemoryDatasource

The MemoryDatasource allows you to manually define the geospatial data, which appears on the map. To use a MemoryDatasource, you first create a `mapnik.Context` object that defines the attributes you want to associate with each feature:

```
context = mapnik.Context()
context.push("NAME")
context.push("ELEVATION")
```

You then create a `mapnik.Feature` object for each of the features you want to include on the map, like this:

```
feature = mapnik.Feature(context, id)
```

In the preceding feature, `id` is a unique integer ID value for this feature.

Once the feature has been created, you can define the feature's attributes as if it was a Python dictionary:

```
feature['NAME'] = "Hawkins Hill"
feature['ELEVATION'] = 1624
```

These attributes can be used by rules to select which features to display, and they can also be used by a TextSymbolizer to draw an attribute's value onto the map.

Each feature can have one or more geometries associated with it. The easiest way to set the feature's geometry is to use the `add_geometries_from_wkt()` method, like this:

```
feature.add_geometries_from_wkt("POINT (174.73 -41.33)")
```

Finally, you can add the feature to the MemoryDatasource using the `add_feature()` method:

```
datasource = mapnik.MemoryDatasource()
datasource.add_feature(feature)
```

Rules, filters, and styles

As we saw earlier in this chapter, Mapnik uses **rules** to specify which particular symbolizers will be used to render a given feature. Rules are grouped together into a **style**, and the various styles are added to your map and then referred to by name when you set up your layer. In this section, we will examine the relationship between rules, filters and styles, and see just what can be done with these various Mapnik classes.

Let's take a closer look at Mapnik's `Rule` class. A Mapnik rule has two parts: a set of **conditions**, and a list of **symbolizers**. If the rule's conditions are met, then the symbolizers will be used to draw the matching features onto the map.

There are four types of conditions supported by a rule:

- A mapnik **filter** can be used to specify an expression that must be met by the feature if it is to be drawn.

- The rule itself can specify minimum and maximum **scale denominators** which must apply. This can be used to set up rules that are only used if the map is drawn at a given scale.

- The rule can have an **else** condition, which means that the rule will only be applied if no other rule in the style has had its conditions met.

- The rule can have an **also** condition, which means that the rule will only be applied if at least one other rule in the style has had its conditions met.

If all the conditions for a rule are met, then the associated list of symbolizers will be used to render the feature onto the map.

Let's take a look at these conditions in more detail.

Filters

Mapnik's `Filter()` constructor takes a single parameter, a string defining an expression which the feature must match if the rule is to apply. You then store the returned Filter object into the rule's `filter` attribute:

```
rule.filter = mapnik.Filter("...")
```

Let's consider a very simple filter expression, comparing a field or attribute against a specific value:

```
filter = mapnik.Filter("[level] = 1")
```

String values can be compared by putting single quote marks around the value, like this:

```
filter = mapnik.Filter("[type] = 'CITY'")
```

Note that the field name and value are both case-sensitive, and that you must surround the field or attribute name with square brackets.

Of course, simply comparing a field with a value is the most basic type of comparison you can do. Filter expressions have their own powerful and flexible syntax for defining conditions, similar in concept to an SQL `where` expression. The following syntax diagram describes all the options for writing filter expression strings:

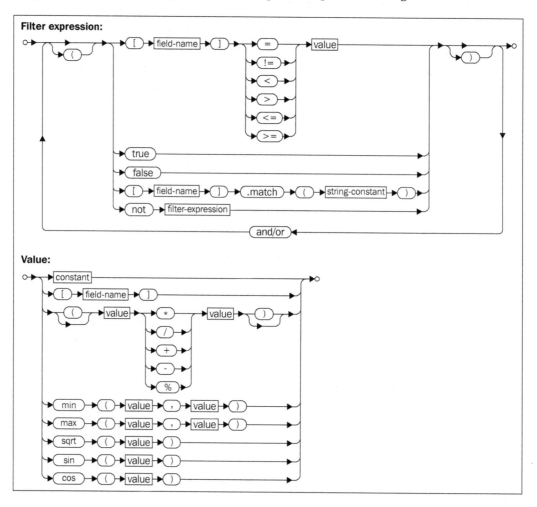

Mapnik also allows you to filter on the type of geometry, using a special syntax:

```
filter = mapnik.Filter("[mapnik::geometry_type] = point")
```

The following geometry types are supported by this filter expression:

- `point`
- `linestring`

- polygon
- collection

Scale denominators

Consider the following two maps:

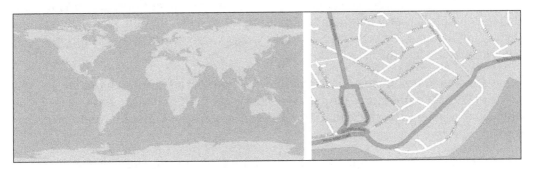

Obviously, there's no point in drawing streets onto a map of the entire world. Similarly, the country outlines shown on the world map are at too large a scale to draw detailed coastlines for an individual city. But if your application allows the user to zoom in from the world map right down to an individual street, you will need to use a single set of Mapnik styles to generate the map regardless of the scale at which you are drawing it.

Mapnik allows you to do this by selectively displaying features based on the map's scale denominator. If you had a map printed on paper at 1:100,000 scale, then the scale denominator would be the number after the colon (100,000 in this case). Drawing maps digitally makes this a bit more complicated, but the idea remains the same.

A Mapnik rule can have a minimum and maximum scale denominator value associated with it:

```
rule.min_scale = 10000
rule.max_scale = 100000
```

If the minimum and maximum scale denominators are set, then the rule will only apply if the map's scale denominator is within this range.

You can also apply minimum and maximum scale factors to an entire layer:

```
layer.minzoom = 1.0/100000
layer.maxzoom = 1.0/200000
```

Note that rules use scale denominators while layers use scale factors. This can be rather confusing, as the relationship between the two is not straightforward. For more information on scale factors and scale denominators, please refer to `http://trac.mapnik.org/wiki/ScaleAndPpi`.

The whole layer will only be displayed when the map's current scale factor is within this range. This is useful if you have a data source that should only be used when displaying the map at a certain scale—for example, only using high-resolution shoreline data when the user has zoomed in.

Scale denominators can be used intuitively, for example a scale denominator value of 200,000 represents a map drawn at roughly 1:200,000 scale. But this is only an approximation; the actual calculation of a scale denominator has to take into account two important factors:

- Because Mapnik renders a map as a bitmapped image, the size of the individual pixels within the image comes into play. Since bitmapped images can be displayed on a variety of different computer screens with different pixel sizes, Mapnik uses a "standardized rendering pixel size" as defined by the Open Geospatial Consortium to define how big a pixel is going to be. This value is 0.28 mm, and is approximately the size of a pixel on modern video displays.

- The map projection being used can have a huge effect on the calculated scale denominator. Map projections always distort true distances, and a projection which is accurate at the equator may be wildly inaccurate closer to the poles.

Depending on the projection being used, the formula Mapnik uses to calculate the scale denominator can get rather complicated. Rather than worrying about the formulas, it is much easier just to ask Mapnik to calculate the scale denominator and scale factor for us:

```
map = mapnik.Map(width, height, projection)
map.zoom_to_box(bounds)
print map.scale_denominator(), map.scale()
```

You can then zoom the map to your desired scale and see what the scale factor and denominator are, which you can then plug into your styles to choose which features should be displayed at a given scale denominator range.

Be careful if you are working with multiple projections. A scale denominator that works for one projection may need to be adjusted if you switch projections.

"Else" rules

Imagine that you want to draw some features in one color, and all other features in a different color. One way to achieve this is by using Mapnik rules, like this:

```
rule1.filter = mapnik.Filter("[level] = 1")
...
rule2.filter = mapnik.Filter("[level] != 1")
```

This is fine for simple filter expressions, but when the expressions get more complicated it is a lot easier to use an "else" rule, like this:

```
rule1.filter = mapnik.Filter("[level] = 1")
...
rule2.set_else(True)
```

If you call `set_else(True)` for a rule, then this rule is to be used if and only if no previous rule in the same style has had its filter conditions met.

Else rules are particularly useful if you have a number of filter conditions and want to have a "catch-all" rule at the end, which will apply if no other rule has been used to draw the feature. For example:

```
rule1.filter = mapnik.Filter("[type] = 'city'")
rule2.filter = mapnik.Filter("[type] = 'town'")
rule3.filter = mapnik.Filter("[type] = 'village'")
rule4.filter.set_else(True)
```

"Also" rules

Imagine that you've defined a series of rules to draw country polygons in different colors depending on the UN region code:

```
rule1 = mapnik.Rule()
rule1.filter = mapnik.Filter("[region] = '002'") # Africa.
rule1.symbols.append(mapnik.PolygonSymbolizer(color1))

rule2 = mapnik.Rule()
rule2.filter = mapnik.Filter("[region] = '019'") # Americas.
rule1.symbols.append(mapnik.PolygonSymbolizer(color2))

rule3 = mapnik.Rule()
rule3.filter = mapnik.Filter("[region] = '142'") # Asia.
rule3.symbols.append(mapnik.PolygonSymbolizer(color3))
```

```
rule4 = mapnik.Rule()
rule4.filter = mapnik.Filter("[region] = '150'") # Europe.
rule4.symbols.append(mapnik.PolygonSymbolizer(color3))

rule5 = mapnik.Rule()
rule5.filter = mapnik.Filter("[region] = '009'") # Oceania.
rule5.symbols.append(mapnik.PolygonSymbolizer(color3))
```

Having filled these polygons, you now want to draw a black line around the polygon boundary. There are two ways you could do this: you could add a LineSymbolizer to each of your five rules, or you could use an **also** rule.

An also rule is basically the opposite of the else rule: the also rule only applies if at least one other rule applies to the feature.

Here is how you could use an also rule to draw a border around all the filled polygons:

```
rule6 = mapnik.Rule()
rule6.set_also(True)
rule6.symbols.append(mapnik.LineSymbolizer(color6, 0.1))
```

This rule would apply if any of the other rules applied to the feature—that is, it would draw a border around any polygon that gets filled in. But if any feature is in a region not covered by the other rules, no border will be drawn.

Symbolizers

Symbolizers are used to draw features onto a map. In this section, we will look at how you can use various types of symbolizers to draw lines, polygons, labels, points, and images.

Drawing lines

There are two Mapnik symbolizers that can be used to draw lines onto a map: LineSymbolizer and LinePatternSymbolizer. Let's looks at each of these in turn.

LineSymbolizer

The **LineSymbolizer** draws linear features and traces around the outline of polygons, as shown in the following diagram:

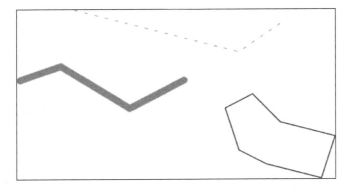

The LineSymbolizer is one of the most useful of the Mapnik symbolizers. Here is the Python code that created the LineSymbolizer used to draw the dashed line in the preceding example:

```
stroke = mapnik.Stroke()
stroke.color = mapnik.Color("#008000")
stroke.width = 1.0
stroke.add_dash(5, 10)
symbolizer = mapnik.LineSymbolizer(stroke)
```

As you can see, the LineSymbolizer uses a Mapnik Stroke object to define how the line will be drawn. To use a LineSymbolizer, you first create the Stroke object and set the various options for how you want the line to be drawn. You then create your LineSymbolizer, passing the stroke object to the LineSymbolizer's constructor:

```
symbolizer = mapnik.LineSymbolizer(stroke)
```

Let's take a closer look at the various line-drawing options provided by the Stroke object.

Line color

By default, lines are drawn in black. You can change this by setting the stroke's `color` attribute to a Mapnik Color object:

```
stroke.color = mapnik.Color("red")
```

For more information about the Mapnik Color object, and the various ways in which you can specify a color, please refer to the *Using Colors* section later in this chapter.

Line width

The line drawn by a LineSymbolizer will be one pixel wide by default. To change this, set the stroke's `width` attribute to the desired width, in pixels:

```
stroke.width = 1.5
```

Note that you can use fractional line widths for fine-grained control of your line widths.

Opacity

You can change how opaque or transparent the line is by setting the stroke's `opacity` attribute:

```
stroke.opacity = 0.8
```

The opacity can range from 0.0 (completely transparent) to 1.0 (completely opaque). If the opacity is not specified, the line will be completely opaque.

Line caps

The line cap specifies how the ends of the line should be drawn. Mapnik supports three standard line cap settings:

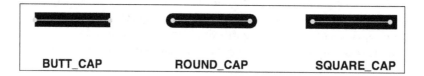

By default, the lines will use `BUTT_CAP` style, but you can change this by setting the stroke's `line_cap` attribute, like this:

```
stroke1.line_cap = mapnik.line_cap.BUTT_CAP
stroke2.line_cap = mapnik.line_cap.ROUND_CAP
stroke3.line_cap = mapnik.line_cap.SQUARE_CAP
```

Line joins

When a line changes direction, the "corner" of the line can be drawn in one of three standard ways:

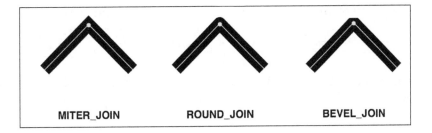

The default behavior is to use MITER_JOIN, but you can change this by setting the stroke's line_join attribute to a different value:

```
stroke1.line_join = mapnik.line_join.MITER_JOIN
stroke2.line_join = mapnik.line_join.ROUND_JOIN
stroke3.line_join = mapnik.line_join.BEVEL_JOIN
```

Dashed and dotted lines

You can add "breaks" to a line to make it appear dashed or dotted. To do this, you add one or more **dash segments** to the stroke. Each dash segment defines a *dash length* and a *gap length*; the line will be drawn for the given dash length, and will then leave a gap of the specified length before continuing to draw the line:

You add a dash segment to a line by calling the stroke's add_dash() method, like this:

```
stroke.add_dash(5, 7)
```

This will give the line a five pixel dash followed by a seven pixel gap.

You aren't limited to just having a single dash segment; if you call add_dash() multiple times, you will create a line with more than one segments. These dash segments will be processed in turn, allowing you to create varying patterns of dashes and dots. For example:

```
stroke.add_dash(10, 2)
stroke.add_dash(2, 2)
stroke.add_dash(2, 2)
```

The preceding code would result in the following repeating line pattern:

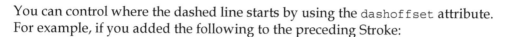

You can control where the dashed line starts by using the `dashoffset` attribute. For example, if you added the following to the preceding Stroke:

```
stroke.dashoffset = -5
```

Your line would now look like this:

As you can see, a negative dash offset shifts the line pattern to the left, while a positive offset shifts the pattern to the right.

Drawing roads and other complex linear features

One thing that may not be immediately obvious is that you can draw a road onto a map by overlying two LineSymbolizers; the first LineSymbolizer draws the edges of the road, while the second LineSymbolizer draws the road's interior. For example:

```
stroke = mapnik.Stroke()
stroke.color = mapnik.Color("#bf7a3a")
stroke.width = 7.0
roadEdgeSymbolizer = mapnik.LineSymbolizer(stroke)

stroke = mapnik.Stroke()
stroke.color = mapnik.Color("#ffd3a9")
stroke.width = 6.0
roadInteriorSymbolizer = mapnik.LineSymbolizer(stroke)
```

This technique is commonly used for drawing street maps. The two symbolizers defined above would then be overlaid to produce a road like this:

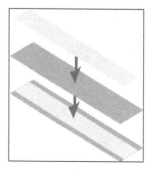

This technique can be used for more than just drawing roads; the creative use of symbolizers is one of the main "tricks" to achieving complex visual effects using Mapnik.

LinePatternSymbolizer

The LinePatternSymbolizer is used in situations where you want to draw a line that can't be rendered using a simple Stroke object. The LinePatternSymbolizer accepts an image file and draws that image repeatedly along the length of the line or around the outline of a polygon. For example, using the following image file:

A LinePatternSymbolizer would draw lines and polygons in the following way:

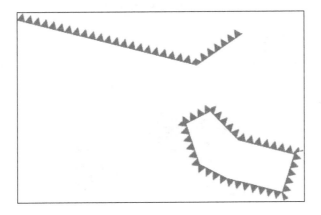

Note that linear features and polygon boundaries have a direction—that is, the line or polygon border moves from one point to the next, in the order in which the points were defined when the geometry was created. For example, the points that make up the line segment in the preceding example were defined from left to right—that is, the leftmost point is defined first, then the center point, and then the rightmost point.

The direction of a feature is important as it affects the way the LinePatternSymbolizer draws the image. If the preceding linestring was defined in the opposite direction, the LinePatternSymbolizer would draw it like this:

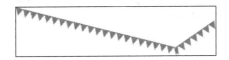

As you can see, the LinePatternSymbolizer draws the image oriented towards the left of the line, as it moves from one point to the next. To draw the image oriented towards the right, you will have to reverse the order of the points within your feature.

To use a LinePatternSymbolizer within your Python code, you create a `mapnik.PathExpression` object that refers to the image file you want to use. You then pass this object to the LinePatternSymbolizer initializer, like this:

```
path = mapnik.PathExpression("path/to/image.png")
symbolizer = mapnik.LinePatternSymbolizer(path)
```

Drawing polygons

Just as there are two symbolizers to draw lines, there are two symbolizers to draw the interior of a polygon: the PolygonSymbolizer and the PolygonPatternSymbolizer. Let's take a closer look at each of these two symbolizers.

PolygonSymbolizer

A PolygonSymbolizer fills the interior of a polygon with a single color:

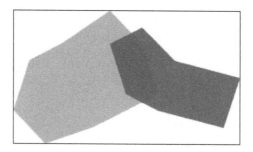

You create a PolygonSymbolizer like this:

```
symbolizer = mapnik.PolygonSymbolizer()
```

Let's take a closer look at the various options for controlling how the polygon will be drawn.

Fill color

By default, a PolygonSymbolizer will draw the interior of the polygon in grey. To change the color used to fill the polygon, set the PolygonSymbolizer's `fill` attribute to the desired mapnik Color object:

```
symbolizer.fill = mapnik.Color("red")
```

For more information about creating Mapnik Color objects, please refer to the *Using Colors* section later in this chapter.

Opacity

By default, the polygon will be completely opaque. You can change this by setting the PolygonSymbolizer's `opacity` attribute, like this:

```
symbolizer.fill_opacity = 0.5
```

The opacity can range from 0.0 (completely transparent) to 1.0 (completely opaque). In the preceding illustration, the left polygon had an opacity of 0.5.

Gamma correction

Gamma correction is an obscure concept, but can be very useful at times. If you draw two polygons that touch with exactly the same fill color, you will still see a line between the two:

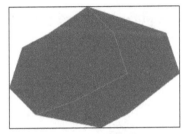

This is because of the way Mapnik anti-aliases the edges of the polygons. If you want these lines between adjacent polygons to disappear, you can add a gamma correction factor, like this:

```
symbolizer.gamma = 0.63
```

This results in the two polygons appearing as one:

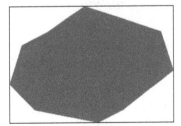

It may take some experimenting, but using a gamma value of around 0.5 to 0.7 will generally remove the ghost lines between adjacent polygons. The default value of 1.0 will mean that no gamma correction will be performed at all.

PolygonPatternSymbolizer

The PolygonPatternSymbolizer fills the interior of a polygon using a supplied image file, like this:

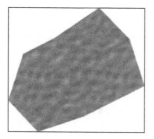

The image will be **tiled**—that is, drawn repeatedly to fill in the entire interior of the polygon:

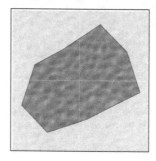

Because the right side of one tile will appear next to the left side of the adjacent tile, and the bottom of the tile will appear immediately above the top of the tile below it (and vice versa), you need to choose an appropriate image that will look good when it is drawn in this way.

Using the PolygonPatternSymbolizer is easy; as with the LinePatternSymbolizer you create a new instance and give it a reference to the image file in a mapnik. PathExpression object:

```
path = mapnik.PathExpression("path/to/image.png")
symbolizer = mapnik.PolygonPatternSymbolizer(path)
```

Drawing labels

Textual labels are an important part of any map. In this section, we will explore the TextSymbolizer, which draws text onto a map.

 The ShieldSymbolizer also allows you to draw labels, combining text with an image. We will look at the ShieldSymbolizer in the section on drawing points.

TextSymbolizer

The TextSymbolizer allows you to draw text onto point, line and polygon features:

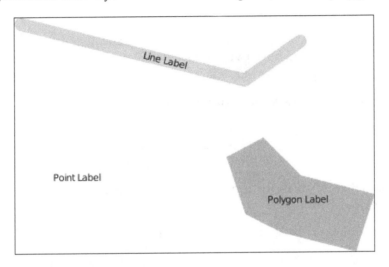

The basic usage of a TextSymbolizer is quite simple. For example, the polygon in the preceding illustration was labeled using the following code:

```
symbolizer = mapnik.TextSymbolizer(
                    mapnik.Expression("[label]"),
                    "DejaVu Sans Book", 10,
                    mapnik.Color("black"))
```

This symbolizer will display the value of the feature's label field using the given font, font size and color. Whenever you create a TextSymbolizer object, you must provide these four parameters.

Let's take a closer look at these parameters, as well as the other options you have for controlling how the text will be displayed.

Specifying the text to be displayed

You select the text to be displayed by passing a `mapnik.Expression` object as the first parameter to the TextSymbolizer's constructor. When creating an Expression, you specify the name of the field or attribute that you want to display. Note that the text to be displayed will always be taken from the underlying data; there is no option for hardwiring a label's text.

> For many data sources the name is case-sensitive, so it is best to ensure that you type in the name of the field or attribute exactly. NAME is not the same as name.

Selecting a suitable font

The label will be drawn using a font and font size you specify when you create the TextSymbolizer object. You have two options for selecting a font: you can use one of the built-in fonts supplied by Mapnik, or you can install your own custom font.

To find out what fonts are available, run the following program:

```
import mapnik
for font in mapnik.FontEngine.face_names():
    print font
```

You can find out more about the process involved in installing a custom font on the following web page:

```
http://trac.mapnik.org/wiki/UsingCustomFonts
```

Note that the font is specified by name, and that the font size is in points.

Drawing semi-transparent text

You can control how opaque or transparent the text is by setting the `opacity` attribute, like this:

```
symbolizer.opacity = 0.5
```

The opacity ranges from 0.0 (completely transparent) to 1.0 (completely opaque).

Controlling text placement

There are two ways in which the TextSymbolizer places text onto the feature being labeled. Using `point` placement (the default), Mapnik would draw labels on the three features shown earlier in the following way:

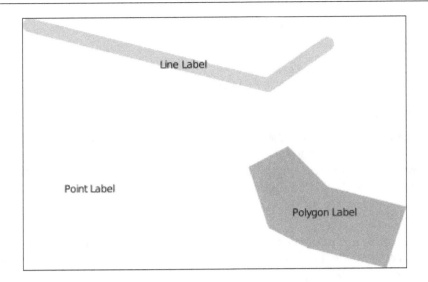

As you can see, the labels are drawn at the center of each feature, and the labels are drawn horizontally with no regard to the orientation of the line. The other option for placing text onto the feature is to use **line placement**. Labeling the preceding features using line placement would result in the following:

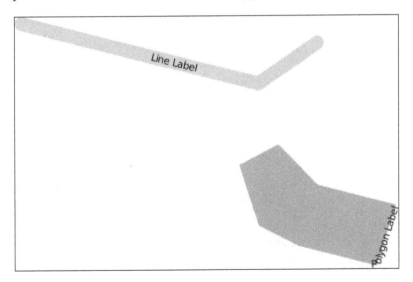

Note that the polygon's label is now drawn along the boundary of the polygon, and the labels now follow the orientation of the line. The point feature isn't labeled at all, since the point feature has no lines within it.

You control the placement of the text by setting the symbolizer's `label_placement` attribute, like this:

```
sym1.label_placement = mapnik.label_placement.POINT_PLACEMENT
sym2.label_placement = mapnik.label_placement.LINE_PLACEMENT
```

Repeating labels

When labels are placed using `LINE_PLACEMENT`, Mapnik will by default draw the label once, in the middle of the line. In many cases, however, it makes sense to have the label repeated along the length of the line. To do this, you set the symbolizer's `label_spacing` attribute, like this:

```
symbolizer.label_spacing = 30
```

Setting this attribute causes the labels to be repeated along the line or polygon boundary. The value is the amount of space between each repeated label, in pixels. Using the preceding label spacing, our line and polygon features would be displayed in the following way:

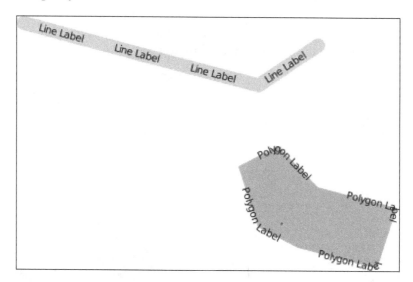

There are several other attributes that can be used to fine-tune the way repeated labels are displayed:

- `symbolizer.force_odd_labels = True`

    This tells the TextSymbolizer to always draw an odd number of labels. This can make the labels look better in some situations.

- `symbolizer.maximum_angle_char_delta = 45`

  This sets the maximum change in angle (measured in degrees) from one character to the next. Using this can prevent Mapnik from drawing labels around sharp corners. For example:

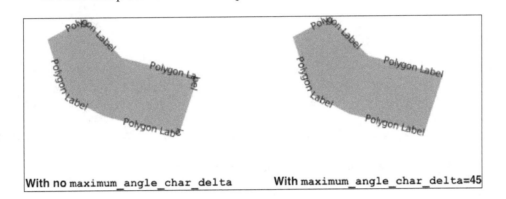

With no `maximum_angle_char_delta`   With `maximum_angle_char_delta=45`

- `symbolizer.minimum_distance = 40`

  The minimum distance between repeated labels, in pixels.

- `symbolizer.label_position_tolerance = 20`

  This sets the maximum distance a label can move along the line to avoid other labels and sharp corners. The value is in pixels, and defaults to `minimum_distance` divided by 2.

Controlling text overlap

By default, Mapnik ensures that two labels will never intersect. If possible, it will move the labels to avoid an overlap. If you look closely at the labels drawn around the boundary of the following two polygons, you will see that the position of the second polygon's labels has been adjusted to avoid an overlap:

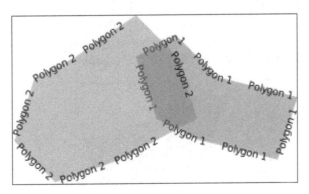

If Mapnik decides that it can't move the label without completely misrepresenting the position of the label, then it will hide the label completely. You can see this in the following illustration, where the two polygons are moved so they overlap:

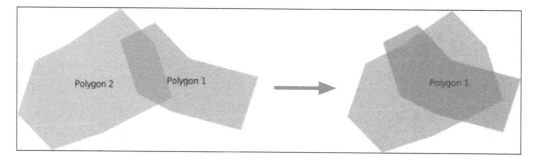

The `allow_overlap` attribute allows you to change this behavior:

```
symbolizer.allow_overlap = True
```

Instead of hiding the overlapping labels, Mapnik will simply draw them one on top of the other:

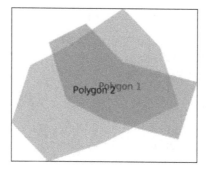

Drawing text on a dark background

The TextSymbolizer will normally draw the text directly onto the map. This works well when the text is placed over a lightly-colored area of the map, but if the underlying area is dark the text can be hard to read or even invisible:

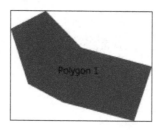

Of course, you could choose a light text color, but that requires you to know in advance what the background is likely to be. A better solution is to draw a "halo" around the text, like this:

The `halo_fill` and `halo_radius` attributes allow you to define the color and size of the halo to draw around the text, like this:

```
symbolizer.halo_fill   = mapnik.Color("white")
symbolizer.halo_radius = 1
```

The radius is specified in pixels; generally a small value such as 1 or 2 is enough to ensure that the text is readable against a dark background.

Adjusting the position of the text

By default, Mapnik calculates the point at which the text should be displayed, and then displays the text centered over that point, like this:

You can adjust this positioning in two ways: by changing the **vertical alignment**, and by specifying a **text displacement**.

The vertical alignment can be controlled by changing the TextSymbolizer's `vertical_alignment` attribute. There are three vertical alignment values you can use:

```
sym1.vertical_alignment = mapnik.vertical_alignment.TOP
sym2.vertical_alignment = mapnik.vertical_alignment.MIDDLE
sym3.vertical_alignment = mapnik.vertical_alignment.BOTTOM
```

`mapnik.vertical_alignment.MIDDLE` is the default, and places the label centered vertically over the point as shown earlier.

If you change the vertical alignment to `mapnik.vertical_alignment.TOP`, the label will be drawn above the point, like this:

Conversely, if you change the vertical alignment to `mapnik.vertical_alignment.BOTTOM`, the label will be drawn below the point:

Your other option for adjusting text positioning is to use the `displacement` attribute to displace the text by a given number of pixels. For example:

```
symbolizer.displacement = (5, 10)
```

This will shift the label five pixels to the right and ten pixels down from its normal position:

Beware

Changing the vertical displacement of a label will also change the label's default `vertical_alignment` value. This can result in your label being moved in unexpected ways, because the vertical alignment of the label is changed as a side-effect of setting the vertical displacement. To avoid this, you should always set the `vertical_alignment` attribute explicitly whenever you change the vertical displacement.

Splitting labels across multiple lines

Sometimes a label is too long to be displayed in the way that you might like:

In this case, you can use the `wrap_width` attribute to force the label to wrap across multiple lines. For example:

```
symbolizer.wrap_width = 70
```

This will cause the preceding label to be displayed like this:

The value you specify is the maximum width of each line of text, in pixels.

Controlling character and line spacing

You can add extra space between each character in a label by setting the `character_spacing` attribute, like this:

```
symbolizer.character_spacing = 3
```

This results in our polygon being labeled like this:

You can also change the spacing between the various lines using the `line_spacing` attribute:

```
symbolizer.line_spacing = 8
```

Our polygon will then look like this:

Both the character spacing and the line spacing values are in pixels.

Controlling capitalization

There are times when you might want to change the case of the text being displayed. You can do this by setting the `text_transform` attribute, like this:

```
symbolizer1.text_transform = mapnik.text_transform.uppercase
symbolizer2.text_transform = mapnik.text_transform.lowercase
```

These two settings will result in the labels being displayed as follows:

Advanced text placement and formatting

If the preceding labeling options aren't enough, you can make use of some amazing new features in Mapnik 2.1 that give you almost infinite control over how your labels are placed and formatted. The `symbolizer.placements.defaults.format_tree` attribute lets you define your own formatting options. For example:

```
format1 = mapnik.FormattingText("[name]")
format1.format.face_name = "DejaVu Sans Book"
format1.format.size = 10

format2 = mapnik.FormattingText("[abbreviation]")
format2.format.face_name = "DejaVu Sans Book"
format2.format.size = 9

formats = mapnik.FormattingList([format1, format2])
textSymbolizer.placements.defaults.format_tree = formats
```

This code sets up two separate formatters, one displaying the `name` attribute in 10 point text, while the second displays the `abbreviation` attribute in 9 point text. When the text symbolizer is set up to use a `FormattingList` object, each of the formats will be tried in turn until a format is found that fits in the available space.

This has the effect of displaying the `name` attribute if there is room, but switching to the `abbreviation` attribute (in a smaller text size) if the name won't fit. The end result would look something like this:

Formatting lists are only one possible way in which the format tree can be used. You can even create your own custom subclass of `mapnik.FormattingNode` and manually calculate the label (and its associated formatting) as each feature is rendered.

To see how these advanced formatting options can be used from within Python, check out the `tests/visual_tests/test_python.py` file in the Mapnik source code.

Drawing points

There are two ways of drawing a point using Mapnik: the PointSymbolizer allows you to draw an image at a given point, and the ShieldSymbolizer combines an image with a textual label to produce a "shield".

Let's examine how each of these two symbolizers work.

PointSymbolizer

A PointSymbolizer draws an image at the point. The default constructor takes no arguments and displays each point as a 4 x 4 pixel black square:

```
symbolizer = PointSymbolizer()
```

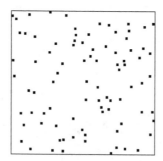

Alternatively, you can supply a path to an image file which the PointSymbolizer will use to draw each point:

```
path = mapnik.PathExpression("path/to/image.png")
symbolizer = PointSymbolizer(path)
```

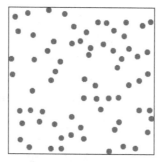

 Be aware that the PointSymbolizer draws the image centered over the desired point. You may have to add transparent space around the image so that the desired part of the image appears over the desired point. For example, if you wish to draw a pin at an exact position, you might need to format the image like this:

The extra (transparent) whitespace ensures that the point of the pin is in the center of the image, allowing the image to be drawn exactly at the desired position on the map.

Whether you supply an image or not, the PointSymbolizer has some attributes, which you can use to modify its behavior:

- `symbolizer.allow_overlap = True`

  If you set this attribute to `True`, all points will be drawn even if the images overlap. The default (`False`) means that points will only be drawn if they don't overlap.

- `symbolizer.opacity = 0.75`

  This attribute controls the amount of opaqueness or transparency used to draw the image. A value of 0.0 will draw the image completely transparent, while a value of 1.0 (the default) will draw the image completely opaque.

- `symbolizer.transform = "..."`

  An SVG transformation expression which you can use to manipulate the image to be displayed. For example, `transform="rotate(45) scale(0.5, 0.5)"` will rotate the image clockwise by 45 degrees and then scale it to 50 percent of its original size.

ShieldSymbolizer

A ShieldSymbolizer draws a textual label and an associated image:

The ShieldSymbolizer works in exactly the same way as having a TextSymbolizer and a PointSymbolizer rendering the same data. The only difference is that the ShieldSymbolizer ensures that the text and image are always displayed together; you'll never get the text without the image, or vice versa.

When you create a ShieldSymbolizer, you have to provide a number of parameters:

```
symbolizer = mapnik.ShieldSymbolizer(fieldExpression,
                                     font, fontSize, color,
                                     imagePath)
```

Following are the components of the preceding code:

- `fieldExpression` is a Mapnik Expression object specifying the field or attribute to display as the textual label
- `font` is the name of the font to use when drawing the text
- `fontSize` of the size of the text, in points
- `color` is a Mapnik Color object that defines the color to use for drawing the text
- `imagePath` is a Mapnik PathExpression object that holds the path to the desired image file

Because ShieldSymbolizer is a subclass of TextSymbolizer, all the positioning and formatting options available for a TextSymbolizer can also be applied to a ShieldSymbolizer. And because it also draws an image, a ShieldSymbolizer also has the `allow_overlap` and `opacity` attributes of a PointSymbolizer.

 To set the opacity of the ShieldSymbolizer's text, use the `text_opacity` attribute.

Be aware that you will most probably need to set the ShieldSymbolizer's `displacement` attribute to position the text correctly, as by default the text appears directly over the point, at the center of the image.

Drawing raster images

The GDAL and Raster data sources allow you to include raster images within a map. The RasterSymbolizer takes this raster data and displays it within a map layer, like this:

Creating a RasterSymbolizer is very simple:

```
symbolizer = mapnik.RasterSymbolizer()
```

A RasterSymbolizer draws the contents of the layer's raster-format data source onto the map. The RasterSymbolizer supports the following options for controlling how the raster data is displayed:

- `symbolizer.opacity = 0.5`

  This controls how opaque the raster image will be. A value of 0.0 makes the image fully transparent, and a value of 1.0 makes it fully opaque. By default, the raster image will be completely opaque.

- `symbolizer.comp_op = mapnik.CompositeOp.hard_light`

  This attribute tells the RasterSymbolizer how to merge the raster data with the previously-rendered map data beneath it. These "compositing" operations are similar to the way layers are merged in image editing programs such as Photoshop or the GIMP. The following compositing operations are supported:

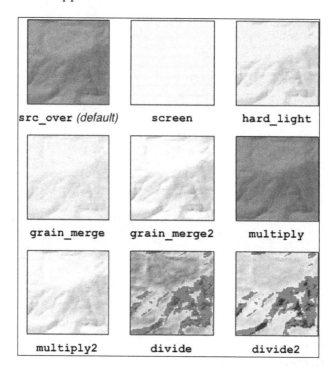

- `symbolizer.scaling = mapnik.scaling_method.bilinear`

  This allows you to control the algorithm used to scale the raster image data. The available options are: `near` (uses the nearest-neighbor algorithm), `bilinear` (uses bilinear interpolation across all four color channels), and `bilinear8` (uses bilinear interpolation for just a single color channel).

- `symbolizer.colorizer = myRasterColorizer`

  This lets you apply a custom palette to the raw raster data, for example to change the coloring of a DEM file. For information on how to set up a raster colorizer in Python, see the documentation for the `RasterColorizer` class on the Mapnik website.

Note that Mapnik does not support on-the-fly reprojection of raster data. If you need to generate a map using a projection that is different from the raster data's projection, you will need to reproject the raster data before it can be displayed, for example by using gdalwarp.

One of the main uses for a RasterSymbolizer is to display a *shaded relief* background such as the one shown earlier. This gives the viewer a good impression of the underlying terrain.

The preceding image was created using a Digital Elevation Map (DEM-format) data file taken from the National Elevation Dataset. This file was processed using the gdaldem utility with the hillshade option to create a shaded relief grayscale image. This image was then displayed using a RasterSymbolizer set to hard_light mode, laid on top of a pale green background with the coastline defined from the GSHHS shoreline database. You may find this process useful if you want to display a shaded relief image as a background for your map.

Using colors

Many of the Mapnik symbolizers require you to supply a color value. These color values are defined using the mapnik.Color class. Instances of mapnik.Color can be created in one of four ways:

- mapnik.Color(r, g, b, a)

  Creates a Color object by supplying separate red, green, blue, and alpha (opacity) values. Each of these values should be in the range 0 to 255.

- mapnik.Color(r, g, b)

  Creates a Color object by supplying red, green, and blue components. Each value should be in the range 0 to 255. The resulting object will be completely opaque.

- mapnik.Color(colorName)

  Creates a Color object by specifying a standard CSS color name. A complete list of the available color names can be found at: http://www.w3.org/TR/css3-color/#svg-color.

- `mapnik.Color(colorCode)`

    Creates a `Color` object using an HTML color code, for example "#806040" is medium brown.

Maps and layers

Once you have set up your data sources, symbolizers, rules and styles, you can combine them into Mapnik layers and place the various layers together onto a map. To do this, you first create a `mapnik.Map` object to represent the map as a whole:

```
map = mapnik.Map(width, height, srs)
```

You supply the width and height of the map image you want to generate, in pixels, and an optional Proj.4-format initialization string in `srs`. If you do not specify a spatial reference system, the map will use "+proj=latlong +datum=WGS84" (unprojected lat/long coordinates on the WGS84 datum).

After creating the map, you set the map's background color, and add your various styles to the map by calling the `map.append_style()` method:

```
map.background_color = mapnik.Color('white')

map.append_style("countryStyle", countryStyle)
map.append_style("roadStyle", roadStyle)
map.append_style("pointStyle", pointStyle)
map.append_style("rasterStyle", rasterStyle)
...
```

 As well as specifying the background color to use for your map, you can also use a background image by setting the map's `background_image` attribute. Note that this currently accepts a string value, rather than a Mapnik PathExpression, though this may change in the future.

You next need to create the various layers within the map. To do this, you create a `mapnik.Layer` object to represent each map layer:

```
layer = mapnik.Layer(layerName, srs)
```

Each layer is given a unique name, and can optionally have a spatial reference associated with it. The `srs` string is a Proj.4 format initialization string; if no spatial reference is given, the layer will use "+proj=latlong +datum=WGS84".

Once you have created your map layer, you assign it a `datasource` and choose the style(s) which will apply to that layer, identifying each style by name:

```
layer.datasource = myDatasource

layer.styles.append("countryStyle")
layer.styles.append("rasterStyle")
...
```

Finally, you add your new layer to the map:

```
map.layers.append(layer)
```

Let's take a closer look at some of the optional methods and attributes of the Mapnik `Map` and `Layer` objects. These can be useful when manipulating map layers, and for setting up rules and layers which are selectively applied based on the map's current scale factor.

Map attributes and methods

The `mapnik.Map` class provides several additional methods and attributes which you may find useful:

- `map.envelope()`

  This method returns a `mapnik.Box2d` object representing the area of the map that is to be displayed. The `mapnik.Box2d` object supports a number of useful methods and attributes, but most importantly includes `minx`, `miny`, `maxx`, and `maxy` attributes. These define the map's bounding box in map coordinates.

- `map.aspect_fix_mode = mapnik.aspect_fix.GROW_CANVAS`

  This controls how Mapnik adjusts the map if the aspect ratio of the map's bounds does not match the aspect ratio of the rendered map image. The following values are supported:

  - `GROW_BBOX` expands the map's bounding box to match the aspect ratio of the generated image. This is the default behavior.
  - `GROW_CANVAS` expands the generated image to match the aspect ratio of the bounding box.
  - `SHRINK_BBOX` shrinks the map's bounding box to match the aspect ratio of the generated image.
  - `SHRINK_CANVAS` shrinks the generated image to match the aspect ratio of the map's bounding box.

- ° `ADJUST_BBOX_HEIGHT` expands or shrinks the height of the map's bounding box, while keeping the width constant, to match the aspect ratio of the generated image.

- ° `ADJUST_BBOX_WIDTH` expands or shrinks the width of the map's bounding box, while keeping the height constant, to match the aspect ratio of the generated image.

- ° `ADJUST_CANVAS_HEIGHT` expands or shrinks the height of the generated image, while keeping the width constant, to match the aspect ratio of the map's bounding box.

- ° `ADJUST_CANVAS_WIDTH` expands or shrinks the width of the generated image, while keeping the height constant, to match the aspect ratio of the map's bounding box.

- `map.scale_denominator()`

  Returns the current scale denominator used to generate the map. The scale denominator depends on the map's bounds and the size of the rendered image.

- `map.scale()`

  Returns the current scale factor used by the map. The scale factor depends on the map's bounds and the size of the rendered image.

- `map.zoom_all()`

  Set the map's bounding box to encompass the bounding box of each of the map's layers. This ensures that all the map data will appear on the map.

- `map.zoom_to_box(mapnik.Box2d(minX, minY, maxX, maxY))`

  Set the map's bounding box to the given values. Note that `minX`, `minY`, `maxX`, and `maxY` are all in the map's coordinate system.

Layer attributes and methods

The `mapnik.Layer` class has the following useful attributes and methods:

- `layer.envelope()`

  This method returns a `mapnik.Box2d` object representing the rectangular area of the map that encompasses all the layer's data. This object has `minx`, `miny`, `maxx`, and `maxy` attributes that hold the coordinates for the layer's bounding box.

- `layer.active = False`

  This can be used to hide a layer within the map.

- `layer.minzoom = 1.0/100000`

  This sets the minimum scale factor which must apply if the layer is to appear within the map. If this is not set, the layer will not have a minimum scale factor.

- `layer.maxzoom = 1.0/10000`

  This sets the maximum scale factor that must apply if the layer is to be drawn onto the map. If this is not set, the layer will not have a maximum scale factor.

- `layer.visible(1.0/50000)`

  This method returns true if this layer will appear on the map at the given scale factor. The layer is visible if it is active and the given scale factor is between the specified minimum and maximum values.

Map rendering

After creating your `mapnik.Map` object and setting up the various symbolizers, rules, styles, data sources, and layers within it, you are finally ready to convert your map into a rendered image.

Before rendering the map image, make sure that you have set the appropriate bounding box for the map so that the map will show the area of the world you are interested in. You can do this by either calling `map.zoom_to_box()` to explicitly set the map's bounding box to a given set of coordinates, or you can call `map.zoom_all()` to have the map automatically set its bounds based on the data to be displayed.

Once you have set the bounding box, you can generate your map image by calling the `render_to_file()` function, like this:

```
mapnik.render_to_file(map, 'map.png')
```

The parameters are the `mapnik.Map` object and the name of the image file to write the map to. If you want more control over the format of the image, you can add an extra parameter, which defines the image format, like this:

```
mapnik.render_to_file(map, 'map.png', 'png256')
```

The supported image formats include the following:

Image format	Description
png	A 32-bit PNG format image
png256	An 8-bit PNG format image
jpeg	A JPEG-format image
svc	An SVG-format image
pdf	A PDF file
ps	A postscript format file

The `render_to_file()` function works well when you want to generate a single image from your entire map. Another useful way of rendering maps is to generate a number of "tiles" which can then be stitched together to display the map at a higher resolution:

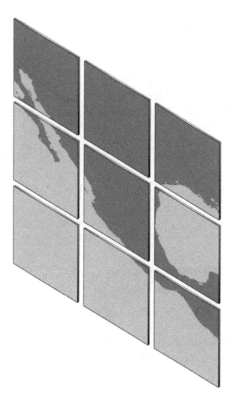

Mapnik provides a helpful function for creating tiles like this out of a single map:

```
def render_tile_to_file(map, xOffset, yOffset, width, height,
                        fileName, format)
```

The parameters to this function are as follows:

- `map` is the `mapnik.Map` object containing the map data
- `xOffset` and `yOffset` define the top-left corner of the tile, in map coordinates
- `width` and `height` define the size of the tile, in map coordinates
- `fileName` is the name of the file to save the tiled image into
- `format` is the file format to use for saving this tile

You can simply call this function repeatedly to create the individual tiles for your map. For example:

```
for x in range(NUM_TILES_ACROSS):
    for y in range(NUM_TILES_DOWN):
        xOffset = TILE_SIZE * x
        yOffset = TILE_SIZE * y
        tileName = "tile_%d_%d.png" % (x, y)
        mapnik.render_tile_to_file(map, xOffset, yOffset,
                                   TILE_SIZE, TILE_SIZE,
                                   tileName, "png")
```

Another way of rendering a map is to use a `Mapnik.Image` object to hold the rendered map data in memory. You can then extract the raw image data from the `Image` object, like this:

```
image = mapnik.Image(MAP_WIDTH, MAP_HEIGHT)
mapnik.render(map, image)
imageData = image.tostring('png')
```

MapGenerator revisited

Now that we have examined the Python interface to Mapnik, let's use this knowledge to take a closer look at the `mapGenerator.py` module used in *Chapter 7, Working with Spatial Data*. As well as being a more comprehensive example of creating maps programmatically, the `mapGenerator.py` module suggests ways in which you can write your own wrapper around Mapnik to simplify the creation of a map using Python code.

The MapGenerator interface

The mapGenerator.py module defines just one function, generateMap(), which allows you to create a simple map which is stored in a temporary file on disk. The method signature for the generateMap() function looks like this:

```
def generateMap(datasource, minX, minY, maxX, maxY,
                mapWidth, mapHeight,
                hiliteExpr=None, background="#8080a0",
                hiliteLine="#000000", hiliteFill="#408000",
                normalLine="#404040", normalFill="#a0a0a0",
                points=None)
```

The parameters are as follows:

- datasource is a dictionary defining the data source to use for this map. This dictionary should have at least one entry, type, which defines the type of data source. The following data source types are supported: "OGR", "PostGIS" and "SQLite". Any additional entries in this dictionary will be passed as keyword parameters to the data source initializer.

- minX, minY, maxX, and maxY define the bounding box for the area to display, in map coordinates.

- mapWidth and mapHeight are the width and height of the image to generate, in pixels.

- hiliteExpr is a Mapnik filter expression to use to identify the feature(s) to be highlighted.

- background is the HTML color code to use for the background of the map.

- hiliteLine and hiliteFill are the HTML color codes to use for the line and fill for the highlighted features.

- normalLine and normalFill are the HTML color codes to use for the line and fill for the non-highlighted features.

- points, if defined, should be a list of (long, lat, name) tuples identifying points to display on the map.

Because many of these keyword parameters have default values, creating a simple map only requires the data source, bounding box, and map dimensions to be specified. Everything else is optional.

The generateMap() function creates a new map based on the given parameters, and stores the result as a PNG format image file in a temporary map cache directory. Upon completion, it returns the name and relative path to the newly-rendered image file.

So much for the public interface to the `mapGenerator.py` module. Let's take a look inside to see how it works.

Creating the main map layer

The module starts by creating a `mapnik.Map` object to hold the generated map. We set the background color at the same time:

```
map = mapnik.Map(mapWidth, mapHeight,
                 '+proj=longlat +datum=WGS84')
map.background_color = mapnik.Color(background)
```

We next have to set up the Mapnik data source to load our map data from. To simplify the job of accessing a data source, the `datasource` parameter includes the type of data source, as well as any additional entries which are passed as keyword parameters directly to the Mapnik data source initializer:

```
srcType = datasource['type']
del datasource['type']

if srcType == "OGR":
    source = mapnik.Ogr(**datasource)
elif srcType == "PostGIS":
    source = mapnik.PostGIS(**datasource)
elif srcType == "SQLite":
    source = mapnik.SQLite(**datasource)
```

We then create our Layer object, and start defining the style, which is used to draw the map data onto the map:

```
layer = mapnik.Layer("Layer")
layer.datasource = source

style = mapnik.Style()
```

We next set up a rule that only applies to the highlighted features:

```
rule = mapnik.Rule()
if hiliteExpr != None:
    rule.filter = mapnik.Filter(hiliteExpr)
```

This rule will use the "highlight" line and fill colors:

```
rule.symbols.append(mapnik.PolygonSymbolizer(
    mapnik.Color(hiliteFill)))
rule.symbols.append(mapnik.LineSymbolizer(
    mapnik.Stroke(mapnik.Color(hiliteLine), 0.1)))
```

We then add this rule to the style, and create another rule that only applies to the non-highlighted features:

```
style.rules.append(rule)

rule = mapnik.Rule()
rule.set_else(True)
```

This rule will use the "normal" line and fill colors:

```
rule.symbols.append(mapnik.PolygonSymbolizer(
    mapnik.Color(normalFill)))
rule.symbols.append(mapnik.LineSymbolizer(
    mapnik.Stroke(mapnik.Color(normalLine), 0.1)))
```

We then add this rule to the style, and add the style to the map and layer:

```
style.rules.append(rule)

map.append_style("Map Style", style)
layer.styles.append("Map Style")
```

Finally, the layer is added to the map:

```
map.layers.append(layer)
```

Displaying points on the map

One of the features of the `generateMap()` function is that it can take a list of points and display them directly onto the map without having to store those points into a database. This is done through the use of a MemoryDataSource data source and a ShieldSymbolizer to draw the points onto the map:

```
if points != None:
    memoryDatasource = mapnik.MemoryDatasource()
    context = mapnik.Context()
    context.push("name")
    next_id = 1
    for long,lat,name in points:
        wkt = "POINT (%0.8f %0.8f)" % (long,lat)
        feature = mapnik.Feature(context, next_id)
        feature['name'] = name
        feature.add_geometries_from_wkt(wkt)
        next_id = next_id + 1
        memoryDatasource.add_feature(feature)
```

```
layer = mapnik.Layer("Points")
layer.datasource = memoryDatasource

style = mapnik.Style()
rule = mapnik.Rule()

pointImgFile = os.path.join(os.path.dirname(__file__),
                            "point.png")

shield = mapnik.ShieldSymbolizer(
            mapnik.Expression('[name]'),
            "DejaVu Sans Bold", 10,
            mapnik.Color("#000000"),
            mapnik.PathExpression(pointImgFile))
shield.displacement = (0, 7)
shield.unlock_image = True
rule.symbols.append(shield)

style.rules.append(rule)

map.append_style("Point Style", style)
layer.styles.append("Point Style")

map.layers.append(layer)
```

> Note that the path to the point.png file is calculated as an absolute path, based on the location of the mapGenerator.py module itself (via the __file__ global). This is done because the module can be called as part of a CGI script, and CGI scripts do not have a current working directory.

Rendering the map

Because the mapGenerator.py module is designed to be used within a CGI script, the module makes use of a temporary map cache to hold the generated image files. Before it can render the map image, the generateMap() function has to create the map cache if it doesn't already exist, and create a temporary file within the cache directory to hold the generated map:

```
scriptDir = os.path.dirname(__file__)
cacheDir = os.path.join(scriptDir, "..", "mapCache")
```

```
if not os.path.exists(cacheDir):
    os.mkdir(cacheDir)
fd,filename = tempfile.mkstemp(".png", dir=cacheDir)
os.close(fd)
```

Finally, we are ready to render the map into an image file, and return back to the caller the relative path to the generated map file:

```
map.zoom_to_box(mapnik.Box2d(minX, minY, maxX, maxY))
mapnik.render_to_file(map, filename, "png")

return "../mapCache/" + os.path.basename(filename)
```

What the map generator teaches us

While in many ways the `mapGenerator.py` module is quite simplistic and designed specifically to meet the needs of the DISTAL application presented in the previous chapter, it is worth examining this module in depth because it shows how the principle of *encapsulation* can be used to hide Mapnik's complexity and simplify the process of map generation. Using the `generateMap()` function is infinitely easier than creating all the data sources, layers, symbolizers, rules, and styles each time a map has to be generated.

It would be a relatively easy task to design a more generic map generator that could handle a variety of data sources and map layers, as well as various ways of returning the results, without having to exhaustively define every object by hand. Designing and implementing such a module would be very worthwhile if you want to use Mapnik extensively from your Python programs. Hopefully this section has given you some ideas about how you can proceed with implementing your own high-level Mapnik wrapper module.

Map definition files

There is one final approach to using Mapnik that is worth examining. In addition to creating your symbolizers, rules, styles, and layers programmatically, Mapnik allows you to store all of this information using a **map definition** file. This is an XML-format file that defines the various Mapnik objects used to generate a map. For example, consider the following Python program to create a simple world map using the World Borders Dataset:

```
import mapnik

map = mapnik.Map(800, 400)
```

```
map.background = mapnik.Color("steelblue")

style = mapnik.Style()
rule = mapnik.Rule()
polySymbolizer = mapnik.PolygonSymbolizer()
polySymbolizer.fill = mapnik.Color("ghostwhite")

stroke = mapnik.Stroke()
stroke.color = mapnik.Color("gray")
stroke.width = 0.1
lineSymbolizer = mapnik.LineSymbolizer(stroke)

rule.symbols.append(polySymbolizer)
rule.symbols.append(lineSymbolizer)
style.rules.append(rule)
map.append_style("My Style", style)

datasource = mapnik.Shapefile(file="TM_WORLD_BORDERS-0.3/" +
                              "TM_WORLD_BORDERS-0.3.shp")

layer = mapnik.Layer("layer")
layer.datasource = datasource
layer.styles.append("My Style")

map.layers.append(layer)

map.zoom_to_box(mapnik.Box2d(-180, -90, +180, +90))
mapnik.render_to_file(map, "map.png")
```

As you can see, this program creates a single rule containing two symbolizers:
a PolygonSymbolizer to draw the interior of the country in the color named
"ghostwhite", and a LineSymbolizer to draw the outlines in gray. This rule is
added to a style named "My Style", and a single layer is created loading the data
from the World Borders Dataset shapefile. Finally, the map is rendered to a file
named map.png.

Here is what the resulting map looks like:

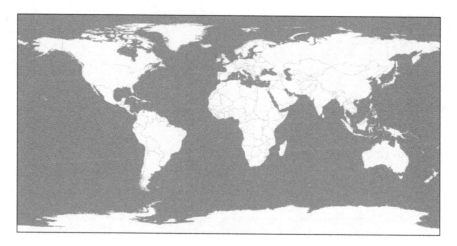

This program was written entirely using Python code. Now, consider the following map definition file, which creates exactly the same map using an XML stylesheet:

```
<?xml version="1.0" encoding="utf-8"?>
<!DOCTYPE Map>

<Map background-color="steelblue"
     srs="+proj=latlong +datum=WGS84">
  <Style name="My Style">
    <Rule>
      <PolygonSymbolizer fill="ghostwhite"/>
      <LineSymbolizer stroke="gray" stroke-width="0.1"/>
    </Rule>
  </Style>

  <Layer name="world" srs="+proj=latlong +datum=WGS84">
    <StyleName>My Style</StyleName>
    <Datasource>
      <Parameter name="type">shape</Parameter>
      <Parameter name="file">TM_WORLD_BORDERS-0.3/ TM_WORLD_BORDERS-
0.3.shp</Parameter>
    </Datasource>
  </Layer>
</Map>
```

To use this stylesheet, you call the `load_map()` function to load the contents of the map definition file into a mapnik `Map` object before rendering it, like this:

```
map = mapnik.Map(800, 400)
mapnik.load_map(map, "mapDefinition.xml")
map.zoom_to_box(mapnik.Box2d(-180, -90, +180, +90))
mapnik.render_to_file(map, "map.png")
```

Which approach you take is up to you. You may prefer to do all your coding in Python (with or without a wrapper module), or you might like the more compact XML stylesheet definition. With only a few exceptions, anything you can do in Python can be done with the XML stylesheets, and vice versa.

Unlike the Python bindings, the format for the XML definition file is thoroughly documented. More information on the syntax of the map definition file can be found at:

```
http://trac.mapnik.org/wiki/XMLConfigReference
```

You don't have to choose between doing all your map definition in XML or doing it all in Python; Mapnik supports a hybrid approach where you can define as much or as little in the XML file, and use Python to do the rest. For example, you might like to define your Mapnik styles in the XML file, and use Python to define the data sources and map layers. To do this, you would set up your map definition file like this:

```
<?xml version="1.0" encoding="utf-8"?>
<!DOCTYPE Map>

<Map background-color="steelblue"
     srs="+proj=latlong +datum=WGS84">
  <Style name="My Style">
    <Rule>
      <PolygonSymbolizer fill="ghostwhite"/>
      <LineSymbolizer stroke="gray" stroke-width="0.1"/>
    </Rule>
  </Style>
</Map>
```

Your Python code would then look like this:

```
import mapnik

map = mapnik.Map(800, 400)
mapnik.load_map(map, "sampleXMLStylesheet.xml")
```

```
datasource = mapnik.Shapefile(file="TM_WORLD_BORDERS-0.3/" +
                              "TM_WORLD_BORDERS-0.3.shp")

layer = mapnik.Layer("layer")
layer.datasource = datasource
layer.styles.append("My Style")

map.layers.append(layer)

map.zoom_to_box(mapnik.Box2d(-180, -90, +180, +90))
mapnik.render_to_file(map, "map.png")
```

Note how we simply exclude the `<Style>` section from the XML file, and then create our map layers using Python.

This hybrid approach has the advantage of separating out the visual representation of the map from the code used to generate it. The XML file defines the various styles to use for rendering the map but doesn't include any map-generation logic itself. Indeed, you can completely change the appearance of the map just by changing the XML stylesheet, without having to change a single line of code in your program. This is very similar to the way HTML templating engines separate form and function within a web application.

Summary

In this chapter, we have explored the Mapnik map-generation toolkit in depth. We learned the following:

- Mapnik is a powerful and flexible toolkit for generating a variety of maps

- Mapnik uses the painter's algorithm to draw the various parts of a map in the correct order

- A map is made up of multiple layers

- Map rendering is controlled using styles

- Styles are defined within the map and are referred to by the layers, allowing styles to be shared between map layers

- Each style consists of one or more rules

- Each rule has a list of symbolizers, telling Mapnik how to draw the layer's features onto the map, and an optional filter which selects the features the rule applies to

- You can use a map definition file as a simpler way of creating maps without having to define all the symbolizers, filters, rules, styles, and layers in Python

- You can use a map definition file as a stylesheet, separating the logic of building a map from the way it is formatted, in the same way that an HTML templating engine separates form and content in a web application

In the next chapter, we will start to build a complete mapping application using PostGIS, Mapnik, and GeoDjango.

9

Putting It All Together – a Complete Mapping System

In the final three chapters of this book, we will bring together all the topics discussed in previous chapters to implement a sophisticated web-based mapping application called **ShapeEditor**.

In this chapter, we will cover the following:

- Designing a geospatial system, and then translating that design into code
- Structuring of Django-based web applications
- Setting up a new Django project and its applications
- Learn how Django represents data structures as objects
- Using GeoDjango's built-in "admin" application to view and edit geospatial data

About ShapeEditor

As we have seen, shapefiles are commonly used to store, make available, and transfer geospatial data. We have worked with shapefiles extensively in this book, obtaining freely-available geospatial data in shapefile format, writing programs to load data from a shapefile, and creating shapefiles programmatically.

While it is easy enough to edit the attributes associated with a shapefile's features, editing the features themselves is a lot more complicated. One approach would be to install a GIS system and use it to import the data, make changes, and then export the data into another shapefile. While this works, it is hardly convenient if all you want to do is make a few changes to a shapefile's features. It would be much easier if we had a web application specifically designed for editing shapefiles.

This is precisely what we are going to implement: a web-based shapefile editor. Rather unimaginatively, we'll call this program ShapeEditor.

The following flowchart depicts the ShapeEditor's basic workflow:

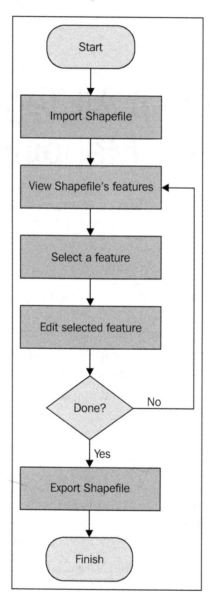

The user starts by importing a shapefile using the ShapeEditor's web interface:

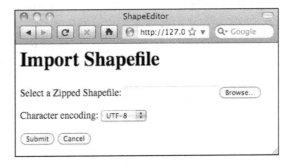

 Our ShapeEditor implementation wasn't chosen for its good looks; instead, it concentrates on getting the features working. It would be easy to add stylesheets and edit the HTML templates to improve the appearance of the application, but doing so would make the code harder to understand. This is why we've taken such a minimalist approach to the user interface. Making it pretty is an exercise left to the reader.

Once the shapefile has been imported, the user can view the shapefile's features on a map, and can select a feature by clicking on it. In this case, we have imported the World Borders Dataset used several times throughout this book:

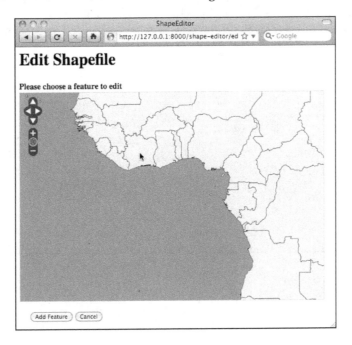

The user can then edit the selected feature's geometry, as well as see a list of the attributes associated with that feature:

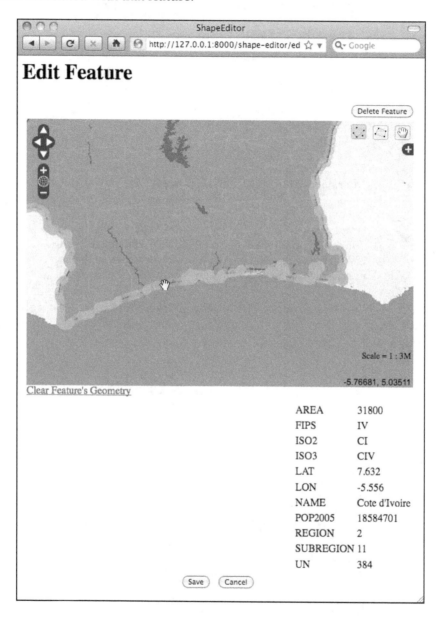

Once the user has finished making changes to the shapefile, he or she can export the shapefile again by clicking on the **Export** hyperlink on the main page:

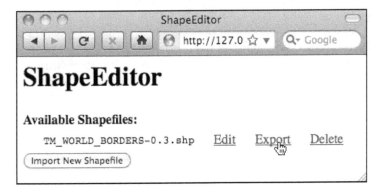

That pretty much covers the ShapeEditor's functionality. It's a comparatively simple system, but it can be very useful if you need to work with geospatial data in shapefile format. And, of course, through the process of implementing the ShapeEditor you will learn how to go about implementing your own complex geospatial web applications using GeoDjango.

Designing ShapeEditor

Let's take a closer look at the various parts of the ShapeEditor, to see what's involved in implementing it. The ShapeEditor is going to support the following activities:

- Importing the geometrical features and attributes from a shapefile
- Allowing the user to select a feature to be edited
- Displaying the appropriate type of editor to allow the user to edit the feature's geometry
- Exporting the geometrical features and attributes back into a shapefile

Let's take a closer look at each of these user activities, to see how they will be implemented within the ShapeEditor system.

Importing a shapefile

When the user imports a shapefile, we have to store the contents of that shapefile in the database so that GeoDjango can work with it. Because we don't know in advance what types of geometries the shapefile will contain, or what attributes might be associated with each feature, we need to have a generic representation of a shapefile's contents in the database rather than defining separate fields in the database for each of the shapefile's attributes.To support this, we'll use the following collection of database objects:

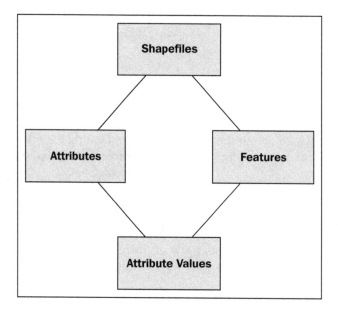

Each imported shapefile will be represented by a single Shapefile object in the database. Each Shapefile object will have a set of Attribute objects, which define the name and data type for each attribute within the shapefile. The Shapefile object will also have a set of Feature objects, one for each imported feature. The Feature object will hold the feature's geometry, and will in turn have a set of AttributeValue objects, holding the value of each attribute for that feature.

To see how this works, let's imagine that we import the World Borders Dataset into the ShapeEditor. The contents of this shapefile would be stored in the database in the following way:

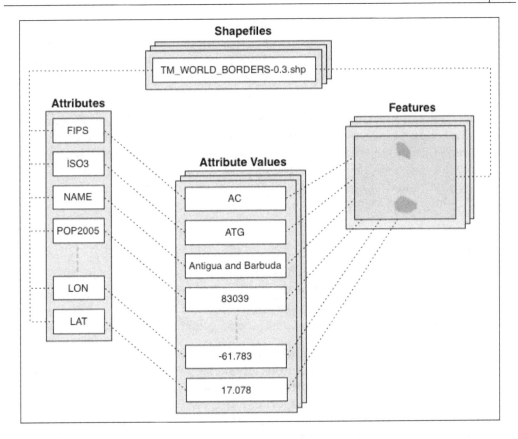

We will use a `Shapefile` object to represent the uploaded shapefile. This object will have a number of `Attribute` objects associated with it, one for each of the shapefile's attributes. There are also a number of `Feature` objects associated with the shapefile; the MultiPolygon geometry for each feature will be stored in the `Feature` object itself, while the attributes for each feature will be stored in a series of `AttributeValue` objects.

While this is a somewhat roundabout way of storing shapefile data in a database (it would be more common to use the `ogrinspect` management command to create a static GeoDjango model out of the shapefile's features and attributes), we have to do it this way because we don't know the shapefile's structure ahead of time, and don't want to have to define a new database table whenever a shapefile is imported.

With this basic model in place to represent a shapefile's data in the database, we can continue designing the rest of the "Import Shapefile" logic.

Because shapefiles are represented on disk by a number of separate files, we will expect the user to create a ZIP archive out of the shapefile and upload the zipped shapefile. This saves us having to handle multiple file uploads for a single shapefile, and makes things more convenient for the user as shapefiles often come in ZIP format already.

Once the ZIP archive has been uploaded, our code will need to decompress the archive and extract the individual files that make up the shapefile. We'll then have to read through the shapefile to find its attributes, create the appropriate `Attribute` objects, and then process the shapefile's features one at a time, creating `Feature` and `AttributeValue` objects as we go. All of this will be quite straightforward to implement.

Selecting a feature

Before the user can edit a feature, we have to let the user select that feature. Unfortunately, GeoDjango's build-in slippy map interface won't allow us to select a feature by clicking on it. This is because GeoDjango can only display a single feature on a map at once, thanks to the way GeoDjango's geometry fields are implemented.

The usual way a GeoDjango application allows you to select a feature is by displaying a list of attributes (for example, city names) and then allowing the user to choose a feature from that list. Unfortunately, that won't work for us either. Because the ShapeEditor allows the user to import any shapefile, there's no guarantee that the shapefile's attribute values can be used to select a feature. It may be that a shapefile has no attributes at all, or has attributes that mean nothing to the end user — or, conversely has dozens of attributes. There is no way of knowing which attribute to display, or even if there is a suitable attribute that can be used to select a feature. Because of this, we really can't use attributes when selecting the feature to edit.

We're going to take a completely different approach. We will bypass GeoDjango's built-in editor and instead use OpenLayers directly to display a map showing all the features in the imported shapefile. We'll then let the user click on a feature within the map to select it for editing.

Here is how we'll implement this particular feature:

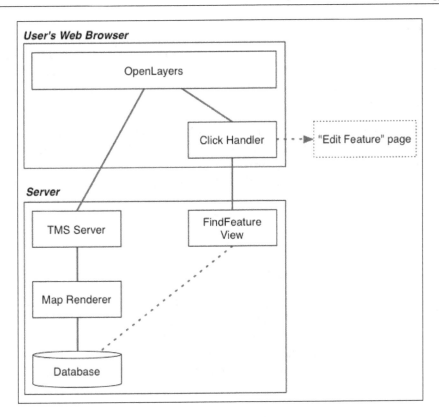

OpenLayers needs to have a source of map tiles to display, so we'll create our own simple **Tile Map Server** (**TMS**) built on top of a Mapnik-based map renderer to display the shapefile's features stored in the database. We'll also write a simple "click handler" in JavaScript that intercepts clicks on the map and sends off an AJAX request to the server to see which feature the user clicked on. If the user does click on a feature (rather than just clicking on the map's background), the user's web browser will be redirected to the "Edit Feature" page so that the user can edit the clicked-on feature.

There's a lot here, requiring a fair amount of custom coding, but the end result is a friendly interface to the ShapeEditor, allowing the user to simply point-and-click at a desired feature to edit it. In the process of building all this, we'll also learn how to use OpenLayers directly within a GeoDjango application, and how to implement our own Tile Map Server built on top of Mapnik.

Editing a feature

To let the user edit the feature, we'll use GeoDjango's built-in geometry editing widget. There is a slight amount of work required here, because we want to use this widget outside of GeoDjango's admin interface and will need to customize the interface slightly.

The only other issue that needs to be dealt with is the fact that we don't know in advance what type of feature we'll be editing. Shapefiles can hold any type of geometry, from Points and LineStrings through to MultiPolygons and GeometryCollections. Fortunately, all the features in a shapefile have to have the same geometry type, so we can store the geometry type in the `Shapefile` object, and use it to select the appropriate type of editor when editing that shapefile's features.

Exporting a shapefile

Exporting a shapefile involves the reverse of the "Import Shapefile" process: we have to create a new shapefile on disk, define the various attributes that will be stored in the shapefile, and then process all the features and their attributes, writing them out to the shapefile. Once this has been done, we can create a ZIP archive from the contents of the shapefile, and tell the user's web browser to download that ZIP archive to the user's hard disk.

Prerequisites

Before you can build the ShapeEditor application, make sure that you have installed the following libraries and tools introduced in *Chapter 3, Python Libraries for Geospatial Development* and *Chapter 6, GIS in the Database*:

- OGR
- Mapnik
- PROJ.4
- pyproj
- PostgreSQL
- PostGIS
- psycopg2

You will also need to download and install Django. Django (`https://djangoproject.com`) comes with GeoDjango built-in, so once you've installed Django itself you're all set to go. Click on the **Download** link on the Django website and download the latest official version of the Django software. We'll be using Django 1.4 for the ShapeEditor.

If your computer runs Microsoft Windows, you may need to download a utility to decompress the `.tar.gz` file before you can use it.

Once you have downloaded it, you can install Django by following the instructions in the Django Installation Guide. This can be found at:

`https://docs.djangoproject.com/en/dev/topics/install`

Once you have installed it, you may want to run through the GeoDjango tutorial (available at `https://docs.djangoproject.com/en/dev/ref/contrib/gis`), though this isn't required to build the ShapeEditor application.

The structure of a Django application

While a complete tutorial on Django is beyond the scope of this book, it is worth spending a few minutes becoming familiar with how Django works. In Django, you start by building a **project** that contains one or more **applications**. Each project has a single database that is shared by the applications within it:

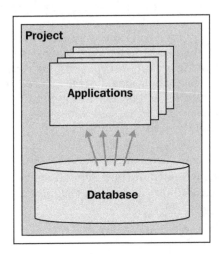

Django comes with a large number of built-in applications that you can include as part of your project, including the following:

- An **authentication** system supporting user accounts, groups, permissions, and authenticated sessions
- An **admin** interface, allowing the user to view and edit data
- A **markup** application supporting lightweight text markup languages including RestructuredText and Markdown
- A **messages** framework for sending and receiving messages
- A **sessions** system for keeping track of anonymous (non-authenticated) sessions
- A **sitemaps** framework for generating site maps
- A **syndication** system for generating RSS and ATOM feeds

The GeoDjango extension is implemented as yet another application within Django that you install when you wish to use it.

Note that applications in Django tend to be fairly small and discrete. Often, an application will implement just one aspect of your system. For example, a complex project may have a `shared` application that defines the shared database tables and commonly-used modules, an `editor` application that allows users to edit data, an `importExport` application that handles importing and exporting, and a `report` application for generating reports. These applications work together to implement the project—for example, the `report` application may make use of data stored in the `shared` application's database models, and the `editor` application may redirect the user to an `importExport` view when they click on the **Import Data** hyperlink.

The project has a **settings** file, which you to use to configure the project as a whole. These settings include a list of the applications you want to include in the project, which database to use, as well as various other project- and application-specific settings.

As we saw in the previous chapter, a Django application has three main components:

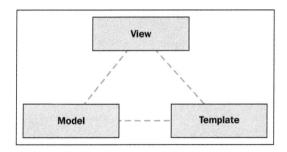

The **models** define your application's data structures, the **views** contain your application's business logic, and the **templates** are used to control how information is presented to the user. These correspond to the data, application, and presentation tiers within a traditional web application stack. Let's take a closer look at each of these in turn.

Models

Because Django provides an object-relational mapper on top of the database, you don't have to deal with SQL directly. Instead, you define a **model** that describes the data you want to store, and Django will automatically map that model onto the database:

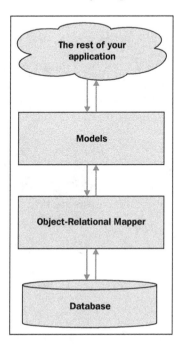

This high-level interface to the database is a major reason why working in Django is so efficient.

 In the ShapeEditor, the database objects we looked at earlier (Shapefile, Attribute, Feature, and AttributeValue) are all models, and will be defined in a file named models.py that holds the ShapeEditor's models.

Views

In Django, a **view** is a Python function which responds when a given URL is called. For example, the ShapeEditor application will respond to the /editFeature URL by allowing the user to edit a feature; the function which handles this URL is called the "edit feature" view, and will be defined like this:

```
def editFeature(request, shapefile_id, feature_id):
```

In general, an application's views will be defined in a Python module named, as you might expect, views.py. Not all of the application's views have to be defined in this file, but it is common to use this file (or a Python package) to hold your application's views.

At its simplest, a view might return the HTML text to be displayed, like this:

```
def myView(request):
    return HttpResponse("Hello World")
```

Of course, views will generally be a lot more complicated, dealing with database objects and returning very sophisticated HTML pages. Views can also return other types of data, for example to display an image or download a file, or to respond to an incoming AJAX request.

URL dispatching

When an incoming HTTP request is sent to a URL within the web application, that request is forwarded to the view in the following way:

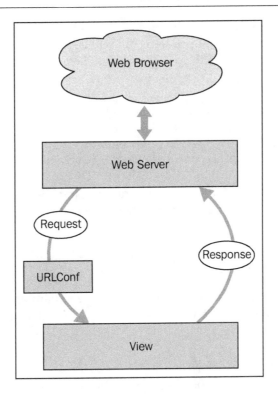

The web server receives the request and passes it on to a URL dispatcher, which in Django parlance is called a **URLConf**. This is a Python module that maps incoming URLs to views. The view function then processes the request and returns a response, which is passed back to the web server so that it can be sent back to the user's web browser.

The URLConf module is normally named `urls.py`, and consists of a list of regular expression patterns along with the views these patterns map to. For example, here is a copy of part of the ShapeEditor's `urls.py` file:

```python
from django.conf.urls.defaults import *

urlpatterns = patterns('geodjango.shapeEditor.views',
        (r'^shape-editor$',
         'listShapefiles'),
    ...
)
```

This tells Django that any URL which matches the pattern `^shape-editor$` (that is, a URL consisting only of the text `shape-editor`) will be mapped to the `listShapefiles` function, which can be found in the `geodjango.shapeEditor.views` module.

This is a slight simplification: the `geodjango.shapeEditor.views` entry in the preceding code example is actually a *prefix*, which is applied to the view name. Prefixes can be anything you like, so long as the prefix plus a period plus the view name yields a fully-qualified reference to your view function.

As well as simply mapping URLs to view functions, the URLConf module also lets you define **parameters** to be passed to the view. Take, for example, the following URL mapping:

```
(r'^shape-editor/edit/(?P<shapefile_id>\d+)$',
 'editShapefile'),
```

The syntax is a bit complicated, thanks to the use of regular expression patterns, but the basic idea is that this entry in the URLConf will match any URL of the following form:

```
shape-editor/edit/NNNN
```

In this URL, NNNN is a sequence of one or more digits. The actual text used for NNNN will be passed to the `editShapefile()` view function as an extra keyword parameter named `shapefile_id`. This means that the view function would be defined like this:

```
def editShapefile(request, shapefile_id):
```

While the URL mapping does require you to be familiar with regular expressions, it is extremely flexible, and allows you to define exactly which view will be called for any given incoming URL, as well as allowing you to include parts of the URL as parameters to the view function.

Remember that Django allows multiple applications to exist within a single project. Because of this, the URLConf module belongs to the project, and contains mappings for all the project's applications in one place. Applications often define their own URLConf modules, which are then imported by the project's URLConf to insert them into the overall system. For example, you might have an application called "editor" that defines its own URLs (/add, /delete, and so on). The project's URLConf might include the editor application's URLs using the /editor prefix. This would have the effect of associating the editor's add() view function with the overall URL /editor/add.

Notice how the editor application only defines its own URLs—it doesn't know about the /editor prefix—and the project then includes all those URLs under the appropriate prefix. This allows different applications to coexist within a single project, without interfering with (or even knowing about) each other's URLs.

Templates

To simplify the creation of complex HTML pages, Django provides a sophisticated templating system. A **template** is a text file that is processed to generate a web page by taking variables from the view and processing them to generate the page dynamically. For example, here is a snippet from the listShapefiles.html template used by the ShapeEditor:

```
<b>Available Shapefiles:</b>
<table>
  {% for shapefile in shapefiles %}
  <tr>
    <td>{{ shapefile.filename }}</td>
    ...
  </tr>
  {% endfor %}
</table>
```

As you can see, most of the template is simply HTML, with a few programming constructs added. In this case, we loop through the shapefiles list, creating a table row for each shapefile, and display (among other things) the shapefile's filename.

To use this template, the view function might look something like this:

```
def myView(request):
    shapefiles = ...
    return render_to_response("listShapefiles.html",
                              {'shapefiles' : shapefiles})
```

As you can see, the `render_to_response()` function takes the name of the template, and a dictionary containing the variables to use when processing the template. The result is an HTML page, which will be displayed to the end user.

 All of the templates for an application are generally stored in a directory named `templates` within the application's directory.

Django also includes a library for working with data-entry **forms**. A form is defined as a Python class defining the various fields to be entered, along with data validation and other behaviors associated with the form. For example, here is the "import shapefile" form used by the ShapeEditor:

```
class ImportShapefileForm(forms.Form):
    import_file = forms.FileField(label="Select a Shapefile")
    character_encoding = forms.ChoiceField(...)
```

`forms.FileField` is a standard Django form field for handling file uploads, while `forms.ChoiceField` is a standard form field for displaying a drop-down menu of available choices. It's easy to use a form within a Django view; for example:

```
def importShapefile(request):
    if request.method == "GET":
        form = ImportShapefileForm()
        return render_to_response("importShapefile.html",
                                  {'form' : form})
    elif request.method == "POST":
        form = ImportShapefileForm(request.POST,
                                   request.FILES)
        if form.is_valid():
            shapefile = request.FILES['import_file']
            encoding = request.POST['character_encoding']
            ...
        else:
            return render_to_response("importShapefile.html",
                                      {'form' : form})
```

If the user is submitting the form (`request.method == "POST"`), we check that the form's contents are valid and process them. Otherwise, we build a new form from scratch. Notice that the `render_to_response()` function is called with the form object as a parameter to be passed to the template. This template will look something like the following:

```html
<html>
  <head>
    <title>ShapeEditor</title>
  </head>
  <body>
    <h1>Import Shapefile</h1>
    <form enctype="multipart/form-data" method="post"
          action="import">
      {{ form.as_p }}
      <input type="submit" value="Submit"/>
    </form>
  </body>
</html>
```

The `{{ form.as_p }}` instruction renders the form in HTML format (embedded within a `<p>` tag) and includes it in the template at that point.

Forms are especially important when working with GeoDjango, because the map editor widgets are implemented as part of a form.

This completes our whirlwind tour of Django. It's certainly not comprehensive, and you are encouraged to follow the tutorials on the Django website to learn more, but we have covered enough of the core concepts for you to understand what is going on as we implement the ShapeEditor. Without further ado, let's start implementing the ShapeEditor by setting up a PostGIS database for our application to use.

Setting up the database

Assuming you have created a PostgreSQL template for PostGIS as described in the *Prerequisites* section of this chapter, setting up the PostGIS database for the ShapeEditor is trivial—simply type the following at the command prompt:

```
% createdb shapeeditor
```

If you don't have PostgreSQL's `createdb` command on your path, you will need to prefix this command with the directory where PostgreSQL's command-line tools are stored.

If your PostgreSQL installation requires you to supply a username when creating a database, you can do this by adding the -U command-line option, like this:

```
% createdb shapeeditor -U <username>
```

You will be prompted to enter the user's password, if it has one.

This will create a new database named shapeeditor, which we will use to hold the data for our ShapeEditor project.

All going well, you should now have a database named shapeeditor on your computer. Open up a command-line client to this database by typing:

```
% psql shapeeditor
```

 You'll need to add a -U command-line option if your PostgreSQL installation requires it.

You should see the PostgreSQL command line prompt:

```
psql (9.1.6)
Type "help" for help.
shapeeditor=#
```

We now need to spatially-enable this database, by installing the PostGIS extension. To do this, type:

```
CREATE EXENSION postgis;
```

If you then type \d and press *Return*, you should see a list of the tables in your new PostGIS database:

```
List of relations
 Schema |        Name        | Type  | Owner
--------+--------------------+-------+-------
 public | geography_columns  | view  | user
 public | geometry_columns   | view  | user
 public | raster_columns     | view  | user
 public | raster_overviews   | view  | user
 public | spatial_ref_sys    | table | user
(5 rows)
```

These five tables are installed automatically by the PostGIS extension. To leave the PostgreSQL command-line client, type \q and then press *Return*:

```
geodjango=# \q
%
```

Congratulations! You have just set up a PostGIS database for the ShapeEditor application to use.

Setting up the ShapeEditor project

We now have to create the Django project which will hold the ShapeEditor system. To do this, cd into the directory where you want the project's directory to be placed, and type:

```
% django-admin.py startproject shapeEditor
```

When you installed Django, it should have placed the django-admin.py program onto your path, so you shouldn't need to tell the computer where this script resides.

All going well, Django will create a directory named shapeEditor, which contains a python program named manage.py. You will use this program to start, stop, and configure your project, and another directory (also called shapeEditor) that holds the files that make up your project. Let's take a closer look at these files:

- __init__.py

  You should be familiar with this type of file; it simply tells Python that this directory holds a Python package.

- settings.py

  This Python module contains various settings for our shapeEditor project. These settings include options for turning debugging on or off, information about which database the Django project will use, where to find the project's URLConf module, and a list of the applications which should be included in the project.

- urls.py

  This is the URLConf module for the project. It maps incoming URLs to views within the project's applications.

- wsgi.py

  This module makes it possible to run your application using the **Web Server Gateway Interface (WSGI)** protocol. You'll use this when deploying your application to a production server.

Now that the project has been created, we next need to configure it. To do this, edit the settings.py file. We want to make the following changes to this file:

- Tell Django to use the PostGIS database we set up earlier for this project
- Add the GeoDjango application to the project, to enable the GeoDjango functionality

To tell Django to use PostGIS, edit the DATABASES variable to look like the following:

```
DATABASES = {
    'default': {
        'ENGINE'   : 'django.contrib.gis.db.backends.postgis',
        'NAME'     : 'geodjango',
        'USER'     : '...',
        'PASSWORD' : '...'
    }
}
```

Make sure you enter the username and password used to access your particular PostgreSQL database.

To enable the GeoDjango functionality, add the following line to the INSTALLED_APPS variable at the bottom of the file:

```
'django.contrib.gis'
```

While we're editing the settings.py file, let's make one more change that will save us some trouble down the track. Go to the MIDDLEWARE_CLASSES setting, and comment out the django.middleware.csrf.CsrfViewMiddleware line. This entry causes the addition of extra error checking when processing forms to prevent cross-site request forgery. Implementing CSRF support requires adding extra code to our form templates, which we won't be doing here to keep things simple.

 If you deploy your own applications on the Internet, you should read the CSRF documentation on the Django website and enable CSRF support. Otherwise you may find your application subjected to cross-site request forgery attacks.

This completes the configuration of our ShapeEditor project.

Defining the ShapeEditor's applications

We now have a Django project for our overall ShapeEditor system. We next need to break down our project into several related applications, following Django's design philosophy of having applications be small and relatively self-contained. Looking back at our design for the overall project, we can see several possible candidates for breaking the functionality into separate applications:

- Importing and exporting shapefiles
- Selecting features
- Editing features
- The Tile Map Server

Let's choose some names for our applications, keeping them short and to the point:

- `importer`
- `exporter`
- `selector`
- `editor`
- `tms`

We will define one more application, which we'll called `shared`, to hold the database models and Python modules that are shared across these applications. For example, we might have a module named `attributeReader.py` that is needed by the importer and editor applications. We'll place this into the `shared` application to make it clear that this code is designed to be used elsewhere in the system.

Creating the shared application

The `shapeEditor.shared` application will hold the core database tables and python modules we use throughout the system. Let's go ahead and create this application now. `cd` into the `shapeEditor` project directory and type the following:

```
python manage.py startapp shapeEditor
```

This will create a directory within the `shapeEditor` project directory named `shared`. This application directory will contain various files Django needs in order to run.

Note that, by default, a new application is placed in the topmost `shapeEditor` directory. This means you can import this application into your Python program like this:

`import shared`

Django's conventions say that applications in the topmost directory (or somewhere else on your Python path) are intended to be *reusable*—that is, you can take that application and use it in a different project. The applications we're defining here aren't like that; they can only work as part of the `shapeEditor` project, and so we need to move the newly-created shared directory inside the `shapeEditor` project's sub-directory, like this:

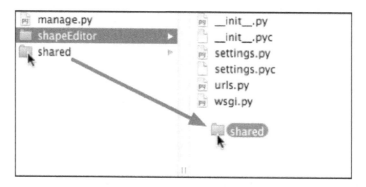

This means we can import our shared application like this:

`import shapeEditor.shared`

or:

`from shapeEditor import shared`

In other words, the `shared` application isn't reusable; it only makes sense within the context of the `shapeEditor` application.

Unfortunately, Django doesn't currently make it easy for you to create non-reusable applications. You have to create the application first, and then move the directory into the project directory to make it non-reusable.

Let's now take a look at what is inside our `shapeEditor.shared` directory:

- `__init__.py`

  This is another Python package initialization file, telling Python that this directory holds a Python package.

- `models.py`

  This Python module will hold the shared application's data models.

- `tests.py`

  This Python module holds various unit tests for your application.
  We won't be using this, so you can delete this file if you wish.

- `views.py`

  This Python module will hold various views for the shared application.
  Once again, we won't be using this, and you can delete this file if you want.

Now that we have created the application itself, let's add it to our project. Edit the `settings.py` file again, and add the following entry to the `INSTALLED_APPS` list:

```
'shapeEditor.shared'
```

Now that we have our `shared` application, let's start to put some useful things into it.

Defining the data models

We already know which database objects we are going to need to store the uploaded shapefiles:

- The `Shapefile` object will represent a single uploaded shapefile.
- Each shapefile will have a number of `Attribute` objects, giving the name, data type, and other information about each attribute within the shapefile.
- Each shapefile will have a number of `Feature` objects, which hold the geometry for each of the shapefile's features.
- Each feature will have a set of `AttributeValue` objects, which hold the value for each of the feature's attributes.

Let's look at each of these in more detail, and think about exactly what information will need to be stored in each object.

Shapefile

When we import a shapefile, there are a few things we need to remember:

- The original name of the uploaded file. We will display this in the "list shapefiles" view, so that the user can identify the shapefile within this list.

- The spatial reference system used by the shapefile's data is present. When we import the shapefile, we will convert it to use latitude and longitude coordinates using the WGS84 datum (EPSG 4326), but we need to remember the shapefile's original spatial reference system so that we can use it again when exporting the features. For simplicity, we're going to store the spatial reference system in WKT format.

- What type of geometry was stored in the shapefile. We'll need this to know which field in the `Feature` object holds the geometry.

- The character encoding used for the shapefile's attributes. Shapefiles don't always come in UTF-8 character encoding, and while we'll convert the attribute values to Unicode when importing the data, we do need to know which character encoding the file was in, so we'll store this information in the shapefile as well. This allows us to use the same character encoding when exporting the shapefile again.

Attribute

When we export a shapefile, it has to have the same attributes as the original imported file. Because of this, we have to remember the shapefile's attributes. This is what the `Attribute` object does. We will need to remember the following information for each attribute:

- The shapefile the attribute belongs to
- The name of the attribute
- The type of data stored in this attribute (string, floating-point number, and so on)
- The field width of the attribute, in characters
- For floating-point attributes, the number of digits to display after the decimal point

All of this information comes directly from the shapefile's layer definition.

Feature

Each feature in the imported shapefile will need to be stored in the database. Because PostGIS (and GeoDjango) uses different field types for different types of geometries, we need to define separate fields for each geometry type. Because of this, the `Feature` object will need to store the following information:

- The shapefile the feature belongs to
- The Point geometry, if the shapefile stores this type of geometry
- The MultiPoint geometry, if the shapefile stores this type of geometry
- The MultLineString geometry, if the shapefile stores this type of geometry
- The MultiPolygon geometry, if the shapefile stores this type of geometry
- The GeometryCollection geometry, if the shapefile stores this type of geometry

Isn't something missing?

If you've been paying attention, you've probably noticed that some of the geometry types are missing. What about Polygons or LineStrings? Because of the way data is stored in a shapefile, it is impossible to know in advance whether a shapefile holds Polygons or MultiPolygons, and similarly if it holds LineStrings or MultiLineStrings. The shapefile's internal structure makes no distinction between these geometry types. Because of this, a shapefile may claim to store Polygons when it really contains MultiPolygons, and similarly for LineString geometries. For more information, see `http://code.djangoproject.com/ticket/7218`.

To work around this limitation, we store all Polygons as MultiPolygons, and all LineStrings as MultiLineStrings. This is why we don't need Polygon or LineString fields in the `Feature` object.

AttributeValue

The `AttributeValue` object holds the value for each of the feature's attributes. This object is quite straightforward, storing the following information:

- The feature the attribute value is for
- The attribute this value is for
- The attribute's value, as a string

For simplicity, we'll be storing all attribute values as strings.

The models.py file

Now that we know what information we want to store in our database, it's easy to define our various model objects. To do this, edit the `models.py` file in the `shapeEditor.shared` directory, and make sure it looks like this:

```python
from django.contrib.gis.db import models


class Shapefile(models.Model):
    filename  = models.CharField(max_length=255)
    srs_wkt   = models.CharField(max_length=255)
    geom_type = models.CharField(max_length=50)
    encoding  = models.CharField(max_length=20)


class Attribute(models.Model):
    shapefile = models.ForeignKey(Shapefile)
    name      = models.CharField(max_length=255)
    type      = models.IntegerField()
    width     = models.IntegerField()
    precision = models.IntegerField()


class Feature(models.Model):
    shapefile = models.ForeignKey(Shapefile)
    geom_point = models.PointField(srid=4326,
                                   blank=True, null=True)
    geom_multipoint = \
        models.MultiPointField(srid=4326,
                               blank=True, null=True)
    geom_multilinestring = \
        models.MultiLineStringField(srid=4326,
                                    blank=True, null=True)
    geom_multipolygon = \
        models.MultiPolygonField(srid=4326,
                                 blank=True, null=True)
    geom_geometrycollection = \
        models.GeometryCollectionField(srid=4326,
                                       blank=True,
                                       null=True)

    objects = models.GeoManager()
```

```
class AttributeValue(models.Model):
    feature   = models.ForeignKey(Feature)
    attribute = models.ForeignKey(Attribute)
    value     = models.CharField(max_length=255,
                                 blank=True, null=True)
```

There are a few things to be aware of here:

- Note that the `from...import` statement at the top has changed. We're importing the GeoDjango models, rather than the standard Django ones.

- We use `models.CharField` objects to represent character data, and `models.IntegerField` objects to represent integer values. Django provides a whole raft of field types for you to use. GeoDjango also adds its own field types to store geometry fields, as you can see from the definition of the `Feature` object.

- To represent relations between two objects, we use a `models.ForeignKey` object.

- Because the `Feature` object will store geometry data, we want to allow GeoDjango to perform spatial queries on this data. To enable this, we define a `GeoManager()` instance for the `Feature` class.

- Note that several fields (in particular, the `geom_xxx` fields in the `Feature` object) have both `blank=True` and `null=True`. These are actually quite distinct: `blank=True` means that the admin interface allows the user to leave the field blank, while `null=True` tells the database that these fields can be set to `NULL` in the database. For the `Feature` object, we'll need both so that we don't get validation errors when entering geometries via the admin interface.

That's all we need to do (for now) to define our database model. After you've made these changes, save the file, `cd` into the topmost project directory, and type:

python manage.py syncdb

This command tells Django to check the models and create new database tables as required. Because the default settings for a new project automatically include the `auth` application, you will also be asked if you want to create a superuser account. Go ahead and create one; we'll need a superuser for the next section, where we explore GeoDjango's built-in admin interface.

There is bug in Django 1.4, which means that geospatial fields aren't created automatically. Instead, you'll see the following error message:

```
Failed to install index for shared.Feature model:
operator class "gist_geometry_ops" does not exist for
access method "gist"
```

Don't worry; if you see this error, you just need to create the spatial fields by hand. We are about to see how to do this.

You should now have a spatial database set up with the various database tables you have created. Let's take a closer look at this database by typing:

`psql geodjango`

When you type \d and press *Return*, you should see a list of all the database tables that have been created:

```
                       List of relations
  Schema |              Name               |   Type    | Owner
 --------+---------------------------------+-----------+-------
  public | auth_group                      | table     | user
  public | auth_group_id_seq               | sequence  | user
  public | auth_group_permissions          | table     | user
  public | auth_group_permissions_id_seq   | sequence  | user
  public | auth_message                    | table     | user
  public | auth_message_id_seq             | sequence  | user
  public | auth_permission                 | table     | user
  public | auth_permission_id_seq          | sequence  | user
  public | auth_user                       | table     | user
  public | auth_user_groups                | table     | user
  public | auth_user_groups_id_seq         | sequence  | user
  public | auth_user_id_seq                | sequence  | user
  public | auth_user_user_permissions      | table     | user
  public | auth_user_user_permissions_id_seq | sequence  | user
  public | django_content_type             | table     | user
  public | django_content_type_id_seq      | sequence  | user
  public | django_session                  | table     | user
```

public	django_site		table	user
public	django_site_id_seq		sequence	user
public	geography_columns		view	user
public	geometry_columns		view	user
public	raster_columns		view	user
public	raster_overviews		view	user
public	shared_attribute		table	user
public	shared_attribute_id_seq		sequence	user
public	shared_attributevalue		table	user
public	shared_attributevalue_id_seq		sequence	user
public	shared_feature		table	user
public	shared_feature_id_seq		sequence	user
public	shared_shapefile		table	user
public	shared_shapefile_id_seq		sequence	user
public	spatial_ref_sys		table	user

(30 rows)

To make sure that each application's database tables are unique, Django adds the application name to the start of the table name. This means that the table names for the models we have created are actually called shared_shapefile, shared_feature, and so on. We'll be working with these database tables directly later on, when we want to use Mapnik to generate maps using the imported Shapefile data.

> If you ran into the bug that prevents Django from creating the spatial fields, you can create them yourself by typing the following commands into pgsql:
>
> ```
> ALTER TABLE shared_feature ADD COLUMN geom_point
> geometry(Point, 4326);
>
> ALTER TABLE shared_feature ADD COLUMN geom_multipoint
> geometry(MultiPoint, 4326);
>
> ALTER TABLE shared_feature ADD COLUMN geom_
> multilinestring geometry(MultiLineString, 4326);
>
> ALTER TABLE shared_feature ADD COLUMN geom_multipolygon
> geometry(MultiPolygon, 4326);
>
> ALTER TABLE shared_feature ADD COLUMN geom_
> geometrycollection geometry(GeometryCollection, 4326);
> ```

Playing with the admin system

Before we can use the built-in admin application, we will need to enable it. This involves adding the admin application to the project, syncing the database, telling the admin application about our database objects, and adding the admin URLs to our `urls.py` file. Let's work through each of these in turn:

- Adding the admin application to the project:

  Edit your `settings.py` file and uncomment the `'django.contrib.admin'` line within the `INSTALLED_APPS` list:

  ```
  INSTALLED_APPS = (
      'django.contrib.auth',
      'django.contrib.contenttypes',
      'django.contrib.sessions',
      'django.contrib.sites',
      'django.contrib.messages',
      # Uncomment the next line to enable the admin:
      'django.contrib.admin',
      'django.contrib.gis',
      'shapeEditor'
  )
  ```

- Resynchronizing the database:

  From the command line, `cd` into your GeoDjango project directory and type the following:

  ```
  python manage.py syncdb
  ```

  This will add the admin application's tables to your database.

- Adding our database objects to the admin interface:

  Next, we need to tell the Admin interface about the various database objects we want to work with. To do this, create a new file in the `shapeEditor.shared` directory named `admin.py`, and enter the following into this file:

  ```
  from django.contrib.gis import admin
  from models import Shapefile, Feature, \
       Attribute, AttributeValue

  admin.site.register(Shapefile, admin.ModelAdmin)
  admin.site.register(Feature, admin.GeoModelAdmin)
  admin.site.register(Attribute, admin.ModelAdmin)
  admin.site.register(AttributeValue, admin.ModelAdmin)
  ```

This tells Django how to display the various objects in the admin interface. If you want, you can subclass `admin.ModelAdmin` (or `admin.GeoModelAdmin`) and customize how it works. For now, we'll just accept the defaults.

 Note that we use an `admin.GeoModelAdmin` object for the `Feature` class. This is because the `Feature` objects include geometries that we want to edit using a slippy map. We'll see how this works shortly.

- Adding the admin URLs to the project:

  Edit the `urls.py` file (in the `shapeEditor` project directory) and uncomment the lines that refer to the admin application. Then change the `from django. contrib import admin` line to read:

  ```
  from django.contrib.gis import admin
  ```

  The following listing shows how this file should end up, with the three lines you need to change highlighted:

  ```
  from django.conf.urls.defaults import *

  # Uncomment the next two lines to enable the admin:
  from django.contrib.gis import admin
  admin.autodiscover()

  urlpatterns = patterns('',
      # Example:
      # (r'^geodjango/', include('geodjango.foo.urls')),

      # Uncomment the admin/doc line below and add 'django.contrib.
  admindocs'
      # to INSTALLED_APPS to enable admin documentation:
      # (r'^admin/doc/', include('django.contrib.admindocs.urls')),

      # Uncomment the next line to enable the admin:
      (r'^admin/', include(admin.site.urls)),
  )
  ```

When this is done, it is time to run the application. `cd` into the main GeoDjango project directory and type:

```
python manage.py runserver
```

This will start up the Django server for your project. Open a web browser and navigate to the following URL:

```
http://127.0.0.1:8000/admin/shared
```

You should see the Django administration **Log in** page as shown in the following screenshot:

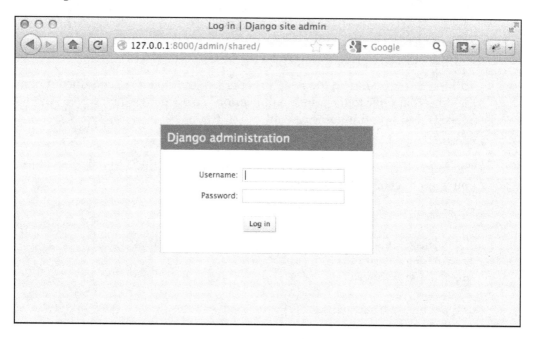

Enter the username and password for the superuser you created earlier, and you will see the main admin interface for the `ShapeEditor.shared` application as shown in the following screenshot:

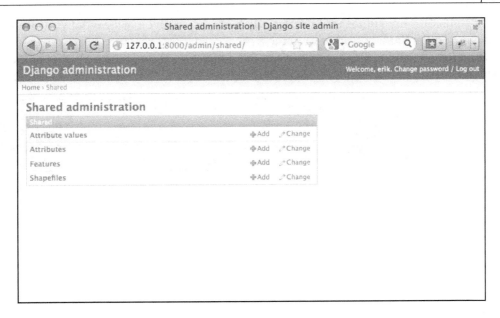

Let's use this admin interface to create a dummy shapefile. Click on the **Add** link on the **Shapefiles** row, and you will be presented with a basic input screen for entering a new shapefile:

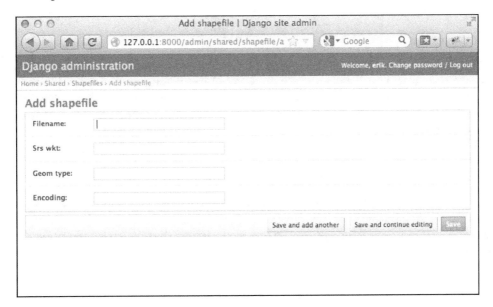

Enter some dummy values into the various fields (it doesn't matter what you enter), and click on the **Save** button to save the new Shapefile object into the database. A list of the shapefiles that are present in the database will be shown. At the moment, there is only the shapefile you just created:

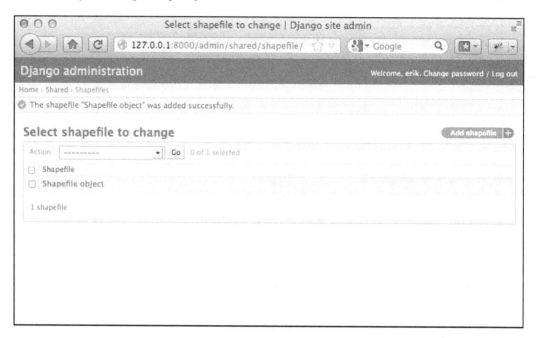

As you can see, the new shapefile object has been given a rather unhelpful label: Shapefile object. This is because we haven't yet told Django what textual label to use for a shapefile (or any of our other database objects). To fix this, edit the shared.models file and add the following method to the end of the Shapefile class definition:

```
def __unicode__(self):
    return self.filename
```

The __unicode__ method returns a human-readable summary of the Shapefile object's contents. In this case, we are showing the filename associated with the shapefile. If you then reload the web page, you can see that the shapefile now has a useful label:

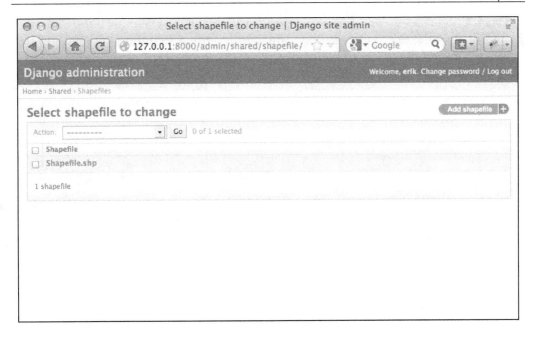

Go ahead and add the __unicode__ methods to the other model objects as well:

```
class Attribute(models.Model):
    ...
    def __unicode__(self):
        return self.name

class Feature(models.Model):
    ...
    def __unicode__(self):
        return str(self.id)

class AttributeValue(models.Model):
    ...
    def __unicode__(self):
        return self.value
```

While this may seem like busywork, it's actually quite useful to have your database objects able to describe themselves. If you wanted to, you could further customize the admin interface, for example by showing the attributes and features associated with the selected shapefile. For now, though, let's take a look at GeoDjango's built-in geometry editors.

Go back to the shared application's administration page (by clicking on the **Shared** hyperlink near the top of the window), and click on the **Add** button in the **Features** row. As with the shapefile, you will be asked to enter the details for a new feature. This time, however, the admin interface will use a slippy map to enter each of the different geometry types supported by the Feature object:

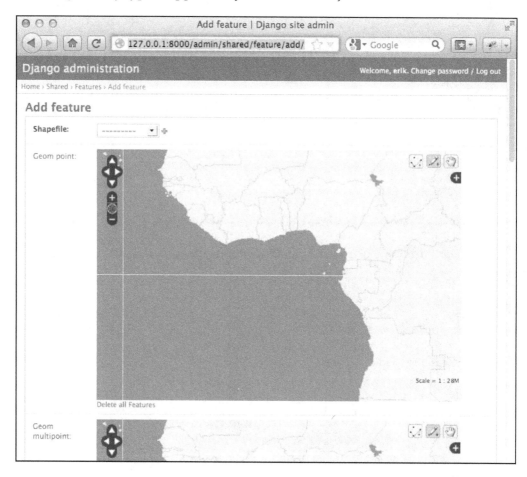

Obviously, having multiple slippy maps like this isn't quite what we want, and if we wanted we could set up a custom GeoModelAdmin subclass to avoid this, but that's not important right now. Instead, try selecting the shapefile with which you want to associate this feature by choosing your shapefile from the pop-up menu, and then scroll down to the Geom Multipolygon field and try adding a couple of polygons to the map.

To do this, click on the map to add points to the current polygon, or hold down the *Shift* key and click to finish the current polygon. The interface can be a bit confusing at first, but it's certainly usable. We'll look at the various options for editing polygons later. For now, just click on **Save** to save your new feature. If you edit it again, you'll see your saved geometry (or geometries) once again on the slippy maps.

Make sure you add at least two polygons. The built-in admin view will show an error if you try to save a single polygon into a MultiPolygon field. Note that this is only a problem with the built-in admin view; when we write the editing code for the ShapeEditor, this limitation won't apply.

That completes our tour of the admin interface. We won't be using this for end users, as we don't want to require users to log in before making changes to the shapefile data. We will, however, be borrowing some code from the admin application so that end users can edit their shapefile features using a slippy map.

Summary

You have now finished implementing the first part of the ShapeEditor application. Even at this early stage, you have made good progress, learning how GeoDjango works, designing the application, and laying the foundations for the functionality you will implement in the next two chapters.

In this chapter, you have learned the following:

- The GeoDjango extension to Django can be used to build sophisticated geospatial web applications
- A Django project consists of a single database and multiple Django applications
- Breaking a complex project into a number of smaller applications and making them all work together
- Django uses objects to represent records in the database
- A Django view is a Python function, which responds when a given URL is called
- The mapping from URLs to views is controlled by a URLConf module named `urls.py` defined at the project level
- Django uses a powerful templating system to simplify the creation of complex HTML pages

- Django allows you to define forms for handling the input of data

- Django form fields make it easy to accept and validate a variety of different types of data

- GeoDjango provides its own set of form fields for editing geospatial data

- An application's data objects are defined in a file called `models.py`

- GeoDjango's built-in "admin" system allows you to view and edit geospatial data using slippy maps

In *Chapter 10, ShapeEditor – Implementing List View, Import, and Export,* we will implement a view to show the available shapefiles, as well as write rather complex code for importing and exporting shapefiles.

10

ShapeEditor – Implementing List View, Import, and Export

In this chapter we continue our implementation of the ShapeEditor application. We will start by implementing a "list" view to show the available shapefiles, and then work through the details of importing and exporting shapefiles via a web interface.

In this chapter, we will learn the following:

- Displaying a list of records using a Django template
- Dealing with the complexities of shapefile data, including issues with geometries and attribute data types
- Importing a shapefile's data using a web interface
- Exporting a shapefile using a web interface

Let's start by implementing the view the user will see when they start running the ShapeEditor.

Implementing the "list shapefiles" view

When the user first opens the ShapeEditor application, we want them to see a list of the previously-uploaded shapefiles, with "import", "edit", "export", and "delete" options. Let's build this list view, which acts as the starting point for the entire ShapeEditor application.

This view is going to be part of the "editor" application, so we first need to create this application within our Django project. To do this, cd into the shapeEditor project directory and type the following:

```
python manage.py startapp editor
```

As usual, Django places the application in the top-level directory, making it a reusable application. We need to move it into our shapeEditor directory so that it becomes specific to our project. Either move the directory manually, or use the following terminal command:

```
mv editor shapeEditor
```

We now need to add our new application to the project. Edit the settings.py module, and add the following line to the end of the INSTALLED_APPS list:

```
'shapeEditor.editor',
```

Because the editor is going to support various URLs, we will want to give the editor its own URLConf module. To do this, create a new file in the shapeEditor/editor directory named urls.py, and enter the following into this file:

```
# URLConf for the shapeEditor.editor application.

from django.conf.urls import patterns, url

urlpatterns = patterns('shapeEditor.editor.views',
    url(r'^$', 'list_shapefiles'),
)
```

This URLConf is going to handle all the URLs for the editor application. At present we have just one entry, that maps the top-level URL (defined using the r'^$' regular expression, which matches an empty string) to the list_shapefiles() view function.

We next need to edit the top-level urls.py module so that the editor application's URLs will be included in the project. Change the top-level urls.py module (at shapeEditor/urls.py) to look like this:

```
from django.conf.urls.defaults import patterns, include, url
from django.contrib.gis import admin
admin.autodiscover()

urlpatterns = patterns('',
    url(r'^editor/', include('shapeEditor.editor.urls')),
)

urlpatterns += patterns('',
    url(r'^admin/', include(admin.site.urls)),
)
```

Notice that we've now got two separate sets of URL patterns, one that places all of the `shapeEditor.editor` application's views into the `editor` URL, and another that places the `django.contrib.gis.admin` application's views into the `admin` URL. This is a very convenient way of splitting up a project's URLs, so that each application has its own section within the URL namespace.

Now that we've set up our URL, let's write the view to go with it. We'll start by creating a very simple implementation of the `list_shapefiles()` view, just to make sure it works. Open the `views.py` module in the `editor` directory and change this file to look like this:

```
from django.http import HttpResponse

def list_shapefiles(request):
    return HttpResponse("in list_shapefiles")
```

If it isn't already running, start up the GeoDjango web server. To do this, open a command-line window, `cd` into the `geodjango` project directory, and type the following:

```
python manage.py runserver
```

Then open your web browser and navigate to the following URL:

```
http://127.0.0.1:8000/editor
```

All going well, you should see in **list_shapefiles** appear on the web page. This tells you that you've successfully created the `list_shapefiles()` view function and have correctly set up the URLConf mappings to point to this view.

We now want to create the view which will display the list of shapefiles. To do so, we'll make use of a Django template. Edit the `views.py` module again, and change this module's contents to look like this:

```
from django.http import HttpResponse
from django.shortcuts import render
from shapeEditor.shared.models import Shapefile

def list_shapefiles(request):
    shapefiles = Shapefile.objects.all().order_by("filename")
    return render(request, "list_shapefiles.html",
                  {'shapefiles' : shapefiles})
```

The `list_shapefiles()` view function now does two things:

- It loads the list of all `Shapefile` objects from the database into memory, sorted by filename

- It passes this list to a Django template (in the file `list_shapefiles.html`), which is rendered into an HTML web page and returned back to the caller

Let's go ahead and create the `list_shapefiles.html` template. Create a directory called `templates` within the `editor` directory, and create a new file in this directory named `list_shapefiles.html`. This file should have the following contents:

```html
<html>
  <head>
    <title>ShapeEditor</title>
  </head>
  <body>
    <h1>ShapeEditor</h1>
{% if shapefiles %}
    <b>Available Shapefiles:</b>
    <table border="0" cellspacing="0" cellpadding="5"
           style="padding-left:20px">
  {% for shapefile in shapefiles %}
      <tr>
        <td>
          <span style="font-family:monospace">{{ shapefile.filename
}}</span>
        </td>
        <td> </td>
        <td>
          <a href="/editor/edit/{{ shapefile.id }}">
            Edit
          </a>
        </td>
        <td> </td>
        <td>
          <a href="/editor/export/{{ shapefile.id }}">
            Export
          </a>
        </td>
```

```
            <td> </td>
            <td>
              <a href="/editor/delete/{{ shapefile.id }}">
                Delete
              </a>
            </td>
          </tr>
      {% endfor %}
        </table>
    {% endif %}
        <button type="button"
                onClick='window.location="/editor/import";'>
          Import New Shapefile
        </button>
      </body>
    </html>
```

This template works as follows:

- If the `shapefiles` list is not empty, it creates an HTML table to display the list of shapefiles
- For each entry in the `shapefiles` list, a new row in the table is created
- Each table row consists of the shapefile's filename (in monospaced text), along with **Edit**, **Export**, and **Delete** hyperlinks
- Finally, an **Import New Shapefile** button is displayed at the bottom

We'll look at the hyperlinks used in this template shortly, but for now just create the file, make sure the Django server is running, and reload your web browser. You should see the following page:

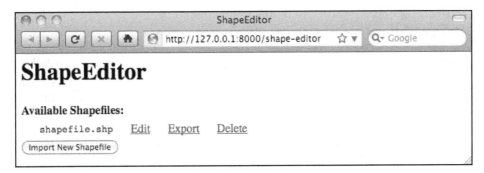

As you can see, the shapefile we created earlier in the admin interface is shown, along with the relevant hyperlinks and buttons to access the rest of the ShapeEditor's functionality:

- The **Edit** hyperlink will take the user to the `/editor/edit/1` URL, which will let the user edit the shapefile with the given record ID

- The **Export** hyperlink will take the user to the `/exporter/export/1` URL, which will let the user download a copy of the shapefile from the server

- The **Delete** hyperlink will take the user to the `/editor/delete/1` URL, which will let the user delete the given shapefile

- The **Import New Shapefile** button will take the user to the `/importer/import` URL, which will let the user upload a new shapefile to the server

You can explore these URLs by clicking on them if you want—they won't do anything other than display an error page, but you can see how the URLs link the various parts of the ShapeEditor's functionality together. You can also take a detailed look at the Django error page, which can be quite helpful in tracking down bugs.

Now that we have a working first page, let's start implementing the core functionality of the ShapeEditor application. We'll start with the logic required to import a shapefile.

Importing shapefiles

The process of importing a shapefile involves the following steps:

1. Displaying a form prompting the user to upload the shapefile's ZIP archive.
2. Decompressing the ZIP file to extract the uploaded shapefile.
3. Opening the shapefile and reading the data out of it into the database.
4. Deleting the temporary files that we have created.

Because of the complexity of this process, we'll use a separate application called `shapefileIO` to handle the behind-the-scenes logic of importing (and later, exporting) the shapefile's contents. This allows us to implement the user interface for importing shapefiles, without having to worry about these behind-the-scenes details.

Let's start by creating the basic framework for the `shapefileIO` application. Using a terminal window, `cd` into the top-level directory and type the following:

```
python manage.py startapp shapefileIO
```

Then move the `shapefileIO` directory into the `shapeEditor` sub-directory, like this:

```
mv shapefileIO shapeEditor
```

While `shapefileIO` is a standard Django application, it won't have a user interface. Instead, it just defines various modules to be used by other parts of the system. For this reason, you can delete the `views.py` module from this application's directory. You can also delete the `tests.py` module, since we won't be defining any unit tests for this application.

> A Django application must have a `models.py` file and an `__init__.py` file. The `models.py` module can be empty if you don't define any database tables for the module, but it must exist or Django won't recognize the package as being an application. The application also needs to be listed in `INSTALLED_APPS` within the project's settings module.

Next, we need to add the `shapefileIO` application to the project. Edit the `settings.py` module, and add the following line to the end of the `INSTALLED_APPS` list:

```
'shapeEditor.shapefileIO',
```

Within the `shapefileIO` directory, create a new module named `importer.py`, and enter the following into this file:

```
def import_data(shapefile, character_encoding):
    return "More to come..."
```

This function will attempt to import the contents of the compressed ZIP archive defined by the `shapefile` parameter, using the given character encoding. If the process fails, this function will return a suitable error message explaining what went wrong. If it succeeds, the `import_data()` function will return `None`.

Now that we've defined the interface to our behind-the-scenes shapefile importer, we can start to implement the user-interface aspects of importing a shapefile. We'll start by defining a view function, and an associated Django form, to let the user import a shapefile.

The "import shapefile" view function

Let's start by creating a placeholder for this view. Edit the `editor` application's `urls.py` module and add a second entry to the `shapeEditor.editor.views` pattern list:

```
urlpatterns = patterns('shapeEditor.editor.views',
        (r'^$', 'list_shapefiles'),
        (r'^import$', 'import_shapefile'),
    )
```

Then edit the `editor` application's `views.py` module and add a dummy `import_shapefile()` view function to respond to this URL:

```
def import_shapefile(request):
    return HttpResponse("More to come")
```

You can test this if you want: run the Django server, go to the main page and click on the **Import New Shapefile** button. You should see the **More to come** message.

To let the user enter data, we're going to use a Django form. **Forms** are custom classes that define the various fields, which will appear on the web page. In this case, our form will have two fields: one to accept the uploaded file, and other to select the character encoding from a pop-up menu. We're going to store this form in a file named `forms.py` in the `editor` directory; go ahead and create this file, and then edit it to look like this:

```
from django import forms

CHARACTER_ENCODINGS = [("ascii",  "ASCII"),
                       ("latin1", "Latin-1"),
                       ("utf8",   "UTF-8")]

class ImportShapefileForm(forms.Form):
    import_file = forms.FileField(label="Select a Zipped Shapefile")
    character_encoding = forms.ChoiceField(choices=CHARACTER_
ENCODINGS, initial="utf8")
```

Our form will contain two fields. The first field is a `FileField`, which accepts uploaded files. We give this field a custom label which will be displayed in the web page. For the second field we'll use a `ChoiceField`, which displays a pop-up menu. Note that the `CHARACTER_ENCODINGS` list shows the various choices to display in the pop-up list; each entry in this list is a `(value, label)` tuple, where `label` is the string to be displayed and `value` is the actual value to be used for that field when the user chooses this item from the list.

Now that we have created the form, go back to the `editor` application's `views.py` module, and replace the implementation of the `import_shapefile()` view function with the following:

```
def import_shapefile(request):
    if request.method == "GET":
        form = ImportShapefileForm()
        return render(request, "import_shapefile.html",
                      {'form'    : form,
                       'err_msg' : None})
```

```
    elif request.method == "POST":
        form = ImportShapefileForm(request.POST,
                                          request.FILES)
        if form.is_valid():
            shapefile = request.FILES['import_file']
            encoding  = request.POST['character_encoding']

            err_msg = importer.import_shapefile(shapefile,
                                                        encoding)

            if err_msg == None:
                return HttpResponseRedirect("/shape-editor")

    else:
        err_msg = None

    return render(request, "import_shapefile.html",
                    {'form'    : form,
                     'err_msg' : err_msg})
```

Also, add the following `import` statements to the top of the module:

```
from django.http import HttpResponseRedirect
from shapeEditor.editor.forms import ImportShapefileForm
from shapeEditor.shapefileIO import importer
```

Let's take a look at what is happening here. The `import_shapefile()` function will initially be called with an HTTP GET request; this will cause the function to create a new `ImportShapefileForm` object, and then call the `render()` function to display that form to the user. When the form is submitted, the `import_shapefile()` function will be called with an HTTP POST request. In this case, the `ImportShapefileForm` will be created with the submitted data (`request.POST` and `request.FILES`), and the form will be checked to see that the entered data is valid. If so, we extract the uploaded shapefile and the selected character encoding.

We then ask the shapefile importer to import the shapefile's data. This will return an error message if something goes wrong. If there is no error, we redirect the user back to the main `/editor` page so that the newly-imported shapefile can be shown.

If the form was not valid, or if the import process failed for some reason, we once again call the `render()` function to display the form to the user, this time with an appropriate error message. Note that Django will automatically display an error message if there is a problem with the form.

To display the form to the user, we'll use a Django template and pass the form object as a parameter. Let's create that template now; add a new file named `import_shapefile.html` in the `editor` application's `templates` directory and enter the following text into this file:

```html
<html>
  <head>
    <title>ShapeEditor</title>
  </head>
  <body>
    <h1>Import Shapefile</h1>
{% if err_msg %}
    <b><i>{{ err_msg }}</i></b>
{% endif %}
    <form enctype="multipart/form-data" method="post"
          action="import">
      {{ form.as_p }}
      <input type="submit" value="Submit"/>
      <button type="button"
              onClick='window.location="/editor";'>
        Cancel
      </button>
    </form>
  </body>
</html>
```

As you can see, this template defines an HTML `<form>` and adds **Submit** and **Cancel** buttons. The body of the form is not specified. Instead, we use `{{ form.as_p }}` to render the form object as a series of `<p>` (paragraph) elements. Near the top of the page, we also display the error message if there is one.

Let's test this out. Start up the Django web server if it is not already running, open a web browser and navigate to the `http://127.0.0.1:8000/editor` URL. Then click on the **Import New Shapefile** button. All going well, you should see the following page:

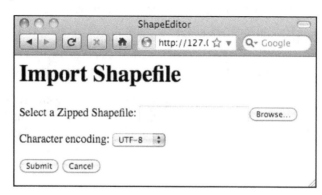

If you attempt to submit the form without uploading anything, an error message will appear saying that the import_file field is required. This is the default error-handling for any form; by default, all fields are required. If you do select a file for uploading, the importer will return the string **More to come...**, so this message should appear near the top of the page.

Now that we've implemented the form itself, let's return to our shapefileIO application and implement the logic needed to process the uploaded shapefile.

Extracting the uploaded shapefile

It is now time for us to write the body of our import_data() function. Go back to the importer.py module within the shapefileIO application, and delete the dummy return statement we added earlier.

When we use a form that includes a FileField, Django returns to us an UploadedFile object representing the uploaded file. Our first task is to read the contents of the UploadedFile object and store it in a temporary file on disk so that we can work with it. Add the following lines to your import_data() function:

```
fd, fname = tempfile.mkstemp(suffix=".zip")
os.close(fd)

f = open(fname, "wb")
for chunk in shapefile.chunks():
    f.write(chunk)
f.close()
```

As you can see, we use the tempfile module from the Python standard library to create a temporary file, and then copy the contents of the shapefile object into it.

Because tempfile.mkstemp() returns both a file descriptor and a filename, we call os.close(fd) to close the file descriptor. This allows us to reopen the file using open() and write to it in the normal way.

We're now ready to open the temporary file and check that it is indeed a ZIP archive containing the files which make up a shapefile. Here is how we can do this:

```
if not zipfile.is_zipfile(fname):
    os.remove(fname)
    return "Not a valid zip archive."

zip = zipfile.ZipFile(fname)

required_suffixes = [".shp", ".shx", ".dbf", ".prj"]
```

```
has_suffix = {}
for suffix in required_suffixes:
    has_suffix[suffix] = False

for info in zip.infolist():
    extension = os.path.splitext(info.filename)[1].lower()
    if extension in required_suffixes:
        has_suffix[extension] = True

for suffix in required_suffixes:
    if not has_suffix[suffix]:
        zip.close()
        os.remove(fname)
        return "Archive missing required "+suffix+" file."
```

Note that we use the Python standard library's zipfile module to check the contents of the uploaded ZIP archive, and return a suitable error message if something is wrong. We also delete the temporary file before returning an error message, so that we don't leave temporary files lying around.

Finally, now that we know that the uploaded file is a valid ZIP archive containing the files that make up a shapefile, we can extract these files and store them into a temporary directory:

```
shapefile_name = None
dst_dir = tempfile.mkdtemp()
for info in zip.infolist():
    if info.filename.endswith(".shp"):
        shapefile_name = info.filename

    dst_file = os.path.join(dst_dir, info.filename)
    f = open(dst_file, "wb")
    f.write(zip.read(info.filename))
    f.close()
zip.close()
```

Note that we create a temporary directory to hold the extracted files before copying the files into this directory. At the same time, we remember the name of the main .shp file from the archive, as we'll need to use this name when we open the shapefile.

Because we've used some of the Python standard library modules in this code, you'll also need to add the following to the top of the module:

```
import os, os.path, tempfile, zipfile
```

Importing the shapefile's contents

Now that we've extracted the shapefile's files out of the ZIP archive, we are ready to import the data from the uploaded shapefile. The process of importing the shapefile's contents involves the following steps:

1. Opening the shapefile.
2. Adding the Shapefile object to the database.
3. Defining the shapefile's attributes.
4. Storing the shapefile's features.
5. Storing the shapefile's attributes.

Let's work through these steps one at a time.

Open the shapefile

We will use the OGR library to open the shapefile:

```
try:
    datasource  = ogr.Open(os.path.join(dst_dir,
                                         shapefileName))
    layer       = datasource.GetLayer(0)
    shapefileOK = True
except:
    traceback.print_exc()
    shapefileOK = False

if not shapefileOK:
    os.remove(fname)
    shutil.rmtree(dst_dir)
    return "Not a valid shapefile."
```

Once again, if something goes wrong we clean up our temporary files and return a suitable error message. We're also using the `traceback` library module to display debugging information in the web server's log, while returning a friendly error message that will be shown to the user.

 In this program, we will be using OGR directly to read and write shapefiles. GeoDjango provides its own Python interface to OGR in the `contrib.gis.gdal` package, but unfortunately GeoDjango's version doesn't implement writing to shapefiles. Because of this, we will use the OGR Python bindings directly, and require you to install OGR separately.

Because this code uses a couple of standard library modules, as well as the OGR library, we'll have to add the following `import` statements to the top of the `importer.py` module:

```
import shutil, traceback
from osgeo import ogr
```

Add the Shapefile object to the database

Now that we've successfully opened the shapefile, we are ready to read the data out of it. First off, we'll create the `Shapefile` object to represent this imported shapefile:

```
src_spatial_ref = layer.GetSpatialRef()
shapefile = Shapefile(filename=shapefile_name,
                      srs_wkt=
                          src_spatial_ref.ExportToWkt(),
                      geom_type="...",
                      encoding=character_encoding)
shapefile.save()
```

As you can see, we get the spatial reference from the shapefile's layer, and then store the shapefile's name, spatial reference, and encoding into a `Shapefile` object, which we then save into the database. There's only one glitch: what value are we going to store into the `geom_type` field?

The `geom_type` field is supposed to hold the name of the geometry type that this shapefile holds. While the OGR shapefile is able to tell us the geometry type as a numeric constant, the `OGRGeometryTypeToName()` function in OGR is not exposed by the Python bindings, so we can't get the name of the geometry directly using OGR.

To work around this, we'll implement our own version of `OGRGeometryTypeToName()`. Because we're going to have a several of these functions, we'll store this in a separate module, which we'll call `utils.py`. Go into the shared application directory and create a new file called `utils.py`. Edit this file, and add the following to it:

```
from osgeo import ogr

def ogr_type_to_geometry_mname(ogr_type):
    return {ogr.wkbUnknown            : 'Unknown',
            ogr.wkbPoint              : 'Point',
            ogr.wkbLineString         : 'LineString',
            ogr.wkbPolygon            : 'Polygon',
            ogr.wkbMultiPoint         : 'MultiPoint',
            ogr.wkbMultiLineString    : 'MultiLineString',
            ogr.wkbMultiPolygon       : 'MultiPolygon',
            ogr.wkbGeometryCollection : 'GeometryCollection',
```

```
      ogr.wkbNone                   : 'None',
      ogr.wkbLinearRing : 'LinearRing'}.get(ogr_type)
```

 Every self-respecting Python program should have a utils.py module; it's about time we added one in the ShapeEditor.

Now that we have our own version of OGRGeometryTypeToName(), we can use this to set the geom_type field in the Shapefile object. Go back to the importer.py module and make the following changes to the end of your import_data() function:

```
    src_spatial_ref = layer.GetSpatialRef()

    geometry_type = layer.GetLayerDefn().GetGeomType()
    geometry_name = \
        utils.ogr_type_to_geometry_name(geometry_type)

    shapefile = Shapefile(filename=shapefileName,
                          srs_wkt=
                            src_spatial_ref.ExportToWkt(),
                          geom_type=geometry_name,
                          encoding=character_encoding)
    shapefile.save()
```

To make this code work, we'll have to add the following import statements to the top of the importer.py module:

```
  from shapeEditor.shared.models import Shapefile
  from shapeEditor.shared import utils
```

Define the shapefile's attributes

Now that we've created the Shapefile object to represent the imported shapefile, our next task is to create Attribute objects describing the shapefile's attributes. We can do this by querying the OGR shapefile; add the following code to the end of the import_data() function:

```
    attributes = []
    layer_def = layer.GetLayerDefn()
    for i in range(layer_def.GetFieldCount()):
        field_def = layer_def.GetFieldDefn(i)
        attr = Attribute(shapefile=shapefile,
                         name=field_def.GetName(),
                         type=field_def.GetType(),
                         width=field_def.GetWidth(),
                         precision=field_def.GetPrecision())
        attr.save()
        attributes.append(attr)
```

Note that, as well as saving the `Attribute` objects into a database, we also create a separate list of these attributes in a variable named `attributes`. We'll use this later on, when we import the attribute values for each feature.

Don't forget to add the following `import` statement to the top of the module:

```
from geodjango.shapeEditor.models import Attribute
```

Store the shapefile's features

Our next task is to extract the shapefile's features and store them as `Feature` objects in the database. Because the shapefile's features can be in any spatial reference, we need to transform them into our internal spatial reference system (EPSG 4326, unprojected latitude, and longitude values) before we can store them. To do this, we'll use an OGR `CoordinateTransformation()` object.

Here is how we're going to scan through the shapefile's features, extract the geometry from each feature, transform it into the EPSG 4326 spatial reference, and convert it into a GeoDjango GEOS geometry object so that we can store it into the database:

```
dst_spatial_ref = osr.SpatialReference()
dst_spatial_ref.ImportFromEPSG(4326)

coord_transform = osr.CoordinateTransformation(src_spatial_ref,
                                               dst_spatial_ref)

for i in range(layer.GetFeatureCount()):
    src_feature = layer.GetFeature(i)
    src_geometry = src_feature.GetGeometryRef()
    src_geometry.Transform(coord_transform)
    geometry = GEOSGeometry(src_geometry.ExportToWkt())
```

So far so good; we now have a GEOS geometry object which we can store into the `Feature` object. Unfortunately, we are now faced with a couple of problems. First, the inability of Shapefiles to distinguish between Polygons and MultiPolygons (and between LineStrings and MultiLineStrings) as described in the previous chapter means that we have to *wrap* a Polygon geometry inside a MultiPolygon, and a LineString geometry inside a MultiLineString, so that all the features in the shapefile will have the same geometry type. This is kind of messy, so we'll write a `utils.py` function to do this. Add the following line to the end of your `import_data()` function (along with the code above, if you haven't already typed this in) to wrap the geometry:

```
geometry = utils.wrap_geos_geometry(geometry)
```

The second problem we have is that we need to decide which particular field within the Feature object will hold our geometry. When we defined the Feature object, we had to create separate geometry fields for each of the geometry types; we now need to decide which of these fields will be used to store a given type of geometry.

Because we sometimes have to wrap up geometries, we can't simply use the geometry name to identify the field. This is another messy function that we'll implement in utils.py. For now, just add the following line to the end of your import_data() function:

```
geometry_field = utils.calc_geometry_field(
                    geometry_name)
```

Now that we've sorted out these problems, we're finally ready to store the feature's geometry into a Feature object within the database:

```
args = {}
args['shapefile'] = shapefile
args[geometry_field] = geometry
feature = Feature(**args)
feature.save()
```

Note that we use keyword arguments (**args) to create the Feature object. This lets us store the geometry into the correct field of the Feature object with a minimum of fuss. The alternative, using a series of if...elif...elif statements would have been much more tedious.

Before we move on, we'd better implement those two extra functions in the utils. py module. Here is the implementation for the wrap_geos_geometry() function:

```
def wrap_geos_Geometry(geometry):
    if geometry.geom_type == "Polygon":
        return MultiPolygon(geometry)
    elif geometry.geom_type == "LineString":
        return MultiLineString(geometry)
    else:
        return geometry
```

Here is the implementation for the calc_geometry_field() function:

```
def calc_geometry_field(geometry_type):
    if geometry_type == "Polygon":
        return "geom_multipolygon"
    elif geometry_type == "LineString":
        return "geom_multilinestring"
    else:
        return "geom_" + geometry_type.lower()
```

You're also going to have to add the following `import` statement to the top of the `utils.py` module:

```
from django.contrib.gis.geos.collections \
    import MultiPolygon, MultiLineString
```

Finally, in the `importer.py` module, you'll have to add the following `import` statements:

```
from django.contrib.gis.geos.geometry import GEOSGeometry
from osgeo import osr
from geodjango.shapeEditor.models import Feature
```

Store the shapefile's attributes

Now that we've dealt with the feature's geometry, we can now look at importing the feature's attributes. The basic process involves iterating over the attributes, extracting the attribute value from the OGR feature, creating an `AttributeValue` object to store the value, and then saving it into the database:

```
for attr in attributes:
    value = ...
    attr_value = AttributeValue(feature=feature,
                                attribute=attr,
                                value=value)
    attr_value.save()
```

The challenge is to extract the attribute value from the feature. Because the OGR `Feature` object has different methods to extract different types of field values, we are going to have to check for the different field types, call the appropriate `GetFieldAs()` method, convert the resulting value to a string, and then store this string into the `AttributeValue` object. `NULL` values will also have to be handled appropriately. In addition, we have to deal with character encoding; any string values will have to be converted from the shapefile's character encoding into Unicode text so that they can be saved into the database. Because of this complexity, we'll define a new `utils.py` function to do the hard work, and simply call that function from `import_data()`.

Note that, because the user might have selected the wrong character encoding for the shapefile, the process of extracting the attribute value can actually fail. Because of this, we have to add error-handling to our code. To support error-handling, our utility function, `get_ogr_feature_attribute()`, will return a `(success, result)` tuple, where `success` will be true if and only if the attribute was successfully extracted, and `result` will either be the extracted attribute value (as a string), or an error message explaining why the operation failed.

Let's add the necessary code to our `import_data()` function to store the attribute values into the database and gracefully handle any conversion errors that might occur:

```
for attr in attributes:
    success,result = utils.getOGRFeatureAttribute(
                            attr, srcFeature,
                            character_encoding)
    if not success:
        os.remove(fname)
        shutil.rmtree(dst_dir)
        shapefile.delete()
        return result

    attr_value = AttributeValue(feature=feature,
                                attribute=attr,
                                value=result)
    attr_value.save()
```

Note that we pass the `Attribute` object, the OGR feature, and the character encoding to the `get_ogr_feature_attribute()` function. If an error occurs, we clean up the temporary files, delete the shapefile we created earlier, and return the error message back to the caller. If the attribute was successfully extracted, we create a new `AttributeValue` object with the attribute's value, and save it into the database.

> Note that we use `shapefile.delete()` to remove the partially-imported shapefile from the database. By default, Django will also automatically delete any records that are related to the record being deleted through a `ForeignKey` field. This means that the `Shapefile` object will be deleted, along with all the related `Attribute`, `Feature`, and `AttributeValue` objects. With one line of code, we can completely remove all references to the shapefile's data.

Now let's implement that `get_ogr_feature_attribute()` function. Add the following to `utils.py`:

```
def getOGRFeatureAttribute(attr, feature, encoding):
    attr_name = str(attr.name)

    if not feature.IsFieldSet(attr_name):
        return (True, None)

    needs_encoding = False
    if attr.type == ogr.OFTInteger:
        value = str(feature.GetFieldAsInteger(attr_name))
```

```
    elif attr.type == ogr.OFTIntegerList:
        value = repr(feature.GetFieldAsIntegerList(attr_name))
    elif attr.type == ogr.OFTReal:
        value = feature.GetFieldAsDouble(attr_name)
        value = "%*.*f" % (attr.width, attr.precision, value)
    elif attr.type == ogr.OFTRealList:
        values = feature.GetFieldAsDoubleList(attr_name)
        str_values = []
        for value in values:
            str_values.append("%*.*f" % (attr.width,
                                         attr.precision,
                                         value))
        value = repr(str_Values)
    elif attr.type == ogr.OFTString:
        value = feature.GetFieldAsString(attr_name)
        needs_encoding = True
    elif attr.type == ogr.OFTStringList:
        value = repr(feature.GetFieldAsStringList(attr_name))
        needs_encoding = True
    elif attr.type == ogr.OFTDate:
        parts = feature.GetFieldAsDateTime(attr_name)
        year,month,day,hour,minute,second,tzone = parts
        value = "%d,%d,%d,%d" % (year,month,day,tzone)
    elif attr.type == ogr.OFTTime:
        parts = feature.GetFieldAsDateTime(attr_name)
        year,month,day,hour,minute,second,tzone = parts
        value = "%d,%d,%d,%d" % (hour,minute,second,tzone)
    elif attr.type == ogr.OFTDateTime:
        parts = feature.GetFieldAsDateTime(attr_name)
        year,month,day,hour,minute,second,tzone = parts
        value = "%d,%d,%d,%d,%d,%d,%d,%d" % (year,month,day,
                                             hour,minute,
                                             second,tzone)
    else:
        return (False, "Unsupported attribute type: " +
                        str(attr.type))

    if needs_encoding:
        try:
            value = value.decode(encoding)
        except UnicodeDecodeError:
            return (False, "Unable to decode value in " +
                    repr(attr_name) + " attribute.  " +
                    "Are you sure you're using the right " +
                    "character encoding?")

    return (True, value)
```

There's a lot of ugly code here, relating to the extraction of different field types from the OGR feature. Don't worry too much about these details; the basic concept is that we extract the attribute's value, convert it to a string, and perform character encoding on the string if necessary.

Finally, we'll have to add the following `import` statement to the top of the `importer.py` module:

```
from geodjango.shapeEditor.models import AttributeValue
```

Cleaning up

Now that we've imported the shapefile's data, all that's left is to clean up our temporary files and tell the caller that the import succeeded. To do this, simply add the following lines to the end of your `import_data()` function:

```
os.remove(fname)
shutil.rmtree(dst_dir)
return None
```

That's it!

To test all this out, grab a copy of the TM_WORLD_BORDERS-0.3 shapefile in ZIP file format. You can either use the original ZIP archive that you downloaded from the World Borders Dataset website, or you can recompress the shapefile into a new ZIP archive. Then run the ShapeEditor, click on the **Import New Shapefile** button, click on **Browse...** and select the ZIP archive you want to import.

Because the World Borders Dataset's features use the Latin1 character encoding, you need to make sure that this encoding is selected from the popup menu. Then click on **Submit**, and wait a few seconds for the shapefile to be imported. All going well, the world borders dataset will appear in the list of imported shapefiles:

If a problem occurs, check the error message to see what might be wrong. Also, go back and make sure you have typed the code in exactly as described. If it works, congratulations! You have just implemented the most difficult part of the ShapeEditor. It gets easier from here.

Exporting shapefiles

Next, we need to implement the ability to export a shapefile. The process of exporting a shapefile is basically the reverse of the "import" logic, and involves the following steps:

1. Create an OGR shapefile to receive the exported data.

2. Save the features into the shapefile.

3. Save the attributes into the shapefile.

4. Compress the shapefile into a ZIP archive.

5. Delete our temporary files.

6. Send the ZIP file back to the user's web browser.

All this work will take place in the `shapefileIO` application, with help from some `utils.py` functions. Before we begin, let's create an exporter module to handle the exporting process. Go to the `shapefileIO` directory, and create a new module named `exporter.py`. Initially, we're just going to add a dummy function to this module:

```
def export_data(shapefile):
    return "More to come..."
```

This function will take a desired `Shapefile` object, and return an `HttpResponse` that can be returned by the view function. This `HttpResponse` object will send the contents of the exported shapefile back to the user's web browser, where it can be saved to disk.

Now let's create the view function that will call the exporter and return the HTTP response back to the caller. Go to the `editor` application's `views.py` module, and add the following new function:

```
def export_shapefile(request, shapefile_id):
  try:
    shapefile = Shapefile.objects.get(id=shapefile_id)
  except Shapefile.DoesNotExist:
    return HttpResponseNotFound()

    return exporter.export_data(shapefile)
```

This view function takes the record ID of the desired shapefile, loads the `Shapefile` object into memory, and passes it to the `export_data()` function for processing. The resulting `HttpResponse` object is then returned to the caller, allowing the exported file to be downloaded to the user's computer.

While we are editing this file, add the following additional `import` statements to the top:

```
from django.http import HttpResponseNotFound
from shapeEditor.shapefileIO import exporter
```

Note that the `export_shapefile()` view function takes an additional parameter, named `shapefile_id`. This parameter will be taken from the URL used to access the view, so that for example if the user accesses the URL `http://127.0.0.1:8000/editor/export/1`, the `shapefile_id` parameter will be set to the value 1.

This is done by adding a special type of entry to the `editor` applications `urls.py` module. Edit this file, and add the following entry to the `urlpatterns` list:

```
url(r'^export/(?P<shapefile_id>\d+)$', 'export_shapefile'),
```

Our `list_shapefiles.html` template already makes use of this URL, adding the shapefile's record ID to the URL when the user clicks on the **Export** hyperlink:

```
<a href="/editor/export/{{ shapefile.id }}">
  Export
</a>
```

Now that we've written our view function, we can start to implement the behind-the-scenes logic required to export and download the shapefile. All of this will be implemented in the `exporter.py` module.

Defining the OGR shapefile

We'll use OGR to create the new shapefile that will hold the exported features. Let's start by creating a temporary directory to hold the shapefile's contents; replace your placeholder version of `export_data()` with the following:

```
def exportData(shapefile):
    dst_dir = tempfile.mkdtemp()
    dst_file = str(os.path.join(dst_dir, shapefile.filename))
```

Now that we've got somewhere to store the shapefile (and a filename for it), we'll create a spatial reference for the shapefile to use, and set up the shapefile's datasource and layer:

```
dst_spatial_ref = osr.SpatialReference()
dst_spatial_ref.ImportFromWkt(shapefile.srs_wkt)

driver = ogr.GetDriverByName("ESRI Shapefile")
datasource = driver.CreateDataSource(dst_file)
layer = datasource.CreateLayer(str(shapefile.filename),
                               dst_spatial_ref)
```

Note that we're using `str()` to convert the shapefile's filename to an ASCII string. This is because Django uses Unicode strings, but OGR can't handle unicode filenames. We'll need to do the same thing for the attribute names.

Now that we've created the shapefile itself, we next need to define the various fields which will hold the shapefile's attributes:

```
for attr in shapefile.attribute_set.all():
    field = ogr.FieldDefn(str(attr.name), attr.type)
    field.SetWidth(attr.width)
    field.SetPrecision(attr.precision)
    layer.CreateField(field)
```

Note how the information needed to define the field is taken directly from the `Attribute` object; Django makes iterating over the shapefile's attributes easy.

That completes the definition of the shapefile. We're now ready to start saving data into the newly-created shapefile.

Saving the features into the shapefile

Because the shapefile can use any valid spatial reference, we'll need to transform the shapefile's features from the spatial reference used internally (EPSG 4326) into the shapefile's own spatial reference. Before we can do this, we'll need to set up an `osr.CoordinateTransformation` object to do the transformation:

```
src_spatial_ref = osr.SpatialReference()
src_spatial_ref.ImportFromEPSG(4326)

coord_transform = osr.CoordinateTransformation(
                        src_spatial_ref, dst_spatial_ref)
```

We'll also need to know which geometry field in the `Feature` object holds the feature's geometry data:

```
geom_field = \
        utils.calc_geometry_field(shapefile.geom_type)
```

With this information, we're ready to start exporting the shapefile's features:

```
for feature in shapefile.feature_set.all():
    geometry = getattr(feature, geom_field)
```

Right away, however, we encounter a problem. If you remember when we imported the shapefile, we had to "wrap" a Polygon or a LineString geometry into a MultiPolygon or MultiLineString so that the geometry types would be consistent in the database. Now that we're exporting the shapefile, we need to *unwrap* the geometry so that features that have only one Polygon or LineString in their geometries are saved as Polygons and LineStrings rather than MultiPolygons and MultiLineStrings. We'll use a `utils.py` function to do this unwrapping:

```
geometry = utils.unwrap_geos_geometry(geometry)
```

We'll implement this `utils.py` function shortly.

Now that we've unwrapped the feature's geometry, we can go ahead and convert it back into an OGR geometry again, transform it into the shapefile's own spatial reference system, and create an OGR feature using that geometry:

```
dst_geometry = ogr.CreateGeometryFromWkt(geometry.wkt)
dst_geometry.Transform(coord_transform)

dst_feature = ogr.Feature(layer.GetLayerDefn())
dst_feature.SetGeometry(dst_geometry)
```

Finally, we need to add the feature to the layer and call the `Destroy()` method to save the feature (and then the layer) into the shapefile:

```
layer.CreateFeature(dst_feature)
dst_feature.Destroy()

datasource.Destroy()
```

Before we move on, let's add our new `unwrap_geos_geometry()` function to `utils.py`. This code is quite straightforward, pulling a single Polygon or LineString object out of a MultiPolygon or MultiLineString if they contain only one geometry:

```
def unwrap_geos_geometry(geometry):
    if geometry.geom_type in ["MultiPolygon",
                              "MultiLineString"]:
        if len(geometry) == 1:
            geometry = geometry[0]

    return geometry
```

So far so good; we've created the OGR feature, unwrapped the feature's geometry, and stored everything into the shapefile. Now we're ready to save the feature's attribute values.

Saving the attributes into the shapefile

Our next task is to save the attribute values associated with each feature. When we imported the shapefile, we extracted the attribute values from the various OGR data types and converted them into strings so they could be stored into the database. This was done using the `utils.get_ogr_feature_attribute()` function. We now have to do the opposite: storing the string value into the OGR attribute field. As before, we'll use a `utils.py` function to do the hard work; add the following highlighted lines to the bottom of your `export_data()` function:

```
    . . .

    dst_feature = ogr.Feature(layer.GetLayerDefn())
    dst_feature.SetGeometry(dst_geometry)

    for attr_value in feature.attributevalue_set.all():
        utils.set_ogr_feature_attribute(
                attr_value.attribute,
                attr_value.value,
                dst_feature,
                shapefile.encoding)

    layer.CreateFeature(dst_feature)
    dst_feature.Destroy()

datasource.Destroy()
```

> You may be wondering what `feature.attributevalue_set.all()` does. Because the `AttributeValue` object includes a foreign key linking each attribute value to the associated `Feature` object, the `Feature` object can refer to the set of attribute values that link back to it, using `attributevalue_set`. Using this technique, we can scan through the list of attribute values for a feature using `feature.attributevalue_set.all()`.
>
> If you want to learn more about these "reverse" foreign key lookups, see `https://docs.djangoproject.com/en/dev/topics/db/queries/#related-objects`.

Now let's implement the `set_ogr_feature_attribute()` function within `utils.py`. As with the `get_ogr_feature_attribute()` function, `set_ogr_feature_attribute()` is rather tedious but straightforward: we have to deal with each OGR data type in turn, processing the string representation of the attribute value and calling the appropriate `SetField()` method to set the field's value. Here is the relevant code:

```
def set_ogr_feature_attribute(attr, value, feature, encoding):
    attr_name = str(attr.name)
    if value == None:
```

```
        feature.UnsetField(attr_name)
        return

    if attr.type == ogr.OFTInteger:
        feature.SetField(attr_name, int(value))
    elif attr.type == ogr.OFTIntegerList:
        integers = eval(value)
        feature.SetFieldIntegerList(attr_name, integers)
    elif attr.type == ogr.OFTReal:
        feature.SetField(attr_name, float(value))
    elif attr.type == ogr.OFTRealList:
        floats = []
        for s in eval(value):
            floats.append(eval(s))
        feature.SetFieldDoubleList(attr_name, floats)
    elif attr.type == ogr.OFTString:
        feature.SetField(attr_name, value.encode(encoding))
    elif attr.type == ogr.OFTStringList:
        strings = []
        for s in eval(value):
            strings.append(s.encode(encoding))
        feature.SetFieldStringList(attr_name, strings)
    elif attr.type == ogr.OFTDate:
        parts = value.split(",")
        year  = int(parts[0])
        month = int(parts[1])
        day   = int(parts[2])
        tzone = int(parts[3])
        feature.SetField(attr_name, year, month, day,
                         0, 0, 0, tzone)
    elif attr.type == ogr.OFTTime:
        parts  = value.split(",")
        hour   = int(parts[0])
        minute = int(parts[1])
        second = int(parts[2])
        tzone  = int(parts[3])
        feature.SetField(attr_name, 0, 0, 0,
                         hour, minute, second, tzone)
    elif attr.type == ogr.OFTDateTime:
        parts = value.split(",")
        year   = int(parts[0])
        month  = int(parts[1])
        day    = int(parts[2])
        hour   = int(parts[3])
        minute = int(parts[4])
        second = int(parts[5])
        tzone  = int(parts[6])
        feature.SetField(attr_name, year, month, day,
                         hour, minute, second, tzone)
```

Compressing the shapefile

Now that we've exported the desired data into an OGR shapefile, we can compress it into a ZIP archive. Go back to the `exporter.py` module and add the following to the end of your `export_data()` function:

```
temp = tempfile.TemporaryFile()
zip = zipfile.ZipFile(temp, 'w', zipfile.ZIP_DEFLATED)

shapefile_base = os.path.splitext(dstFile)[0]
shapefile_name = os.path.splitext(shapefile.filename)[0]

for fName in os.listdir(dst_dir):
    zip.write(os.path.join(dst_dir, fName), fName)

zip.close()
```

Note that we use a temporary file, named `temp`, to store the ZIP archive's contents. We'll be returning `temp` to the user's web browser once the export process has finished.

Deleting temporary files

We next have to clean up after ourselves by deleting the shapefile that we created earlier:

```
shutil.rmtree(dst_dir)
```

Note that we don't have to remove the temporary ZIP archive, as that's done automatically for us by the `tempfile` module when the file is closed.

Returning the ZIP archive to the user

The last step in exporting the shapefile is to send the ZIP archive to the user's web browser so that it can be downloaded onto the user's computer. To do this, we'll create an `HttpResponse` object which includes a Django `FileWrapper` object to attach the ZIP archive to the HTTP response:

```
f = FileWrapper(temp)
response = HttpResponse(f, content_type="application/zip")
response['Content-Disposition'] = \
    "attachment; filename=" + shapefileName + ".zip"
response['Content-Length'] = temp.tell()
temp.seek(0)
return response
```

As you can see, we set up the HTTP response to indicate that we're returning a file attachment. This forces the user's browser to download the file rather than trying to display it. We also use the original shapefile's name as the name of the downloaded file.

This completes the definition of the `export_data()` function. There's only one more thing to do: add the following `import` statements to the top of the `exporter.py` module:

```
from django.http import HttpResponse
from django.core.servers.basehttp import FileWrapper
```

We've finally finished implementing the "Export Shapefile" feature. Test it out by running the server and clicking on the **Export** hyperlink beside one of your shapefiles. All going well, there'll be a slight pause and you'll be prompted to save your shapefile's ZIP archive to disk:

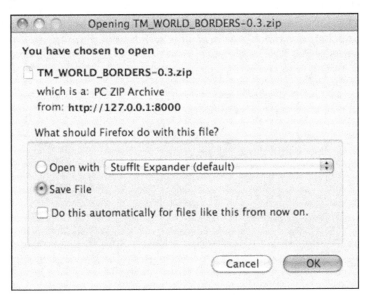

Summary

In this chapter, we continued our implementation of the ShapeEditor by adding three important functions: the "list" view, and the ability to import and export shapefiles. While these aren't very exciting features, they are a crucial part of the ShapeEditor.

In the process of implementing these features, we have learned the following:

- Using Django's templating language to display a list of records within a web page.

- Using the zipfile standard library module to extract the contents of an uploaded shapefile before opening that shapefile using OGR.

- You will need to "wrap" Polygon and LineString geometries when importing data from a shapefile into a PostGIS database, to avoid problems caused by a shapefile's inability to distinguish between Polygons and MultiPolygons, and between LineStrings and MultiLineStrings.

- When you call the object.delete() method, Django automatically deletes all the linked records for you, simplifying the process of removing a record and all its associated data.

- You can use OGR to create a new shapefile, and the zipfile library module to compress it, so that you can export geospatial data using a web interface.

With this functionality out of the way, we can now turn our attention to the most interesting parts of the ShapeEditor: the code that displays and lets the user edit geometries using a slippy map interface. This will be the main focus for the final chapter of this book.

11
ShapeEditor – Selecting and Editing Features

In this final chapter, we will implement the remaining features of the ShapeEditor application. A large part of this chapter will involve the use of OpenLayers and the creation of a Tile Map Server so that we can display a map with all the shapefile's features on it, and allow the user to click on a feature to select it. We'll also implement the ability to add, edit, and delete features, and conclude with a exploration of how the ShapeEditor can be used to work with geospatial data, and how it can serve as the springboard for your own geospatial development efforts.

In this chapter, we will learn:

- How to implement a Tile Map Server using Mapnik and GeoDjango
- How to use OpenLayers to display a slippy map on a web page
- How to write a custom click-handler for OpenLayers
- How to use AJAX requests within OpenLayers
- How to perform spatial queries using GeoDjango
- How to use GeoDjango's built-in editing widgets in your own application
- How to edit geospatial data using GeoDjango's built-in editing widgets
- How to customize the interface for GeoDjango's editing widgets
- How to add and delete records in a Django web application

Let's get started with the code that lets the user select the feature to be edited.

Selecting a feature to edit

As we discussed in the section on designing the ShapeEditor, GeoDjango's built-in map widgets can only display a single feature at a time. In order to display a map with all the shapefile's features on it, we will have to use OpenLayers directly, along with a Tile Map Server and a custom AJAX-based click handler. The basic workflow will look like this:

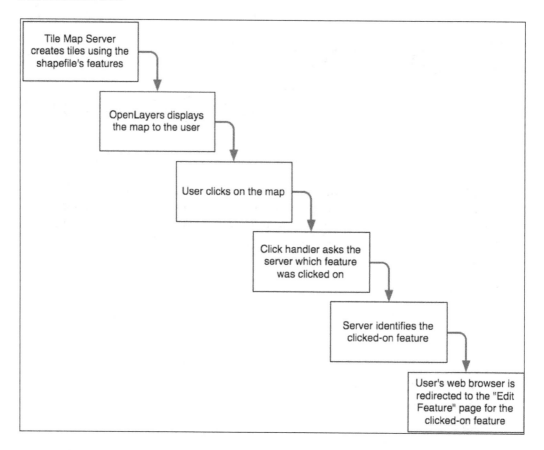

Let's start by implementing the Tile Map Server, and then see what's involved in using OpenLayers, along with a custom click-handler and some server-side AJAX code, to respond when the user clicks on the map.

Implementing Tile Map Server

As we discussed in *Bonus chapter, Web Frameworks for Python Geospatial Development* (Download link available in preface) the **Tile Map Server Protocol** is a simple RESTful protocol for serving map tiles. The TMS protocol includes calls to identify the various maps which can be displayed, along with information about the available map tiles, as well as providing access to the map tile images themselves.

Let's briefly review the terminology used by the TMS protocol:

- A **Tile Map Server** is the overall web server which is implementing the TMS protocol.

- A **Tile Map Service** provides access to a particular set of maps. There can be multiple Tile Map Services hosted by a single Tile Map Server.

- A **Tile Map** is a complete map of all or part of the Earth's surface, displaying a particular set of features or styled in a particular way. A Tile Map Service can provide access to more than one Tile Map.

- A **Tile Set** is a collection of tiles displaying a given Tile Map at a given zoom level.

- A **Tile** is a single map image representing a small portion of the map being displayed by the Tile Set.

This may sound confusing, but it's actually not too bad. We'll be implementing a Tile Map Server with just one Tile Map Service, which we'll call the "ShapeEditor Tile Map Service". There will be one Tile Map for each shapefile that has been uploaded, and we'll support Tile Sets for a standard range of zoom levels. Finally, we'll use Mapnik to render the individual Tiles within the Tile Set.

Following the Django principle of breaking a large and complex system down into separate self-contained applications, we will implement the Tile Map Server as a separate application within the shapeEditor project. Start by cd'ing into the shapeEditor project directory and type the following:

```
python manage.py startapp tms
```

This creates our tms application in the top-level directory, making it a reusable application. Move the newly-created directory into the shapeEditor sub-directory, either using the mouse or by typing the following command:

```
mv tms shapeEditor
```

This makes the Tile Map Server specific to our project. We then have to enable the application by editing our project's `settings.py` module and adding the following entry to the end of the `INSTALLED_APPS` list:

```
'shapeEditor.tms',
```

Next, we want to make our Tile Map Server's URLs available as part of the shapeEditor project. To do this, edit the global `urls.py` module (located inside the main shapeEditor directory), and add the following highlighted line to the first `urlpatterns = ...` statement:

```
urlpatterns = patterns('',
    url(r'^editor/', include('shapeEditor.editor.urls')),
    url(r'^tms/', include('shapeEditor.tms.urls')),
)
```

We now want to define the individual URLs provided by our Tile Map Server application. To do this, create a new module named `urls.py` inside the `tms` directory, and enter the following into this module:

```
# URLConf for the shapeEditor.tms application.

from django.conf.urls import patterns, url

urlpatterns = patterns('shapeEditor.tms.views',
        url(r'^$',
            'root'), # "/tms" calls root()
        url(r'^(?P<version>[0-9.]+)$',
            'service'), # eg, "/tms/1.0" calls service(version="1.0")
        url(r'^(?P<version>[0-9.]+)/' +
            r'(?P<shapefile_id>\d+)$',
            'tileMap'), # eg, "/tms/1.0/2" calls
                        # tileMap(version="1.0", shapefile_id=2)
        url(r'^(?P<version>[0-9.]+)/' +
            r'(?P<shapefile_id>\d+)/(?P<zoom>\d+)/' +
            r'(?P<x>\d+)/(?P<y>\d+)\.png$',
            'tile'), # eg, "/tms/1.0/2/3/4/5" calls
                        # tile(version="1.0", shapefile_id=2, zoom=3, x=4,
y=5)
)
```

These URL patterns are more complicated than those we've used in the past, because we're now extracting parameters from the URL. For example, consider the following URL:

```
http://127.0.0.1:8000/tms/1.0
```

This will be matched by the second regular expression in our `tms` application's `urls.py` module:

```
^(?P<version>[0-9.]+)$
```

This regular expression will extract the `1.0` portion of the URL and assign it to a parameter named `version`. This parameter is then passed on to the view function associated with this URL pattern, as follows:

```
tileMap(version="1.0")
```

In this way, each of our URL patterns maps an incoming RESTful URL to the appropriate view function within our `tms` application. The included comments give examples of how the regular expressions will map to the view functions.

Let's now set up these view functions. Edit the `views.py` module inside the `tms` directory, and add the following to this module:

```python
from django.http import HttpResponse

def root(request):
    return HttpResponse("Tile Map Server")

def service(request, version):
    return HttpResponse("Tile Map Service")

def tileMap(request, version, shapefile_id):
    return HttpResponse("Tile Map")

def tile(request, version, shapefile_id, zoom, x, y):
    return HttpResponse("Tile")
```

Obviously these are only placeholder view functions, but they give us the basic structure for our Tile Map Server.

To test that this works, launch the `ShapeEditor` server by running the `python manage.py runserver` command, and point your web browser to `http://127.0.0.1:8000/tms`. You should see the text you entered into your placeholder `root()` view function.

Let's make that top-level view function do something useful. Go back to the `tms` application's `views.py` module, and change the `root()` function to look as follows:

```python
def root(request):
    try:
        baseURL = request.build_absolute_uri()
```

```
        xml = []
        xml.append('<?xml version="1.0" encoding="utf-8" ?>')
        xml.append('<Services>')
        xml.append('   <TileMapService ' +
                   'title="ShapeEditor Tile Map Service" ' +
                   'version="1.0" href="' + baseURL + '/1.0"/>')
        xml.append('</Services>')
        return HttpResponse("\n".join(xml), mimetype="text/xml")
    except:
        traceback.print_exc()
        return HttpResponse("Error")
```

You'll also need to add the following import statement to the top of the module:

```
import traceback
```

This view function returns an XML-format response describing the one-and-only Tile Map Service supported by our TMS server. This Tile Map Service is identified by a version number, 1.0 (Tile Map Services are typically identified by version number). If you now go to `http://127.0.0.1:8000/tms`, you'll see the TMS response displayed in your web browser:

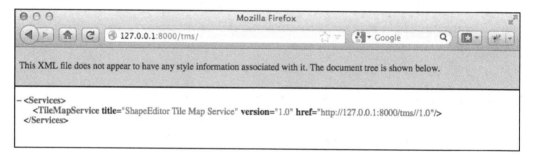

As you can see, this provides a list of the Tile Map Services which this TMS server provides. OpenLayers will use this to access our Tile Map Service.

Error handling

Notice that we've wrapped our TMS view function in a `try...`
`except` statement, and used the `traceback` standard library
module to print out the exception if anything goes wrong.
We're doing this because our code will be called directly by
OpenLayers using AJAX; Django helpfully handles exceptions
and returns an HTML error page to the caller, but in this case
OpenLayers won't display that page if there is an error in your
code. Instead, all you'll see are broken image icons instead of a
map, and the error itself will remain a mystery.

By wrapping our Python code in a `try...except` statement,
we can catch any exceptions in our Python code and print them
out. This will cause the error to appear in Django's web server
log, so we can see what went wrong. This is a useful technique
to use whenever you write AJAX request handlers in Python.

We're now ready to implement the Tile Map Service itself. Edit the `view.py` module
again, and change the `service()` function to look like this:

```python
def service(request, version):
    try:
        if version != "1.0":
            raise Http404

        baseURL = request.build_absolute_uri()
        xml = []
        xml.append('<?xml version="1.0" encoding="utf-8" ?>')
        xml.append('<TileMapService version="1.0" services="' +
                   baseURL + '">')
        xml.append('    <Title>ShapeEditor Tile Map Service' +
                   '</Title>')
        xml.append('    <Abstract></Abstract>')
        xml.append('    <TileMaps>')
        for shapefile in Shapefile.objects.all():
            id = str(shapefile.id)
            xml.append('        <TileMap title="' +
                       shapefile.filename + '"')
            xml.append('                 srs="EPSG:4326"')
            xml.append('                 href="'+baseURL+'/'+id+'"/>')
        xml.append('    </TileMaps>')
        xml.append('</TileMapService>')
```

```
            return HttpResponse("\n".join(xml), mimetype="text/xml")
    except:
        traceback.print_exc()
        return HttpResponse("Error")
```

You'll also need to add the following `import` statements to the top of the module:

```
from django.http import Http404
from geodjango.shapeEditor.models import Shapefile
```

Notice that this function raises an `Http404` exception if the version number is wrong. This exception tells Django to return a HTTP 404 error, which is the standard error response when an incorrect URL has been used.

Assuming the version number is correct, we iterate over the various `Shapefile` objects in the database, listing each uploaded shapefile as a Tile Map.

If you save this file and enter `http://127.0.0.1:8000/tms/1.0` into your web browser, you should see a list of the available tile maps, in XML format:

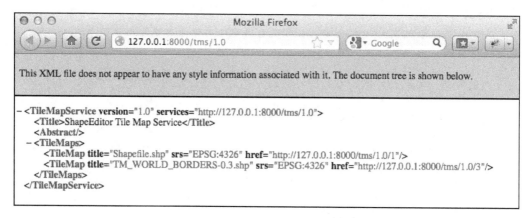

We next need to implement the `tileMap()` function to display the various Tile Sets available for a given Tile Map. Before we can do this, though, we're going to have to learn a bit about the notion of zoom levels.

As we have seen, a slippy map lets the user zoom in and out to view the map's contents. This zooming is done by controlling the map's zoom level. Typically, a zoom level is specified as a simple number: zoom level zero is when the map is fully zoomed out, zoom level 1 is when the map is zoomed in once, and so on.

Let's start by considering the map when it is zoomed out completely (in other words, zoom level 0). In this case, we want the entire Earth's surface to be covered by just two map tiles:

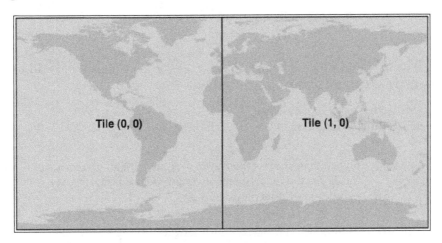

Each map tile at this zoom level would cover 180 degrees of latitude and longitude. If each tile was 256 pixels square, this would mean that each pixel would cover 180 / 256 = 0.703125 map units, where in this case a "map unit" is a degree of latitude or longitude. This number is going to be very important when it comes to calculating the Tile Maps.

Now, whenever we zoom in (for example by going from zoom level 0 to zoom level 1), the width and height of the visible area is halved. For example, at zoom level 1 the Earth's surface would be displayed as the following series of eight tiles:

Tile (0, 1)	Tile (1, 1)	Tile (2, 1)	Tile (3, 1)
Tile (0, 0)	Tile (1, 0)	Tile (2, 0)	Tile (3, 0)

Following this pattern, we can calculate the number of map units covered by a single pixel on the map, for a given zoom level, using the following formula:

$$\text{Map units per pixel} \quad = \quad \frac{0.703125}{2^{\text{zoom level}}}$$

Since we'll be using this formula in our TMS server, let's go ahead and add the following code to the end of our `tms.py` module:

```
def _unitsPerPixel(zoomLevel):
    return 0.703125 / math.pow(2, zoomLevel)
```

 Notice that we start the function name with an underscore; this is a standard Python convention for naming "private" functions within a module.

You'll also need to add an `import math` statement to the top of the file.

Next, we need to add some constants to the top of the module to define the size of each map tile, and how many zoom levels we support:

```
MAX_ZOOM_LEVEL = 10
TILE_WIDTH     = 256
TILE_HEIGHT    = 256
```

With all this, we're finally ready to implement the `tileMap()` function to return information about the available Tile Sets for a given shapefile's Tile Map. Edit this function to look as follows:

```
def tileMap(request, version, shapefile_id):
    if version != "1.0":
        raise Http404

    try:
        shapefile = Shapefile.objects.get(id=shapefile_id)
    except Shapefile.DoesNotExist:
        raise Http404

    try:
        baseURL = request.build_absolute_uri()
        xml = []
```

```
xml.append('<?xml version="1.0" encoding="utf-8" ?>')
xml.append('<TileMap version="1.0" ' +
            'tilemapservice="' + baseURL + '">')
xml.append('  <Title>' + shapefile.filename + '</Title>')
xml.append('  <Abstract></Abstract>')
xml.append('  <SRS>EPSG:4326</SRS>')
xml.append('  <BoundingBox minx="-180" miny="-90" ' +
            'maxx="180" maxy="90"/>')
xml.append('  <Origin x="-180" y="-90"/>')
xml.append('  <TileFormat width="' + str(TILE_WIDTH) +
            '" height="' + str(TILE_HEIGHT) + '" ' +
            'mime-type="image/png" extension="png"/>')
xml.append('  <TileSets profile="global-geodetic">')
for zoomLevel in range(0, MAX_ZOOM_LEVEL+1):
    unitsPerPixel = _unitsPerPixel(zoomLevel)
    xml.append('    <TileSet href="' +
                baseURL + '/' + str(zoomLevel) +
                '" units-per-pixel="'+str(unitsPerPixel) +
                '" order="' + str(zoomLevel) + '"/>')
xml.append('  </TileSets>')
xml.append('</TileMap>')
return HttpResponse("\n".join(xml), mimetype="text/xml")
except:
    traceback.print_exc()
    return HttpResponse("Error")
```

As you can see, we start with some basic error checking on the version and shapefile ID, and then iterate through the available zoom levels to provide information about the available Tile Sets.

If you save your changes and enter `http://127.0.0.1:8000/tms/1.0/2` into your web browser, you should see the following information about the Tile Map for the shapefile object with record ID 2:

Notice that we provide a total of eleven zoom levels, from zero to ten, with an appropriately-calculated `units-per-pixel` value for each zoom level.

We have now implemented three of the four view functions required to implement our own Tile Map Server. For the final function, `tile()`, we are going to write our own tile renderer. The `tile()` function accepts a Tile Map Service version, a shapefile ID, a zoom level, and the X and Y coordinates for the desired tile:

```
def tile(request, version, shapefile_id, zoom, x, y):
    ...
```

This function needs to generate the appropriate map tile and return the rendered image back to the caller. Before we implement this function, let's take a step back and think about what the map rendering should look like.

We want the map to include the outline of the various features within the given shapefile. However, by themselves these features won't look very meaningful:

It isn't until these features are shown in context, by displaying a **base map** behind the features, that we can see what they are supposed to represent:

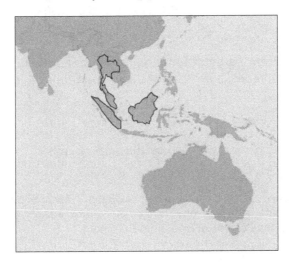

Because of this, we're going to have to display a base map on which the features themselves are drawn. Let's build that base map, and then we can use this, along with the shapefile's features, to render the map tiles.

Setting up the base map

For our base map, we're going to use the World Borders Dataset we've used several times throughout this book. While this dataset doesn't look great when zoomed right in, it works well as a base map on which we can draw the shapefile's features.

We'll start by creating a database model to hold the base map's data. Because the base map will be specific to our Tile Map Server application, we want to add a database table specific to this application. To do this, edit the `models.py` module inside the `tms` application directory, and change this file to look like the following:

```
from django.contrib.gis.db import models

class BaseMap(models.Model):
    name     = models.CharField(max_length=50)
    geometry = models.MultiPolygonField(srid=4326)

    objects = models.GeoManager()

    def __unicode__(self):
        return self.name
```

 Don't forget to change the `import` statement at the top of the file.

As you can see, we're storing the country names as well as their geometries, which happen to be MultiPolygons. Now from the command line, `cd` into your project directory and type:

% python manage.py syncdb

This will create the database table used by the `BaseMap` object.

 Remember that there's a bug in Django 1.4 that prevents the geospatial fields from being created automatically. To fix this, run the Postgresql command-line client:

```
$ psql shapeeditor
```

You can then manually add the missing `geometry` field and its associated spatial index by typing in the following commands:

```
ALTER TABLE tms_basemap ADD COLUMN geometry
geometry(MultiPolygon, 4326);

CREATE INDEX tms_basemap_geometry_id ON tms_
basemap USING GIST(geometry);
```

Now that we have somewhere to store the base map, let's import the data. Place a copy of the World Borders Dataset shapefile somewhere convenient, open up a command line window, and `cd` into your `shapeEditor` project directory. Then type:

```
% python manage.py shell
```

This runs a Python interactive shell with your project's settings and paths installed. Now create the following variable, replacing the text with the absolute path to the World Borders Dataset's shapefile:

```
>>> shapefile = "/path/to/TM_WORLD_BORDERS-0.3.shp"
```

```
Then type the following:
```

```
>>> from django.contrib.gis.utils import LayerMapping
```

```
>>> from shapeEditor.tms.models import BaseMap
```

```
>>> mapping = LayerMapping(BaseMap, shapefile, {'name' : "NAME",
'geometry' : "MULTIPOLYGON"}, transform=False, encoding="iso-8859-1")
```

```
>>> mapping.save(strict=True, verbose=True)
```

We're using GeoDjango's `LayerMapping` module to import the data from this shapefile into our database. The various countries will be displayed as they are imported, which will take a few seconds.

Once this has been done, you can check the imported data by typing commands into the interactive shell, for example:

```
>>> print BaseMap.objects.count()
```

```
246
```

```
>>> print BaseMap.objects.all()
```

```
[<BaseMap: Antigua and Barbuda>, <BaseMap: Algeria>, <BaseMap:
Azerbaijan>, <BaseMap: Albania>, <BaseMap: Armenia>, <BaseMap: Angola>,
<BaseMap: American Samoa>, <BaseMap: Argentina>, <BaseMap: Australia>,
<BaseMap: Bahrain>, <BaseMap: Barbados>, <BaseMap: Bermuda>, <BaseMap:
Bahamas>, <BaseMap: Bangladesh>, <BaseMap: Belize>, <BaseMap: Bosnia and
Herzegovina>, <BaseMap: Bolivia>, <BaseMap: Burma>, <BaseMap: Benin>,
<BaseMap: Solomon Islands>, '...(remaining elements truncated)...']
```

Feel free to play some more if you want; the Django tutorial includes several examples of exploring your data objects using the interactive shell.

Because this base map is going to be part of the ShapeEditor project itself (the application won't run without it), it would be good if Django could treat that data as part of the project's source code. That way, if we ever had to rebuild the database from scratch, the base map would be reinstalled automatically.

Django allows you to do this by creating a **fixture**. A fixture is a set of data that can be loaded into the database on demand, either manually, or automatically when the database is initialized. We'll save our base map data into a fixture so that Django can reload that data as required.

Create a directory named `fixtures` within the `tms` application directory. Then, in a terminal window, `cd` into the `shapeEditor` project directory and type:

```
% python manage.py dumpdata tms > shapeEditor/tms/fixtures/initial_data.
json
```

This will create a fixture named `initial_data.json` for the `tms` application. As the name suggests, the contents of this fixture will be loaded automatically if Django ever has to re-initialize the database.

Now that we have a base map, let's use it to implement our tile rendering code.

Tile rendering

Using our knowledge of Mapnik, we're going to implement the TMS server's `tile()` function. Our generated map will consist of two layers: a **base layer** showing the base map, and a **feature layer** showing the features in the imported shapefile. Since all our data is stored in a PostGIS database, we'll be using a `mapnik.PostGIS` datasource for both layers.

Our `tile()` function will involve five steps:

1. Parse the query parameters.
2. Set up the map.
3. Define the base layer.
4. Define the feature layer.
5. Render the map.

Let's work through each of these in turn.

Parsing the query parameters

Edit the `tms` application's `views.py` module, and delete the dummy code we had in the `tile()` function. We'll add our parsing code one step at a time, starting with some basic error-checking code to ensure the version number is correct and that the shapefile exists, and once again wrapping our code in a `try...except` statement to catch typos and other errors:

```
try:
    if version != "1.0":
        raise Http404

    try:
        shapefile = Shapefile.objects.get(id=shapefile_id)
    except Shapefile.DoesNotExist:
        raise Http404
```

We now need to convert the query parameters (which Django passes to us as strings) into integers so that we can work with them:

```
zoom = int(zoom)
x    = int(x)
y    = int(y)
```

We can now check that the zoom level is correct:

```
if zoom < 0 or zoom > MAX_ZOOM_LEVEL:
    raise Http404
```

Our next step is to convert the supplied x and y parameters into the minimum and maximum latitude and longitude values covered by the tile. This requires us to use the `_unitsPerPixel()` function we defined earlier to calculate the amount of the Earth's surface covered by the tile for the current zoom level:

```
xExtent = _unitsPerPixel(zoom) * TILE_WIDTH
yExtent = _unitsPerPixel(zoom) * TILE_HEIGHT

minLong = x * xExtent - 180.0
minLat  = y * yExtent - 90.0
maxLong = minLong + xExtent
maxLat  = minLat  + yExtent
```

Finally, we can add some rudimentary error checking to ensure that the tile's coordinates are valid:

```
if (minLong < -180 or maxLong > 180 or
    minLat < -90 or maxLat > 90):
    raise Http404
```

Setting up the map

We're now ready to create the `mapnik.Map` object to represent the map. This is trivial:

```
map = mapnik.Map(TILE_WIDTH, TILE_HEIGHT,
                 "+proj=longlat +datum=WGS84")
map.background = mapnik.Color("#7391ad")
```

Defining the base layer

We now want to define the layer which draws our base map. To do this, we have to set up a `mapnik.PostGIS` datasource for the layer:

```
dbSettings = settings.DATABASES['default']
datasource = \
    mapnik.PostGIS(user=dbSettings['USER'],
                   password=dbSettings['PASSWORD'],
                   dbname=dbSettings['NAME'],
                   table='tms_basemap',
                   srid=4326,
                   geometry_field="geometry",
                   geometry_table='tms_basemap')
```

As you can see, we get the name of the database, the username, and the password from our project's `settings` module. We then create a PostGIS datasource using these settings. With this data source, we can now create the base layer itself:

```
baseLayer = mapnik.Layer("baseLayer")
baseLayer.datasource = datasource
baseLayer.styles.append("baseLayerStyle")
```

We now need to set up the layer's style. In this case, we'll use a single rule with two symbolizers: a `PolygonSymbolizer` which draws the interior of the base map's polygons, and a `LineSymbolizer` to draw the polygon outlines:

```
rule = mapnik.Rule()

rule.symbols.append(
```

```
        mapnik.PolygonSymbolizer(mapnik.Color("#b5d19c")))
    rule.symbols.append(
        mapnik.LineSymbolizer(mapnik.Color("#404040"), 0.2))

    style = mapnik.Style()
    style.rules.append(rule)
```

Finally, we can add the base layer and its style to the map:

```
    map.append_style("baseLayerStyle", style)
    map.layers.append(baseLayer)
```

Defining the feature layer

Our next task is to add another layer to draw the shapefile's features onto the map. Once again, we'll set up a `mapnik.PostGIS` datasource for the new layer:

```
    geometry_field = utils.calc_geometry_field(shapefile.geom_type)

    query = '(select ' + geometry_field \
            + ' from "shared_feature" where' \
            + ' shapefile_id=' + str(shapefile.id) + ') as geom'

    datasource = \
        mapnik.PostGIS(user=dbSettings['USER'],
                       password=dbSettings['PASSWORD'],
                       dbname=dbSettings['NAME'],
                       table=query,
                       srid=4326,
                       geometry_field=geometryField,
                       geometry_table='shared_feature')
```

In this case, we are calling `utils.calc_geometry_field()` to see which field in the `shared_feature` table contains the geometry we're going to display.

We're now ready to create the new layer itself:

```
    featureLayer = mapnik.Layer("featureLayer")
    featureLayer.datasource = datasource
    featureLayer.styles.append("featureLayerStyle")
```

Next, we want to define the styles used by the feature layer. As before, we'll have just a single rule, but in this case we'll use different symbolizers depending on the type of feature we are displaying:

```
rule = mapnik.Rule()

if shapefile.geom_type in ["Point", "MultiPoint"]:
    rule.symbols.append(mapnik.PointSymbolizer())
elif shapefile.geom_type in ["LineString", "MultiLineString"]:
    rule.symbols.append(
        mapnik.LineSymbolizer(mapnik.Color("#000000"), 0.5))
elif shapefile.geom_type in ["Polygon", "MultiPolygon"]:
    rule.symbols.append(
        mapnik.PolygonSymbolizer(mapnik.Color("#f7edee")))
    rule.symbols.append(
        mapnik.LineSymbolizer(mapnik.Color("#000000"), 0.5))

style = mapnik.Style()
style.rules.append(rule)
```

Finally, we can add our new feature layer to the map:

```
map.append_style("featureLayerStyle", style)
map.layers.append(featureLayer)
```

Rendering the map tile

We looked at using Mapnik to render map images in *Bonus Chapter, Web Frameworks for Python Geospatial Development*. The basic process of rendering a map tile is the same, except that we won't be storing the results into an image file on disk. Instead, we'll create a `mapnik.Image` object, convert it into raw image data in PNG format, and return that data back to the caller using an `HttpResponse` object:

```
map.zoom_to_box(mapnik.Box2d(minLong, minLat,
                             maxLong, maxLat))
image = mapnik.Image(TILE_WIDTH, TILE_HEIGHT)
mapnik.render(map, image)
imageData = image.tostring('png')

return HttpResponse(imageData, mimetype="image/png")
```

All that's left now is to add our error-catching code to the end of the function:

```
except:
    traceback.print_exc()
    return HttpResponse("Error")
```

That completes the implementation of our Tile Map Server's `tile()` function. Let's tidy up and do some testing.

Completing the Tile Map Server

Because we've referred to some new modules in our `views.py` module, we'll have to add some extra import statements to the top of the file:

```
from django.conf import settings
import mapnik
import utils
```

In theory, our Tile Map Server should now be ready to go. Let's test it out. If you don't currently have the Django web server running, `cd` into the `shapeEditor` project directory and type:

% python manage.py runserver

Start up your web browser and enter the following URL into your browser's address bar:

```
http://127.0.0.1:8000/tms/1.0/2/0/0/0.png
```

All going well, you should see a 256 x 256 pixel map tile appear in your web browser:

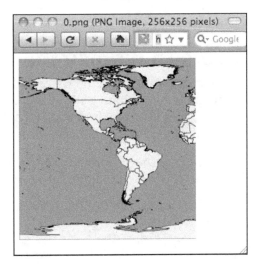

Problems?

If an error occurs, there are two likely causes: you might have made a mistake typing in the code, or you might have the record ID of the shapefile wrong. Check the web server log in the terminal window you used to run the `python manage.py runserver` command; when a Python exception occurs, the traceback will be printed out in this window. This will tell you if you have a syntax error, some other error, or if an `Http404` exception was raised.

If you do get an `Http404` exception, it's most likely because you're using the wrong record ID for the shapefile. The URL is structured like this:

```
http://path/to/tms/<version>/<shapefile_
id>/<zoom>/<x>/<y>.png
```

If you've been working through this chapter in order, the record ID of the World Borders Dataset shapefile you imported earlier should be 2, but if you've imported other shapefiles in the meantime, or created more shapefile records while playing with the admin interface, you may need to use a different record ID. To see what record ID a given shapefile has, go to `http://127.0.0.1:8000/editor` and click on the **Edit** hyperlink for the desired shapefile. You'll see a `Page Not Found` error, but the final part of the hyperlink will be the record ID of the shapefile. Replace the record ID in the previous URL with the correct ID, and the map tile should appear.

Once you've reached the point of seeing the previous image in your web browser, you deserve a pat on the back: congratulations, you have just implemented your own working Tile Map Server!

Using OpenLayers to display the map

Now that we have our TMS server up and running, we can use the OpenLayers library to display the rendered map tiles within a slippy map. This slippy map will be used within our `edit shapefile` view function to display all the shapefile's features, allowing the user to select a feature within the shapefile to edit.

Let's implement this `edit shapefile` view. Edit the `urls.py` module within the `editor` application, and add the following highlighted entry to this file:

```
urlpatterns = patterns('shapeEditor.editor.views',
    url(r'^$', 'list_shapefiles'),
    url(r'^import$', 'import_shapefile'),
```

```
    url(r'^export/(?P<shapefile_id>\d+)$', 'export_shapefile'),
    url(r'^edit/(?P<shapefile_id>\d+)$',
'edit_shapefile'),
)
```

This will pass any incoming URLs of the form /editor/edit/N to the edit_shapefile() view function.

Let's implement that function. Edit the editor application's views.py module and add the following code:

```
def edit_shapefile(request, shapefile_id):
    try:
        shapefile = Shapefile.objects.get(id=shapefile_id)
    except Shapefile.DoesNotExist:
        return HttpResponseNotFound()

    tms_url = "http://"+request.get_host()+"/tms/"

    return render(request, "select_feature.html",
                  {'shapefile' : shapefile,
                   'tms_url'    : tms_url})
```

As you can see, we obtain the desired Shapefile object, calculate the URL used to access our TMS server, and pass both on to a template called select_feature.html. That template is where all the hard work will take place.

Now we need to write the template. Start by creating a new file named select_feature.html in the editor application's templates directory, and enter the following into this file:

```
<html>
  <head>
    <title>ShapeEditor</title>
    <style type="text/css">
      div#map {
        width:  600px;
        height: 400px;
        border: 1px solid #ccc;
      }
    </style>
  </head>
  <body>
    <h1>Edit Shapefile</h1>
```

```
<b>Please choose a feature to edit</b>
<br/>
<div id="map" class="map"></div>
<br/>
<div style="margin-left:20px">
  <button type="button"
          onClick='window.location="/editor";'>
    Cancel
  </button>
</div>
</body>
</html>
```

This is only the basic outline for this template, but it gives us something to work with. With the Django development server running (python manage.py runserver in a terminal window), go to http://127.0.0.1:8000/editor click on the **Edit** hyperlink for a shapefile. You should see the basic outline for the select feature page:

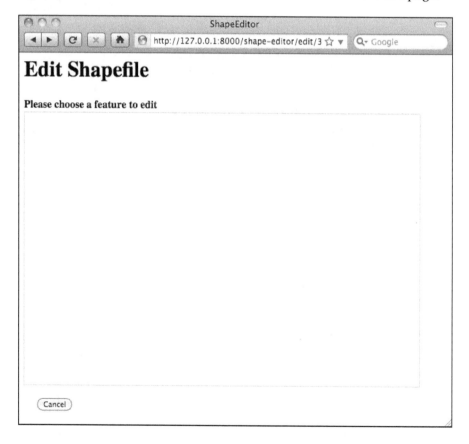

Notice that we created a `<div>` element to hold the OpenLayers map, and we use a CSS stylesheet to give the map a fixed size and border. The map itself isn't being displayed yet, because we haven't written the JavaScript code needed to launch OpenLayers. Let's do that now.

Add the following `<script>` tags to the `<head>` section of your template:

```
<script src="http://openlayers.org/api/OpenLayers.js">
</script>
<script type="text/javascript">
  function init() {}
</script>
```

Also, change the `<body>` tag definition to look like this:

```
<body onload="init()">
```

Notice that there are two `<script>` tags: the first loads the `OpenLayers.js` library from the `http://openlayers.org` website, while the second will hold the JavaScript code that we'll write to create the map. We've also defined a JavaScript function called `init()` which will be called when the page is loaded.

Let's implement that initialization function. Replace the line which says `function init() {}` with the following:

```
function init() {
  map = new OpenLayers.Map('map',
                {maxResolution: 0.703125,
                 numZoomLevels: 11});
  layer = new OpenLayers.Layer.TMS('TMS',
                "{{ tms_url }}",
                {serviceVersion: "1.0",
                 layername: "{{ shapefile.id }}",
                 type: 'png'});
  map.addLayer(layer);
  map.zoomToMaxExtent();
}
```

Even if you haven't used JavaScript before, this code should be quite straightforward: the first instruction creates an `OpenLayers.Map` object representing the slippy map. We then create an `OpenLayers.Layer.TMS` object to represent a map layer that takes data from a TMS server. Then we add the layer to the map, and zoom the map out as far as possible so that the user sees the entire world when the map is first displayed.

Notice that the Map object accepts the ID of the <div> tag in which to place the map, along with a dictionary of options. The maxResolution option defines the maximum resolution to use for the map, and the numZoomLevels option tells OpenLayers how many zoom levels the map should support.

For the Layer.TMS object, we pass in the URL used to access the Tile Map Server (which is a parameter passed to the template from our Python view), along with the version of the Tile Map Service to use and the name of the layer—which in our Tile Map Server is the record ID of the shapefile to display the features for.

That's all we need to do to get a basic slippy map working with OpenLayers. Save your changes, start up the Django web server if it isn't already running, and point your web browser to http://127.0.0.1:8000/editor. Click on the **Edit** hyperlink for the shapefile you imported, and you should see the working slippy map:

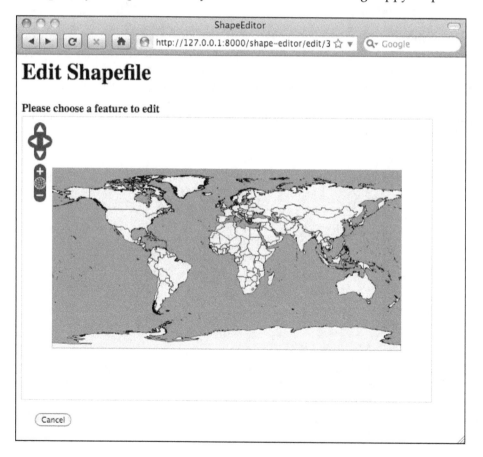

You can zoom in and out, pan around, and click to your heart's content. Of course, nothing actually works yet (apart from the **Cancel** button), but we have got a slippy map working with our Tile Map Server and the OpenLayers JavaScript widget. That's quite an achievement!

What if it doesn't work?

If the map isn't being shown for some reason, there are several possible causes. First, check the Django web server log, as we are printing any Python exceptions there. If that doesn't reveal the problem, look at your web browser's error console window to see if there are any errors at the JavaScript level. Because we are now writing JavaScript code, error messages will appear within the web browser rather than in Django's server log. In Firefox, you can view JavaScript errors by selecting the **Error Console** item from the **Tools** menu. Other browsers have similar windows for showing JavaScript errors.

JavaScript debugging can be quite tricky, even for people experienced with developing web-based applications. If you do get stuck, you may find the following article helpful: `http://www.webmonkey.com/2010/02/javascript_debugging_for_beginners`

Intercepting mouse clicks

When the user clicks on the map, we want to intercept that mouse click, identify the map coordinate that the user clicked on, and then ask the server to identify the clicked-on feature (if any). To intercept mouse clicks, we will need to create a custom `OpenLayers.Control` subclass. We'll follow the OpenLayers convention of adding the subclass to the OpenLayers namespace, by calling our new control `OpenLayers.Control.Click`. Once we've defined our new control, we can create an instance of the control and add it to the map so that the control can respond to mouse clicks.

All of this has to be done in JavaScript. The code can be a bit confusing, so let's take this one step at a time. Edit your `selectFeature.html` file and add the following code to the `<script>` tag, immediately before your `init()` function:

```
OpenLayers.Control.Click = OpenLayers.Class(
    OpenLayers.Control, {
        defaultHandlerOptions: {
            'single'        : true,
            'double'        : false,
```

```
            'pixelTolerance' : 0,
            'stopSingle'      : false,
            'stopDouble'      : false
        },

        initialize: function(options) {
          this.handlerOptions = OpenLayers.Util.extend(
            {}, this.defaultHandlerOptions);
          OpenLayers.Control.prototype.initialize.apply(
            this, arguments);
          this.handler = new OpenLayers.Handler.Click(
            this, {'click' : this.onClick}, this.handlerOptions);
        },

        onClick: function(e) {
          alert("click")
        }
      }
    );
```

Don't worry too much about the details here—the `initialize()` function is a bit of black magic that creates a new `OpenLayers.Control.Click` instance and sets it up to run as an OpenLayers control. What is interesting to us is the `defaultHandlerOptions` dictionary, and the `onClick()` function.

The `defaultHandlerOptions` dictionary tells OpenLayers how you want the click handler to respond to mouse clicks. In this case, we want to respond to single clicks, but not double clicks (as these are used to zoom further in to the map).

The `onClick()` function is actually a JavaScript method for our `OpenLayers.Control.Click` class. This method will be called when the user clicks on the map—at the moment, all we're doing is displaying an alert box with the message **Click**, but that's enough to ensure that the click control is working.

Now that we've defined our new click control, let's add it to the map. Add the following lines immediately before the closing } for the `init()` function:

```
var click = new OpenLayers.Control.Click();
map.addControl(click);
click.activate();
```

As you can see, we create a new instance of our `OpenLayers.Control.Click` class, add it to the map, and activate it.

With all this code written, we can now reload the `Select Feature` web page and see what happens when the user clicks on a map:

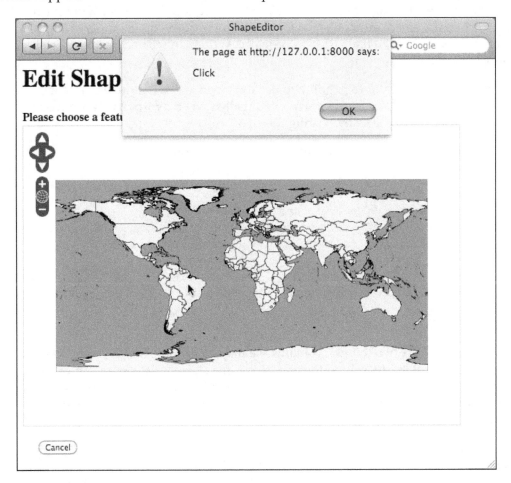

So far so good. Notice that our click handler only intercepts single clicks; if you double-click on the map, it will still zoom in.

If your map isn't working, you may have made a mistake typing in the JavaScript code. Open your browser's JavaScript console or log window, and reload the page. An error message will appear in this window if there is a problem with your JavaScript code.

Let's now implement the real `onClick()` function to respond to the user's mouse-click. When the user clicks on the map, we're going to send the clicked-on latitude and longitude value to the server using an AJAX request. The server will return the URL of the edit feature page for the clicked-on feature, or an empty string if no feature was clicked on. If a URL was returned, we'll then redirect the user's web browser to that URL.

To make the AJAX call, we're going to use the `OpenLayers.Request.GET` function, passing in a callback function which will be called when a response is received back from the server. Let's start by writing the AJAX call.

Replace our dummy `onClick()` function with the following:

```
onClick: function(e) {
    var coord = map.getLonLatFromViewPortPx(e.xy);
    var request = OpenLayers.Request.GET({
        url       : "{{ find_feature_url }}",
        params    : {shapefile_id : {{ shapefile.id }},
                     latitude      : coord.lat,
                     longitude     : coord.lon},
        callback : this.handleResponse
    });
}
```

This function does two things: it obtains the map coordinate that corresponds to the clicked-on point (by calling the `map.getLonLatFromViewPortPx()` method), and then it creates an `OpenLayers.Request.GET` object to send the AJAX request to the server and call the `handleResponse()` callback function when the response is received.

Notice that the `OpenLayers.Request.GET()` function accepts a set of query parameters (in the `params` entry), as well as a URL to send the request to (in the `url` entry) and a callback function to call when the response is received (in the `callback` entry). We're using a template parameter, `{{ find_feature_url }}`, to select the URL to send the request to. This will be provided by our `edit_shapeFile()` view function when the template is loaded. When we make the request, the query parameters will consist of the record ID of the shapefile and the clicked-on latitude and longitude values.

While we're editing the `select_feature.html` template, let's go ahead and implement the callback function. Add the following function to the end of the `OpenLayers.Control.Click` class definition (immediately below the closing } for the `onClick()` function):

```
handleResponse: function(request) {
  if (request.status != 200) {
    alert("Server returned a "+request.status+" error");
    return;
  };
  if (request.responseText != "") {
    window.location.href = request.responseText;
  };
}
```

 Make sure you add a comma after the `onClick()` function's closing parenthesis, or you'll get a JavaScript error. Just as with Python, you need to add commas to separate dictionary entries in JavaScript.

Even if you're not familiar with JavaScript, this function should be easy to understand: if the response didn't have a status value of 200, an error message is displayed. Otherwise, we check that the response text is not blank, and if so we redirect the user's web browser to that URL.

Now that we've implemented our callback function, let's go back to our view module and define the `find_feature_url` parameter which will get passed to the template we've created. Edit the `view.py` module to add the following highlighted lines to the `edit_shapefile()` function:

```
def edit_shapefile(request, shapefile_id):
  try:
    shapefile = Shapefile.objects.get(id=shapefile_id)
  except Shapefile.DoesNotExist:
    return HttpResponseNotFound()

  tms_url = "http://"+request.get_host()+"/tms/"
  find_feature_url = "http://" + request.get_host() \
              + "/editor/find_feature"
```

```
        return render(request, "select_feature.html",
                    {'shapefile'        : shapefile,
                     'find_feature_url' : find_feature_url,
                     'tms_url'          : tms_url})
```

The `find_feature_url` template parameter will contain the URL the click handler will send its AJAX request to. This URL will look like the following:

```
http://127.0.0.1:8000/editor/find_feature
```

Our `onClick()` function will add `shapefile_id`, `latitude` and `longitude` query parameters to this request, so the AJAX request sent to the server will look like the following:

```
http://127.0.0.1:8000/editor/find_feature?shapefile_id=1
&latitude=-38.1674&longitude=176.2344
```

With our click handler up and running, we're now ready to start implementing the `find_feature()` view function to respond to these AJAX requests.

Implementing the find feature view

We now need to write the view function which receives the AJAX request, checks to see which feature was clicked on (if any), and returns a suitable URL to use to redirect the user's web browser to the "edit" page for that clicked-on feature. To implement this, we're going to make use of GeoDjango's **spatial query functions**.

Let's start by adding the `find_feature` view itself. To do this, edit `views.py` again and add the following placeholder code:

```
def find_feature(request):
    return HttpResponse("")
```

Returning an empty string tells our AJAX callback function that no feature was clicked on. We'll replace this with some proper spatial queries shortly. First, though, we need to add a URL pattern so that incoming requests will get forwarded to the `find_feature()` view function. Open up the `editor` application's `urls.py` module and add the following entry to the URL pattern list:

```
url(r'^find_feature$', 'find_feature'),
```

You should now be able to run the ShapeEditor, click on the **Edit** hyperlink for an uploaded shapefile, see a map showing the various features within the shapefile, and click somewhere on the map. In response, the system should do—absolutely nothing! This is because our find_feature() function is returning an empty string, so the system thinks that the user didn't click on a feature and so ignores the mouse-click.

 In this case, "absolutely nothing" is good news. As long as no error messages are being displayed, either at the Python or JavaScript level, this tells us that the AJAX code is running correctly. So go ahead and try this, even though nothing happens, just to make sure that you haven't got any bugs in your code. You should see the AJAX calls in the list of incoming HTTP requests being received by the server.

Before we implement the find_feature() function, let's take a step back and think what it means for the user to "click on" a feature's geometry. The shapeEditor supports a complete range of possible geometry types: Point, LineString, Polygon, MultiPoint, MultiLineString, MultiPolygon, and GeometryCollection. Identifying if the user clicked on a Polygon or MultiPolygon feature is straightforward enough: we simply see if the clicked-on point is inside the polygon's bounds. But because lines and points have no interior (their area will always be zero), a given coordinate could never be "inside" a Point or a LineString geometry. It might get infinitely close, but the user can never actually click inside a Point or a LineString.

This means that a spatial query of the form:

```
SELECT * FROM features WHERE ST_Contains(feature.geometry,
clickPt)
```

This is not going to work, because the click point can never be inside a Point or a LineString geometry. Instead, we have to allow for the user clicking close to the feature rather than within it. To do this, we'll calculate a search radius, in map units, and then use the DWithin() spatial query function to find all features within the given search radius of the clicked-on point.

Let's start by calculating the search radius. We know that the user might click anywhere on the Earth's surface, and that we are storing all our features in lat /long coordinates. We also know that the relationship between map coordinates (latitude/longitude values) and actual distances on the Earth's surface varies widely depending on whereabouts on the Earth you are: a degree at the equator equals a distance of 111 kilometers, while a degree in Sweden is only half that far.

To allow for a consistent search radius everywhere in the world, we will use the PROJ.4 library to calculate the distance in map units given the clicked-on location and a desired linear distance. Let's add this function to our `shared.utils` module:

```
def calc_search_radius(latitude, longitude, distance):
    geod = pyproj.Geod(ellps="WGS84")

    x,y,angle = geod.fwd(longitude, latitude, 0, distance)
    radius = y-latitude

    x,y,angle = geod.fwd(longitude, latitude, 90, distance)
    radius = max(radius, x-longitude)

    x,y,angle = geod.fwd(longitude, latitude, 180, distance)
    radius = max(radius, latitude-y)

    x,y,angle = geod.fwd(longitude, latitude, 270, distance)
    radius = max(radius, longitude-x)

    return radius
```

This function calculates the distance, in map units, of a given linear distance measured in meters. It calculates the lat/long coordinates for four points directly north, south, east, and west of the starting location and the given number of meters away from that point. It then calculates the difference in latitude or longitude between the starting location and the end point:

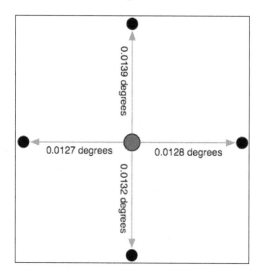

Finally, it takes the largest of these differences and returns it as the search radius, which is measured in degrees of latitude or longitude.

Because our `utils.py` module is now using `pyproj`, add the following import statement to the top of this module:

```
import pyproj
```

With the `calc_search_radius()` function written, we can now use the `DWithin()` spatial query to identify all features *close to* the clicked-on location. The general process of doing this in GeoDjango is to use the `filter()` function to create a spatial query, as follows:

```
query = Feature.objects.filter(geometry__dwithin=(pt, radius))
```

This creates a query set that returns only the `Feature` objects which match the given criteria. GeoDjango cleverly adds support for spatial queries to Django's built-in filtering capabilities; in this case, the `geometry__dwithin=(pt, radius)` parameter tells GeoDjango to perform the `dwithin()` spatial query using the two supplied parameters on the field named `geometry` within the `Feature` object. Thus, this statement will be translated by GeoDjango into a spatial database query which looks something as follows:

```
SELECT * from feature WHERE ST_DWithin(geometry, pt, radius)
```

 Note that the `geometry__dwithin` keyword parameter includes two underscore characters; Django uses a double-underscore to separate the field name from the filter function's name.

Knowing this, and having the `utils.calc_search_radius()` function implemented, we can finally implement our `find_feature()` view function. Edit `views.py` and replace the body of the `find_feature()` function with the following:

```
def find_feature(request):
    try:
        shapefile_id = int(request.GET['shapefile_id'])
        latitude     = float(request.GET['latitude'])
        longitude    = float(request.GET['longitude'])

        shapefile = Shapefile.objects.get(id=shapefile_id)
        pt = Point(longitude, latitude)
        radius = utils.calc_search_radius(latitude, longitude, 100)
```

```
          if shapefile.geom_type == "Point":
              query = Feature.objects.filter(
                  geom_point__dwithin=(pt, radius))
          elif shapefile.geom_type in ["LineString", "MultiLineString"]:
              query = Feature.objects.filter(
                  geom_multilinestring__dwithin=(pt, radius))
          elif shapefile.geom_type in ["Polygon", "MultiPolygon"]:
              query = Feature.objects.filter(
                  geom_multipolygon__dwithin=(pt, radius))
          elif shapefile.geom_type == "MultiPoint":
              query = Feature.objects.filter(
                  geom_multipoint__dwithin=(pt, radius))
          elif shapefile.geom_type == "GeometryCollection":
              query = feature.objects.filter(
                  geom_geometrycollection__dwithin=(pt, radius))
          else:
            print "Unsupported geometry: " + shapefile.geom_type
            return HttpResponse("")

          if query.count() != 1:
            return HttpResponse("")

          feature = query[0]
          return HttpResponse("/editor/edit_feature/" +
                              str(shapefile_id)+"/"+str(feature.id))
      except:
        traceback.print_exc()
        return HttpResponse("")
```

There's a lot here, so let's take this one step at a time. First off, we've wrapped all our code inside a `try...except` statement:

```
def find_feature(request):
  try:
    ...
  except:
    traceback.print_exc()
    return HttpResponse("")
```

This is the same technique we used when implementing the Tile Map Server; it means that any Python errors in your code will be displayed in the web server's log, and the AJAX function will return gracefully rather than crashing.

We then extract the supplied query parameters, converting them from strings to numbers, load the desired Shapefile object, create a GeoDjango Point object out of the clicked-on coordinates, and calculate the search radius in degrees:

```
shapefile_id = int(request.GET['shapefile_id'])
latitude     = float(request.GET['latitude'])
longitude    = float(request.GET['longitude'])

shapefile = Shapefile.objects.get(id=shapefile_id)
pt = Point(longitude, latitude)
radius = utils.calc_search_radius(latitude, longitude, 100)
```

Note that we use a hardwired search radius of 100 meters; this is enough to let the user select a point or line feature by clicking close to it, without being so large that the user might accidentally click on the wrong feature.

With this done, we're now ready to perform the spatial query. Because our Feature object has separate fields to hold each different type of geometry, we have to build the query based on the geometry's type:

```
if shapefile.geom_type == "Point":
  query = Feature.objects.filter(
            geom_point__dwithin=(pt, radius))
  elif shapefile.geom_type in ["LineString", "MultiLineString"]:
  query = Feature.objects.filter(
            geom_multilinestring__dwithin=(pt, radius))
  elif shapefile.geom_type in ["Polygon", "MultiPolygon"]:
query = Feature.objects.filter(
            geom_multipolygon__dwithin=(pt, radius))
  elif shapefile.geom_type == "MultiPoint":
  query = Feature.objects.filter(
            geom_multipoint__dwithin=(pt, radius))
  elif shapefile.geom_type == "GeometryCollection":
  query = feature.objects.filter(
            geom_geometrycollection__dwithin=(pt, radius))
else:
  print "Unsupported geometry: " + shapefile.geom_type
  return HttpResponse("")
```

In each case, we choose the appropriate geometry field, and use __dwithin to perform a spatial query on the appropriate field in the Feature object.

Once we've created the appropriate spatial query, we simply check to see if the query returned exactly one `Feature`. If not, we return an empty string back to the AJAX handler's callback function, to tell it that the user did not click on a feature:

```
if query.count() != 1:
    return HttpResponse("")
```

If there was exactly one matching feature, we get the clicked-on feature and use it to build a URL redirecting the user's web browser to the "edit feature" URL for the clicked-on feature:

```
feature = query[0]
return HttpResponse("/shape-editor/editFeature/" +
                    str(shapefile_id)+"/"+str(feature.id))
```

After typing in the previous code, add the following `import` statements to the top of the `views.py` module:

```
import traceback
from django.contrib.gis.geos import Point
from shapeEditor.shared.models import Feature
from shapeEditor.shared import utils
```

This completes the `find_feature()` view function. Save your changes, run the Django web server if it is not already running, and try clicking on a shapefile's features. If you click on the ocean, nothing should happen—but if you click on a feature, you should see your web browser redirected to a URL of the form:

```
http://127.0.0.1:8000/shape-editor/editFeature/X/Y
```

where X is the record ID of the shapefile, and Y is the record ID of the clicked-on feature. Of course, at this stage you'll get a **Page Not Found** error, because you haven't written that page yet. But at least you can click on a feature to select it, which is a major milestone in the development of the ShapeEditor application. Congratulations!

Editing features

Now that we know which feature the user wants to edit, our next task is to implement the edit feature page itself. To do this, we are going to have to create a custom form with a single input field, named `geometry`, that uses a map-editing widget for editing the feature's geometry.

To create this form, we're going to borrow elements from GeoDjango's built-in "admin" interface, in particular the `django.contrib.gis.admin.GeoModelAdmin` class. This class provides a method named `get_map_widget()` which returns an editing widget which we can then include in a custom-generated form.

The process of building this form is a bit involved, thanks to the fact that we have to create a new `django.forms.Form` subclass on-the-fly to be handle the different types of geometries which can be edited. Let's put this complexity into a new function within the `shared.utils` module, which we'll call `get_map_form()`.

Edit the `utils.py` module and type in the following code:

```
def get_map_form(shapefile):
    geometry_field = calc_geometry_field(shapefile.geom_type)
    admin_instance = admin.GeoModelAdmin(Feature, admin.site)
    field          = Feature._meta.get_field(geometry_field)
    widget_type    = admin_instance.get_map_widget(field)

    class MapForm(forms.Form):
        geometry = forms.CharField(widget=widget_type(),
                                   label="")

    return MapForm
```

You'll also need to add the following `import` statements to the top of the file:

```
from django import forms
from django.contrib.gis import admin
from shapeEditor.shared.models import Feature
```

The `get_map_form()` function makes use of a `GeoModelAdmin` instance. We met `GeoModelAdmin` earlier in this chapter when we explored GeoDjango's built-in admin interface; here we are using it to generate an appropriate map widget for editing the type of geometry stored in the current shapefile.

Using the `GeoModelAdmin` instance, the `get_map_form()` function creates and returns a new `django.forms.Form` subclass with the appropriate widget type used to edit this particular shapefile's features. Note that the `get_map_form()` function returns the `MapForm` *class*, rather than an instance of that class; we'll use the returned class to create the appropriate `MapForm` instances as we need them.

With this function behind us, we can now implement the rest of the edit feature view. Let's start by setting up the view's URL; open the `editor` application's `urls.py` module and add the following to the list of URL patterns:

```
url(r'^edit_feature/(?P<shapefile_id>\d+)/' +
    r'(?P<feature_id>\d+)$', 'edit_feature'),
```

We're now ready to implement the view function itself. Edit the `views.py` module and start defining the `edit_feature()` function:

```
def edit_feature(request, shapefile_id, feature_id):
    try:
        shapefile = Shapefile.objects.get(id=shapefile_id)
    except ShapeFile.DoesNotExist:
        return HttpResponseNotFound()

    try:
        feature = Feature.objects.get(id=feature_id)
    except Feature.DoesNotExist:
        return HttpResponseNotFound()
```

So far this is quite straightforward: we load the `Shapefile` object for the current shapefile, and the `Feature` object for the feature we are editing. We next want to load into memory a list of that feature's attributes, so these can be displayed to the user:

```
attributes = []
for attr_value in feature.attributevalue_set.all():
    attributes.append([attr_value.attribute.name,
                       attr_value.value])
attributes.sort()
```

This is where things get interesting. We need to create a Django `Form` object (actually, an instance of the `MapForm` class created dynamically by the `get_map_form()` function we wrote earlier), and use this form instance to display the feature to be edited. When the form is submitted, we'll extract the updated geometry and save it back into the `Feature` object again, before redirecting the user back to the edit shapefile page to select another feature.

As we saw when we created the `import shapefile` form, the basic Django idiom for processing a form is as follows:

```
if request.method == "GET":
    form = MyForm()
```

```
        return render(request, "template.html",
                      {'form' : form})
    elif request.method == "POST":
        form = MyForm(request.POST)
        if form.is_valid():
            # Extract and save the form's contents here...
            return HttpResponseRedirect("/somewhere/else")
        return render(request, "template.html",
                      {'form' : form})
```

When the form is to be displayed for the first time, `request.method` will be set to GET. In this case, we create a new form object and display the form as part of an HTML template. When the form is submitted by the user, `request.method` will be set to POST. In this case, a new form object is created that is bound to the submitted POST arguments. The form's contents are then checked, and if they are valid they are saved and the user is redirected back to some other page. If the form is not valid, it will be displayed again along with a suitable error message.

Let's see how this idiom is used by the `edit feature` view. Add the following to the end of your new view function:

```
geometry_field = \
    utils.calc_geometry_field(shapefile.geom_type)
form_class     = utils.get_map_form(shapefile)

if request.method == "GET":
  wkt = getattr(feature, geometry_field)
  form = form_class({'geometry' : wkt})

  return render(request, "edit_feature.html",
                {'shapefile'  : shapefile,
                 'form'       : form,
                 'attributes' : attributes})
elif request.method == "POST":
  form = form_class(request.POST)
  try:
    if form.is_valid():
      wkt = form.cleaned_data['geometry']
      setattr(feature, geometry_field, wkt)
      feature.save()
```

```
            return HttpResponseRedirect("/editor/edit/" +
                                        shapefile_id)
    except ValueError:
      pass


    return render(request, "edit_feature.html",
                  {'shapefile'  : shapefile,
                   'form'       : form,
                   'attributes' : attributes})
```

As you can see, we call `utils.get_map_form()` to create a new `django.forms.Form` subclass which will be used to edit the feature's geometry. We also call `utils.calc_geometry_field()` to see which field in the `Feature` object should be edited.

The rest of this function pretty much follows the Django idiom for form-processing. The only interesting thing to note is that we get and set the geometry field (using the `getattr()` and `setattr()` functions, respectively) in WKT format. GeoDjango treats geometry fields as if they were character fields which hold the geometry in WKT format. The GeoDjango JavaScript code then takes that WKT data (which is stored in a hidden form field named `geometry`) and passes it to OpenLayers for display as a vector geometry. OpenLayers allows the user to edit that vector geometry, and the updated geometry is stored back into the hidden `geometry` field as WKT data. We then extract that updated geometry's WKT text, and store it back into the Feature object again.

So much for the `edit_feature()` view function. Let's now create the template used by this view. Create a new file named `edit_feature.html` within the `editor` application's `templates` directory, and enter the following text into this file:

```
<html>
  <head>
    <title>ShapeEditor</title>
    <script src="http://openlayers.org/api/OpenLayers.js">
    </script>
  </head>
  <body>
    <h1>Edit Feature</h1>
    <form method="POST" action="">
      <table>
        {{ form.as_table }}
        <tr>
```

```
            <td></td>
            <td align="right">
              <table>
{% for attr in attributes %}
                <tr>
                  <td>{{ attr.0 }}</td>
                  <td>{{ attr.1 }}</td>
                </tr>
{% endfor %}
              </table>
            </td>
          </tr>
          <tr>
            <td></td>
            <td align="center">
              <input type="submit" value="Save"/>
               
              <button type="button" onClick='window.location="/editor/
edit/{{ shapefile.id }}";'>
                Cancel
              </button>
            </td>
          </tr>
        </table>
      </form>
    </body>
</html>
```

This template uses an HTML table to display the form, and uses the `form.as_table` template function call to render the form as HTML table rows. We then display the list of feature attributes within a sub-table, and finally include **Save** and **Cancel** buttons at the bottom.

With all this code written, we are finally able to edit features within the ShapeEditor:

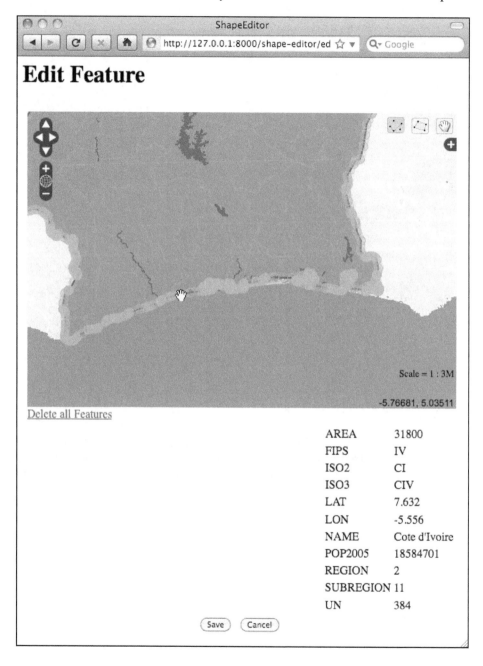

Within this editor, you can make use of a number of GeoDjango's built-in features to edit the geometry:

- You can click on the **Edit Geometry** tool ( ) to select a feature for editing.
- You can click on the **Add Geometry** tool ( ) to start drawing a new geometry.
- When a geometry is selected, you can click on a dark circle and drag it to move the endpoints of a line segment.
- When a geometry is selected, you can click on a light circle to split an existing line segment in two, making a new point which can then be dragged.
- If you hold the mouse down over a dark circle, you can press the *Delete* key (or type *D*) to delete that point. Note that this only works if the geometry has more than three points.
- You can click on the **Delete all Features** hyperlink to delete the current feature's geometries. We'll look at this hyperlink in more detail shortly.

Once you have finished editing the feature, you can click on the **Save** button to save the edited features, or the **Cancel** button to abandon the changes.

While this is all working well, there is one rather annoying quirk: GeoDjango lets the user remove the geometries from a map by using a hyperlink named **Delete all Features**. Since we're currently editing a single feature, this hyperlink is rather confusingly named: what it actually does is delete the *geometries* for this feature, not the feature itself. Let's change the text of this hyperlink to something more meaningful.

Go to the copy of Django that you downloaded, and navigate to the contrib/gis/ templates/gis/admin directory. In this directory is a file named openlayers. html. Take a copy of this file, and move it into your editor application's templates directory, renaming it to openlayers-custom.html.

Open your copy of this file, and look near the bottom for the text Delete all Features. Change this to Clear Feature's Geometry, and save your changes.

So far so good. Now we need to tell the GeoDjango editing widget to use our custom version of the openlayers.html file. To do this, edit your utils.py module and find your definition of the get_map_form() function. Replace the line which defines the admin_instance variable with the following highlighted lines:

```
def get_map_form(shapefile):
    geometry_field = calc_geometry_field(shapefile.geom_type)

    class CustomGeoModelAdmin(admin.GeoModelAdmin):
        map_template = "openlayers-custom.html"
```

```
adminInstance = CustomGeoModelAdmin(Feature, admin.site)
field         = Feature._meta.get_field(geometry_field)
widget_type   = admin_instance.get_map_widget(field)

class MapForm(forms.Form):
    geometry = forms.CharField(widget=widget_type(),
                               label="")

return MapForm
```

If you then try editing a feature, you'll see that your customized version of the `openlayers.html` file is being used:

By replacing the template, and by creating your own custom subclass of `GeoModelAdmin`, you can make various changes to the appearance and functionality of the built-in editing widget. If you want to see what is possible, take a look at the modules in the `django.contrib.gis.admin` directory.

Adding features

We'll next implement the ability to add a new feature. To do this, we'll put an **Add Feature** button onto the `edit shapefile` view. Clicking on this button will call the "edit feature" URL, but without a feature ID. We'll then modify the `edit feature` view so that if no feature ID is given a new `Feature` object is created.

Open the `editor` application's `views.py` module, find the `edit_shapefile()` function, and add the following highlighted lines to this function:

```
def editshapefile(request, shapefile_id):
    try:
        shapefile = Shapefile.objects.get(id=shapefile_id)
    except Shapefile.DoesNotExist:
        raise Http404

    tms_url = "http://"+request.get_host()+"/tms/"
    find_feature_url = "http://" + request.get_host() \
                  + "/editor/find_feature"
    add_feature_url = "http://" + request.get_host() \
                  + "/editor/edit_feature/" \
                  + str(shapefile_id)
```

```
        return render(request, "select_feature.html",
                    {'shapefile'        : shapefile,
                     'find_feature_url' : find_feature_url,
                     'add_feature_url'  : add_feature_url,
                     'tms_url'          : tms_url})
```

Then edit the `select_feature.html` template and add the following highlighted lines to the body of this template:

```
<body onload="init()">
 <h1>Edit Shapefile</h1>
 <b>Please choose a feature to edit</b>
 <br/>
 <div id="map" class="map"></div>
 <br/>
 <div style="margin-left:20px">
   <button type="button"
   onClick='window.location="{{ add_feature_url }}";'>
    Add Feature
   </button>
   <button type="button"
     onClick='window.location="/shape-editor";'>
     Cancel
   </button>
  </div>
</body>
```

This will place an **Add Feature** button onto the "select feature" page. Clicking on that button will call the URL `http://127.0.0.1:8000/editor/edit_feature/N` (where `N` is the record ID of the current shapefile).

We next need to add a URL pattern to support this URL. Open the `editor` application's `urls.py` module and add the following entry to the URL pattern list:

```
url(r'^edit_feature/(?P<shapefile_id>\d+)$',
  'edit_feature'), # feature_id = None -> add.
```

Then go back to `views.py` and edit the function definition for the `edit_feature()` function. Change the function definition to look as follows:

```
def editFeature(request, shapefile_id, feature_id=None):
```

Notice that the `feature_id` parameter is now optional. Now find the following block of code:

```
try:
   feature = Feature.objects.get(id=feature_id)
```

```
except Feature.DoesNotExist:
  return HttpResponseNotFound()
```

You need to replace this block of code with the following:

```
if feature_id == None:
  feature = Feature(shapefile=shapefile)
else:
  try:
    feature = Feature.objects.get(id=feature_id)
  except Feature.DoesNotExist:
    return HttpResponseNotFound()
```

This will create a new `Feature` object if the `feature_id` is not specified, but still fail if an invalid feature ID was specified.

With these changes, you should be able to add a new feature to the shapefile. Go ahead and try it out: run the Django web server if it's not already running and click on the **Edit** hyperlink for your imported shapefile. Then click on the **Add New Feature** hyperlink, and try creating a new feature. The new feature should appear on the `Select Feature` view:

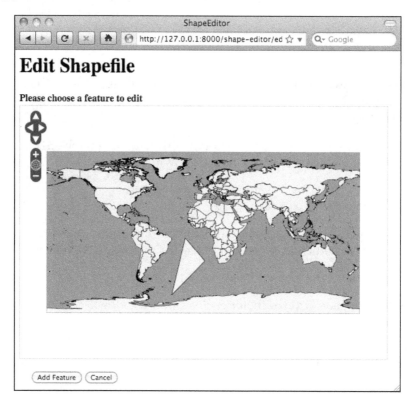

Deleting features

We next want to let the user delete an existing feature. To do this, we'll add a **Delete Feature** button to the `edit feature` view. Clicking on this button will redirect the user to the `delete feature` view for that feature.

Edit the `edit_feature.html` template, and add the following highlighted lines to the `<form>` section of the template:

```
<form method="POST" action="">
  <table>
    <tr>
      <td></td>
      <td align="right">
        <input type="submit" name="delete"
               value="Delete Feature"/>
      </td>
    </tr>
    {{ form.as_table }}
    ...
```

Notice that we've used `<input type="submit">` for this button. This will submit the form, with an extra POST parameter named `delete`. Now go back to the `editor` application's `views.py` module again, and add the following to the top of the `edit_feature()` function:

```
if request.method == "POST" and "delete" in request.POST:
    return HttpResponseRedirect("/editor/delete_feature/" +
                                shapefile_id+"/"+feature_id)
```

We next want to create the `delete feature` view. Open the `editor` application's `urls.py` and add the following to the list of URL patterns:

```
url(r'^delete_feature/(?P<shapefile_id>\d+)/' +
    r'(?P<feature_id>\d+)$', 'delete_feature'),
```

Next, create a new file named `delete_feature.html` in the templates directory, and enter the following text into this file:

```
<html>
    <head>
        <title>ShapeEditor</title>
    </head>
    <body>
```

```
        <h1>Delete Feature</h1>
        <form method="POST">
            Are you sure you want to delete this feature?
            <p/>
            <button type="submit" name="confirm"
                    value="1">Delete</button>
             
            <button type="submit" name="confirm"
                    value="0">Cancel</button>
        </form>
    </body>
</html>
```

This is a simple HTML form that confirms the deletion. When the form is submitted, the POST parameter named `confirm` will be set to 1 if the user wishes to delete the feature. Let's now implement the view which uses this template. Open the `editor` application's `views.py` and add the following new view function:

```
def delete_feature(request, shapefile_id, feature_id):
  try:
    feature = Feature.objects.get(id=feature_id)
  except Feature.DoesNotExist:
    return HttpResponseNotFound()

  if request.method == "POST":
    if request.POST['confirm'] == "1":
      feature.delete()
    return HttpResponseRedirect("/editor/edit/" +
                                shapefile_id)

  return render(request, "delete_feature.html")
```

As you can see, deleting features is quite straightforward.

Deleting shapefiles

The final piece of functionality we'll need to implement is the Delete shapefile view. This will let the user delete an entire uploaded shapefile. The process is basically the same as for deleting features; we've already got a **Delete** hyperlink on the main page, so all we have to do is implement the underlying view.

Go to the `editor` application's `urls.py` module and add the following entry to the URL pattern list:

```
url(r'^delete/(?P<shapefile_id>\d+)$', 'delete_shapefile'),
```

Then edit `views.py` and add the following new view function:

```
def delete_shapefile(request, shapefile_id):
    try:
        shapefile = Shapefile.objects.get(id=shapefile_id)
    except Shapefile.DoesNotExist:
        return HttpResponseNotFound()

    if request.method == "GET":
        return render(request, "delete_shapefile.html",
                      {'shapefile' : shapefile})
    elif request.method == "POST":
        if request.POST['confirm'] == "1":
            shapefile.delete()
        return HttpResponseRedirect("/editor")
```

Notice that we're passing the `Shapefile` object to the template. This is because we want to display some information about the shapefile on the confirmation page.

> Remember that `shapefile.delete()` doesn't just delete the `Shapefile` object itself; it also deletes all the objects associated with the `Shapefile` through `ForeignKey` fields. This means that the one call to `shapefile.delete()` will also delete all the `Attribute`, `Feature`, and `AttributeValue` objects associated with that shapefile.

Finally, create a new template named `delete_shapefile.html`, and enter the following text into this file:

```
<html>
  <head>
    <title>ShapeEditor</title>
  </head>
  <body>
    <h1>Delete Shapefile</h1>
    <form method="POST">
      Are you sure you want to delete the
```

```
         "{{ shapefile.filename }}" shapefile?
         <p/>
         <button type="submit" name="confirm"
                 value="1">Delete</button>
          
         <button type="submit" name="confirm"
                 value="0">Cancel</button>
     </form>
   </body>
</html>
```

You should now be able to click on the **Delete** hyperlink to delete a shapefile. Go ahead and try it; you can always re-import your shapefile if you need it.

Using ShapeEditor

Congratulations! You have just finished implementing the last of the ShapeEditor's features, and you now have a complete working geospatial application built using GeoDjango. Using the ShapeEditor, you can import shapefiles, view their features and the feature attributes, make changes to the feature geometries, add and delete features, and then export the shapefile again.

This is certainly a useful application. Even if you don't have a full-blown GIS system installed, you can now make quick and easy changes to a shapefile's contents using the ShapeEditor. And, of course, the ShapeEditor is a great starting point for the development of your own geospatial applications.

Further improvements and enhancements

As with any new application, there are a number of ways in which the ShapeEditor could be improved. For example:

*   Adding user signup and login, so that each user has his or her own private set of shapefiles, rather than every user seeing the entire list of all the uploaded shapefiles.

*   Adding the ability to edit a feature's attribute values.

*   Using a higher resolution base map. An obvious candidate for this would be the GSHHS high-resolution shoreline database.

- Adding a tile cache for our TMS server.

- Using JavaScript to add a **please wait** pop-up message while a shapefile is being imported or exported.

- Improving the reusability of the ShapeEditor's codebase. We've concentrated on learning how to use GeoDjango to build a working system, but with a suitable redesign the code could be made much more generic so that it could be used in other applications as well.

Feel free to make these improvements; you will learn a lot more about GeoDjango, and about geospatial development in general. As you work with the ShapeEditor, you'll probably come up with your own list of things you'd like to improve.

Summary

In this chapter, we finished implementing a sophisticated geospatial web application using GeoDjango, Mapnik, PostGIS, OGR, and pyproj. This application is useful in its own right, as well as being a springboard to developing your own geospatial web applications.

We have learned:

- That we can easily create our own Tile Map Server using Mapnik and GeoDjango.

- That we can include OpenLayers on our own web pages, independent of GeoDjango, and display map data from our Tile Map Server.

- How to create a custom "click handler" to respond to mouse-clicks within an OpenLayers map.

- That we can use AJAX calls to have the server respond to events within the web browser.

- That GeoDjango provides a powerful query language for performing spatial queries without writing a single line of SQL.

- How to "borrow" geometry editing widgets from GeoDjango and use them within your own web application.

- That you can create your own GeoModelAdmin subclass to change the appearance and functionality of GeoDjango's geometry editing widgets.

- That you can use a simple HTML form to confirm the deletion of a record.

This completes our exploration of GeoDjango, and also completes this book. Hopefully you have learned a lot about geospatial development, and how to create geospatial applications using Python. With these tools at your disposal, you are now ready to start developing your own complex geospatial systems. Have fun!

Index

L

labels
  drawing 319
Landsat
  about 94
  data format 95
Landsat imagery
  obtaining 95-97
Layer objects 287
layers 336
Layers, Mapnik 73
libspatialite extension
  loading 176
linear distance 25
linear ring 38
LinearRing class 68
line-drawing options
  dashed and dotted lines 313
  line caps 312
  line color 311
  line joins 312
  line width 312
  opacity 312
LinePatternSymbolizer 315
lines
  drawing, onto map 310
linestring 38
LineString class 67
LineSymbolizer
  about 288, 310
  using 311
Linux
  SpatiaLite, installing 174
list_countries() function 235
list shapefiles view
  implementing 393-397
list_shapefiles() view function 394-396
locations
  about 22
  measuring 22-24
LULC datafiles 127

M

Mac OS X
  SpatiaLite, installing 174

map definition file 346-350
Map Definition File 291
MapGenerator
  about 341
  interface 342
  main map layer, creating 343, 344
  map, rendering 345
  points, displaying on map 344, 345
mapGenerator.generateMap() function 246
mapGenerator.py module 342
Mapnik
  about 16, 71, 285, 286
  availability 76
  data sources 296, 297
  design 72
  documentation 76
  example code 74, 75
  example map, creating 292-296
  features 71, 287
  filters 304
  layers 336
  map, generating 287
  map rendering 339, 341
  maps 336
  Polygons layer 290
  Python documentation 296
  rules 304
  styles 304
  symbolizers 310
  URL 76, 286
Mapnik Datasource object
  setting up 296, 297
mapnik.Layer class
  methods 338
mapnik.Map class
  attributes 337, 338
  methods 337, 338
mapnik.Shapefile() function 297
mapnik.SQLite() function 302
Mapnik Wiki
  URL 76
map rendering 339
maps 336
MapServer 16
markup application, Django application
    364
MBRContains() function 165

Universal Transverse Mercator (UTM)
    projection 127
unprojected coordinates 11
unprojected coordinate system 34
unwrap_geos_geometry() function 417
uploaded shapefile
  extracting 403, 404
URLConf 367
URL dispatching, Django 366, 367
usability 262
US Census Bureau
  URL 41
utils.calc_geometry_field() 464
utils.get_map_form() 464
utils.get_ogr_feature_attribute() function
    418

V

vector format data
  about 40
  coverage 40
  shapefile 40
  simple features 40
  TIGER/Line 40
vector-format geospatial data
  about 80
  sources 80
view, Django 366
Virtual Datasource (VRT) format 301

W

WCS 18
WebGIS website
  URL 127
Well-known Binary (WKB) format 40, 136
Well-known Text (WKT) format 40, 135
WFS 18
WGS 84 37
WMS 18
World Borders Dataset
  about 92, 93, 216, 218
  data format 93
  downloading 112
  obtaining 93
World Data Bank II 90
world reference system (WRS) 96
World Vector Shoreline 90

X

XCode
  about 65
  installing 65

Thank you for buying
Python Geospatial Development: Second Edition

About Packt Publishing

Packt, pronounced 'packed', published its first book "*Mastering phpMyAdmin for Effective MySQL Management*" in April 2004 and subsequently continued to specialize in publishing highly focused books on specific technologies and solutions.

Our books and publications share the experiences of your fellow IT professionals in adapting and customizing today's systems, applications, and frameworks. Our solution based books give you the knowledge and power to customize the software and technologies you're using to get the job done. Packt books are more specific and less general than the IT books you have seen in the past. Our unique business model allows us to bring you more focused information, giving you more of what you need to know, and less of what you don't.

Packt is a modern, yet unique publishing company, which focuses on producing quality, cutting-edge books for communities of developers, administrators, and newbies alike. For more information, please visit our website: www.packtpub.com.

About Packt Open Source

In 2010, Packt launched two new brands, Packt Open Source and Packt Enterprise, in order to continue its focus on specialization. This book is part of the Packt Open Source brand, home to books published on software built around Open Source licences, and offering information to anybody from advanced developers to budding web designers. The Open Source brand also runs Packt's Open Source Royalty Scheme, by which Packt gives a royalty to each Open Source project about whose software a book is sold.

Writing for Packt

We welcome all inquiries from people who are interested in authoring. Book proposals should be sent to author@packtpub.com. If your book idea is still at an early stage and you would like to discuss it first before writing a formal book proposal, contact us; one of our commissioning editors will get in touch with you.

We're not just looking for published authors; if you have strong technical skills but no writing experience, our experienced editors can help you develop a writing career, or simply get some additional reward for your expertise.

Python Geospatial Development

Build a complete and sophisticated mapping application from scratch using Python tools for GIS development

Erik Westra   [PACKT] open source*

Python Geospatial Development

ISBN: 978-1-849511-54-4   Paperback: 508 pages

Build a complete and sophisticated mapping application from scratch using Python tools for GIS development

1. Build applications for GIS development using Python

2. Analyze and visualize Geo-Spatial data

3. Comprehensive coverage of key GIS concepts

4. Recommended best practices for storing spatial data in a database

Quick answers to common problems

Programming ArcGIS 10.1 with Python Cookbook

Over 75 recipes to help you automate geoprocessing tasks, create solutions, and solve problems for ArcGIS with Python

Eric Pimpler   [   ]

Programming ArcGIS 10.1 with Python Cookbook

ISBN: 978-1-849694-44-5   Paperback: 304 pages

Over 75 recipes to help you automate geoprocessing tasks, create solutions, and solve problems for ArcGIS with Python

1. Learn how to create geoprocessing scripts with ArcPy

2. Customize and modify ArcGIS with Python

3. Create time-saving tools and scripts for ArcGIS

Please check **www.PacktPub.com** for information on our titles